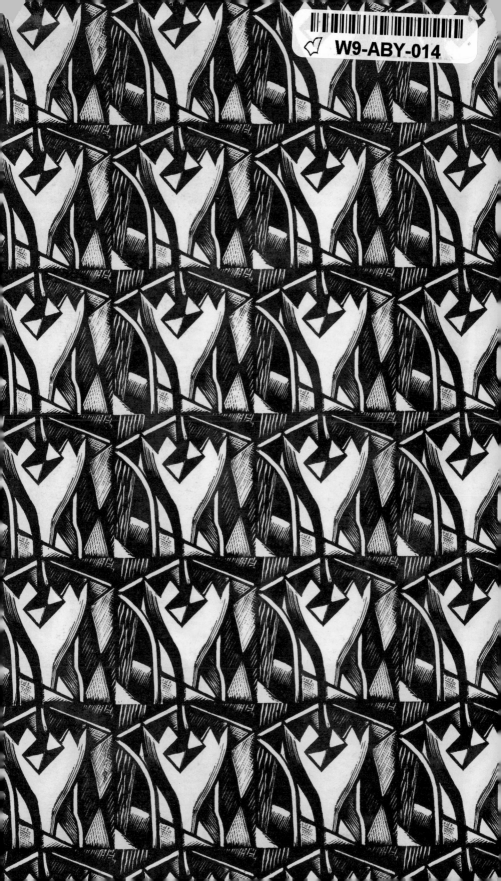

We can make our minds so like
still water that beings gather
about us that they may see, it may
be, their own images, and so live for
a moment with a clearer, perhaps
even with a fiercer life because of
our quiet.

W. B. Yeats.

Paul Nash:
The Portrait of an Artist

November Moon. 1942
Oil

PAUL NASH

The Portrait of an Artist

by

ANTHONY BERTRAM

As a man is, so he sees.
—WILLIAM BLAKE

Paul Nash's work will last because
it has aesthetic integrity. It will be
loved because it creates a world of
harmony and of magic. It will survive
our poor attempts to explain its
mystery.
—SIR HERBERT READ

FABER AND FABER
24 Russell Square
London

First published in mcmlv
by Faber and Faber Limited
24 Russell Square London W.C. 1
Printed in Great Britain by
R. MacLehose and Company Limited
The University Press Glasgow

Contents

CONTENTS

Illustrations

9

ILLUSTRATIONS

Acknowledgements

M y principal written sources, in addition to those given in the
Bibliography and the footnotes, have been Paul Nash's
letters. I want to thank all those who have lent me original
letters or sent me copies, and who have patiently answered many
questions arising out of them. I regret that in the end I was unable
to use so much of this material for which I had pestered them. I had
to cut my first draft almost in half in order to bring the book down to
an economic price; but a great deal that is not now quoted or directly
referred to has none the less been of immense indirect value and their
kindness has not been wasted.

The following is the list of letters, with executors' names in
brackets where the recipients were dead before I began work. Unhappily several have died since. The figure following each name
gives the number of letters received. The figures in brackets indicate
that I have only seen copies. Those marked (1) were sent as literatim
copies or the passages quoted have been since checked to make them
so. Those marked (2) are copies which have obviously been 'tidied'
in spelling, punctuation and so on. In all other cases I saw the
originals and made my own literatim copies.

Lady Agnew 1 (2), Conrad Aiken 7, Martin Armstrong 9, Michael
Ayrton 1, Anthony Bertram and wife 44, Nell Bethell (Major H. le
F. F. Harvey) 20, John Betjeman 9, Darcy Bradell 1, Mrs Bradhurst
(Mrs Fitzgerald) 1, Edward Burra 16, Robert Byron (Mrs Butler) 4,
Carnegie Institute, Pittsburgh (letters to various officials lent by John
O'Connor) 17, Ruth Clark 20 (1), Raymonde Collignon 1, Cecil
Collins 1, Alice Daglish (2), Mrs Earl 7 (2), Margot Eates 2 (1),
John Gould Fletcher (Norman H. Pearson) 14 (1), Desmond Flower
6, Sybil Fountain 1, Viola Garvin 1, Mrs Basil Gray 3, F. E. Halliday
3, Maurice Hare and wife 6 (2), Mrs Hilda Harrisson 1, D. W.
Herdman 4, Imperial War Museum (letters to various officials on
files of I. W. M.) 12 (2), Philip James 1, P. H. Jowett 1, Rex Nan

ACKNOWLEDGEMENTS

Kivell 45, Sir Allen Lane and Eunice Frost of Penguin Books 13 (2), Elspeth Little now Mrs Edward Burder 23 (2), Sir Edward Marsh 55 (2), Enid Marx 3, Henry Moore 3, Mrs George Mortimer 6, Catherine Munro now Mrs J. N. Macdonald 5 (2), Barbara Nash 1, John Nash 9, Margaret Nash (extracts, excluding those printed in *Outline*) 39 (2), Peter Nash 1, Clare Neilson 45 (1), Eric Newton 2, Mercia Oakley now Mrs Grimsdale 50, Hon. Arnold Palmer 18, Velona Pilcher 1, John Piper 4, E. Hartley Ramsden 26 (1), Sir Herbert Read 2, James Ross 2, Sir William Rothenstein (Sir John Rothenstein) 48, Archibald G. B. Russell and wife 7 (2), Sir Michael Sadler (Michael Sadleir) 10, Richard Seddon 36, George Bernard Shaw 3 (2), Lancelot de G. B. Sieveking and wife 67, Oliver Simon 9 (2), Messrs Tooths' file (various addressees, chiefly Richard Smart and Dudley Tooth) 395, C. S. Lisle Trask 3, Audrey Withers now Mrs Victor Kennett 50 (2), Percy Withers and wife (Mrs Kennett) 34 (2).

I want also to thank the following: the authorities of various schools, art schools and colleges, the Air Ministry (Information Dept.), the War Office (Records D), the Arts Council (Mr Philip James) and the Imperial War Museum (Mr W. Philip Mayes) for information and in the last case for supplying copies of all letters I wanted; Professor A. W. Lawrence and Messrs Jonathan Cape for permission to quote from the letters of T. E. Lawrence; the late Sir Desmond Macarthy, Mrs Dewhurst, Miss Margot Eates, Mr Philip Moss, Mr Oliver Simon, Fr. Victor White O.P. and the late Kenneth Romney Towndrow for help in research work; all those who have given me their memories of Nash verbally or in writing; Miss Ruth Clark and Mr Lancelot Sieveking for reading my manuscript and making many useful suggestions; Mr John Nash R.A. and other members of the Nash family for giving me every possible help and my wife for patient and frequent assistance in the drudgery of checking, listing and indexing.

But my chief debt of gratitude must naturally be to Mrs Paul Nash. It is obvious that my work could not have been done at all without her constant and close cooperation. This, however, must not be taken to imply that she necessarily agrees with all my interpretations of her husband's motives and beliefs. Indeed, in certain cases, she holds quite different opinions and must not be associated with conclusions for which I am alone responsible.

Bignor, Pulborough, Sussex   A. B.

'Outline'

In the year before his death Paul Nash borrowed a drawing called *Night in Bird Garden*[1] which he had made when he was a little over twenty. It had been bought at his first exhibition by its present owner, Mrs. George Mortimer; and now, in April 1945, he wrote to her:

'I think it's awfully good! I have been studying its technique which I had forgotten, and as I looked closely into the drawing all my early life of those days and nights came creeping back into memory and I remembered the sensation of doing that drawing of the night shrubs and trees and how I wanted to give the true feeling of a nocturnal scene and must get the sky that elusive colour—that luminous darkness.'

Such experiences were frequent with him during the last few years of his life. It is impossible to know when he first suspected that his death was near, but his behaviour after 1940 suggests that it was about then. During these last six years he was living at three levels of time. He was examining his past, creating in his present and ordering his papers for the future. He was collecting the material for a survey of all his work, tracing old pictures, borrowing them, having them photographed; and at the same time he was working on his autobiography, which he had begun in 1938. Like his ordering for the future, it was never finished.

In his last years Nash found his most intense imaginative experiences in a sky that was inhabited by bombers and by flowers. At the same time he was peering back into the skies of his childhood and youth, and recording them in his book with particular clarity. For he found like Rossetti that

> *life all past*
> *Is like the sky when the sun sets in it,*
> *Clearest when furthest off.*[2]

[1] Particulars of all the pictures that are mentioned in the text will be found in the Index of Pictures.
[2] *A Last Confession.*

13

While he was painting his late series of *The Sun Descending*, under a renewed stimulus from Blake, his interest had also gone back to Rossetti, who had been the first strong influence on him.

This fragment of autobiography which ends abruptly in 1913 was published posthumously with the title which Nash had chosen:

'Since it is impossible to give a full picture of any life by means of an autobiography suitable for publication, I have called this personal history *Outline*. But there is another reason. Although it is an autobiography, it aims at telling the story of the development of an artist's life, a development which, on looking back, appears to have a curious "inevitable" quality, like a line of fate in the palm of the hand. I do not wish to exaggerate the significance of this impression, or to suggest anything mystical.'

These explanations from the unfinished preface, which he must have begun drafting when he already knew that he might not finish the book, can be exactly applied to this biography. The biographer who writes when many of his subject's closest friends and relations still live, must always also have certain material which is not 'suitable for publication'. I do not mean only scandalous or libellous material, but I mean also that which might hurt feelings or desecrate intimacies. Because this is obvious, certain people always suspect that the biographer must have something to hide. It may often be so, but in this case I want to say that I know of nothing in Nash's life that the majority of men today would feel it necessary to hide. Indeed he was a man of exceptional integrity. He did not accept the whole code of orthodox Christian morals, but he did accept higher standards than most of his contemporaries. I shall not hide the few instances of his falling below them.

But there is, of course, material that I cannot use, or do not wish to. I chiefly regret suppressing some of his wittiest letters. His delight in the ridiculous often led him to describe casual acquaintances in a way which they would not appreciate. They were not written in malice but to entertain his friends. He was a kind man and it would hurt his memory as much as their feelings, if I printed them.

For different reasons I shall not give any depth to my account of his relations with his wife. That is my only important restriction. It is important because a marriage which lasted through most of his working life—from 1914 until his death—cannot possibly be considered irrelevant to his art. But it would be intolerable to intrude on such an intimacy while his wife is alive, and I must leave future writers to estimate the influence of her resolute companionship and help, particularly in the long difficult years of his illness. The general character of their relations will, I hope, emerge, but I confine myself to quoting one passage from an intimate letter to suggest, once for all, Nash's attitude to her on the deeper level. It was written about 1931: 'My thought of you is what we call God's thought of all men—the best and truest. . . . I do not set out to be even a small god, but my attitude to you is, so far as this goes, divine!'

Apart from his work, Nash's life is of no public interest. He had no adventures except in the imagination: he travelled little except in the skies, which he never entered in any machine: he was not active in affairs. But the significance of an artist's life in relation to his work has nothing to do with the intrinsic value of his actions except as the revelation of the kind of man he was, what he felt and thought rather than what he did; for it is from that that his work springs. *L'artiste est devant une mer immense et déserte*

> *sans mâts, sans mâts ni fertiles îlots,*

et le miroir qu'il lui présente n'est pas plus grand que son cœur.[1]

The artist's mirror at any moment, is what, up to that moment, he has made of himself. It includes and summarizes all his past, even what he has shed, as a tree draws life from its own decayed leaves. Like Rossetti and Blake, Nash had the vision of poet and painter—not two visions, but a double vision, inseparable, as I hope to show; but the fields of contemplation could be separate. As I have said, when, in his last years, he was painting new experiences, he was writing in his autobiography of his earliest; and he was finding that they were related.

'Some day, no doubt,' Sir Herbert Read wrote in his editorial preface, 'the outline will be completed and filled in, but as it stands, in the artist's own handwriting, the composition holds together, and from it emerges the portrait of an artist.' It is that portrait I am trying to complete and fill in, but there must be some discrepancy between the part of his life covered by *Outline*[2] and the remainder. I shall do my best to reduce that by the fullest possible use of his letters, so that the voice which spoke so revealingly of twenty-four years may continue to sound intermittently to the end.

[1] Jacques Maritain, *Art et Scolastique*, ed. 1935, p. 75.
[2] The book, however, also includes a selection from Nash's letters to his wife and his notes for the continuation of his autobiography. I shall use both, distinguishing the latter as *Outline: Notes*.

I

Childhood and Schooldays
1889-1906

i. Parentage

Paul Nash was born in London on the eleventh of May 1889, at a house then called Ghuznee Lodge but now 2 Sunningdale Gardens. It is in Kensington, south-west of the Gardens and a few minutes walk from them. But his family belonged to the Home Counties and the sea.

His father was William Harry Nash, who was born in Buckinghamshire in 1848, admitted to the Inner Temple in January 1871, and called to the bar in November 1873. He was to become revising barrister for Gloucestershire and Recorder of Abingdon. His younger brother, Francis, was a barrister of the same Inn, two of his nephews and one of his great-nephews are solicitors; but it was only in his generation that any of the Nash family had taken to the law, although two of his aunts had married lawyers. The tradition of the family was agricultural.

That is a background which Paul Nash felt to be important: it may indeed explain the peculiarly English character of his work and its preoccupation with cultivated nature. He wrote of his first visit to his grandfather's house in Buckinghamshire: 'It was like finding my own home, my true home, for somehow it was far more convincing than our so-called home in London. I realized, without expressing the thought, that I belonged to the country.'[1] Indeed he did, and to one county for as long as could matter in heredity. He apparently traced his family back to a Henrie Nash of the fifteenth century at Oving in

[1] All passages quoted without a reference are from *Outline*.

north Buckinghamshire. In the sixteenth century the family appears in the records of Nash and Quainton, two neighbouring villages near Stony Stratford.[1] This began a consistent move to the South which only stopped at the border of the county. By the end of the seventeenth century they seem to have reached the district that was to play so large a part in forming Nash's outlook, the area which is bounded at its four corners by Gerrard's Cross, Uxbridge, Colnbrook and Slough. From 1704 we can trace their rise, in three wills, from the rank of husbandmen through yeoman to gentleman. The last of these, a William Nash, owned Upton Lea and lived at Upton Court in Slough; and he was sufficiently well-to-do to buy a new estate for his son, another William, on his marriage. This consisted of the Rectory of Langley Marish, with its lands and adjacent farms and the great tithes of the parish, which was about seven miles long and ran from Horsemoor Green, between Colnbrook and Slough, to George Green, between Slough and Uxbridge, and contained three villages. The possession of these tithes gave the head of the Nash family the position of Lay Rector but the work of the parish was done by a Perpetual Curate with the courtesy title of Vicar.

This William of Langley (1778–1838), Nash's great-grandfather, was the only Nash before the present generation to leave the Church of England. While continuing to draw the tithes, he built a chapel in his farmyard and instituted a nonconformist minister. His wife was the narrowest type of Protestant and her diary attributes all the troubles of her life to having visited a theatre. I believe this ugly tradition in the family had its effect on Paul Nash's attitude to religion. Their youngest surviving son, Henry Fleetwood, inherited Upton Lea and produced eleven cousins for Paul Nash. Their eldest, another William, who succeeded to Langley, appears in *Outline* as the sporting great-uncle William who 'did nothing except lose money in rather a grand way quite beyond the resources of the family'. When he died at thirty-eight his widow was obliged to sell Langley; but fortunately his brother, Zachary, the Vicar of Christchurch in Hampshire, was able to buy it and rent it to another brother, John, who established himself there in 1851. This was Nash's grandfather who will appear later in this chronicle.

Paul Nash's mother was Caroline Maud, daughter of Captain John Millbourne Jackson, a naval officer who died before Nash's birth. The Jackson family was of an established naval tradition, but

---

[1] When not specified, my sources for the early history of the family are *Outline* and an unpublished account by Miss Olive Nash, the daughter of Nash's eldest uncle.

Nash took more interest in the fact that a great-great-uncle, James Grey Jackson, and an uncle, Lt. Col. Hubert Jackson, were both good amateur painters.[1] Nash's maternal grandmother was Caroline Cattley, whose family were Hull timber merchants trading to Russia.

It will be apparent that I have done little research into the Nash and Jackson families. I cannot believe that further knowledge would help us to understand Nash's character and art, which is our business. Indeed I should have given an even shorter account had I not wished to reflect Nash's own interest in them.

We can now return to the point at which this chapter began—the birth of Paul Nash in Kensington.

ii. Early Childhood

My account of Nash's life before he left school can be little more than a summary of the first two chapters of *Outline*; but there are some facts to add, others to correct or enlarge, some commentaries to make. We can begin firmly enough with the date of his birth, but for the next nine years it is impossible to establish any exact chronology. It does not matter. The imaginative memories of childhood are far more valuable than dated events.

It is a critical commonplace to remark on the absence of people from his work and on his preoccupation with places. But in fact his places are very fully peopled, though not with bodies. The bodies had been there but have withdrawn and left their mark like a footprint on the landscape. It is, as it were, the presence of the absent such as we feel, without any business of ghosts, in contemplating a familiar empty chair. But people are bodily present and acutely observed in *Outline*, as in his letters and the caricatures with which he decorated them.

Most of the people in *Outline* are relations and most of the places are connected with them. They begin with his parents and Ghuznee Lodge. His father first appears only as an awaited step and the sound of a front-door key. His mother is first associated only with an evening hour in the drawing-room, which has survived as perpetual winter, a shut-in and difficult hour. Mrs. Nash was always anxious. She had to manage on very limited means: she was delicate: she was worried over her children, over their laziness and stupidity. She took nothing easily. Nash would look up from his game on the floor at 'her

---

[1] See the aquatint by James Grey, *Outline*. p. 48. On the same plate is an engraving of him incorrectly captioned as a great-uncle.

beautiful dark head with its agate eyes and abundant hair. Her mouth would be parted rather sadly'. The dusk gathered and only the firelight warded off the darkness until she roused herself and rang for the lamp just before the step and the key sounded.

That sombre drawing-room looked on to a conservatory full of withered plants. Such withered plants, and the dry, brown, ever-lasting plants, were to occupy Nash's pictorial imagination in a whole series of pictures in the later nineteen-twenties—an aspect of his recurrent but not too obsessive sympathy with the stillness of winter and with objects whose growth had ceased, dead wood and stones.

In 1893 Nash's brother, John Northcote, was born, and in 1895 his sister, Barbara Millbourne. This completed the family. In spite of the six years between them they soon played well together. They had plenty of imagination and plenty of toys. In particular there was a neighbour called Mr. Day who gave them a great many soldiers. Among Nash's papers there is a letter which had come with the Christmas present of 1898—cavalry and infantry and a rag doll for Barbara. His keeping that letter for nearly fifty years is the interesting point.

The toys were for the world of the day-nursery. In the night-nursery Nash dreamt. I must quote his account of certain dreams because of their bearing on his art. Of one, he says:

'The horror consisted in being hemmed in by vast perpendiculars of changing dimensions, as though the building of walls and columns might begin a deliberate animation, like a slow-motion film, its archi-tectural features changing position, eccentrically. Yet all the while height, breadth and thickness were increasing—not to the release of the dreamer into wider spaces and restful perspectives, but always in some way encroaching, towering and massive, until, at length, about to envelop and overwhelm one.'

Nash defeated these aggressive forms on the whole. They appear rarely in his work, though perhaps we may recognize them in his designs for *King Lear* and in the vast perpendiculars of his mega-liths and monoliths. But they did not overwhelm him: he was safely released into the wider spaces of the sky where he could meet death serenely.

Of a second dream he says: 'There was a dreadful moment ahead when I would find myself in a tunnel which was either closing in or had narrowed imperceptibly, and I was trapped, horribly, unable to squeeze through or to back out.' This tunnel does not appear in his work as a threat but rather as an invitation. He invites us to explore, to push through to the light. It most often takes the form of the path through the wood, which is related, of course, to Dante's image; but Nash's 'way' is much less alarming and there is nowhere in his imaginative world the place where the sun is silent, *là dove'l sol tace*. But there was a beast to stand in his way, not Dante's lion or leopard but a black dog. Nash did not dream this still and silent creature, but was awake when he felt its threat at a dark corner of the landing. He also defeated this and it became only a memory. There is disquiet in Nash's late work, but no horror, no nightmare. The only childish dream which seems to have persisted in later life is of quite a different sort—a pleasant and triumphant dream.

'It consisted, simply, of flying or floating, usually downstairs and round about the top of the hall. Sometimes, I would find myself in other places, unknown country perhaps, easily traversed by a process of leaping and, by some act of will, keeping afloat for a good distance before sinking slowly to earth, when another spring from the purchase of the ground would carry me up again and again unaccountably onward, slightly twirling at times like a leaf on the still air, but always able, just sufficiently, to steer a course.

. . . No other adventure of sleep is so disappointing to wake from and so bitterly relinquished as "unreal ".'

This flying dream is common enough, but the interest of it in Nash's case is the important part its imagery was to play in his conscious imagination and in his work.

The dominant activity of his conscious imagination as a child was to invest places with personality. The first Place characterized in this way was in Kensington Gardens. There he escaped from the confining walls of Ghuznee Lodge and the invisible lead on which a child was led through the streets; and there he discovered the country. 'I became aware of trees,' he wrote, 'felt the grass for the first time, saw an expanse of water, listened to a new kind of silence.' He enjoyed all that in a perfectly ordinary way. He played Red Indians and sailed his boat. But it was there also that he found what he described as his first Authentic Place:

'This place of mine was not remarkable for any unusual feature which stood out. Yet there was a particular spacing in the disposal of the trees or it was their height in relation to these intervals, which suggested some inner design of very subtle purpose, altogether defeating the conventional lay-out of the gardens. . . . Simply, it was not the same as the rest. In addition, it was strangely beautiful and excitingly unsafe! . . . Whatever happened to me there throughout my life I

21

was conscious always of the influence of the place at work upon my nerves—but never in any sinister degree, rather with a force gentle but insistent, charged with sweetness beyond physical experience, the promise of a joy utterly unreal.'

He goes on to say that perhaps this Place was not on the map at all, but only within himself. I do not think so. It will be found in his pictures that his imagination has always, or almost always, been stimulated by a real place or object. Nature was his spring-board, as it was Wordsworth's. But there is so much that is Wordsworthian in his attitude to nature that it is odd how little he seems to have read him. It is perhaps because Wordsworth's effects are slow and cumulative and Nash was not a steady reader. In an essay called 'The Life of the Inanimate Object'[1] he associated Wordsworth with the surrealist fear of the inanimate object, and quoted from the famous boating episode in Book I of *The Prelude*. He admitted that he was quoting at second hand, but he was clearly so vague about Wordsworth that he merely referred to the passage as 'from Wordsworth's early poems'. In fact, it is quoted from the version of 1850. I doubt whether Nash was capable of reading *The Prelude*. He picked here and there among books for what would feed his own creative imagination, and did not make the sustained effort of absorbing the creation of others. He sought, in literature as in nature, for material; and at first it was in literature rather than in nature. Few painters have been so positively stimulated by their reading, and therefore, from time to time, we must take notice of what he read.

It begins with Lewis Carroll, Grimm and Hans Andersen, whose *Snow Queen* particularly delighted him, and indeed the story has remarkable affinities with his future life and work. There is the small manageable garden on the roof-tops. Nash was always to love gardens and later to become an enthusiastic gardener on a small scale. His gardens had the rigid boundaries and the tidiness of the window-box. There is the persistent contrast of the intense winter and of flowers, both themes recurrent throughout his work. There is Kay's flight with the Snow Queen through the moonlit sky with the woods and lakes and snow under him, a whole collection of images that were to become frequent with him. There is the vision of the Dreams, and we have already seen what they meant to him. Indeed, we shall tire of the word 'dream' before we have finished with his youth.

Even as an adult, Nash was able to accept fairies, magic, the legendary and the mythological, at least imaginatively. These were

---

[1] *Country Life*, 1 May 1937.

ancient faiths and he was drawn to them. He came to distinguish them sharply from the self-conscious and apologetic modern fabrications of improbabilities; but he was mistaken, when he wrote *Outline*, in thinking that he had always made that distinction. He was careful to explain that his experience of the Place in Kensington Gardens had been before Barrie took them over. 'You could look at a tree without misgiving; it was unlikely ever to resolve into something by Mr. Rackham. The place was not *infested* by fairies.' From the same adult view point he described his dislike of Kipling's *Just So Stories* for 'the first whiff of quaintness ... the faint odour of whimsicality' which they had brought to his nostrils. But in his adolescence he delighted in far worse whimsies—a fact which I am convinced he genuinely forgot. I shall speak of that later, but in the meantime, it is pleasanter to speak of Edward Lear.

Nash's connection with Edward Lear was through 'Aunt Gussie', an indomitable woman whose personality and presence are still legendary among great-nieces and nephews. She was the Hon. Augusta Bethell, a daughter of the first Baron Westbury, Lord Chancellor in 1861–65. Lear, who was a friend of the family, fell in love with her, but thought himself too old and ugly to propose. She married a cripple. After his death she visited Lear in San Remo, but he could still not make up his mind. Within a year, he was dead, still in love.[1] In 1890, when she was fifty-two, she married her father's biographer, Nash's uncle, Thomas Arthur. Nash gives an admirable description of her in *Outline* and of how she would read him Lear's nonsense verses in her drawing-room at 60 Elm Park Gardens, which was full of his 'dry, luminous water-colours'. They were among the first pictures he ever saw. The very first, since there is no word of his ever being taken to any kind of exhibition, must have been those of his military uncle, which crowded the walls of his mother's drawing-room. He describes them as 'tender, limpid paintings' and these are qualities which would have appealed to him. It is easy to imagine what pleased him in Lear's drawings, not in the finished topographical renderings of the picturesque for his volumes of Excursions, Journals and Views, but in his more fluid and lively sketches. Their strict 'bounding line' and subordinated colour-wash, and a particular rhythmic handling of trees may well have influenced Nash's early work.[2]

[1] *Edward Lear* by Angus Davidson, Murray, 1928, pp. 164 and 262.
[2] See, for example, Plates VI, VII and VIII in the catalogue of *One Hundred Landscape Drawings by Edward Lear* issued by Craddock & Barnard, Tunbridge Wells, 1937.

But neither Nash nor his brother seems to have shown any precocious interest in art nor any special talent, though like most children they both drew in pencil and waxy chalks, and even had 'bouts of smearing and daubing with cheap water-colours'.

There were, of course, other people and places in Nash's childhood besides these London memories. He gives some account of them in *Outline*, but all I need repeat here is what he wrote of his first encounter with the sea: '(They) must have been spring or winter seas, for I associate them with cold and cruel waters usually in a threatening mood, pounding and rattling along the shore.' In that, perhaps, the ground was laid for the imagery of his Dymchurch series.

A clearer memory remained of a visit with his brother to a house at Botley in Hampshire, which his maternal grandmother had rented. It became a Place for him. 'If ever a house could be said to be haunted —in the abstract—without the illustration of a ghost, The Grange was haunted,' he wrote. 'Or, was it I who was haunted?' At any rate, he was in a very sensitive state, and he records many things in this strange Place which troubled him, particularly the presence of snakes. On one occasion a snake rose up under his hand, hissing, when he bent to pick up an apple. The incident impressed itself on him as the symbol of evil concealed at the heart of innocence. The snake was to find its way later into the garden at Madams and many other innocent places in his work.

The end of this state of nervous excitement was the first 'vision' which he has recorded. If the ghosts in The Grange remained comparatively abstract, they did not in the villa, to which he was removed because of whooping-cough. That, he says, 'was *peopled* with ghosts'. This distinction seems to relate to what I have called the presence of the absent in his imaginative world. If I understand him correctly, he is suggesting that at The Grange the *beings* were not there at all, but only the feeling of their possibility and of their having been there: but that at the villa, they *were* there, yet physically absent. 'They seemed unsubstantial presences, featureless bodies,' he writes.

But terrified, on one occasion, by his intuition of these formless presences, he ran to catch his nurse's hand, when something drew his attention to the window. 'I looked over my shoulder', he wrote, 'at the space of sky. A cloud mounting up, parted, and I saw a figure in white lean out looking at me, it seemed, and holding up a warning finger.... After that apparition I do not remember any more horrors.'

The incident is of the highest importance. 'Visions' in the sky were to recur for him at frequent intervals and in particular to be associated with his first love, with war and with his approaching death. In so far as they were of a religious character, and since Nash discovered his affinity with Yeats early in his life, it is not irrelevant to recall Yeats's statement that all his religious emotions were connected with clouds and cloudy glimpses of luminous sky.[1]

An account which Nash gives of another country visit introduces another experience which was to appear frequently in his work, a particular feeling for woods, and the paths and the streams through them. The visit was to Mrs. George Chapman, his father's sister, Susan Mary, who appears in *Outline* as Aunt Molly. She lived at Yateley in north Hampshire. During this visit Nash attended a dame's school at Cricket Hill, where he was the only boy. All that he remembered learning was not to be afraid of girls and how to get things done for him. I do not find that he ever forgot either lesson.

But what was more important was the walk to school and particularly a little path which entered a spinney at a stile.

'On the other side of the stile the path continued under very different conditions. Whereas in the open fields it seemed to run unhindered at top speed, abreast of the hedgerow, it now appeared to falter and creep along in the twilight of the wood. Its colour changed from a bright resilient tone to a purplish brown. Its surface now became heavy, damp and unsure, its form confused by dead leaves or encroaching undergrowth. I, too, was influenced by the atmosphere of the wood. Here I trod more circumspectly, glancing from side to side. It was very quiet and still.'

Before he had left the spinney, he started to run. He is careful to explain that this was not panic, but only an impulse to reach the open space quickly. The tunnel of his dream was now forming itself into the significant but less fearful 'path through the wood'. On the return journey, his aunt would meet him with a black dog, which he speaks of with great affection and no thought of the black dog on the landing at home.

This fertile visit also awakened his love of winter country. He remembered 'the brittle ice pools with their dark thin rushes . . . the dripping trees in the deep lanes . . . the colour of faded, rotting paling in the pure distilled beam of the winter sun'. These elements appear constantly in his work, the paling most persistently or some equivalent in hedge or fence. But we cannot know whether these things—

[1] *Autobiography*, London, 1938, p. 25.

the path through the wood, winter sea or winter pools, the inhabited sky itself—were so significant to him at the time. We have no witness but his memory of some forty years later. Unquestionably, it will have played its usual tricks, and peering back into the past, he will have seen everything through the filter of his experiences and his work in the intervening years. He will not have invented these experiences, because that was not in his character; but he will certainly have given them greater weight and precision than they had for the child. But if there had not been some particular quality in them, if they had not already acquired some unconsciously apprehended symbolism for the child, then why indeed did they ever do so?

We may, of course, believe that his imagination was dipping into the collective subconscious; or that he did not, in fact, experience such emotions at the time, but attached them afterwards to the remembered path or pattern of cloud. I do not know. That there *are* these archetypal symbols seems probable, but we are not concerned with psychological theory but with incidents which illumine Nash as an artist—I mean, of course, incidents in the imagination—and if the same incidents are common to mankind, that does not make them less valid in any one man. If the path which each man takes through the wood were his path only and the wood only his mystery, there would be no communication possible, and therefore no art. The path of each original artist *is* his own path through his own wood, and I am tracing Nash's. But it is also every man's, and that is why we can recognize his.

iii. Langley Marish

My account of the Nash family broke off at the generation of Paul's grandfather. It must now be resumed. In 1846 he married Susanna Dodd of Peppard in Oxfordshire. The Dodds were a cultivated family, descended from the learned and reverend William Dodd who was executed for forgery in 1777, in spite of Dr. Johnson's support.[1] Susanna insisted that her children should be well educated. The boys were all at public schools, two of them were at the Temple and two of them at Oxford: the girls were finished abroad. Nash never knew this grandmother, who died in 1875, and his grandfather was an old man when he first met him. Born in the year before Waterloo, he had already ruled at Langley Rectory for over forty years.

The house, of which the oldest part is dated 1664, still stands at the

[1] See Boswell under that year.

end of a drive whose gates face the inn at George Green.[1] When Nash first went there it was a substantial, hospitable house with its carriages and riding horses; and its master was an autocratic but benevolent landowner. He had the reputation among his fellows of being a subversive radical because he had improved the local water supply, built three bedrooms in his new cottages and, as a member of the Eton Board of Guardians, agitated about the conditions of workhouse children. Nash was devoted to him, but he recognized that he was not a man to be contradicted or disobeyed. It was a devotion composed of love for his kindness, respect for his authority and amusement at his endearing eccentricity

When Nash first visited at Langley, his aunt, Edith Sara, ran the house, and two of his uncles lived there. One was the gay Uncle Hubert, his 'favourite uncle', a great beagler with a passion for betting, who once, I am told, laid odds on the undertaker's men dropping the coffin at a family funeral. The second was Uncle Rowland, 'a strange, rather uneasy being, difficult to get to know.'

On weekdays at Langley Nash would drive round the estate with his grandfather and afterwards accompany him to his study where samples of produce had been collected for his inspection. They always included a clutch of hen's eggs. When Nash came to write of this he realized that it had been particularly important to him:

'Ever since I can remember sensation I have been delighted by the sight and feel of birds' eggs. They represent for me a kind of beauty which to this day nothing supplants. To take an egg from the larder and hold it in my hand gives me the same pleasure as touching and contemplating a piece of perfect sculpture or ... pottery, with its supreme glaze covering the lovely solid form. The fact that it is potentially alive I do not think ever interested me. I experience only an aesthetic emotion.'

Nash was self-deceived about this. The potential bird may not have been in his conscious mind when he was enjoying the formal quality of its egg; but his life-long concern with birds, with flight and with the inhabited sky suggests that it was these associations which gave a particular significance to the egg-shape. It is not a shape that occurs frequently in his work, but sometimes it is very conspicuous—in *Salome* (Plate XIII), for example—and it contains the bird in a very particular way in *Mansions of the Dead* (Plate XIV). It was at Langley that Nash first learnt to recognize birds and their nests, and to

[1] A water-colour of the house is reproduced in *Outline*, facing p. 33. It is now called Westmoor House.

collect their eggs. Uncle Hubert taught him this, and how to make catapults and how to fish.

The pattern of Sundays at Langley was quite different. Nash was rarely to like church-going, because, I think, of the arid form in which it was first offered to him. But a more beautiful form could move him deeply, at least on occasions. Years later, he gave his wife an account of a service at St. George's, Windsor:

'The choir performs the extraordinary feat of marching round the Chapel singing unaccompanied by music, the Trinity hymn—'Holy, Holy, Holy'! The effect is exquisite. . . . So pure were the boys' voices and the music altogether so poignant, that tears gushed into my eyes and I felt indeed thrilled. The whole service was reverent and refined in the extreme—really impressive and inviting to holy humble worship and prayer. I feel I cannot go to the parish business ever again' (8 June 1914).

But he also enjoyed Langley church-going, although for different reasons. The drive from George Green in the family brougham through smiling and curtseying villagers appealed to his taste for the grand manner. In thanking Conrad Aiken for the dedication of his poem *Landscape West of Eden*,[1] he wrote: 'I am established for all time among those wealthy and pleasant people, the Landed Gentry. A Landscape West of Eden, the seat of Paul Nash, Esquire . . .[2] it sounds good.' He went on to say that he had read the letter to his wife, who had laughed at him for being so eighteenth century, and he added: 'Never mind, it comes from my eighteenth century guts' (1 November 1934).

Langley had set him off along these lines. Langley was not only his father's home, but his grandfather's and great-grandfather's: it was a tradition. He could wrap himself in it with some dignity. Today there are the Nash brasses in the church and their graves in the churchyard, but it is difficult to find anybody who remembers the family.

The end of the day at Langley, weekdays or Sundays, was the same. Lying in bed, Nash would hear his grandfather mounting the stairs to the landing where he thumped three times with his stick. The house fell silent. Then the old man called loudly: 'Are all the windows closed and all the doors fastened?' Then the child heard the distant chorus of reassurance and finally his grandfather's very loud: 'Goodnight, everybody' and the answer and the crash of his door.

[1] J. M. Dent, 1934.
[2] No omission.

John Nash died a few weeks before Queen Victoria. He was buried on the twentieth of December 1900. The next morning, being St. Thomas's Day, the poor widows came with their baskets to beg for wheat, oatmeal, corn and milk. It was the last Thomasing at Langley.

The eldest son, John Hartopp Nash, succeeded, but the estate was still heavily encumbered from the days of the extravagant and sporting William. He was not a farming man. His interests were in public works and his son, Bernard, who at first left Eton to help him, preferred to enter the Church. Langley was sold out of the family in 1907, three years before the centenary of its purchase.

iv. Schooldays

In January 1898 Nash went to Colet Court, the preparatory school for St. Paul's. The whole eight years of his school life are covered in seventeen pages of *Outline*. 'In those years', he wrote, 'I suffered greater misery, humiliation and fear than in all the rest of my life. It is for that reason, perhaps, that I do not wish to dwell upon this period.' He suffered from the usual bullying, which, he is careful to say, was unknown to the masters. It taught him a lesson about himself. 'I knew then', he said, 'that cruelty was what I could not stand.' He was to defeat the cruelty of war by the purge of artistic expression: he defeated the leader of the school bullies by making his nose bleed, although he had to jump for it.

Then he learnt a second lesson about himself: that he suffered from a nervous anxiety which often prevented him from making full use of his natural capacities. He ran well, but always failed to get off the mark promptly, and he was bad at cricket for the same reason; but at football he was carried through by the momentum and he could use his skill. The air of confidence and self-possession which he displayed as a man must have been the result of self-discipline, of a deliberate defeat of this weakness. Perhaps it was the remains of that effort, a certain constraint, which made him sometimes appear cold and aloof to strangers.

But it was another handicap which he discovered in himself, a remarkable inaptitude for mathematics, which mattered most at the time. He was intended for the Navy and it was entirely because of this that the intention was defeated. 'I have seen mathematical teachers', he said, 'reduced to a sort of awe by my imbecility.' And yet this does not make *The Times* critic look foolish for saying that 'the probability is that he has the mathematician's rather than the painter's mind'. That was in 1932,[1] and his art at that time did reflect a second and more successful effort to tackle this inaptitude. The discipline of mathematical order, which he could not acquire by calculation in numbers, he did to some extent realize in the creation of geometrical images; but it remained foreign to his naturally organic sensibility.

Soon after the summer holidays of 1900, which Nash had spent at Swanage, that was to be so important a Place in his later work, he had to meet sorrow and anxiety. First there was his grandfather's death and then his mother's illness. She had changed. She had become irritable and detached, and even more troubled. His father decided that they would move into the country, and he bought a site at Iver Heath, near Langley. It was in Wood Lane, which runs south from the Uxbridge-Slough road. When in 1943 Nash found the word 'suburban' used of this district, in a draft account of his life, he altered it to 'country' and added the remark: '*suburban*, actually, was just what all that was not in 1900.' At the end of 1901, they moved into the house which was to be his father's permanent home and his own for many years. It stands back from the road on a semi-circular drive and is a typical, inoffensive villa of the period, built in brick and roughcast, with a touch of *art nouveau* in the tiled open fireplaces and the white overmantel. There were four reception rooms and six bedrooms, small stables and an acre and a half of garden, including a croquet lawn. That is the sort of place—a pleasant, comfortable, ordinary house such as a modest barrister might build himself at the beginning of this century. The character it acquired for Nash and for all the family was a human affair, and an affair of trees and birds, not of bricks and mortar. It was the house with the Bird Garden where Paul and John Nash grew into artists.

One effect of this move was to make Nash a boarder at Colet Court, which had many satisfactory results. He gained a new self-confidence by being in the football first eleven and a cox in Bewsher's Four, but more importantly for us by his lead in a school craze for theatricals and model theatres. He carried this activity into the holidays. The programmes of family theatricals for 1901 and 1906 have survived, and they show Nash in the parts of a bad fairy and a wizard and as a singer of comic songs. He was to act many times afterwards, and he always retained a gift for imitation. His imitation of Roger Fry was to be most imposing. But what concerns us more is that his chief rôle at school, the designing and painting of sets, was the beginning

[1] 4 November.

of the interest which produced the theatre designs of the nineteen twenties.

Nash went on to St. Paul's for the autumn term of 1903, but was then transferred to a crammer's at Greenwich. The bullying here was far worse than anything he had yet known, and it was supplemented by the indiscriminate brutality of the headmaster, a retired commander, who unfortunately took mathematics. But Nash was able to transform his position quite suddenly by a success at football, and became a favourite with the commander and his wife. This amazing woman who, in her Sunday best, 'seemed to radiate a faint blue light from her diamond encirclements', was particularly prominent at church parade when she punished dirty ears by using her rings as knuckle-dusters. Once again Nash was driven to dissociate religion from church-going.

But neither the bullying nor the favouritism improved Nash's mathematics. He failed his entrance examination for the Navy and was returned to St. Paul's in the autumn term of 1904. He was put on the science side, for which apparent insanity he gives no reason; but I suspect that he was also bad at classics. He had no gift for any language but his own, which he came to speak and write very beautifully although he never mastered its spelling and punctuation. It was now proposed that he should be an architect, but again he was defeated by mathematics; and his father was then advised to give up all idea of a profession and put him in a bank. Nash felt that he was the victim of a foolish conspiracy to involve him with figures; but however foolish, it was unpleasant to be considered a failure.

He left St. Paul's in July 1906, when he was just eighteen. He had not enjoyed his school life. 'I emerged from it impaired in body and spirit,' he wrote, 'more or less ignorant and equipped for nothing.' He seems to have had no further contact with his school until 1941, when the High Master founded a school collection of works by Old Paulines. Nash joined the advisory board and attended a luncheon, which was the nearest approach he ever made to any kind of old boys' reunion. It showed that he bore no malice and indeed he could not well do so, for it was not the fault of St. Paul's that he was a bad subject for a public school education.

The last impression of his schooldays which Nash recorded was of coming upon Eric Kennington drawing a bust of Caesar in one of the corridors. He watched and envied him. Kennington had already decided to be an artist, but it did not occur to Nash at the moment that that might be his profession too. 'No drawing I had ever done', he wrote, 'could be said to justify such a hope.' Indeed, he had no natural facility and the education for his professional life had not yet begun. But that does not mean, of course, that his education as an artist had not begun. That is why I have treated his childhood in some detail: it supplied so many images that he was to use in his mature work. For the same reason, I shall treat his adolescence in even more detail.

Gordon Bottomley[1] was to write to him, shortly after he left the Slade: 'Our own parish is the only place we need when we would find subjects for our art; but we have to go round the world and enter our own parish anew from the other side before we can see those subjects' (19 August 1912).

Nash's way round was to be through an attempt to conform with an aesthetic which was alien to his nature, a valuable discipline in the classic attitude which purged his romanticism of sentimentality. The pattern of this book must be largely the story of his wanderings and of his return to Ithaca.

[1] See p. 37.

II

Early Visions and Poems
1906-1912

————————⊰⊷⊙⊕⊙⊶⊱————————

i. The Letters of Paul Nash

From this chapter onward I have the use of Nash's letters, and therefore it is here that I should comment on them in general. Many or all may be published, and therefore I give the name of the recipient and dates or conjectural dates of all extracts, even if they are not relevant to the text. They will serve as references should this happen. At present only those to his wife printed in *Outline* and the correspondence between him and Gordon Bottomley are available.[1]

Nash had an old-fashioned view of the importance of letters in human relationships. He never wrote with the idea of publication or the convenience of his biographer in mind. His letters are completely natural: they were his way of talking at a distance. And it was for this quality that he praised the letters of others.

He wrote to Conrad Aiken,[2] for example: 'There are very few people who can write a letter which can speak, as it were, in which you can so plainly hear the writers voice and see him or her before you in the minds eye that the whole experience of reading the letter is a vivid pleasure' [Between August 1939 and July 1940].[3] And he told Edward Burra[4] that he was 'one of the rare few who *can* write a letter without it being apparent that its being written' [3 August 1937].

[1] *Poet and Painter*, ed. by C. Colleer Abbott and Anthony Bertram, Oxford University Press, 1955. But see also p. 37 n. 1 and p. 39.
[2] The American poet and novelist, who was to be a close friend of Nash's after about 1930.
[3] Dates in square brackets are conjectural or from postmarks.
[4] The painter, with whom Nash's intimacy also began about 1930.

In the other direction, Gordon Bottomley, who had probably received more of Nash's letters than anybody else, wrote to him in the year before his death: 'You don't age—not in your letters at any rate; your perfect phrasing defies time, and continually delights me' [27 August 1945].

Nash was not a regular correspondent and his apologies for this are recurrent and disarming, particularly in later years. One example will be enough here, from a letter to Lance Sieveking:[1] 'Now you need have no qualms and queasies about being a champ non-letter writer. i am the worst, lowest most crawling abject nonletter writer to a dear friend as ever existed in any walk of life [1942 c. January].

Nash did not systematically date his letters, but neither did he systematically not date them. Generally speaking, he more often dated to men than to women; but he usually dated his first letters to either sex. In effect, the nearer a letter reached to intimate talk, the less he treated it as a document.

Nash's spelling, punctuation and use of capitals were most idiosyncratic. But even his incorrectness was not consistent, and the difference, in this respect, even between letters written in the same year, is so remarkable as to be significant. It was never easy for him even to be nearly correct: he had to make a certain deliberate intellectual effort. At his best, he expressed himself intuitively. The letter moved with his feelings and the texture varied according to the person he was writing to. In so far as his idiosyncrasies seem to have a definite value for those reasons, I shall transcribe the letters exactly, but I shall correct mere habitual misspellings such as the reversed e and i after c, occasionally insert or remove punctuation marks where the meaning is not immediately clear and italicize the titles of pictures and books.[2]

Nash's letters were also a form of visual expression in the deliberate pattern-making of their lay-out and the beauty and clarity of the handwriting, which Bottomley found so like Rossetti's. They were also frequently illustrated with sketch caricatures, decorative designs and even drawings pushed to a certain finish with coloured pencils, in which he also sometimes wrote the text, changing from one to another in the course of the same letter. These visual qualities must necessarily be lost in printing; but so much excellence remains in the literary expression that I shall, as I have said, make the fullest possible use of them.

[1] See p. 86.
[2] In some cases I have not seen the originals. See Acknowledgments.

ii. Chronicle

However modestly Nash may have contemplated Eric Kennington at work, he very soon decided that he was made to be some kind of artist. But, at this time, he was almost as much attracted by literature as by the visual arts, which is probably why he now proposed to become an illustrator. His father not only accepted the idea, but encouraged it. He was a churchwarden and chairman of the parish council: his profession was the law and his relaxation was croquet. He did not understand art or poetry. But he became Nash's champion against the less tolerant uncles. Nash's gratitude never failed, nor did his sense of the immediate duty that it imposed on him. Nearly forty years later he wrote to Richard Seddon:[1] 'Your position is not unlike my own when I was beginning. I had to make my work justify itself as a profession in the eyes of my father, altho he never pressed me or embarrassed me. . . . It is a matter for oneself and the world' [1944 c. October].

On the seventeenth of December 1906 Nash registered at the Chelsea Polytechnic. At first he seems only to have been a part-time student but later to have taken the full course, including the life classes.[2] At the same time he began to illustrate Stanley Weyman's novels for practice, and he approached a publisher to whom his father introduced him. But nothing came of that except a memory that rankled, and years later he wrote to Audrey Withers[3]: 'I know how irritated I used to get when influential old people used to give me important interviews and introductions on the strength of being my Father's son' [c. 1924]. He could not understand why anything should be done for anyone except on their own merit. He was always prepared to push his own, but he was firmly independent from the beginning. He was also always anxious to help others by bringing them to the attention of influential people, but he wanted them to be helped because of their merit and not because of his patronage.

Nash was not to any romantic degree a poor student: he was in no danger of starvation in a garret. But there was some financial pressure: his mother's illness was expensive and his father's income modest. And it was largely because he wanted to relieve him as soon as possible that he left the Polytechnic for the more commercial

[1] Now (1955) Director of the Sheffield Art Galleries, but then a young painter and disciple.
[2] The present Principal informs me that the organization of the school has so changed that he can only guess what is implied by the registry entries.
[3] See p. 112.

atmosphere of a London County Council school at 6 Bolt Court, Fleet Street. He began work there in the autumn term of 1908 and remained for two years. The atmosphere was brisk and practical with no room for dilletantism. The students were there to learn 'art' for the sole purpose of making a living.

Nash began by working very much on his own, but after a time he attracted the attention of the masters and found their technical advice very useful. He was struggling to learn correctness and to counteract his tendency to exaggerated idealization. But that did not last. He soon fell under what he calls 'the disintegrating charm of Pre-Raphaelitism, or, rather, of Dante Gabriel Rossetti'.

In the February of 1909 Nash had his first recorded illness. 'I am in bed', he wrote to Nell Bethell,[1] 'with a mouth full of absysses (I *cant* spell that awful word!). . . . I am suffering *literally* from swelled head caused rather by acute colds in nerves than conceit . . . and I'm just rather fed up with everything all round' [1 March 1909]. He was to be in the presence of illness during most of his life. His mother's had already shadowed his youth. He was to be with his father at terrible moments. His wife and himself were to be so frequently attacked that long stretches of his life appear as the history of a hopeless campaign against it. But not until his body was defeated by death did he cease to work with astonishing imaginative vitality. The sickness of his body could interrupt but never permanently weaken his activity as an artist.

While he was at Bolt Court he began to attract attention. At one of the monthly Sketch Club exhibitions a drawing of his interested Selwyn Image. This was a link with the Pre-Raphaelites, for Image had attended Ruskin's lectures as Slade Professor at Oxford, a post he was shortly to hold himself. He invited Nash to his house, an event which Nash describes as his first entry into a new world. But, through a later exhibition, he was to make a more permanent entry. He exhibited what he refers to as 'my river composition', which was *Flumen Mortis* (1910). The judge, William Rothenstein, rather sensationally gave this drawing full marks; and Nash went up to him afterwards 'glowing with happy excitement'.[2] From that moment his debt to Rothenstein began. 'You have been a true friend,' he wrote to him years later, 'you were the first to acknowledge my work and to give me encouragement. I have never forgotten that' [1931 c. August].

[1] See p. 42.
[2] *Men and Memories, Recollections of William Rothenstein,* 1900-1922, 2 vols., Faber, 1932. Pp. 184 and 185 give a full account of this incident. So does *Outline,* pp. 82-3.

Shortly after their first meeting, Nash visited Rothenstein and was overwhelmed by what he calls 'a new visual experience'. He 'was in the presence of taste'. Nash was to be very sensitive to 'the room', to make many beautiful rooms of his own, to write on room-design, to be always alive to the possibilities of beauty in everything. It seems as if it were this visit which directed his interest to all uses of design.

Nash first submitted a poster for Rothenstein's criticism, which was that though the idea might be good, the expression was neither clear nor simple. The few designs which survive from that early date certainly suggest that that criticism was justified, and Nash accepted it and acted on it. He then submitted a collection of the drawings which resulted, and when Rothenstein had examined them, he told him that he should go to the Slade and learn to draw. When Nash objected that he could not ask his father to keep him any longer and pay higher fees, Rothenstein simply asked him why he did not earn them for himself; so that Nash left Hampstead full of exaltation and in the proper attitude of mind.

He soon wrote to Rothenstein: 'I'm racking all my brains and tapping all the sources and raising all the wind to produce enough for the fees! You were very right about the feeling which comes—the desire to draw for the sake of drawing. I begin to feel it but as yet I am very uneasy and laborious' (13 July 1910)[1]

In the meantime Nash had made another friend, who was to have an even more lasting and profound influence on him, the poet and dramatist, Gordon Bottomley. It was also an influence of a wholly different kind. While the painter's contribution was to help the young artist to a clearer and more accomplished expression, the poet's was to stimulate his vision.

A neighbour at Iver Heath, a Mrs. Goldsworthy, lent Nash Bottomley's *The Crier by Night*, the first edition printed at the Sign of the Unicorn in 1902. Nash was deeply stirred by the book and, without considering that it was not his, began to illustrate and decorate it. He made two small pen and ink drawings and a geometrical border round the title-page, and pasted in a full-page drawing in pencil and ink with touches of white body colour.[2] On another page are the faint remains of an erased pencil drawing. When Nash

---

[1] The complete letter is printed in *Men and Memories*.
[2] Reproduced in *Outline*, p. 92. I shall not generally refer to where reproductions are to be found. That information is given in the Index of Pictures.

returned it to Mrs. Goldsworthy with apologies, she sent it to Bottomley. The result was the beginning of an immense correspondence; the typescript made from it occupies over five hundred and fifty pages.

It was just before this correspondence began that Nash suffered his first great sorrow. On 14 February 1910, his mother died at the age of forty-nine, and was buried four days later at Iver Heath. She had been ill some ten years, often away from home and even when there increasingly withdrawn into herself, almost a stranger, it seems, in her own family. But that did not lessen the shock or the horror of the circumstances. John and Barbara Nash were at school, and Paul was alone with his father. He has said very little of this event and I shall say little more. In only one letter that I have seen does he refer to it, and that was not written until the autumn. He was glad for his mother, he wrote to Nell Bethell, 'for she came to the end of all life'; and of his own first experience of the great commonplace he said very simply: 'I cannot tell you how terrible death is' (17 September 1910).

It was a hard responsibility for a boy of twenty-one to be his father's only support in the following months and it was made more difficult by the fact that just at the time when his father returned from the Temple, Nash left for his evening classes and was not back until about eleven. It was only then that they could sit together for an hour.

The affection between these two men, with their totally different outlooks and values and interests, was based on the recognition by each of the other's integrity and on deep sympathy and respect between them. Thirty years later, recalling his beginnings at the Polytechnic, Nash was to write in *Outline*: 'How I should have felt had my father's support weakened or had he shown signs of losing faith in me I do not know. But he never wavered, nor, apparently, did he worry. Without offering either criticism or advice he waited with a confidence which I now realise was the greatest encouragement I received during those early years.'

Now it was the father who found support in the son. They made the adjustment together. Nash absorbed his first experience of death, and it was never again to be a stranger. When his own death became a presence to which he must grow accustomed, the symbol he was to find was the aerial flower and never 'death's worst, winding sheets, tombs and worms and tumbling to decay'. He listened to the Golden Echo though what he heard could not have Hopkins's clarity because he never achieved Hopkins's faith.

38

CHRONICLE

At the end of August, Nash went to Normandy and Brittany for about a fortnight with his uncle Tom and 'Aunt Gussie'. It was his first journey abroad. The diary which he kept of it is lost—the only diary I have ever heard of—and there remains nothing but the vague enthusiastic letter which Rothenstein printed in his *Men and Memories* —talk of 'tremendous churches and cathedrals', of 'twelve towns and incidentally a thousand beautiful things'. He came back full of ideas and with a few drawings which he hoped to make something of. In October he entered the Slade. He began with four days a week, drawing from the Antique; but by December he was admitted to the Life Class.

Those, of course, were the days of Henry Tonks. There is no need to give an account of that remarkable teacher: he is familiar in so many memoirs and in the excellent biography by Joseph Hone. Nash's first encounter with him was like that of most students. Tonks knew the breed: he had been at the Slade some eighteen years when Nash arrived. This tall and aquiline man, heavily lined, remote, capable of great rudeness and even cruelty, could place the new student exactly in his place. Nash exposed his drawings and invoked the impressive names of Rothenstein and Bottomley. This is his account of what happened then:

'Tonks cared nothing for other authorities and he disliked self-satisfied young men. . . . His surgical eye raked my immature designs. With hooded stare and sardonic mouth, he hung in the air above me, like a tall question mark, moreover . . . of a derisive, rather than an inquisitive order. In cold discouraging tones he welcomed me to the Slade. It was evident he considered that neither the Slade, nor I was likely to derive much benefit.'

But Hone has said that though the first effect of Tonks was like a cold douche, if the student took it well, he soon felt 'that he was being folded under the shadow of a wing'. Apparently Nash did take it well, for before the end of his first month, he could write to Nell Bethell: 'The great Tonks cares for us and preaches "Art" in large letters all the day he is beautifully mad' (20 October 1910): and by Christmas he was telling various correspondents that he liked him more and more, that he was a splendid man, really great and full of care for the strugglers. He was falling under that spell which Sir Muirhead Bone has said never broke—the spell of trying to gain Tonks's approval. At one point at least he seems indeed to have gained it, but the undated letter to Mercia Oakley[1] has no indication of

[1] See p. 44.

when it was. 'I had a great triumph at the Slade today a picture created a little stir and the great Tonks was very nice on it and congratulated me!!'

According to Hone it was Tonks's opinion that 'a painter who is not a poet ought to be put in the stocks', but it was also his opinion that that was nothing to do with the teacher. 'All I can do', he said to his students, 'is to give you a few *facts* about drawing.' Bottomley was afraid that this insistence on facts might interfere with the poetry in Nash, but it was precisely what he needed. Tonks must have criticized his work on practically the same points as Rothenstein had done, for Nash was to assure Bottomley within a year that he had taught him 'a greater feeling for form and shapes and a way of seeing things more simply, more as a whole' (11 September 1911).

In *Outline* Nash described the Slade as being like 'a typical English Public School seen in a nightmare', with C. R. W. Nevinson as the school bully. But that was not quite how he reacted at the time, when he found it 'frightfully exciting'; he was 'loving it'; it was 'absorbing'. His letters were full of such phrases.

It was one of the recurrent periods of Slade brilliance, and his contemporaries included Stanley Spencer, Mark Gertler, William Roberts, Edward Wadsworth and Ben Nicholson. Nash's friendship with Nicholson began in those early days. He was soon taken to his father's house in Mecklenburgh Square, another important 'interior' for him. Sir William Nicholson was then at the height of his celebrity, and that was impressive. So were the blue ceilings and the black mirrors and the whole Whistlerian atmosphere. Nash spent the Easter vacation of 1911 at the Nicholsons' house in Rottingdean,[1] and had Nicholson with him at Iver Heath in June. Of course he had other Slade friends at this time, or shortly afterwards, such as Ivan Wilkinson Brooks, known as 'Wilkie', Claughten Pellew-Harvey, Claude Miller and Rupert Lee.

Nash returned to the Slade in the autumn term of 1911 but only attended three days a week. In December he left for good. In the meantime, in the second half of October, he had settled in London. This came about through a neighbour at Iver Heath, the Hon. Mrs. Audrey Handcock,[2] who was to become his stepmother.

She was of a peculiar and impressive ugliness, but she had great presence and kindliness. Nash was very fond of her and regretted

---

[1] For an account of this visit see Nash's letter to Bottomley of 16 April 1911.
[2] Not Hancock as given in *Outline*. She was the daughter of the third Lord Tenterden and widow of Major Robert Gordon Handcock, grandson of the second Lord Castlemaine.

when 'the bloom of her ugliness was passed'.[1] She died some six months before him.

But her sister-in-law, Mrs. Harry Taylor,[2] was a very different person. She had been a society beauty of the late nineteenth century and is reported to have sat to Burne Jones, Poynter and Sir William Richmond. Nash met her at Mrs. Handcock's in the summer of 1911. She became interested in him and began sowing seeds. She dazzled him with her background of fashion and aristocracy, high politics and expensive painters. He concluded that it was most important that he should move to London and enter 'select circles'. He was not at all embarrassed by the idea and he expressed his views with naïve frankness in a letter to Mercia Oakley:

'I have met some interesting people here and there and men who hold the keys of the select circles where I long to move one day. I am to be introduced to many artists and writers and I am glad to have the chance because it is an opportunity to get known. So far I have got to know men because they have seen my work which is more creditable than by patronising introductions of friends' [21 July 1911].

Mrs. Handcock encouraged all this. He must meet people, she said, Poynter, Alma-Tadema, above all, it seems, Sir William Richmond. The first two were old and ill and could not see him, but Richmond was to have an important influence on his career.

In October of 1911, then, Nash took rooms in Chelsea, at 19 Paultons Square. He found it wonderful to be alone and free, but he was a little uneasy—'shocked and hurt with myself', he told Bottomley, 'to find I am so happy away from home'; but he kept the feeling that he could go home whenever he liked—'that is a touch like a hand stretched out to meet yours in the night' [1911 c. October].[3] But Chelsea was to last a very short time. Nash was on the verge of deserting all that it then stood for—the Chelsea of Rossetti and his associates—although he did not yet seem artistically aware of the disruptive forces which had rushed into Bloomsbury to fill the vacancy when the Pre-Raphaelites emigrated to the west. He knew, of course, that there had been the first Post-Impressionist exhibition in November 1910. He had heard Tonks fulminating in a set speech in which he appealed to his students' instincts. He could not keep them away from the Grafton Galleries; but he had warned them and said how

---

[1] A remark of Nash's remembered by her niece, Viola Garvin.
[2] She had married the son of the poet and dramatist, Sir Henry Taylor.
[3] For a full description of his lodging, see his letter to Bottomley, 22 November 1911.

very much better he would be pleased if they did not risk contamination. But the speech had made no difference either way to Nash. He was untouched.[1] In the autumn of 1911 Chelsea seemed to him the proper place for a young artist: but he left it in May 1912.

iii. Letters to Nell Bethell and Mercia Oakley

There is a large batch of letters, written during the years we have been surveying, from which I have already quoted passages to illustrate the chronicle of events; but now I want to use them to display the growth of Nash's imagination and character, which they do most vividly and intimately. They were written to two girls, and I shall treat them separately so that his relation with each of them is distinct.

The first letter of his which I have been able to find at all is the first of these. It is dated 15 January 1909, and is to his cousin Eleanor Love Slingsby Bethell, the daughter of Lord Westbury's second son and therefore a niece of Nash's 'Aunt Gussie'. She lived with her mother at Brighton. Nash described her in *Outline* as intelligent, pretty and with a fascinating stammer. His second letter to her, dated 21 January 1909, is a 'declaration'. It is the ordinary love-letter of a young man of his day, diffident and sensitive. Nell answered with a kind but firm refusal. Nash accepted the situation and apologised. 'I'm only a boy and not sentimental at that and it was quite an unnecessary thing to do', he told her; and he added that he was glad she would allow him to be her friend and write to her sometimes (31 January 1909). It is a sad and common little incident of wasted feelings, with no very serious meaning, and I have not considered it as his first love; but it must have coloured their relations when they met during the second war, both middle-aged and both near death. After this, the interest of the letters, which continue for about three years at fairly regular intervals, is almost confined to Nash's reading. They evidently shared the same taste, and it was deplorable.

There was great enthusiasm for *The Beloved Vagabond* by W. J. Locke. 'I think if I failed in this life (and I dont mean to),' Nash said, 'I should gather all my worldly goods and having raked in a little money—take to the High Road. . . . Think of such a glorious existence if you really loved the open air and knew about the woods and fields, as I do a very little' (9 March 1909). But of course vagabondage was not Nash's line at all, though the influence was not to

[1] There is some confusion in *Outline*. Nash gives this speech as following the *second* Post-Impressionist exhibition, but he had left the Slade by that time.

disappear at once; it was later to be more respectably derived from
Borrow.

Then there was a series of Hindu fairy stories translated by F. W.
Bain, which he loved because they dealt with 'fantastic creeds and
fabulous happenings' (1 March 1903). They suited his appetite: the
very titles obviously suggest the inhabited sky—*The Descent of the Sun*,
A Heifer of the Dawn, A Digit of the Moon and so on.

But then there appears a very regrettable book indeed, E. F.
Benson's *Angel of Pain*. What affected Nash in this drab mosaic of
clichés was the mystic affair of its hero, a simple-lifer, who hears the
pipes of Pan and ends up by being very properly trampled to death
by a goat. 'That last', said Nash, 'was horrid and cruel but this man
learnt too much. . . . I quite believe in Pan and when I should be cast
upon the hospitality of the woods and hedgerows I should study
Nature and make never ending drawings' (9 March 1909). But it is
understandable that three things in this book appealed to him—the
symbolism of birds, an empty wood filled with a presence, and a curtain uneasily stirred by a presence just the other side—the presence
of the absent.

The next book mentioned is a volume of Keats' letters which he
gave Nell. She evidently rated him for spending his money and that
annoyed him:

'It is frightfully sweet of you to exercise a motherly care for me and
doubtless it is convenient to treat me as a schoolboy but it sometimes
rather hurts! I say this just in sorrow not in any conceit. I want to be
considered seriously because I am absolute master of my own
affairs . . . Then on the other hand . . . I still love to play the Ass and
have a weakness for futile games and all children and pretending
things and anything childish—I dont know what I want but I do
know that it is very galling to be thanked at all for every twopenny
halfpenny book I send you' (25 April 1909).

Unfortunately the Keats level was not maintained. Another distressing enthusiasm arose—this time for the works of Algernon Blackwood. Nash first particularly praised *John Silence*, which certainly
contains a good deal of what was to be characteristic Nash imagery—
haunted woods, Druidic circles, mystic flying and again the curtain
which threatens to lift on the hidden presence. Then he found *The
Education of Uncle Paul*. 'These are the things I have felt and thought
upon . . .' he says 'I for one anyhow am proud to confess I understand and sympathise in each thought and idea. The book has helped
me and done me good' (6 May 1911). It is a story of Paul Rivers,

43

whom the author describes as 'a dumb poet—a dreamer of dreams that bear no fruit'. We shall soon find Nash fancying himself in that part at moments of depression. The dumb poet's niece is a child called Nixie, a terrible child who continually disappears with 'a fluttering as of white wings'. She tells her uncle in a dream, for she gets about a good deal in an occult sort of way, that he contains the sun, moon, stars, wind, rain, dawns and sunsets, moonrise and wild flowers. Then she happily dies and Rivers takes up social work. It is amazing that this twaddle should have fed an imagination so athletic as Nash's. But it certainly did: we cannot fail to be struck by that accumulation of images from nature, which is almost a list of his themes. And the white wings were also to play their part.

That is the last book referred to. The letters peter out in trivialities, but I shall quote from others later. The last which has survived was written on Christmas Eve 1912. But Nell Bethell returns to the chronicle after thirty years.

The second series of letters also begins in 1909. There are fifty of them, and all but one were written before the end of 1912. They were to Mercia Oakley. She has long been married but, as with Nell Bethell, I shall use the name by which she was known to Nash. They met because Mercia's godmother, with whom she often stayed, lived next to the Nashes at Iver Heath. There was no question of a love affair between them. She was 'a sort of "she-comrade" ', as Nash told Bottomley (8 April 1912).[1] The nearest to anything of the sort was a regret that they were not in love:

'Mercia Im going to say a quaint thing. it has been a thought to me since my stay at Wings. . . .[2]

'If only I could have been that man you met and fell in love with and you the girl I was destined to meet and know for my dream and desire. Instead of you being in love with a man who don't care and I meeting a girl who dont give me a thought.[3] It seems a muddle. . . . I feel more easy to have told you for honesty between true friends is a great thing towards true friendship' [? 1912].

I think it is necessary, although a little painful, to give one long extract from a letter that is nearly three times as long. It shows Nash's romantic sentimentality in its most extreme form; but under

---

[1] The passage is cut in *Poet and Painter*.
[2] Mercia's home at Winkton near Christchurch in Hampshire. A plaque on the front was inscribed: *William Wing 1719*. It was burnt down in 1915.
[3] Sybil Fountain. Nash's mistake will be explained later.

the flowery language we can perceive the sincerity and sensitivity of
his immature excited imagination and we can hear the echoes of all
his unfortunate reading. And if we find it embarrassing, we must
remember that it was written before the first war when youth was not
afraid to let itself go:

> *Sister, comrade, girl of the sunshine, friend,*
> *Fawn, wild bird, wind flower, kid and little devil*
> *I am your brother to the old world's end*
> *I will be your tree your friend thro good and evil.*

'Now if that aint an inspiring verse strike me comic! Do you realise
the full significance of "tree" or what it would *try* to mean to you. A
shelter, a shade, a consoling old thing, a strong kind friend to come
to thats what I *want* to be. As yet I'm rather young and not too wise
but some day I hope to grow up to that ideal. . . . In you I have found
something appealing to all of me and ready to sympathise with all of
me. I have *never* never found it before either in man or woman it is
the rarest and most priceless treasure a man who is an artist or strives
to become an artist can find. As you know I am not a person who
dangles after women and can only find sympathy and companionship in feminine society. . . . I despise and hate effeminacy tho' I
realise how easy it is for an artist and a poet to become effeminate
but man cannot live with men alone at least not an artist I know
many women and I *consider* I have once been in love now I feel less
selfish I want to give and take a great broad buxsom gorgeous love I
must and I shall. You are going to be one who will stand with outstretched hands upon a hill—wind-blown sun-kissed one with the
great earth, a dreamer who can dream into my dreams, understand,
grip and feel deep. At the same time one who can talk the sublimest
nonsense with me and go mad with the winds you are to be my sister
thro the magical compelling touch of Nature thro' that touch which
thrills in our beings, which we call sympathy . . .

'When you read this letter much of it may seem extravagant I have
written almost unconsciously yet with an irresistible certain force in
my mind driving my pen there is no affectation anywhere. . . . This is a
muddled world. Read some Stevenson he's a tonic for sore hearts. I
wish I was with you Id be so damned funny and amusing Id make
you laugh the skies down!' [undateable].

Clearly Nash was in a very susceptible and excitable state in those
years. He was rushing about to parties and dances and wrote Mercia
ecstatic accounts of them. The Three Arts Ball, for example, was

'simply the final word in' happy nights everyone so gay and fanciful —all the nuts there and many quaint and beautiful folk' [1909 or 1911]. The enthusiasm and the language carry us back into a different kind of youth from any we know today, but the experience can become cloying, and I need quote no more.

But there are two images which recur throughout the letters and have more significance. The name of Mercia's home, Wings, continually excited him and there are constant references to the Silver Hands. They had seen a curious cloud formation one evening like a pair of silver hands meeting across the sky and it became one of the things which 'belonged' to them, as she has expressed it. This is another example of that preoccupation with the inhabited sky which we have already noted and shall not cease to note until we leave the last pictures.

I now want to take the letters to Mercia as the opportunity for three digressions. The very first is concerned with Mercia's singing and it touches on a subject which need hardly arise again. Nash liked music and was later to have a good taste; but we may accept the competent and yet obviously sympathetic judgment of John Nash that his brother was not in the fullest sense musical.

His earliest liking was for drawing-room ballads and hymns. The Sunday evening hymn-singing at Iver Heath had been 'a fairly loud outcry' with his father making 'a queer indeterminate noise' through his pipe. He constantly refers to Mercia's singing, but one quotation will be enough. It is not in his most pleasing manner. 'Aye, we must hear those little waves of Breffney. What I love about your singing is the birdyness of it and the wavyness in it and the wildness o' it. You are a true singer you sing because you must, for joy, or for sorrow or for very pity' [? 1909].

After his marriage, Nash found a great deal of pleasure in singing to his wife's accompaniment on an early piano. He had a baritone voice which was true and flexible, but not very rich. It was an unpretentious performance and it also gave a great deal of pleasure to their intimate friends. He sang English music mostly—Elizabethan and eighteenth century. Indeed his lasting affection was for the English composers, particularly Purcell; and it was appropriate that the concert arranged by the Arts Council for the opening of his Memorial Exhibition in 1948 should have included his work and Thomas Morley's and Orlando Gibbons's.

The dreadful little waves of Breffney were heard no more after his youth, and by the middle of the nineteen twenties at the latest he had discovered his other lasting enthusiasm—for Bach. He speaks of it in a letter to Audrey Withers:

'Christine [Mrs John Nash] has just been playing Bach. . . . What is the secret of the extraordinary magic of Prelude 8 1st. Book. I heard it long ago—when it first enthralled me—played by Rupert [Lee] on his little old piano in Chelsea. The riddle of it haunts me still—how terribly moving it is. The first cold chords initiating one into that sweet yet frightening mystery. There was never such music, such unutterable things—said—what is it hidden in that Prelude, Audrey?' [c. 1925].

A few years later, Nash developed a taste for American jazz and an enthusiasm for the gramophone, and he would ask Lance Sieveking to give him 'a spot of jazz . . . or a foxtrot vocal melody called—Shes such a comfort to me' [3 January 1930].

Another letter to Mercia introduces the second digression—on Nash's appearance. It proposes a birds'-nesting expedition and raises the question of a chaperone, and then goes on: 'I dont know how to flirt and dont suppose you do. . . . In the springtime my thoughts invariably lightly turn to thoughts of summer suitings and my mood is a revolving kaleidoscope of blue checks and black and white stripes' [6 May 1910]. Nobody who ever met Nash failed to recognize his 'presence' and how that was augmented by his clothes. He took the same care of his appearance that he did of everything around him. It was a subject like another for his artistry, a means of personal expression. But he did not take it too seriously: his account of his clothes in Outline is detached and self-mocking. Their conventionality at the Slade led Nevinson to make a public exhibition of him by asking if he were an engineer. In spite of this, he appeared at his first private view in 1912 wearing a silk hat, snuff-coloured trousers, a black jacket and white spats; and carrying a silver-headed malacca cane.

But Nash soon remedied this conventionality. He acquired a sealskin waistcoat, a fawn Stetson and a brown tweed cloak. With this remarkable get-up he wore a red silk scarf knotted sailor-fashion, smoked a cherry-wood pipe and carried a long ebony shepherd's crook. His hair flowed and he had small side whiskers. For best, he wore a black coat, wide oatmeal trousers and black patent leather shoes with red heels. But after the war Sieveking introduced him to his tailor: there was no more nonsense. The following extract from a letter to Clare Neilson[1] shows how discreet he became in later years. He is explaining why he cannot wear the gay pull-over she had knitted him:

[1] Mrs. Charles Neilson. See p. 220.

'You know, we gents are so reserved in our garments! If my tailor caught me wearing a blue silk pullover he'd probably insist on my paying his account and going elsewhere! Not but other chaps sporting bloods and all sorts dont wear silk pulls but Mary sent me a book at Christmas called *The Middle aged Man on the Flying Trapeze* and that reminder steadied me a bit. Dear Clare, it sounds beastly of me ...[1] but what I want terribly badly is a woven bed wooly' [4 January 1936].

In general, Nash evolved a style of dress that combined the artist with the man-about-town, and at the same time achieved a vaguely eighteenth-century and naval look. 'He carried over'... as Herbert Read expressed it, 'some of the swagger of the rejected career—art, for him, was to be a Senior Service. His clothes were not conventional, but they were always well-cut'.[2] He would, for example, allow himself a dark velvet dinner-jacket but it had to be excellently tailored.[3]

But all this, of course, was only the 'finish' of his appearance. The man himself was never dominated by his clothes: there was never the faintest suggestion of the tailor's advertisement. He was, in Oliver Simon's phrase, 'a natural dandy'. His dandyism was not assumed with his clothes, but was naturally present in the whole poise of his body, in his admirable good manners, in his quiet, hesitant way of speaking which seemed to select each word with care and offer it for approval. It is difficult to convey this without giving an impression of his being finical and even affected: but in his presence there was no such impression. The carefulness, one felt, came from a deep integrity, the power of a whole personality ceaselessly occupied with choosing the best, even in the most trivial matters. This objectivity, even towards the very words he used or the way he knotted a coloured scarf, the way he spread out a piece of paper or drank a glass of wine, the judgment he exercised on any opinion that was offered him, this objectivity sometimes produced at first meeting an impression that he was aloof, that he lacked spontaneity and easy conversation. There was, indeed, a certain reserve in his attitude to strangers and he could even occasionally chill his friends by a fastidious disapproval. But there were three characteristics which counteracted this: the steady penetrating look of his blue eyes which 'carried immediate conviction of clarity of vision and integrity of purpose';[4] the absorbed interest he

---

[1] No omission.
[2] *Nash: Eates*, p. 9. Cf. also Margot Eates, p. 5, Reference abbreviations will be found in the Bibliography, II A.
[3] See a description of him in 1922 by Oliver Simon, *Signature*, No. 15, New Series, 1952.
[4] Archibald Russell, Clarenceux King of Arms, in *The Times*, 23 July 1946.

1b. The Three. 1911
Pen and wash

1a. Our Lady of Inspiration. 1910
Ink and chalk

2a. Margaret Nash. c. 1934
Photograph by Paul Nash

2b. Facsimile postcard
to Lancelot de G. Sieveking
from Paul Nash with
self-caricature. 13 August
1923

displayed in whatever he was concerned with at the moment, an interest which far transcended the nice making of conversation; and his sense of fun and delight in the ridiculous. He could, when the occasion was fitting, direct his wit to hurt, but usually it was applied to indifferent subjects and the general tone of his manner was of sympathetic kindness and courtesy. In fact, he looked and behaved like what he was: an artist and a gentleman. It is a pity that, with his habitual conscious artistry in every detail of his life and work, he sometimes over-posed for his photographs, so that many of them seem affected, which, as I have said, his presence never did.[1] He never sat for a formal portrait, and the only drawings of him which I know were those by Rupert Lee,[2] William Rothenstein[3] and Edmond X. Kapp.[4] His only self-portrait, apart from the frequent caricatures in his letters, is the woodcut which acted as frontispiece to my first book on him.

My third digression is a return to the subject of Nash's early reading. The occasion is the following passage from a letter to Mercia:

'Do you know this from the "Hills of Dream"? "Long, long ago, a white merle flew out of Eden. Its song has been in the world ever since but few there are who have seen the flash of its white wings thro' the green gloom of the living wood, the sun splashed, rain drenched, mist girt, storm-beat wood of human life."

'But today, as I came thro the wood, under an arch of tempest and led by lightenings, I passed into a green sun splashed place. There, there I heard the singing of a rapt song of joy! there ah there I saw the flash of white wings' (5 March 1912).

Here again Nash has chosen to copy out a 'Wings' passage and the image remained so fixed in his imagination, although his memory may long have lost its origin, that about 1942 he painted the *Vale of the White Blackbird*. At that date he would have shuddered at the word 'merle', but it is the same thing and the same symbol.

The Hills of Dream set me a puzzle which I have not solved. I can trace no such book. *The Hill of Dreams* by Arthur Machen seemed a likely guess, but the passage is not to be found in it. And yet the book corresponds so exactly at so many points to Nash's imagery and imaginative life at that time that he must certainly have read it, and confused the title and source of his quotation.

[1] Photographs may be easily found in the following sources: *Unit One*, p. 78; *Nash: Read*, frontispiece; *Nash: Penguin*, p. 6; *Nash: Eates*, frontispiece; *Outline*, facing pp. 18, 96, 144, 208, 221; *Poet and Painter*, plate xv.
[2] Collection of Mrs. Paul Nash. Reproduced *Outline*, facing p. 124, and 'Century of British Painting' by Anthony Bertram, *Studio* 1951, Plate 111.
[3] Present whereabout unknown. Reproduced *Nash: B.A.F.*, p. 1.
[4] Present whereabout unknown. Mr. Kapp believes that it has never been reproduced.

It is the story of a youth who has some kind of Pannish vision or experience in an ancient earthwork. This place became for him very much what Wittenham Clumps were to be for Nash. There are many passages which are almost descriptions of certain pictures. The following extract is assembled from three of them:

'In the hedge of the lane there was a gate on which he used to lean and look down south to where the hill surged up so suddenly, its summit defined on summer evenings not only by the rounded ramparts but by the ring of dense green foliage that marked the circle of oak trees. . . . The image of it grew more intense as the symbol of certain hints and suggestions. . . . The streaming fire of the great full moon glowed through the bars of the weird oaks, and made a halo shine about the hill.'[1]

This corresponds closely in mood to the late Clumps series painted from Boars Hill and to Nash's description of the Clumps in *Outline* (p. 122).

There are many other correspondences but it will be enough to draw attention to one more. It is the account of trees in the 'haunted wood' below the earthwork. There were 'forms that imitated the human shape, and faces and twining limbs that amazed him . . . here and there an oak stripped of its bark, white and haggard and leprous'. These are Nash's Monster Trees and the subjects of many photographs in *Fertile Image*.

I am not suggesting that Nash took his later images from this book; they came from something much deeper. But I do suggest that we see him shaping them to some extent in this type of reading. It is probable that he quite forgot that he had ever delighted in it. Certainly his account in *Outline* of his reading at this time is very different. He speaks of the *Morte d'Arthur*—by way of Rossetti, of course —and of Tennyson, Morris, Keats, Whitman, Blake and Coleridge; of Stevenson, Carlyle and Borrow. In the letters there are also references to Poe, Patmore, W. H. Davies, Belloc, Milton and Browning; and in the later letters to Peacock, de Quincy and Wordsworth.

He only makes one reference to Shakespeare and none to the Bible, but Mrs. Nash assures me that he knew them both well when they first met and that he never ceased to read them. Dante, who should have been his author above all others, is only mentioned twice in his letters and the references are trivial. He certainly read *in* Rossetti's *Early Italian Poets*, for he took the theme of a drawing from it; but that does not guarantee that he read all of it, including the transla-

---

[1] *Hill of Dreams*, ed. 1907, pp. 15, 46, 70.

tion of the *Vita Nuova*. But even if he had, it is not the *Vita Nuova* which would have most enthralled him; and he never once refers to *The Divine Comedy*. His poem on *The Passing of Dante*[1] obviously derives from Rossetti. It is, therefore, particularly interesting that he urged his students at the Royal College of Art to read Dante. I can only imagine that being aware of Dante through Rossetti and Blake, he instinctively felt his immensity; but disliking translations and unable to read Italian, and being, as he says in *Outline*, 'a lazy, incurious reader', he left it at that.

iv. *Sybil Fountain*

Only one letter to Sybil Fountain has survived. It must have been written in the summer of 1912, and it begins: 'O formosa dea, will you wonder I have not written before or not—no you are not given to wondering. Many times I have been on the point of writing and then have thought it was not worth while: you dont want letters and I dont know that I want to write 'em so wheres the use of them.' Then Nash goes on to announce his first exhibition, which she will not see because she will be in Switzerland. 'I wish you could be there at the opening day—I shall miss you I think.'

But indeed he had already missed her: or perhaps, imaginatively, he had not. She remains bound up in the most profoundly personal and, I believe, the most important part of his work. I am happy in the graciousness which allows me to use a real name in a matter of such intimacy; and the selflessness which writes: 'I really don't feel it matters at my age. . . . It's the book that matters and it's truth to Paul.'

The story of Nash's relations with Sybil Fountain is curiously without dates. It remains as an experience, in which the sharp edges of fact have all been lost, an experience of clouds in the sky. It seems that their grandparents had been friends. Did they meet, perhaps, over theatricals? Nobody remembers. In after life, Nash had a memory of a waggonette arriving at Iver Heath and unloading Mrs. Fountain and her three daughters, and of his being overcome with shyness. It was their first meeting, but was it in 1906 or later? Nobody can be more precise. And when did Nash fall in love? That can at least be placed in a particular period. When he was at the art school in Bolt Court he used to bicycle home from Uxbridge station. The road

[1] *A Book of Verse*, MS. of 1910. See p. 63.

crossed the Alderbourne by a little bridge, where he was accustomed to halt and listen to the stream talking. 'For talk it did, most convincingly,' he wrote in *Outline*, 'nor was its voice the only one I could hear, as I leaned on the parapet.' Nash has said that he knew almost every poem of Rossetti's by heart. He must have remembered one passage, surely, at this time:

> *What thing unto mine ear*
> *Wouldst thou convey,—what secret thing,*
> *O wandering water ever whispering?*
> *Surely thy speech shall be of her.*
> *Thou water, O thou whispering wanderer,*
> *What message dost thou bring?*[1]

And indeed he fancied that it spoke to him of a girl, for he says that the memory of this Place was connected with his first love.

'Henceforth,' he wrote, 'my world became inhabited by images of a face.' He saw it when asleep and when awake. He saw it, most importantly, in the sky.[2] I shall discuss the nature of this 'vision' later; for the moment I am only concerned with it in the limited sense, that this face in the sky was Sybil Fountain's. There is not enough of Nash's work which has survived from this period to judge how literal his statement was meant to be. But I do not think it must be taken to suggest that his world was *exclusively* inhabited by one face. We have not here Rossetti's obsession, as his sister described it:

> *One face looks out from all his canvases,*
> *One selfsame figure sits, walks, leans,*[3]

although Nash described the face as of 'the new Beata Beatrix'. But it does not appear that he drew or wrote about it alone. There was no other specific face, perhaps, but there were other 'visions'. Nash, I think, was running two experiences side by side, perhaps even three. But for the moment, I am chronicling, not speculating; I am concerned with the incarnate Sybil Fountain and not 'the face in the sky'. She became now what Nash calls 'the human subject of my inspiration', but he did not speak directly to her about his feelings. He only sent her his poems. At each meeting, he seems to have expected *her* to speak. Naturally, she did not. There was one awkward, ill-chosen moment, in the hall of a house, when he did declare his love and she told him to be quiet because other people could hear.

---

[1] *The Stream's Secret.*
[2] The relevant passages from *Outline* are quoted on p. 58.
[3] *In an Artist's Studio.*

Finally there was the embarrassed break which he describes in *Outline*. 'The face in the night sky, the voice by the bridge of the Alderbourne had, as I feared, been only a dream.' He died still believing that. But now Sybil Fountain writes to me: 'It is time to say that I think I should have married him if he had really asked me to and persisted a little. That was my feeling when, at sixty, I read his book with so much astonishment. . . . I should have told Paul all this, had I read his book before he died.'

Nash's diffidence, his naïvety, had waited for some romantic sign which did not come. He could not see what was there. 'I did lots of things yesterday,' he wrote to Mercia Oakley in a letter that is postmarked 15 March 1912. 'I broke my dream for one thing. . . . I have been in love with an idea. That was because I was a poet and a fool.' And in another undated letter, he returns to the subject:

'I am such a patchwork mixture that I can do such a thing as I have just done—break a dream which has been for over three years; which at times was all absorbing and simply I believe life itself but which was like a stream strong at first and high but which grew stiller and stiller under the freezing sky. . . . At last after struggles innumerable it grew dead and the ice covered it. . . . Perhaps had I been a simpler stronger nature the stream would have born up. . . . I realised suddenly she thought I would pester her with my presence and would bore her. I was furious, pride rose like a wave and drowned everything . . . oh lord thats enough, forgive such a history. All I know is that I suddenly freed myself and stood alone, untrammeled; perhaps a coward, a weakling! God judge me' [1912].

The face faded from the sky. For years, the sky was to remain uninhabited, except by natural birds and sun and moon. It was not again to be the centre of his vision until death appeared in it, first in the shape of the bombers which he called aerial creatures, then of the parachute, as the Rose of Death, and lastly of the aerial flowers and the sunflower which passed into the sun and was eclipsed.

v. Drawings and Poems

When in 1922 I was preparing the material for a book on Paul Nash,[1] he told me of his early period under the influence of Rossetti, and of the visionary drawings and poems that belonged to it; but he would not allow any of them to be reproduced nor even show them to me. But it is clear from *Outline* and from what he had chosen for

[1] *Nash: A.B.*

reproduction in it, that he changed his mind. He wrote to Bottomley of the *Crier* drawing: 'I still feel I should not be ashamed of its publication' [*c.* 26 May 1944]., and in more general terms: 'I hope you dont think I do not value my first drawings. I am nearer to them today in one sense than I was ten years ago' [26 June 1944]. My full justification, however, for recalling this early work from oblivion is in a letter to the painter, Cecil Collins (24 December) [1944]. He outlined the book on his life's work which he then had in mind and for which he hoped Collins would write the text and he called the first section by the name I have adopted for this chapter—'Early Visions and Poems'.

It has been difficult to trace any very early work. The first example I have seen is the drawing for a bookplate designed for the late George Mortimer, K.C. It is clearly dated September 1907 in Nash's hand. This is disconcerting because two bookplates which Nash designed in 1909 are in exactly the same manner. There can be no doubt about their dates: they were for Ada Lance and Christine Bradhurst, both of whom he met at the Colchester Pageant in that year and one of them is dated. It is frail evidence but it does suggest, as far as it goes, that Nash made no progress in nearly two years of training.

All three designs depict a pseudo-mediaeval library, with a paraphernalia of ink-horns and quill-pens, Tudor chairs, heaped folios and so on. Each is surrounded by elaborate floral patterns and two of them include angels derived from Burne-Jones. The whole effect is of careful, patient and not very skilful exercises in the Rossetti-Morris-Crane manner. It is impossible now to discover how many bookplates Nash designed, but it seems to have been a regular activity between 1907 and his going to the Slade in 1910.[1]

I have not seen any drawing except Mrs. Mortimer's that can be dated before 1910. About 1907, he says in *Outline*, he did an illustration to Rossetti's *Staff and Scrip*,[2] and in 1909, he told Nell Bethell, 'an ambitious water colour drawing' based on Boccaccio's sonnet *Of Fiammetta Singing* which he found in Rossetti's *Early Italian Poets*. 'The colour is rich', he said, 'and rather foreign and I think more successful because I absolutely disregarded all rules and conventions and painted piece by piece like a stain glass window' (9 March 1909).

Obviously he had been reading or hearing about Pre-Raphaelite methods. But we must remember that for him Pre-Raphaelite meant,

---

[1] An example is reproduced in *Outline*, p. 65. Nash exhibited some at the Curwen Press Exhibition 1937, and the C.E.M.A. travelling exhibition 1943. Another proof that he outgrew any shame of them.

[2] Not, of course, 'Script' as it is printed in *Outline*, p. 81—the only evidence of this drawing.

not the early Holman Hunt and Millais, but Rossetti; and this seems the occasion for saying something about his influence on Nash. It had begun early in 1909, and how strong it was a year later is sufficiently witnessed in a letter to Bottomley:

'Rossetti to me is a very great man and I would rather see a picture of his painting than that of any other artist. Whatever sense of beauty or line I may have or may develope I seem to owe to him. And I have only to look at his designs to feel a burning desire to create something beautiful. The wonderful sweetness and strength of his work is like stimulant and inspiration to me and I can never be sufficiently grateful to his memory' [1910 c. April].

Nash seems in particular to have been attracted by Rossetti's double activity as poet and painter, what he calls in *Outline* his 'dual expression'. But there were many other affinities between them. Much of their imagery was the same. The sun, moon, stars and clouds are recurrent in Rossetti and The Blessed Damosel inhabited the sky.

Kerrison Preston quotes William Michael Rossetti on his brother's character in a passage which, he writes, 'might very nearly have been said of Blake'. It could as well be said of Nash.

'Certainly he had some sentiment; he may have been a mystic, and he had a passion for art in various forms. But it is not the less true that he was full of vigour and buoyancy, full of élan, well alive to the main chance, capable of enjoying the queer as well as the grave aspects of life, by no means behindhand in contributing his quota to the cause of high spirits—and generally a man equally natural and genial.'[1]

In William Michael's preface to his brother's poems, he mentions many other characteristics which were also Nash's. 'He was always and essentially of a dominant turn, in intellect and in temperament a leader. . . . Constant and helpful as a friend . . . free-handed and heedless of expenditure . . . in family affection warm and equable . . . self-centred always, and brushing aside whatever traversed his purpose or his bent. He was very generally and very greatly liked by persons of extremely diverse character.'

It seems possible to isolate a group of artists to whom Nash was linked by the 'dual expression', and who were all, except Nash, directly dependent on Dante. We know that Rossetti was deeply sympathetic to Blake and Botticelli[2] and that all three illustrated Dante. Blake, of course, like Rossetti, had the 'dual expression'. It is true that we know of no poetry by Botticelli, but he frequently took

[1] *Blake and Rossetti*, De la More Press, 1944, p. 69.
[2] For a connection between Nash and Botticelli, see p. 165.

his subjects from poetry. We know Blake's admiration for Michelangelo and that Michelangelo also had the 'dual expression' and rated Dante above all men.

Simil uom né maggior non nacque mai.[1]

As to the central figure, Dante himself, it is true that we know of no drawing by him, but he said that he drew an angel—*disegnava un angelo sopra certe tavolette*;[2] Leonardo Bruni states that he drew; and there is a mass of evidence and commentary on his close relation to the visual arts.[3]

There is, of course, no question of ranking Nash with Blake and Botticelli, Michelangelo and Dante; but we can at least claim that he belonged to the high company of these poetic painters and visual poets.

It was the fashion not long ago to deride the 'literary' painter: it is now no longer necessary to defend him. But it is perhaps necessary to recall that Nash did, at the height of that fashion, try to conform to it and did profess its doctrines. We shall discuss that when the time comes. But the point of recalling it at the moment is that so much of what we know about his early literary influences comes from his own late writing in *Outline*. By the time he had begun to write that, he was no longer ashamed of his early work but fascinated by it. He was happily back in his parish.

On the other hand Nash was always intensely alert visually, a tireless and acute observer. Rossetti was not. He told the truth about himself when he wrote:

I shut myself in with my soul,
And the shapes come eddying forth.[4]

However 'visionary' Nash might be and however much, in the last years, he was shut in with his soul, his shapes were always taken from nature. Nature never ceased to be his dictionary, once he had discovered her; which however was not yet.

But it may be that he turned away from Rossetti because he felt a need for more defined images, because he already realized that the image in art should be as closely observed as the emotion it images. He found that it was so in Blake. On the other hand, it may be, as

---

[1] *Le Rime*, ed. Valentino Piccoli, 1944, CLIV. See also CXLII.
[2] *Vita Nuova*, XXXV.
[3] See *Iconografia Dantesca* by Ludwig Volkmann, Grevel, London, 1899. Introduction and Bibliography.
[4] Fragment from Section called *Versicles and Fragments* in W. M. Rossetti's ed., 1900.

Bottomley was to say years later, that it was the mystic in Nash that made him turn from Rossetti to Blake (16 July 1941). The two influences seem to have overlapped in 1910 and 1911; but that he lectured on Rossetti's poetry to the London University Literary Society in the latter year is practically his last concern with Rossetti for thirty years. Blake's influence certainly lasted through the period of his love for Sybil Fountain, although after he had 'broken that dream' it was to fade for a time. But the impulse to the 'dual expression' never died out, though his writing was to become prose instead of verse; and Blake's influence was to revive, although it was no longer to shape his visual expression. His very last paintings, which were totally unlike Blake's, were admittedly derived from his poetry.

I must now try to substantiate what I have been saying from the small body of work which has survived from 1910 and 1911. We can take three productions as examples of the direct influence of Rossetti. The first is the *Sleeping Beauty* (1910). When, thirty years later, Nash borrowed this and other early drawings which belonged to Bottomley, he wrote to him: 'I am overwhelmed, and quite staggered to find what I was capable of. When Margaret[1] saw the Sleeping Princess she exclaimed indignantly *its cheating*—meaning I suppose, I had been cribbing from D G R which of course I most incredibly had!' [12 May 1942]. And indeed he had, for the drawing[2] is little more than a weak *copy* of Rossetti. The second is a pen drawing, *Legend of the Christmas Rose*, of a peasant girl offering the rose to Our Lady and the Infant Jesus. The design is a little freer and less crowded than the bookplates', but has nothing of Nash in it except the imagery of the rose and a bird that flies below an arc of stars. The third is a short story in manuscript, dated January 1911, called *The Dream Room*.[3] The story, vaguely set in 'the middle ages', is of a painter, a thwarted lover, who lives in a tower overlooking the sea. It is packed with Nash symbols such as: 'There were times at evening when there came a beautiful soft light into the sky, like the coming of angels with grey wings' and 'the great red swords of the sunset', which particularly foreshadows the skies of his first-war paintings. His hero, who is obviously himself, has a vision of a girl, whose eyes are obscured with

---

[1] His wife.

[2] The present whereabouts of pictures, where known, will be found in the Index of Pictures.

[3] In Miss Fountain's collection. He sent a copy to Bottomley and described it as his 'latest effort' (20 February 1911). There is an etching, clearly related to the story, also in Miss Fountain's collection; but when he sent a print of this to Bottomley with a letter dated Christmas Eve 1911, he described it as 'my first and only etching, perpetrated the year before last'. It is indeed in the manner of 1909, so that it appears that the idea first took visual form.

birds. She calls him up a winding stair 'filled with wings—a great many rose wings'. At the top is a door, which he forces open to find himself before the 'great quiet face of the evening sky' and he falls from the tower to death. The girl is called Margaret. He wrote this, we must remember, three years before he met his future wife. We must also remember that a Margaret is a flower, so that this Margaret is his first aerial flower and symbol of death.

I must now digress to examine Nash's 'visions' and make some attempt to define their nature, not because of the immature drawings that were their immediate result, but because they were the seed of his most mature and most original work.

The relevant passage in *Outline*, to which I previously referred, follows the description of his experiences on the bridge over the Alderbourne:

'Henceforth, my world became inhabited by images of a face encircled with blue-black hair, with eyes wide-set and luminous, and a mouth, like an immature flower, about to unfold. But the whole countenance, as I saw it so often in my dreams, seemed remote, untouched by human warmth, lit only by some other radiance which poured out of the eyes in their steady gaze—unaware of the mundane world; certainly unaware of me.'

Nash then describes his desertion of 'those little close rooms of Rossetti's', from which, he says, 'I emerged into open spaces. Led by the voice of Lavengro I followed on to the heath.' It is true that that movement was to come soon, but the immediate movement was into the visionary skies of Blake; which indeed he recognizes by passing at once to the effect on him of certain verses which he quotes—the opening thirty-two lines of *To my friend Butts I write*. . . . He resumes:

'The strange import of this poem, which has even more meaning for me to-day, penetrated my consciousness insidiously. I began to form a habit of visual expansion 'into regions of air'. I believed that by a process of what I can only describe as inward dilation of the eyes I could increase my actual vision. I seemed to develop a power of interpenetration which disclosed strange phenomena. I persuaded myself I was seeing visions.

'These generally took the form of faces and figures in the night sky.'

W. B. Yeats was to ask Nash: 'Did you really see these things?' and we must repeat the question. On that occasion, Nash says that in the presence of 'the master of visions' he felt it 'necessary to be uncompromising', from which I presume that he answered Yes. But it is implicit that the real answer was not so simple as that. Perhaps we can best get at it by an attempt to distinguish the poet's from the mystic's vision; for Nash's, I think, was poetic vision only.

The poet's vision, in its proper nature, is not of reality but of the image of reality: even Dante, even St Teresa and St John of the Cross, as poets, are obliged to employ the medium of the image. But the reality is not what is seen, but what is not seen. It is loose talk to speak of an artist as mystical. An artist may, of course, be a mystic, as he may be a cricketer: but *as artist* be cannot be a mystic.[1] Nash is careful, in the passage I have quoted, to speak of the face in the sky, as *seeming* to be lit by 'some other radiance'. He does not claim to see the radiance, but only an image which seems to reflect it: not to see the sun, nor even its light reflected in the moon, but only an image of the moon.

We see only with 'the hindered eye', but the poet unceasingly struggles to recover the full vision. I take that to be the meaning of Emily Dickinson's enormously evocative lines:

> *Oh, poor and far, oh, hindered eye*
> *That hunted for the day.*[2]

That hindered eye sees only the image clearly, but the reality as in the image, darkly; and it is that duality which Elizabeth Browning described in *Aurora Leigh*:

> *But man, the twofold creature, apprehends*
> *The twofold manner, in and outwardly,*
> *And nothing in the world comes single to him,*
> *A mere itself.*

We must distinguish between this conception of the 'double vision', in Blake's parallel phrase, and the single vision of memory which Wordsworth meant by

> *that inward eye*
> *Which is the bliss of solitude.*

This is only the *oculus imaginationis*. Wordsworth's 'inward eye' *in that poem* is not Blake's: the daffodils remain daffodils to his inward as they were to his outward eye. But that is not the case with Blake's double vision, to which we were bound to come in the end. The familiar lines once again demand our attention.

> *For double the vision my Eyes do see,*
> *And a double vision is always with me.*

[1] But see the fuller discussion of this in Chapter VII, v.
[2] *Bolts of Melody*, Cape, 1945, No. 40.

With my inward Eye 'tis an old Man grey;
With my outward, a Thistle across my way.[1]

The thistle, in passing from the outward to the inward eye, changes: in the inward eye it is no longer a thistle nor even a remembered thistle, like Wordsworth's daffodils, but an old man grey. But both are seen in the present tense. When I said 'passing' I was using a metaphor: there is no time for passing. It is Blake, rather, who passes, because of an unhappy compulsion to write in time, so that two different but instantaneous experiences, which make one, must be expressed one after the other and so divided.

Or, of course, there may be more than two experiences. The expression of these experiences in symbol is commonly described as having 'layers' of meaning, but that is surely a misleading metaphor. In allegory there are layers because the images *stand for* the concepts; but in true poetic symbol the images *are* the concepts. It may therefore be exceedingly difficult to distinguish the pure sensation—the experience of the object with the outward eye—from the vision of the inward. As an object seen by the outward eye may be filled with the significance of an inward vision and thus wholly change its character—thistle into old man—so, I suspect, an inward vision may project itself imaginatively into the world normally apprehended by the outward eye. In this way the visionary 'sees' it, not as an hallucination but as something which he knows all the time to be only an emanation from within.

It might be expected that the visual artist would be more liable to this experience than the poet, because of the special sensitivity of his outward eye. But I do not believe this is so. On the contrary, that very sensitivity makes him experience the thistle—the thistle itself, 'the mere itself'—with such intensity that there is often no room for a second *visual* image of inward origin to intrude. His intuition of what is more than 'the mere itself' usually remains within the appearance of 'the mere itself', or at least approximately. His painted thistle will not be the camera's record, but it will be an equivalent for a thistle: it will *not* be an old man grey. The poet, on the other hand, is not specialized visually. Could this explain why, for Blake, who was poet-and-painter, a poetic visual experience of the inward eye could be strong enough to displace the physical visual image? Nash was also a poet, although never successfully articulate in verse, but is that not all the more likely to explain his face in the sky? I suppose that his

---

[1] *Letter to Thomas Butts,* 22 November 1802.

hindered poetic eye projected a *visual* equivalent for what he failed to express in verse, that his 'visions' were substitutes for poetry. If he had stopped at that point, he would have failed; but his subsequent work was a discipline in which, by concentrating on nature with his outward eye, he learnt to find his poetry in the image, instead of trying to find the image for his poetry. And then it becomes *his* poetry indeed, whereas these 'visionary' drawings are no more than his reaction to the poetry of others.

In a letter to Mercia Oakley, he said: 'So you too have seen Our Lady of the Stars. So have I Mercia I wish I could show you the picture I made of her a quaint man bought it because it moved him to tears![1] ... I didnt see any birds but of course they would be there undoubtedly' (5 March 1912).

It was precisely the birds he next learnt to see and ultimately the aerial flowers; but he would no longer fancy he saw Our Lady.

Nash's immature 'visionary' drawings and verses do not, in themselves, justify the attention I am giving them: I am giving it because of the light they throw on what came after. He was himself to find *Angel and Devil or The Combat* 'the best of its kind', and even rather surprisingly included it in his Retrospective Exhibition at the Oxford Arts Club in 1931, a date which is at the very beginning of the return to his parish. The drawing shows a domed hill such as we are to find in all the Wittenham Clumps[2] pictures; but here in place of the Clumps—which helps to explain their significance for him—is a crudely drawn angel who fights with his sword against a monster, which has a hawk's head and wings but human legs. Nash could not have read Yeats's play *At the Hawk's Well* because it was not yet written, but it is a comment on his affinity to Yeats that the scene is described there:

> *As I came hither*
> *A great grey hawk swept down out of the sky . . .*
> *It flew*
> *As though it would have torn me with its beak,*
> *Or blinded me, smiting with that great wing.*
> *I had to draw my sword to drive it off. . . .*

If, as I believe, his aerial flowers were to be his symbol of death—and certainly *The Rose of Death* was—we have here his first fumbling for such a symbol. He was to find the Rose very shortly after. There

---

[1] A banker who lived at Iver Heath.
[2] See pp. 69 and 70.

was originally a poem on the same sheet as the drawing. I give it here from a copy.

> *A place of gibbet-shapen trees and black abyss*
> *Where gaunt hills brooded dark and evil*
> *Girdled by dense wet woods and rushing streams*
> *A dread place only seen in dreams*
> *In which there is no history but this*
> *That on yon' stony shouldered tor*
> *An angel fought a devil.*[1]

Vision at Evening [1911], which contains the face in the sky, was also accompanied by a poem in which the face is compared to a rose.[2] The treatment of the landscape is much freer and more organic than in *Angel and Devil* or *Our Lady of Inspiration* (Plate I.a). Both these are undoubtedly of 1910 and completely under Pre-Raphaelite influence. On the other hand, there was a drawing, also undoubtedly of 1910, which showed the full Blake influence. Nash described the design in *Outline*.

'I imagined a wide, slow-moving river flowing between fields of poppies and orchard trees. The surface of the stream was covered with human heads upturned in sleep. . . . The fields were being scythed by winged reapers and above the distant hills a huge dolorous face appeared with hair streaming across the sky and threaded with the feathers of its flat outstretched wings. Underneath this design I wrote "a poem" of sentimental symbolism which later I regretted and destroyed.'[3]

This was the drawing which attracted Rothenstein and I have very little doubt that it was *Flumen Mortis*, which he sent for Bottomley's inspection in the first half of 1910. It is difficult not to believe that he derived this from Blake's *River of Life*.

I have already mentioned another drawing of this year—the illustration to Bottomley's *Crier by Night*. Bottomley's first letter to Nash has been lost, but we can deduce his opinion of the drawing from Nash's answer, in which he says of Blanid's figure, 'I *did* shirk drawing her feet and purposely because I wanted to try and make you see her *swaying* sick with terror and loathing. . . . I didnt dare draw

---

[1] For Bottomley's astonishingly high opinion of these verses, see his letters to Nash of 14 April and 2 August 1910. *Poet and Painter*, pp. 2 and 7.

[2] It is in Sybil Fountain's *Book of Verses*, dated 1910, but a later letter to Mercia speaks of a *proposed* drawing for it. There is a striking resemblance detween this and the second drawing described in *Jane Eyre* Chapter XIII.

[3] It survives, however, in the *Book of Verses* as *The River of Rest*.

in her feet even if I could. Also her arms are out of drawing I think but I wanted to get her strained, intense, wrung' (9 April) [1910].

It is most illuminating to find Nash, at that date, justifying an expressive distortion, when he was at the same time struggling to acquire the power of drawing accurately, as he said in a later letter to Bottomley:

'I am grinding along slowly with my drawing. . . . I have made very slow progress I think but already comes a little greater facility, and at the least, a great *desire* to draw. . . . I find painful difficulties in drawing from the model! I know what I want to express—all that I can see beautiful of line and expression, and away goes the correctness—the true proportion! It wont do. So I gave up drawing from life and went back to the solid expressionless casts. . . . It was better. I forced myself to draw accurately' (14 July 1910).

The last drawings of this year which I have traced are in Nash's manuscript *A Book of Verses* dated 11 May 1910.[1] Apart from *Places*, published in 1922, it was his only complete attempt at the form of Blake's 'dual expression'. He composed, wrote and decorated it himself. The full-page frontispiece is *Our Lady of Inspiration* (Plate I.a) and the chief decorations are birds and roses, and a knocker in the figure of a snake swallowing its own tail, a symbol which he may have found in Blake, although there are plenty of other possible sources. The verses are full of the images we have already found, and so is a separate poem preserved by Sybil Fountain, *The Hands of the Evening*, decoratively written out and dated June 1910. The major image here is the rose of the sunset sky—'The rose of an hour that grows on the grave of the sun'—which is ravished by the silver hands of evening. It seems that only one of Nash's poems was ever published, and that was written in the same year or early in 1911. It was called *Under a Picture* and appeared in a periodical edited from University College, London.[2] We find the familiar images again—an angel in rose and silver with long green hair who appears to Nash in a tree.

It was certainly in 1910 that he made his most serious effort to be a poet. 'I should cry like a kid I believe if I ever heard myself called a poet', he wrote to Bottomley; but even then he knew that verse was not his proper medium, for he goes on to speak of it as the art to which he was not called [1910 c. April].

In 1911 Nash's new phase began, and there are several drawings of that year, which must be discussed in the next chapter: I have seen

[1] Made for Miss Fountain who still owns it.
[2] U.C.L. *Union Magazine*, vol. v, No. 1, March 1911, p. 158.

none which properly belong to this. There are, however, many references in letters to drawings with titles which suggest that they were 'visionary', and we can be certain that he persisted with such drawings throughout the year and into 1912, when he did at least two which must be treated here. The first is *Pyramids in the Sea*. Nash gave an interesting account to Bottomley of its sudden arrival:

'I have spent nearly three weeks making pictures which, unknown to me, are from the first, doomed; and when my eyes are opened to this tearing them up and beginning anew and muddling for days and tearing up again. Then when I was tired of that game I started a new outdoor drawing—but the devil or someone said 'no you dont', and at half hour intervals I was interrupted by heavy rain—this lead eventually to another up-tearing. So I began some 'imaginative' landscapes indoors, they went most damnably wrong: my brain seemed a hollow tunnel thro' which stupid meaningless trains of thought rushed, or just aimless winds of nothing at all. At last I nearly wept; indeed I did *cry* inside and made an attempt at weeping but returned soon to my board and suddenly did a queer drawing of pyramids crashing about in the sea in uncanny eclipsed moonlight' (21 August) [1912].

The embryo of the idea can be found in a bookplate of 1910,[1] but in this the pyramids are reflected in water, as they might naturally be if they stood at its very edge. Above them is the face in the sky and round this group is a 'Pre-Raphaelite' tangle of briar roses. But *Pyramids in the Sea* is free from these decorative elements and is a far more original and striking design, to which the pervading blue gives a strange, almost spectral atmosphere. Here we meet for the first time a mark of Nash's work which is to recur in many forms—an image of the interpenetration of images. In this case the image of durable geometrical order stands firm—it is not 'crashing about' at all—in the perpetual movement of the sea. It expresses the meeting of Kant's concept of the Mathematical and Dynamic Sublime. The desert beyond moves in parallel wave-motion, which breaks down the isolation of phenomena—another recurrent theme—and prepares the way for *Stone Sea*, *Wood Sea* and many similar pictures. That the drawing also contains the moon and a group of trees on a domed hill brings it into further relationship with typical Nash imagery.

But this drawing is not only interesting as a forerunner. It can stand on its own as the first free expression of Nash's particular vision, not least because the face has withdrawn from the sky, as all

[1] Reproduced in *Outline*, p. 65.

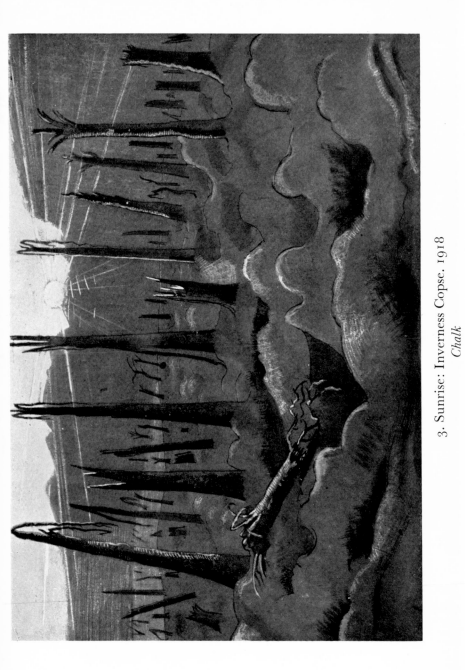

3. Sunrise: Inverness Copse. 1918
Chalk

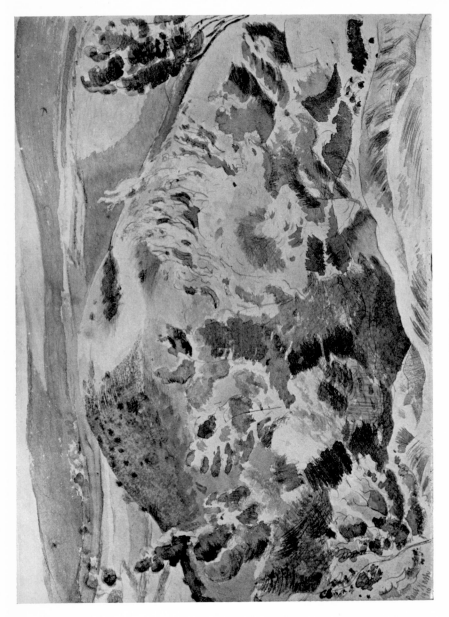

4. Windy Hill. 1919

figures were soon to withdraw from his work. The world of this drawing is inhabited by an event, a dramatic encounter between the work of man and the sea. The pyramids meet it, as the Wall was to meet and hold it in the Dymchurch series.

The second drawing derived its theme from Borrow—*Lavengro Teaching Isopel Armenian in the Dingle*. Nash has described in *Outline* how he used Mercia Oakley for Isopel, though he does not name her; how he evolved the dingle from sketches made in Richmond Park; and how, after much searching, he found the model for Lavengro in Rupert Lee, a fellow-student at the Slade and thereafter a close friend. The following extracts from letters to Bottomley give the story of its troubled progress.

'The picture said at the end of each day—"ah! youre beaten now, Im like nothing on earth Im a beastly mess, you *cant* right me, tear me up." But I said Im damned well *going* to right you, so goodnight and blew out the light. And at last I got its back broken and now its comparatively docile though a little odd' [26 March 1912].

'Alas alas the Lavengro drawing has failed. But Im going to begin it anew directly and tackle it in pen and wash. I became muddled you know and dreadfully un-simple Oh it was heartbreaking' (8 April 1912).

'That picture I started last year for "Lavengro".... I had spoilt it and consigned it to the failure drawer when one day I realised its possibilities so took and washed it and built it up' [c. end of November 1912].

The drawing is a firm geometrical design, a composition of pyramids, which successfully conveys the massive quiet of the evening and of the meditative figures. The play of light, too, is well managed—the glow of the fire and of the stars.[1]

We have now finished with Nash's derivative work, the direct influences of Rossetti, Blake and Borrow; and we have finished, for the moment, with his visions. The face had faded from the sky, only to return years later in disguise. But very shortly he was to make a drawing, *The Rose Cloud*, which laid up the prototype, as it were, for the last inhabitants of his sky during the long discipline of observation and design on which he was now to enter. He described the circumstance of this drawing in a letter to his future wife:

'This evening a wonderful cloud formed in the sky like the bubbling of pale rose leaves in a bowl—terribly exciting, Bunty. After a little it

[1] The latter are most oddly reversed in the *Outline* reproduction, where they appear as black smudges on a light ground. There is a better reproduction in *Nash: A.B.*

grew to the shape of a great rose itself, it might almost have been the shadow of that "far off and most sweet inviolate rose"[1] Yeats is ever writing about. I was painting in a field and saw the cloud behind me and ran back home to get more paper to try to draw it' [25 May 1913].

The Rose Cloud was the first item in the catalogue of his 1915 exhibition, but now it is lost. There is not even a photograph.

[1] A misquotation, of course. Yeats wrote 'Far-off, most secret, and inviolate Rose' (*The Secret Rose*). It is odd that Nash, who was so particular about the reproduction of his own work, persistently misquoted the work of poets.

III

Poetic Landscape
1912-1917

i. Chronicle

I broke off my chronicle of Nash's life at the end of 1911, when he moved to rooms in Chelsea. That was about the time at which the second phase of his work began. If any single event could precisely mark its beginning, it would be his first visit to Sir William Richmond, but I have failed to date that exactly. It was probably in the late summer or autumn of 1911, but I can only say with certainty that it was before March 1912. Richmond's link with Blake, Samuel Palmer and the Pre-Raphaelites[1] must have been very attractive to Nash, far more attractive than Richmond's own depressing work, of which indeed he seems to have been quite unaware except for his horrified memory of the mosaics at St. Paul's School. Richmond was simply for him an old man who knew the way. He found him rather like one of Blake's immensely bearded Ancients with such a booming voice as one might imagine they had. But, however alarming, Nash found him always 'wise and kind'. He was certainly practical. His advice was above all to learn drawing by copying nature. He was not, as Bottomley suspected, turning Nash away from visionary work because he disliked it; he was advising what he thought good for him at that time. He set him a weekly 'exercise' in still-life or anatomy, which he criticized on Sundays; but he also criticized the visionary drawings, and it was after his close study of the landscape in one of

---

[1] See *The Richmond Papers from the Correspondence and Manuscripts of George Richmond, R.A., and his Son Sir William Richmond, R.A., K.C.B.,* by A. M. W. Stirling (Heinemann 1926).

these[1] that, according to Nash's account, he said: 'My boy, you should go in for Nature.'

The idea of a pure landscape was not, however, entirely new to Nash. Richmond only pressed the trigger. In the autumn of 1911, his Slade friend Pellew-Harvey had stayed at Iver Heath and tried to interest him in certain features of the country, particularly ricks and stooks. 'At first,' he said, 'I was unable to understand an almost devotional approach to a haystack and listened doubtfully to a rhapsody on the beauty of its form. Such objects, and, indeed, the whole organic life of the countryside were still, for me, only the properties and scenes of my "visions". Slowly, however, the individual beauty of certain things, trees particularly, began to dawn upon me.' He examined the elms that lined the boundary of his father's property, and particularly three of them that stood apart; but for the moment, they eluded him. 'Yet', he went on, 'I was shaken within; a new vibration had been set up.' And after Richmond pressed the trigger he returned at once to the contemplation of his three elms and wondered how they would look in a picture 'with no supernatural inhabitants of the earth or sky, with no human figures with no story'. But he told Bottomley that, in spite of his new pursuit, 'imaginative inventive drawings still happen' [July 1912], and, about a month later, that he was beginning a big imaginative design based on Psalm xxiv, verse 7—Lift up your heads, O ye gates. . . .[2] But it was the results of the new pursuit that excited Richmond. Nash was bewildered. He could not see why they excited him but he continued the pursuit. Richmond began to talk of an exhibition and Nash bubbled over to his friends. For example, he wrote to Nell Bethell with boyish exuberance:

'I have found my direction or one of them. You know I believe that Billy Richmond took me up. . . . One day I took him some queer drawings from Nature not sheep in the shade or cows in the cool or anything natural like that but trees as I saw 'em and a great vague drawing of massy forms half seen and a splash of spring sunlight down a lane. Billy is excited . . . and thinks I shall be a great landscape painter bow, wow. And I am to have a show Nell all to myself in London and a real printed catalogue and tea and coffee and a beadle and become quite famous—or not. Isnt it fun' [May 1912].

But there was one person who was not pleased with what Rich-

---

[1] Mrs. Nash tells me that it was *Vision at Evening.*
[2] He was to describe the significance this phrase had for him in *Sermons by Artists* (1934). See p. 207.

mond had done. That was Bottomley. He never ceased to accuse him of having turned Nash away from his imaginative figure drawing. He harped on it in letter after letter. He returned to it as late as 1941, for example: 'That goblin Sir William Pauvremond interfered with your psychology. For your feeling that you don't "find a place for figures in your pictorial expression" never occurred to you until that Academic tempter insinuated his oily whisper in your ear' (12 August 1941). Nash protested against this: 'The old man never said a word *against* my figures only *for* my backgrounds' (15 August 1941). But Nash was always aware that the direction he took under Richmond's stimulus was not the one which Bottomley and perhaps some others had hoped he would take. That is why he expressed anxiety over the success of one of his later exhibitions in a letter to Percy Withers:

'You see I am an investment Imagine the dreadful responsibility of a gilt edged security! Not that I am worried by people investing their money in me—its their faith. . . . Think of poor Gordon. Gordon haunts me at times with great reproachful eyes and denouncing beard. I know I failed him and I know I shall fail others who have made up their minds what I should be. I beg you never do that for I shall always change' [undateable].

Every autumn the Nash family visited relations in Berkshire for the shooting. This was at Sinodun House, the home of Alfred Wells,[1] who had married a sister of Nash's paternal grandmother. It was on these visits that Nash learnt to know his most persistently emotive Place. About two miles north-west of Wallingford in the Sinodun range are two domed or mammiform hills. One of them is a hill-fort of the early iron age. They do not rise to much above two hundred feet, but they are very conspicuous in this relatively flat district. Both are crowned with compact clumps of trees which are known as the Wittenham Clumps. In describing the whole countryside to Mercia, Nash wrote of 'grey hallowed hills crowned by old old trees, Pan-nish places down by the river wonderful to think on, full of strange enchantment . . . a beautiful legendary country haunted by old Gods long forgotten' (23 September 1911). This is the language of *The Hill of Dreams*, which he was soon to outgrow; but the description he was to send Dudley Tooth in 1943 is substantially the same.[2] At that date they had returned to his work in person, as it were; but their influence was recurrent throughout his life in all those pictures to which we might give the generic name of *The Wood on the Hill*.

[1] Not Welles as given in *Outline*.
[2] See p. 292.

It was in this autumn of 1912 that he was first to capture the image. One day when he was out with the guns and saw the dogs pointing, he had a sudden experience of pursuit. At first it was the memory of his pursuit of a Clouded Yellow in his childhood. 'Then, as now,' he said, 'I had paused in the midst of pursuit.' His reverie was interrupted by a shot; but what he had had, I believe, at the obscure centre of the experience, although he does not say it in these terms, was a revelation of his part in the universal pursuit for which our perpetual hunger never ceases to make images. He was to capture his own Golden Fleece and Holy Grail and Celestial City. The day of the borrowed image was over.

The next morning he set out for the Clumps. 'I wanted an image of them', he wrote, 'which would express what they meant to me. . . . There was one aspect which, had I the wit to perceive it, would convey the strange character of the place, one image which, in its form, would contain the individual spirit. . . . I hunted my quarry, I watched and waited.'

The drawing which he then captured may have been Bottomley's *Wittenham Clumps* or *The Wood on the Hill*.[1] In either case we are surprised and relieved to find them quite free from the whimsy of his description to Mercia. He was maturing faster than he yet showed himself in letters. Both are 'straight' landscape drawings, studies for those future images of Wittenham Clumps through which he would express an enriched and personal vision.

The Wood on the Hill was included among the drawings at his first exhibition. This was held at the Carfax Gallery in November 1912. Nash has given an entertaining account of how he took the manager by storm and arranged this exhibition. It is an example of his gift for getting what he wanted. As soon as he had won, he became feverishly active. 'I have to write, write, write,' he told Mercia. 'I'm to have all the glory of press notices', he told Sybil, 'and a private view and such like amusements and become famous or ridiculous or just neither. Aint it exciting!'

And when the private view was in sight, he reported to Mercia the results of his energetic mobilisation of support:

'And think you a moment what a day it will be for me. My first real chance in life and see how blest I am beyond other men that on *that* day I can have all those I love and who care for me about me

---

[1] The latter is dated 1911 in *Outline* and *Nash: Eates*. Either this must be wrong or Nash was wrong in placing his account of it after he left the Slade. I have followed his chronology as I have no other evidence. He was at Sinodun in both years.

sharing in my joy. Oh I feel it deeply. *Everyone* has been wonderful promising to come, promising to help in every way they can—driving people to the show, sending out cards for me, hunting up odd journalistic friends to write me up—impressing dull rich friends with the importance of buying—writing me charming I-am-so-glad letters—I am most moved at times to think of it all. . . . I am like one unfurling a banner round which I am proud to gather my true friends' [Early autumn 1912].

He had tried to enlist Rothenstein to whip up the critics for him, but he was unable to visit the exhibition until the end. 'But,' Nash was to write to him nineteen years later, 'you did the kindest and most impressive thing. You bought a Drawing[1] and it was without exaggeration one of the thrills of my life'.[2]

I have given this compressed summary of Nash's extensive campaign because, being the first, it seems the proper place for a digression on his 'salesmanship' and on his attitude to publicity and criticism. Nash was ambitious. He believed in the value of his work and he believed in his fame. But he was practical enough to know that fame does not look after itself among the loud and ephemeral reputations of today; and he always took pains to ensure that his work was advantageously presented. Sometimes he pushed the demand for this to unreasonable extremes, as when he insisted on particular mounts even in the most difficult times of the second war. Sometimes he could be too ready with accusations of 'treachery to artists' and 'abusing trust', so that a publisher of reproductions after his work once answered: 'I do wish you didn't always think that we were trying to play a dirty trick on you one way or another. If I wasn't so fond of you both I'd be cross. Do I look like a rogue?' But Nash rarely exceeded the proper respect an artist should have for his own work; when there was trouble, it generally came from an improper lack of respect in others, who were not artists.

I do not agree with the extreme opinion of some who had dealings with him , that he would do anything for publicity short of modifying his work. This is to underrate his fastidiousness. He was indifferent to the ordinary press notice, or at least he soon became so; but he was intensely interested in what critics of standing might say and in how he was presented to the public in substantial articles. This indeed was part of his pride. He considered the mere report or the vulgar 'puff' beneath his notice. His press-cutting books are witnesses to this dis-

[1] *The Falling Stars.*
[2] From a rough undated copy sent me by Lady Rothenstein.

tinction. He naturally kept even the most trivial report of his earliest exhibitions, but after 1918 he only kept the more important articles.

Nash did not like adverse criticism. If it came from insignificant sources he was contemptuously amused; but if it came from responsible sources, he could be very angry; and, of course, he could persuade himself that it was unjust and based on ignorance or malice. Probably it was sometimes, but certainly not always. One example will be enough: it is from a letter to Richard Smart[1] and refers to a criticism in an important London paper:

'Who is this ill-educated provincial reporter who has been exalted to the place of art critic to that once august and conscientious newspaper? I seem a particular bogie in his (or her?) eyes. With inveterate dull mindedness I am damned with faint contemptuous praise every time I exhibit. I have noticed on the other hand the sort of thing that comes in for eulogy so I am not very impressed' [April 1941].

But when Nash was convinced that there was no prejudice, he could discuss an adverse criticism reasonably although he might maintain his position. Again one example will be enough. In the early twenties he drew Souldern Church while staying with Percy Withers. Withers told him that the colour of the stone was wrong. Nash answered:

'I cannot offer to help you over the Church difficulty. So I saw it, so it must remain—at least until I can see it again when I promise you I will seriously reconsider its appearance. There was at the moment of vision a pale glow distinctly warm amid those trees, that was what interested me. Architectural substantial form did not show forth, in fact I had to peer for *any* detail. My over emphasis of the warm tints may have been right or wrong but it was probably instinctive. I of course think it is right from the point of view of its relation to the other colour surrounding it and that is to me the important thing. I was not setting out to make a portrait of a medieval church' (25 July) [*c*. 1923].

In spite of the ardour of Nash's campaign for his first exhibition, it did not begin well. 'The pictures hang there looking silly' he wrote to Bottomley, 'and I am rather miserable. I have heard many praises from great people but no real general excitement as I hoped—vainly and foolishly hoped, I suppose. . . . I am being a disappointed discontented pig' [November 1912]. In the end he had good notices and made thirty pounds, which he asked for in gold. But he was sobered by the fact that most of his sales were to friends. Altogether

[1] A director of Messrs. Tooths Gallery, when they were his agents in later life.

he was encouraged but not thrown off his balance. What he had written to Rothenstein was still true—'Oh Lord what a work I have before me' (14 May 1912)—and for a time he went back to school and again attended night classes at Bolt Court to draw the figure.

In the November of that year, 1912, Nash first met Gordon Bottomley. The Bottomleys were staying with the poet, Robert Trevelyan, at his home in Surrey, The Shiffolds, Holmbury St. Mary, one of the houses associated with the Roger Fry circle. Nash was delighted with the 'select company' into which he was now indeed getting, but where he was not yet a familiar, for, when Trevelyan mentioned 'Roger', he was still innocent enough to ask 'Roger who?' He has described this visit in *Outline*;[1] it is a long entertaining passage, but I need only quote his description of Bottomley:

'No print or picture had quite conveyed that big, benign presence. Otherwise he was pre-eminently Victorian, and with his mane of black hair, fine profile, and great red beard could have taken his place alongside Tennyson, Watts or any other of the bearded giants of the last century. He was a good deal of a giant himself. But for his defective lung he must have been a Viking of a man. . . . He gave, always without stint. His encouragement, his praise, his sympathy, flowed out in the fullest measure and ran over. . . . Gordon's [features] seemed moulded like his own undulating hills. His slightly flattened, black crest, roofing his broad sloping brows, together with the longer sweep of his great red beard, all suggested rather the flow of polished, sculptured planes. Since very little could be seen of his mouth, he seemed to have acquired a special power of smiling with his large blue eyes which, otherwise, had an introspective, deeply contemplative look.'

It was on this visit that Nash made the first drawing of Bottomley reproduced in *Poet and Painter* (Plate V). Five years later, Bottomley wrote that it no longer represented either of them. Nash's 'deftness and certainty of handling' had increased and he himself was no longer the invalid he appears in it (19 September 1917).

'I am what the servants call "flummuxed" . . .' Nash wrote to Bottomley early in 1913. 'I have met the woman I am going to marry and marvel of marvels she loves me—and that is all to tell' [c. March]. Clearly, of course, it was not and he went on to describe her. 'And

[1] pp. 159-64. Nash has telescoped two visits, making the first 1913 instead of 1912. See Bottomley's letter to Nash, 16 July 1941, and Nash's answer.

there my dear Gordon (forgive the liberty!) you have it, and I am so damn happy I dont know what to do.' And then he went on again.

Nash had met his future wife in Rupert Lee's studio at 3 Old Church Street, Chelsea.[1] That had been in February. Within a month they were engaged. She was Margaret Theodosia, only child of the Rev. N. Odeh and Mary Ann Eleanore, daughter of John Gilchrist Dickson of Dumfries. She was born in Jerusalem where her father was chaplain to the Anglican bishop; but as he was shortly afterwards transferred to St. Mary's Mission at Cairo, she spent her early childhood and received the beginning of her education there. In 1902, when she was fifteen, she was sent to the Cheltenham Ladies' College and in 1905, having been awarded the Hay Scholarship, she went up to St. Hilda's. Her parents joined her later at Oxford, where Mr. Odeh set up as an independent tutor in Arabic, with T. E. Lawrence among his pupils. But he was living in London at the time when Nash met his daughter, although soon after he became Chaplain to the Infirmary at Hillingdon in Middlesex. On leaving Oxford in 1908 with an honours degree in modern history, Margaret Odeh began teaching, but she found the life did not suit her health. In 1912 she became assistant to the organizing secretary of the Tax Resistance League (Women's Suffrage Society) and in 1913 organizing secretary to the Committee of Social Investigation and Reform.[2]

During the period between Nash's engagement and the outbreak of war he was living and working eagerly, but there are few events to record. He was drawing landscapes, but he had not given up his idea of illustrating books or his 'visionary' interests. In particular he called on Yeats to discuss illustrating *The Wind among the Reeds*, a choice which suggests that he was still attracted by the songs 'covered with embroideries'; and he wrote to Rothenstein as late as April 1913 of his 'ideas for psychic portraiture'. But he added that he was also engaged in mundane portraiture, 'because', he said, 'I am anxious to get some commissions but more because I love this form of expression'. Clearly he was not yet exclusively following Richmond's advice to 'go in for Nature'.

In the late summer Nash visited Rothenstein at his Gloucestershire farm, and his letter to Margaret Odeh on that occasion contains one passage of particular interest:

'I told Will all my hopes and fears and found in him great comfort

---

[1] See *Outline*, pp. 140 et seq., for a full account of the occasion.
[2] I owe most of these particulars to Mrs. Paul Nash, the Bursar at Cheltenham, and St. Hilda's College Register 1948.

and encouragement, especially in my half articulated scheme of things for establishing artists in a real status in the business of life (life that is as *a living*). If we will all work at producing drawings, paintings, decorated furniture, etc, and make a real effort to produce new and beautiful things in these directions (that was my plan) he would lend us his house in town to hold a show, he would write a preface, get the press there and send his friends. . . .

'Of course it is absolutely magnificent. Now all of us can start experimenting, building, creating in new directions for an individual expression and in a year perhaps have things for a show' (24 September 1913).

That passage foreshadows a characteristic activity: Nash was to give a great deal of his time and thought to the problem of organizing the artist's economic life.

It was about this time that Nash spent an evening at the Café Royal with Gordon Craig, Rupert Lee, John Cournos, Robert Gibbings and 'a group of eager, slightly spellbound students'. These are the last words of the broken sentence with which *Outline* ends. The first event which I must record with no help from that source is an exhibition of water-colours which he and his brother held in November 1913 at the small Dorien Leigh Gallery adjoining South Kensington station, which they hired for eight days at £2 10s. 0d. It was a success, particularly in attracting the attention of two notable collectors—Charles Rutherston, founder of the Rutherston Loan Collection at Manchester,[1] and Sir Michael Sadler, at that time Vice-Chancellor of Leeds University.[2] A third and even more imposing visitor, though not a buyer, was Roger Fry. Nash described him to Bottomley:

'I thought I knew who he was so I up and spoke to him and he was simply delightful. Of course he's the most persuasive and charming person you could ever meet. Dangerous to work with or for but frightfully shrewd and brilliant brain and pleasant as a green meadow. He was obviously *very* pleased with our work and stayed some time talking and inspecting' [27 December 1913].

Fry's admiration seems to have been more than politeness in the artist's presence, for he told Robert Trevelyan that the Paul Nashes were the only things he liked at the New English Art Club's exhibition of the same year,[3] and he invited Nash to design for the Omega

[1] It now owns two oils and sixteen water-colours by Paul Nash.
[2] For an account of Sadler see *Michael Ernest Sadler. A Memoir by his Son*, Constable, 1949.
[3] Reported by Bottomley (17 July 1913).

workshops. This organization for producing furniture, textiles, pottery and so forth, had been started by Fry in the July of 1913.[1] Nash began working for it in the second half of February, 1914, but although he wrote to Edward Marsh about that time of 'making endless notes and sketches for designs destined for Omega', his association with it was to be very slight. It is evident from Nash's account of their meeting that he distrusted Fry's influence from the outset. He was not prepared to follow any 'leader' and he must have felt, though perhaps only obscurely at the time, that Fry would expect of him greater conformity with his theories than he could accord. He did later accept them in part, as we shall see; but not as a personal disciple. There was no quarrel, but they were certainly never friends. Nash was not one of Bloomsbury's 'favourite painters', although for the moment he and his brother were to be labelled Post-Impressionists. In an enthusiastic letter to Rothenstein about the success of the exhibition, in which he particularly acknowledged the help of Rothenstein's brother, the painter Albert Rutherston, Nash wrote:

'And to crown all Spencer Gore has taken six of Jacks and 6 of mine for his show at Brighton now beginning (under the title of an exhibition of English Post Impressionists and Cubists) This is amusing to us—so we're Post Impressionists and Cubists are we? Well its something to give as a reply to the damn silly enquiries we have had as to what we are, to what school do we belong, are we not very Japanese. etc. etc!' [1913 c. December].

Gore was at that time president of the Camden Town Group. This invitation therefore associated Nash with those painters who were to form the London Group, with which he was to exhibit for many years. He was moving rapidly. He has said in *Outline* that as recently as the spring of 1913 he had still considered that the New English Art Club 'represented all that was most typical of modern art in England'.

In the early spring of 1914, Nash met another notable patron of artists and poets, the late Sir Edward Marsh. Although he had begun collecting pictures from about 1900, it was only in the last two or three years that Marsh had concentrated on contemporary work. His main activity in that field was to come, but he was already a distinguished civil servant and had edited the first volume of *Georgian Poetry*. By the time he completed the series in 1922 he had given a name to an epoch of English literature.

Eddie Marsh—it is impossible for men of my generation to be more

---

[1] See *Roger Fry* by Virginia Woolf, Hogarth Press, 1940. I quote Nash's opinion of Omega on p. 186.

formal—had a particular genius for friendship in many different circles. Nash was quickly admitted to one of them and became a regular visitor to those chambers in Raymond Buildings, Gray's Inn, which were for so long the gathering place of young painters and poets. Eddie Marsh's diary for March 1914 has a number of entries in which Nash is involved and which, even in their bare records, recall that lost period: dinners at the Chanticleer and Moulin d'Or, visits to the Coliseum where Adeline Genée was dancing, meetings with Rupert Brooke, W. H. Davies and Siegfried Sassoon.

The last event for Nash before the outbreak of war was a visit with Margaret Odeh to the Bottomleys at their home in Silverdale near Carnforth. He described it to Eddie Marsh:

'I found Gordon quite splendid. It is surprising to realise how absolutely sound and healthy he is save in but one weak and fatal spot. I enjoyed his good company and profited hugely by basking in the light of such a fine intellect as Gordon possesses. I came away I believe, a rather humbler and wiser man. Their house is a treasure box of books and pictures within, and surrounded by an enchanted jungle without. Its windows command the silver bay and grey hills one way and look east across fine stony, stumbly, grey green country to the Mountains.[1] You can't think with what awe and apprehension I regarded those distant Mountains—I who had never yet met a mountain. Soon we approached them and got to grips and they turned out kindly green and brown fellows, not really formidable. But some lakes were terrific with their guardian hills—my aunt you should see them at night and evening! There is no doubt about them then. My pictures are promising for later developments but individually rather nice and gentlemanly: still, I feel I have given a jump right away from "Nash trees" ' [August 1914].

They broke the journey south to visit Sadler at Leeds and Charles Rutherston at Manchester, and after his return Nash wrote enthusiastic letters about their collections. 'I felt v proud', he said to Bottomley, 'to see my drawing hung up there. Charles very much liked the big Orchard drawing and I think would have had it if War had not just broken out and caused everyone to think twice about buying a thing' [1914. Mid August to early September].

[1] See Edward Thomas's poem, *The Sheiling*, written during a visit to the Bottomleys in December 1916, as Bottomley told Nash (7 January 1917).

ii. Drawings

The drawings which we must now consider overlap at the beginning with his last visionary period and extend up to his departure for
the front in February 1917. They are the result of his 'going in' for
nature under Richmond's impulse. By the end of these five years he
had finally rid his work of the figure as protagonist. 'When I came to
look at the landscape for itself I found it enough. I had then no use
for figures,' he wrote to Bottomley in 1941. 'That has gone on until
this day' (15 August). But even then he did not consider the question
settled. 'I do not mean I shall leave it at that . . .' he went on.
Indeed in the preceding letter, earlier in the month, he had said:
'From time to time, and particularly recently, people, and even
painters, have nagged me to pull myself together and consider figures
or parts of them as subjects for pictures. . . . Well, I am vaguely trying. . . . I need a method perhaps I shall find one. Someone suggested I should draw people like landscapes—there is something in
that dont you think'. It is, of course, exactly the opposite that was
one of his particular achievements—to draw landscapes like people,
to reveal personality in what Blake called the Vegetable World. But
at intervals throughout most of his life, Nash tried to introduce the
figure if not as protagonist, at least in a major supporting rôle. The
most important example was a large oil which he painted in 1923 and
called *The Lake*. It had a recumbent nude in the foreground, with
which he was thoroughly dissatisfied. 'Its got to look a damn sight
better than it looks now at its best before I've done with it,' he wrote
to me (6 December 1923). And indeed it was to be a very long time—
fifteen years. In its final state and with the new title *Chestnut Waters* it
had no figure.[1]

But Nash's failure to introduce the figure into his 'public' work was
not due to any lack of interest in human beings. *Outline* and his letters
are full of an observant, sympathetic and humorous delight in them;
but his visual expression of that was almost confined to frequent
caricatures in his letters and to the substantial number of straight portrait drawings which were and have mostly remained 'private'.[2] In
general I agree with Herbert Read that they show 'great talent in
this direction',[3] but they never suggest anything more than talent

[1] The original design can be seen in the woodcut *Meeting Place*, which is the frontispiece
of *Places* (1922).
[2] A few have been reproduced, notably of Margaret Nash, his father and Bottomley in
Outline and two of Bottomley in *Poet and Painter*.
[3] *Nash: Eates*, p. 10.

and we cannot regret that he did not exploit it. He had other fish to fry. His only surviving oil portrait, so far as I know, is that of Alice Daglish (1921).[1] It is treated in exactly the manner of his landscapes at the time. The structure of the forms takes precedence over the psychological revelation.

There is, however, one figure drawing to which I want to draw particular attention, *Nude: Iver Heath* (1914). A girl, naked to the waist and with her long hair loose, is moving down a garden path. She bends her head towards her right and stretches out her right arm tenderly over the flowers. In her other hand she carries a bunch of long grass. The path and the borders end abruptly just behind her. Beyond and on each side of the borders are tall seeding grasses and the background is closed by thick foliage. It is a strange drawing. The scene was a garden in Buckinghamshire: the model was Margaret Odeh. But the *feel* of the drawing is exotic, as of a Ruth amid the alien corn. The girl seems to guard and caress, contemplatively and sadly, the trim path and borders cut out of the wilderness. She is a rare embodiment in Nash's work. But take her away and the drawing would be typical and the presence of her absence expressed in the marks of human intervention.

In the beginning of Nash's landscape two dominant themes announce themselves. One is precisely the garden, the enclosed world of Bird Garden, where this drawing was made. The garden was to recur in Nash's life and work to the end. The making of gardens themselves was often to absorb him, but not as an activity separated from his work. 'I realise', he wrote to his brother, 'that in my only exercise "hobby" I am *making pictures out of the garden* It is only a projection from actual painting' [1941 *c.* October]. The gardens which interested him were usually enclosed by trees, walls or fences: it was only in his last and most adventurous painting that he used a high garden which opened to a distant view, where Wittenham Clumps rose into the sky. The significance of that development is not easily missed.

The first garden which became a Place for him, after Kensington Gardens had ceased to be more than a memory, was at Iver Heath. It was an area of rough grass outside the morning-room window planted with trees, flowering shrubs and daffodils. It came to be known as Bird Garden. In *Outline* Nash described its particular

---

[1] The canvas is dated. Nash gave the date 1923 for *Nash: Bertram*. It will not, however, be possible to draw attention to all the misdating in earlier books on Nash. For Mrs. Daglish, see p. 107.

magic, which was 'the soul of its design' as being evoked by a sensitive and dramatic response to changing lights.

'There were moments when, through this agency, the place took
on a startling beauty, a beauty to my eyes wholly unreal. It was this
"unreality", or rather this reality of another aspect of the accepted
world, this mystery of clarity which was at once so elusive and so
positive, that I now began to pursue and which from that moment
drew me into itself and absorbed my life.'

That, of course, is the sophisticated expression of thirty years later:
it is interesting to compare it with what he wrote to Bottomley at the
time: 'I turned to landscape not for the landscape sake but for the
"things behind" the dweller in the innermost: whose light shines
thro' sometimes. I went out to try and give a hint in my drawings of
those sometimeses' [1912. *c.* 1 August].

The phrase in the passage I have just quoted—'mystery of clarity'
—derived from one used by Bottomley in his first surviving letter to
Nash: 'the greatest mystery comes by the greatest definiteness' (14
April 1910). Nash was often to refer to it and I believe that it influenced him deeply by setting him to pursue the concrete image, and
to observe it closely. The idea, of course, recurs continually in Blake,
and led to his insistence on the pre-eminent importance of outline, a
teaching which Nash adopted. There is a good exposition of this in
G. K. Chesterton's *William Blake*, which, as it appeared in 1911, at
the height of Nash's Blake enthusiasm, he may well have read. If so,
he would have been struck by two statements. First, that 'there is one
element always to be remarked in the true mystic, however disputed
his symbolism, and that is its brightness of colour and clearness of
shape';[1] and secondly, that 'the Christian decorators being true
mystics, were chiefly concerned to maintain the reality of objects.
For the highest dogma of the spiritual is to affirm the material'.

I do not, at this stage, want to say any more on the so-called
'mystical' quality in Nash. But the concept which he introduced so
directly in connexion with Bird Garden—the mystery of clarity—
need not be exclusively applied to the 'true mystic': it can also be
applied to the true symbol. The symbol itself must have material
reality and be clearly defined, if it is to give visible form to the spiritual reality symbolized. The garden was in fact such a symbol for
Nash. It is part of his mythology revealed by his own intuition; but

---

[1] This is the third element necessary to beauty as defined by St. Thomas Aquinas—
claritas: unde quae habent colorem nitidum, pulchra esse dicuntur (Sum. Theol. I. q. 39. a. 8. Cf.
Aristotle, *Metaphysics*, XII, 3). For a discussion of, Nash's nitid colour see p. 162.

it is also, of course, part of folk mythology, the *pratum felicitatis*.[1] Nash succeeded in getting his image of the garden clear and definite; but not his image of its divine inhabitant. The presence of the absent man, which I have already more than once referred to, is paralleled by the presence of the absent God. Because he knew man, his footprint is also clear and definite, but God's though implicit is not marked.

The series of drawings that were directly of the Bird Garden, or may be associated with it, includes *Bird Garden* [1911], *Bird Chase* and *The Field before the Wood*. But none of these achieves the beauty and emotional fullness of *Night in Bird Garden*, with which this book began. Here there is poetic fusion: the drawing is *one* in form and feeling and yet its parts are sufficiently distinguished. The mystery is made clear. And here, almost alone among all the drawings of this period, there are no birds. I mean, no birds are drawn; but their presence is implicit in the sheltering trees and the deep stillness of the dark blue night. Probably the last of the series was *Summer Garden* (1914), where a new conscious formalization appears, a decorative pattern-making. It is more sophisticated. The rhymes and scansion are more marked, each tree and flower more botanically defined, but the poetry has shyly withdrawn.

The second dominant theme of this period was the personality of trees, which we find particularly in a group of drawings made from those elms at Iver Heath which had set Nash wondering how they would look in a picture with no supernatural inhabitants, no figures, no story. That was the beginning of a lasting devotion. What he wrote to Bottomley in 1912, he might have written in 1946: 'I have tried . . . to paint trees as tho they were human beings . . . because I sincerely love and worship trees and know they *are* people and wonderfully beautiful people' [*c.* 1 August]. But this does not, of course, mean that he drew trees like people. He immediately knew that the image of the personality of the tree must be revealed through the tree as tree. He was in no danger of being a second Arthur Rackham.

His first drawing of isolated trees was probably *The Three* (Plate I.b), which was made before October 1911. It is a lovely design, far more deeply infused with poetic feeling than any of the contemporary Bird Garden series. The design is simple and grand. Nothing intrudes on the image of the three trees drawing together and standing firm in the centre of the immense space round them. They are

---

[1] This is discussed on p. 210.

persons: but they are also just elms. *The Three in the Night* [1913] is a more accomplished drawing of them, and subtler in design, but it does not quite escape sentimentality.

But Nash did not confine himself to rendering the poetic personality of these trees. He soon began to discover their possibilities as elements in a more formalized design. The most familiar example of this is the *Elms* (1914) where he sets going a swinging rhythm of dome-like forms, which he develops rather mechanically in such other cases as *Orchard* [1915]. This drawing, however, introduces an interplay of curving trees with the straight lines of ladders which he was to explore more successfully later. Another future theme—the avenue—is foreshadowed in the vista established by the elms in *Landscape at Wood Lane*.[1]

Some of these drawings began with 'visionary' elements. When Bottomley complained of the state of *Falling Stars*, for example, Nash explained that 'the holes and scars are the places where a moon, some too-many stars, two embracing figures, and a fairy have been not quite successfully obliterated' (August 21) [1912]. The drawing now called *Night Landscape* is another example. It was originally called *The Archer*, but the archer has disappeared with the name.[2]

Of course, the whole of Nash's production in this period was not of variants on Bird Garden and the Iver Heath elms. Quite as important in the history of his development, if not in themselves, are the drawings connected with Sinodun, of which *Wittenham Clumps* is the most impressive. One Clump only appears and it is very near the centre of the drawing, remote against the bird-filled sky, cut off from us by a hedge which runs right across the foreground and by a further straight barrier made by a fold in the ground. The solitary awfulness of the Clump is more powerfully conveyed than in *The Wood on the Hill*. But in place of the enclosure of *Bird Garden* we experience the high open place and the wide earth in both of them. Two drawings— *Sunset in a Corn Valley* and *Sunset below Wittenham*—are broadly similar in feeling, but the rich harvest and the heavy sun introduced an imagery which prepares for Nash's farthest future, his last concern with the masterful presence of the sun, on whose eclipse he died.

I suspect that the lovely drawing *Under the Hill* must also belong to

---

[1] I mean the attractive drawing at Manchester (see *Nash: Eates*, pl. 8) and not the rather stilted one, wrongly given the same title, in *Outline*, p. 129, but really *Elm Trees: Wood Lane*.

[2] It was drawn about Christmas 1912, as stated by Nash in a letter to Rothenstein. The date, 1911, given in *Outline* is therefore wrong. So is 1914, given in *Nash: Eates*, p. 44. It was exhibited in 1913.

Wittenham. The great massed trees of the wood which we are invited
to enter by an opening—the path through the wood—seem precisely
that 'part of the early forest where the polecat still yelled in the night
hours' which Nash spoke of in *Outline* as being at the foot of Sinodun.
It is the mythological forest he must pass through, the place of trials
and encounters.[1]

There is one work in this period of an altogether different character, but which also heralds a whole series—the richly coloured
Lake in a Wood, probably drawn in 1915 or 1916. It is convenient to
postpone discussing the formal elements of this drawing[2] and I confine myself here to pointing out two symbolic elements which we
shall frequently meet—the enclosed water and the barrier across the
foreground.

I have reserved to the end an early drawing, *Spring at the Hawk's
Wood*, which seemed to Nash of such importance in his progress that
he gave four pages of *Outline* to describing the occasion and execution
of it. It is dated 1911 and 1912 in Nash's hand, but the whole story
of his development as he gives it in *Outline* and as it is confirmed by
contemporary letters, makes the later date the only possible one. The
drawing was made in a district near his home which was suffused
with particular, happy memories of childhood. The fact that he describes these minutely shows how fully he was aware of its 'personality', of its subjective existence. It was this heightened feeling for the
concrete image which led to a technique being, as it were, 'given' to
him for the problem he had set himself. He had no technique ready
to hand: he had not yet learnt to draw. Indeed there is a sense in
which he never did learn to draw. He never, that is, had the facility
which could made the *expression* of each new phase in his imaginative
development a secondary problem. There was a struggle each time.
In about 1928 he wrote to Audrey Withers: 'O that next phase what
could not be written of it, the difficulties, doubts terrible risks, daring
decisions hopes and fears, and then perhaps a long anxious waiting
and another phase or *perhaps* the crowning of all endeavour, the
sudden completion when there is no more to be said—victory—or a
beastly mess.'

That struggle goes back to his early days. 'But oh I wish I could
draw' he would break out suddenly to Mercia [1911 *c.* July]. But
faced with the Hawk's Wood, and the intensity of his desire to draw
it, he had a new experience: a technique grew out of his concentra-

[1] See p. 209.
[2] See p. 154.

83

tion. 'An instinctive knowledge seemed to serve me as I drew, enabling my hand to convey my understanding...' he wrote in *Outline*. 'There stole through me a peculiar thrill as I realized the forms taking life under my hand.' This power, surging up under the pressure of emotion, pushed him to a new experiment. Hitherto he had confined himself to black and white, or he had tinted with one colour, usually blue. Suddenly, on this occasion, he began to use full colour, while yet keeping that outline which seemed to him so vital.

This was a moment of assurance, but his struggles were not over. He wrote to Rothenstein in the following year:

'I have had difficulties lately in managing colour. I want all the colour but all the drawing and definite outline too. . . . I find no *way* to do things, it is terribly wearying to have to consider the way to do each picture but I have to—for tho' my end is clear to me and object in mind I find the means a great struggle being obliged to experiment over and over on each new work. I suppose it is good in a way too—it is certain I shall never be facile!' [1913. Before September].

But gradually he learnt that there is no 'way' to be found, that technique has a vitality of its own, which must be accepted but disciplined. Near the end of his life he wrote to Richard Smart:

'I fear I have let you down but one cant always be sure of drawings you know—they sometimes "take over" or take *on* (like females) and then hours are wasted reasoning with them or struggling to keep ones end up' [1940 *c.* January].

If it is felt that I have given undue space to Nash's very early drawings, I have at least his own authority for doing so—an extract from a letter he wrote to Bottomley when, a year before his death, he was surveying his life's work:

'When I came to look into the early drawings I lived again that wonderful hour. I could feel myself making those drawings—in some ways the best I ever did to this day. And because of this I suddenly saw the way to finish my "life". . . . I feel I could make a complete thing by taking it up to 1914—just up to the war. After that it was another life, another world' [*c.* late July 1945].

IV

The War
1914-1918

————⟫∘⟪————

i. Chronicle

Nash's first reactions to the war can be given in extracts from two letters. The first is to Eddie Marsh and it is dated 'Bloody August 1914'.

'God bless my soul, what a horrible state of things is come to pass. . . . Everyone is so damned excited and those who arn't gone to the war all seem to be doing other peoples business or writing to the Times for advice. I have as yet held myself back from becoming a soldier as I am more inclined to Red X work and gathering in the harvest or guarding the Railway. . . . However I daresay I shall get dragged in for the war before long. . . . But really the whole business is most bloody stupid.'

The second letter is to Bottomley:

'I am not keen to rush off and be a soldier. The whole damnable war is too horrible of course and I am all against killing anybody, speaking off hand, but beside all that I believe both Jack and I might be more useful as ambulance and red cross men and to that end we are training. There may be emergencies later and I mean to get some drilling locally and learn to fire a gun but I dont see the necessity for a gentleminded creature like myself to be rushed into some stuffy brutal barracks to spend the next few months practically doing nothing but swagger about disguised as a soldier *in case* the Germans poor misguided fellows—should land' [September 1914].

Nash had not considered whether the artist had a claim to be exempted from war: it was not the sort of problem that he thought about. Nor had he, apparently, any views on the moral legitimacy of war or of this war in particular. He simply hated all cruelty and violence. This first reaction of his was, I think, simply a futile attempt to brush the intrusion aside. He was busy with his work and with being in love, and his attitude was merely passive and fatalistic—'I dare say I shall get dragged in.' Therefore, on the tenth of September he enlisted as a private in the Artists Rifles; but for home service only.

I doubt whether he was quite easy in his mind about this. He told Bottomley that he had enlisted, and when a letter came which approved his action and the need to fight, he answered as if he were answering himself:

'I should have told you I am only a home defender but it is for many good reasons. Personally I should like to get over to Belgium but in the ordinary way there is no chance of our battallion going and to sign for foreign service simply means you get sent off to Egypt or India and there you stay for 4 years. Now if we are wanted at the front it will be in an emergency at a later date and in that case I shall probably volunteer. . . . I know this sounds selfish but I am only out to do what I can see is my duty and as yet I cant see it to that extent. . . . Of course Bunty dreads the whole thing and that's another reason for *signing* for Home Defence at the beginning. . . . Poor dove she fears much too much for me as it is! I met Rupert Brook[e] tother day fresh home from Antwerp trenches he said it was marvellous. I expect I should hate the slaughter—I know I should but I'd like to be among it all' [1914 ? late October].

Nash did not immediately find himself in 'brutal barracks', but lived at Iver Heath and drilled in Regent's Park or at Hampstead. He enjoyed that and he found many agreeable people in his company, among them the poet, Edward Thomas, who was killed in 1917,[1] and the novelist and radio script-writer, Lancelot de Giberne Sieveking, who was to remain a life-long friend and patron of Nash's.

The most important immediate effect of the war on Nash's life was that he and Margaret Odeh decided against the long engagement they had anticipated. The Bottomleys had heard rumours that they were to be married, and Emily Bottomley wrote in mild dissuasion. 'From the opinion we formed of you and Bunty,' she said, 'we decided you would need quite lots of money to marry happily' [1914 c. late November]. And it is true that the Nashes certainly never gave the impression of being indifferent to the scale of life which only money can assure. Their hospitality was always lavish,

[1] See Nash's letter to Bottomley [4 September 1917].

their clothes and everything about them were handsome. They were to have difficult times, very difficult times, but never to live without style. Or perhaps it was that Nash's personal style covered any shortages. I could imagine him offering a cheap Empire wine with an air that would suggest a château-bottled claret, if I could imagine him ever not finding the money to avoid a cheap Empire wine. He was one of those who can be 'hard up' but never show the makeshifts, whose clothes can be old but never threadbare, whose dinners may have been scraped together but yet hint at a chef and a butler. Even in an army mess in France, Nash was to establish his lordliness. 'A good manservant looks after one hand and foot,' he wrote to his wife, 'and you can imagine the full advantage I have taken of such luxuries. Also I am generally rather extra attended upon because of my infernal managing habits and taste in cooking and the amenities of the Mess. They tell me here I have a good idea of making myself comfortable' (12 May 1917).[1]

At the same time there was, of course, always the romantic idea of poverty to be indulged. Nash had misled the Bottomleys by many such phrases as 'Tonight we are too poor to get dinner' [1913. Early July]. When he now wrote explaining that they had about four hundred pounds a year between them, a comfortable income for a young couple in 1914, Emily Bottomley wrote a letter of mildly ironical complaint [December 1914]. Nash frankly admitted that the misconception had come from his 'unfortunate turn for romancing' [c. early December 1914]. But it seems that Nash was also romancing a little over their income. Margaret Nash does not accept his account of it. She assures me that they had far less, that he never had clear ideas on money and that his 'whole statement to G.B. is fantasy . . . and wishful thinking'. Ruth Clark, who was their closest friend at the time, also assures me that 'they *were* poor and they *were* happy' and that Nash's 'ideas of finance were then as clouded as his mathematics, but he was good at counting chickens before they were hatched'.

One advantage they certainly began with. Margaret Nash had a furnished flat in Alexandra Mansions, Judd Street, which she had shared with Ruth Clark. It was most useful to the Nashes and they were to keep it until 1936. Although very small and not at all elegant, it served them as a London base during their years in the country and its outlook gave Nash the material for several pictures.[2]

The wedding was on 17 December 1914 at St. Martin's-in-the-

---

[1] The letter is printed in *Outline*, p. 203.   [2] See p. 163.

Fields. It seems appropriate at this point to introduce a passage from a letter to his wife, which gives Nash's views at that time on the relations of the sexes, and in particular of his relations to her. He is criticizing Gilbert Cannan's *Mendel*:

'The main cause of the two tragedies in the story is the attitude of the men to women—it is the lowest conceivable.... What a monster sex is ...

'Love of the body is a fearful tyranny and our most precious moments are not of the body. I think I am saved by a passionate tenderness I have always felt for you, and indeed I could not love or live with one who did not stir that in me, it may not be very forceful or robust or belonging to any of the emotions of grand passion, but it is a jewel, a charm that smooths life and keeps one simple and I think humble. Had any of these brilliant young lovers of Cannan heard of humility—no—God comes into their thoughts and speech but never Christ' [1917 *c*. January].

It is not my business to enquire whether Nash always lived up to this Christian view. The spirit matters and not the 'fearful tyranny' of the flesh.

Almost immediately after his honeymoon Nash was moved into 'barracks' at Roehampton, which do not appear as very 'brutal', in the description he gave to his wife:

'The house is a large mansion.... The grounds are most lovely, made splendid by huge cedars and ilex trees. There are little Dutch gardens, Italian gardens, gardens surrounded by huge old brick walls; trees, shrubs, bushes and flowers of all kinds.... It looks as if we ought to be comfortable enough.... The rooms are high, airy and clean, heated by pipes' [28 December 1914].

He was hardly justified in describing this to Eddie Marsh as 'the very real thing at last' (1 January 1915), especially as he was given two or three afternoons' leave a week to continue his work. Indeed his whole experience of the war at this time was remarkably unreal, and not a little self-centred. His complaints were of losing one of his free afternoons or of guard duties at the Tower on Christmas Day 1915, even though his wife did contrive to join him with mince pies. His ambition, he told Michael Sadler, was to be commissioned in the Ordnance Corps, because the pay was high and the work less suicidal than in the Infantry.

He was in one sense, however, becoming an efficient 'old soldier'. There are many circumstances which explain why a fellow-cadet at Denham, where Nash was posted in August to the first O.C.B., remembers him chiefly for 'his cleverness, knowledge of sergeants or just luck in getting sleeping out passes',[1] and why his brother wrote to him from the front: 'You are indeed a wonderful man for working things'. In September he was transferred to the eleventh O.C.B. at Camberley and on the nineteenth of December he was gazetted to a temporary commission as second lieutenant in the Hampshire Regiment. He wrote to Bottomley on New Year's Day:

'It is strange to stand on the edge of the year and look across and think of the extraordinary things that may happen during this new year—what does it hold for me I am wondering. A more crowded life than I have ever lived before, more anxiety, more pain, more excitement, more vivid impressions than I have ever felt before. Or just death. I feel most interested for I cannot say I have premonition of this or that, only I realise a rather dramatic moment, this, at the end of the other years, before the one that really matters, dawns. I wish things didnt matter so much, that I was answerable to none but myself' [1 January 1917].

Soon after that he reported for duty at Gosport, and again he made himself comfortable, living out in pleasant lodgings with his wife. But at last, on the twenty-second of February, he reached France. He was at Le Havre on his way to joining the fifteenth Hampshires in the Ypres salient.

Nash's military life up to this point had not been edifying. His imagination seems to have failed entirely. The war was out of its scope, and he was so preoccupied with the inconvenience it caused him that he set himself to organize his own part in the service with unusual caution. There was not a soldier who, once in, did not take all available means to make himself comfortable, but he was normally not so cautious in advance. It was not then usual, however foolish it may seem to a conscript world, for fit young men of Nash's class and tradition to volunteer only for home defence and to hope for the Ordnance Corps. By the standards of the time, he fell short.

Nash's physical experience of war, when now at last he met it, was not at all exceptional. He made no claims to anything but the minimum war experience. Against a journalist's remark that 'this sensitive youth, torn from his art studies, was exposed to the perils and privations of the front line in Flanders', Nash wrote in his press-cutting book: 'quite untrue privations Tower of London and elsewhere. perils Ypres salient about 3 months.' But his imaginative experience was, of course, tremendous. His imagination, once

_____
[1] Douglas Rowntree in a letter to the author.

89

violently expanded to take in the war, took it in and gave it out with a far greater intensity than any other war artist achieved. This was mainly because he was a better artist, no doubt: but I cannot help believing that his time at the front as an infantry officer, however short and uneventful, was of great value to him. It put him, for his later visit as an official artist, in an altogether superior position to that of the tourist in a staff car. He could feel into the experience and not merely sight-see it. He had been one of the chaps.

The effect of the front on his painting belongs to the next section, but its effect on his writing may be introduced here. He now began to write from direct observation and experience, in language that was fresh and precise. He had at last outgrown the pseudo-poetic and second-hand romanticism of his long adolescence. The poetry, which he had failed to catch in his painstaking verses, now appeared as by accident in his letters, in particular the poetry of that fearful landscape. As Yeats was discarding his embroidered dreams under the impact of Easter 1916, and writing that 'a terrible beauty is born'; as Wilfred Owen was writing: 'My subject is War, and the pity of War. The Poetry is in the pity'; so Nash could write: 'I believe I am happier in the trenches than anywhere out here. . . . Life has a greater meaning here and a new zest, and beauty is more poignant.'[1] I shall quote examples of his written landscapes of war in the next section, but even before he reached the front, a change had taken place. While he was at the Infantry Base Depôt at Rouen, he went for a long walk, away from the drill and the cabarets and 'those indefatigable women on the street', into the unmilitary countryside where he saw a village cemetery. He *saw* it. He did not pull what was before his eyes into the shape of a ready-made vision, but now found a new and personal experience in it. Herbert Read has already drawn attention to the astonishing beauty of his description. 'The whole of Paul Nash's "vision" is in this word-picture, not only his characteristic colours, but even his characteristic symbols.'[2] In this nameless cemetery, he entered his own imaginative world. He 'went absent' into aesthetic experience. At the moment, this was only from the prospect of war: but he was soon able to go absent from the terror of its presence so that he was not afraid. 'I have experienced neither nerves nor fear,' he wrote, 'and there is only one attitude to adopt, that of complete indifference and a rigid fatalism—you are meant to die or not as

[1] All quotations without references in this chapter are from Nash's letters to his wife printed in *Outline*.
[2] *Nash: Eates*, p. 12.

God wills. I have no other belief save in His mercy.' But indeed there was something else—the power of the artist to shield himself in contemplation. 'There is no situation so terrible that it may not be relieved by the momentary pause of the mind to contemplate it aesthetically.'[1] Already, on the boat, Nash had entered into such a pause when he saw the masthead light as 'a kind of guide and spirit of the ship, piercing the dark, greeting the unknown ahead'. There is no such commonplace image in the cemetery passage, which I must now quote:

'As we were about to enter the village we saw a cemetery on the left side perched up on the higher ground outside the village. It was a wonderful sight, little wooden shrines over each grave filled inside with some sort of wire wreaths and small flowering trees, a little bower pale blue and green in colour and always there was floating a little cherub doll upon a thread. Wind and weather had washed white shrines to a moist delicate grey—had faded the bowers to a mysterious pale blue. The wind passing through the place set the cherubs flying gently over the wire trees and flowers—set the foliage whispering and the little doors that had swung open, creaking. Never have I seen such curious beauty connected with graves and burials, the uncompromising slabs, a brown coloured marble, rise before my mind, monstrous piles, a hopeless grey blank granite with chiselled words in gold of some vapid hymn, the circular glass cases filled with white wax flowers, the poisoned-berried yews, all conveying the idea of death for death's sake. I turned from this to the windy churchyard of waving trees and shrubs and little happy tinkling shrines.'[2]

Read has pointed out that this is the origin of the vision which Nash was to use in *Urne Buriall*; but indeed it is also the origin of his latest symbol. Death was to be the aerial flower, the rose of death in the sky; it was to inhabit where the Silver Hands and the face of Sybil had been and the 'aerial creatures' of a second war. For the moment, only the little cherub dolls fly on their threads; and the wire flowers are gravebound. But the whole cemetery was on a windy hill: it was already, as it were, taking off. We shall understand that better when we have finished the roundabout journey we are tracing, whose beginning is not fully illuminated before its end.

From Rouen, Nash joined his battalion in routine trench warfare, at first in the Ypres salient and later in France. Within two months

[1] George Santayana, *The Sense of Beauty*.
[2] This is the version given in *Outline*. It differs slightly from that quoted by Read, *loc. cit.* As I have not been able to check with the original letter, I have chosen the later printing.

he had become angrily involved in the life of the fighting soldier. His
early dislike of war as something ugly and irrelevant that interfered
with his chosen life grew into a passionate hatred. He arrived at a
larger mode of experience and could share the common view. We
can trace this growth in the letters to his wife:

'Apart from any bitter thoughts one may have on the subject, we
are all uneasy out here. The letters of "Eve" drivel on each
week and a new batch of snaky actresses crop up in *The Tatler* and
Sketch—personally I like reading Eve's nonsense and looking at the
legs of the pretty actresses, if I am not thinking of anything at all, but
sometimes I sit up with a start and wonder if we are all mad. As for
the newspapers . . . it just seems as if I heard all the pap being
made and dripping, dripping into the foolish blubber mouth of the
people which greedily laps it up, loving it so—the great brain fodder,
the food of the little gods. . . . It is intolerable—I cannot read the
papers—it's just humbug from beginning to end. We need a spirit to
stamp out cant and lies from England, a race of men and women in
England to supersede a brood of efts and leeches. You speak of a
revolution that will come at home if war grinds us to famine; it would
be a pity to nurse your sorrows and your wrongs until the men return,
that is when revolution would come. Out here men have been thinking,
living so near to silence and death, their thoughts have been furious,
keen, and living has been alive. Hammering in their minds are a
hundred questions, festering in their hearts a thousand wrongs. The
most insistent question is "Why am I here?" The greatest wrong "I
am still here"; but an end will come one day and the next will be a
day of reckoning. Everyone knows that out here—do they know it at
home, I wonder—they will' (April 18).

Towards the end of April he was sent on a course and learnt the
soldiers' lesson—that he would rather be back in the trenches. It was
not only a negative anger he was acquiring, but also a positive pride
and charity. He was suddenly recalled. An offensive was in sight and
there was a three-day forced march 'and not one man fell out', he wrote
triumphantly: 'There is a quiet confident strength, an easy carriage
and rough beauty about these men which would make your heart
jump and give you a lumpy throat with pride. The other day as I
watched them I felt near tears somehow. Poor little lonely creatures
in this great waste.' And then he arrived at patriotism, the positive
counter to his bewildered anger:

'I cannot get things straight at all. What is God about? I have
given up thinking, it is futile. One's mind widens out here alarm-

ingly. I begin to think in much, much larger forms. I confess to you this thing that brings men to fight and suffer together, no matter from what original or subsequent motives, is a very great and healthy force. The cause of war was probably quite futile and mean, but the effect of it is huge. No terrors will ever frighten me into regret. What are the closing lines of Tennyson's "Maude"?—"I have felt I am one with my native land". This is the emotion and it is a satisfying one to rest with when every other has turned bitter and dead' (12 May).[1]

Perhaps when Nash gave a war landscape the title *We are Making a New World*, he was not being wholly ironical. Or perhaps by then he foresaw that the better vision was to fade and the ex-soldier to betray the soldier.

On the twenty-fifth of May,[2] a week before the offensive, Nash fell into a trench and broke a rib, and on the first of June he was admitted to the Swedish War Hospital in London.

As soon as he had arrived at the front, he had begun to draw and by the middle of April he had made twenty drawings. Shortly before his accident, he had written to his wife that he did not think anything he had done was 'of much use' except as 'material for fine things to create afterwards' (12 May 1917). Soon after arriving in hospital he was allowed to work during the day at his Judd Street flat and was able to exhibit twenty drawings at the Goupil Galleries later in the month. The exhibition was well received by the critics and half the drawings were sold. But no praise will have pleased him so much as a pencilled letter from his brother in the front line. He had seen press reproductions only, but he was able to say with typical directness 'We have always liked or not liked each other's work and it has always appeared quite simply either good or bad. They are good and I like them.'

Nash was discharged from hospital on the twenty-first of June, but in July he was sent to the Alexandra Hospital at Cosham with a nasal infection. By the end of August he was again discharged and attached to the Third (Reserve) Battalion of the Hampshires at Gosport, where he lived out with his wife at 19 Clarence Square. From there he wrote to Bottomley.

'You will read the article written by John Cournos. . . . When

---

[1] I think Nash was feeling after Tennyson's larger meaning but his memory slipped. The last lines are:

I have felt with my native land, I am one with my kind,
I embrace the purpose of God, and the doom assign'd.

[2] I take the date from his letter to his wife, *Outline*, p. 205. War Office records give the 30 May.

Cournos first read his essay to me I recognised things—"Someone has described a certain poet's work as possessing the quality of 'accurate mystery' that is, mystery expressed with precision, for in many peoples' minds the idea of *mystery is not disassociated from vagueness and mistiness.*" I am glad that has come into my work. Years ago when you first wrote me those fine letters which did so much to correct my mind you said "the greatest mystery is obtained by the greatest definity" (is there such a word?)[1] I never forgot that lesson and I always knew its truth. I know I am a very, very long way off accomplishing anything greatly significant but to have qualities which make for significance recognised in my drawings has encouraged me much. Oh but I want time and freedom. So far I can but make drawings as I go from place to place. I know how secret and reserved Nature really is and what devotion and homage must be paid to her before she will yield her mysteries. Sometimes I am desperate at my impotence. And I see so much more now: the world is crowded with the most marvellous things; everywhere I see form and beauty in a thousand thousand diversities. Only old Whitman poured out what I feel in his endless magnificat of rapture in the created world' [1917. *c.* 23 August].

In September John Drinkwater held an exhibition of twenty Nash drawings at the Birmingham Repertory Theatre, but only seven were of war. They had met Nash at the Goupil exhibition and Nash had described him to Bottomley in the same letter as 'a new and very dear friend . . . the kindest and most lovable person'.

In the meantime Nash had been campaigning to be sent out again, but this time as an official artist.[2] It is evidence of his growing reputation that he was able to use the support of Eddie Marsh, Rothenstein, Eric Maclagan of the Victoria and Albert Museum and Laurence Binyon; and that he had powerful reserves whose letters still lie among his papers: Claude Phillips, Frank Rutter, A. Clutton Brock, Roger Fry, John Drinkwater, Robert Trevelyan, Henry Tonks, Charles Holmes, Michael Sadler and Gordon Bottomely.

The result of it all was that John Buchan, then Director of Information, though he did not himself like Nash's work but thought him 'a good fellow', wrote to C. F. G. Masterman, who was Director of Propaganda in his department: 'I think we will have to send Paul Nash as one of our artists to the front. There is a tremendous consensus

---

[1] See p. 80.
[2] For an earlier proposal that he should do so, see Rothenstein's *Men and Memories*, Vol. II, p. 307, and an extract from his letter to Rothenstein (20 May 1916) printed in *Nash: Eates*, p. 14.

of opinion about his work.' Nash was therefore seconded to the Department of Information on the twelfth of October.

But Nash had not only been campaigning for himself. He had already tackled the patient and influential Eddie Marsh over all sorts of things his friends and relations wanted. Now it was for his brother, who had been in France for nearly a year without leave and was number one in a bombing squad. 'Can you by any fair or foul means help to get Jack home for a commission. . . . It is unnecessary to speak of Jack's worth and his real value as an English artist and its a damned shame if nothing can be done to extricate him from a position where he is in utmost danger', he wrote. And in a later letter: 'All my own success and happiness turns bitter while I think of Jack in the trenches' (8 January 1918). Nash's first activity on reaching France at the beginning of November was to find his brother, by now a sergeant. He reported to his wife that he was 'a bronzed and tattered soldier, with incredible hands all rough and overgrown with cuticle—his eyes I thought less shy, very blue and bright, thin in the face but not worn or strained; voice rather tired, but giving out the same wit and humour as of old' (5 November 1917).

But now Nash was meeting the 'difficulties of an infantry subaltern behaving like a Staff Captain', as he said in *Outline: Notes* and he added: 'I evolve a technique. Eventually I get where I want to be.'

His technique must have been swift and masterly. He had soon 'set up house' with his car and chauffeur and a batman who was a professional valet and cook, although these comforts were later diminished. 'My excellent chauffeur is leaving,' he wrote, 'and my chef has been precipitated into the wind screen and messed up his mouth. With true spirit and the nice feeling of a faithful servant he only said "How fortunate it wasn't you, sir!" I was much touched.' The record of this is in his reports to Masterman, but what was much more important was that he was also able to report 'fifty drawings of muddy places'. They were only in chalk on brown paper. What he wanted above all from Masterman was time to work them up. On his return he was at first granted some forty days leave, and after that the technique operated so effectively that we hear nothing more of his doing infantry duties for the rest of his service.

In May he held an exhibition of his war drawings at the Leicester Galleries which was a very marked success. The better press was enthusiastic and the buyers were good judges.

In the meantime a grandiose proposal for a memorial museum was being discussed. From its ruins there remains the series of immense canvases which compete with the guns and parachutes in the central hall of the Imperial War Museum. It includes Nash's *Menin Road*.

Nash received the commission for this work in April 1918, and his brother, who had returned to England in the middle of January, had a similar commission. They decided to join forces in the necessary big studio, which they found at Chalfont St. Peter in their native county. There they established themselves with their wives at the beginning of June. Nash described their pleasant life to Bottomley, and then went on:

'France and the trenches would be a mere dream if our minds were not perpetually bent upon those scenes. And yet how difficult it is, folded as we are in the luxuriant green country, to put it aside and brood on those wastes in Flanders, the torments, the cruelty and terror of this war. Well it is on *these* I brood for it seems the only justification of what I do now—if I can help to rob war of the last shred of glory the last shine of glamour . . . I feel very serious about this big picture it is going to have all I can muster. A kind of enlarged and intensified *Void*; I pray I may carry it through' (16 July 1918).

This life continued until the beginning of 1919, when the Paul Nashes returned to Judd Street. *The Menin Road* was finished in various borrowed or rented studios and then Nash's service came to an end. The Ministry of Information, as it had now become, released him on the twelfth of February and the army on the following day.

In the meantime the first publication on his work had appeared in a series called *British Artists at the Front*. It included a pencil portrait by Rothenstein and introductions by C. E. Montague and Jan Gordon, under the pseudonym of John Salis. There had been a proposal that Robert Nichols should write one of these, and that was the occasion of Nash's last letter to Mercia. It was a new world and they were to drift apart.

'Dearest Mercia thank you ever so much for your letter. how sorry I was to hear of your unbecoming illness—do be careful my dear— I expect you were dreadfully bad. However it was nice of you to do it all at Nunney—my God how I should like to be there now! are you still there I wonder—those woods—the larches, I can see them tremulously green and the mystery of the garden in these stirring spring days—what a place of dreams. Something rather odd happened a day or two back. Robert Nichols the poet—do you know his work—you should I think—was here writing notes for his article on Paul and his work which is coming out. So I was showing him all my queer old drawings and he pounced on a sketch of you which I made down at the cottage in that wonderful long ago time So excited and insistent was he that I parted with it thinking perhaps he should have it altho' I hesitated at first—he wants to write a poem on it or some madness. So my dear you go into a poets rooms after all these years and since this young man is rather *the* young man of the time, all sorts and kinds of great and little men will stand and look at you murmuring the words written under the drawing Mercia Oakley, Mercia Oakley—who is she? who was she?' [Early 1918].

ii. War Pictures

The landscape of war had an immediate effect on Nash's visual imagination. He suddenly stopped 'going in' for nature. Nature went in for him, exploded at him, as a meaning of poetry exploded at Hopkins. It was a landscape that had lost its innocence, blasted and dark like the settings of Lear and Macbeth. Even before he had reached the front, he had seen a new landscape; but that was innocent in its beauty like his cemetery. He described it in a letter to his wife which is not among those printed in *Outline*:

'Everywhere are old farms, rambling and untidy, some of course ruined and deserted, all have red or yellow or green roofs and on a sunny day they look fine. The willows are orange, the poplars carmine with buds, the streams gleam brightest blue and flights of pigeons go wheeling about the field. Mixed up with all this normal beauty of nature you see the strange beauty of war. Trudging along the road you become gradually aware of a humming in the air, a sound rising and falling in the wind. You look up and after a second's search you can see a gleaming shaft in the blue like a burnished silver dart, another and then another. Then comes a new noise, two or three cracks from somewhere in the near farms, a second, and as you gaze the blue sky is charmingly speckled by little shining clouds of white. Nothing could be gayer, the clear blue pierced by silver darts and spangled with baby clouds. Nothing whiter, purer, more full of life than these flaky clouds' (21 March 1917).

As he penetrated into this landscape, his pleasure in the ironic prettiness, as of the cherub dolls over the graves, grew into the experience of tragic beauty. There are three passages from the published letters which show this progression:

'Here in the back garden of the trenches it is amazingly beautiful —the mud is dried to a pinky colour and upon the parapet, and through sandbags even, the green grass pushes up and waves in the

G 97

breeze, while clots of bright dandelions, clover, thistles and twenty other plants flourish luxuriantly, brilliant growth of bright green against the pink earth' (7 March 1917).

'Imagine a wide landscape flat and scantily wooded and what trees remain blasted and torn, naked and scarred and riddled. The ground for miles around furrowed into trenches, pitted with yawning holes in which the water lies still and cold or heaped with mounds of earth, tangles of rusty wire, tin plates, stakes, sandbags and all the refuse of war. . . . A slope rises to a scarred bluff the foot of which is scattered with headless trees standing white and withered, hopeless, without any leaves, done, dead. As shells fall in the bluff, huge spouts of black, brown and orange mould bursts into the air, amid a volume of white smoke. . . . In the midst of this strange country . . . men are living in their narrow ditches' (6 April, Good Friday, 1917).

'No glimmer of God's hand is seen anywhere. Sunset and sunrise are blasphemous, they are mockeries to man, only the black rain out of the bruised and swollen clouds all through the bitter black of night is fit atmosphere in such a land. The rain drives on, the stinking mud becomes more evilly yellow, the shell holes fill up with green-white water, the roads and tracks are covered in inches of slime, the black dying trees ooze and sweat and the shells never cease. . . . They plunge into the grave which is this land; one huge grave, and cast up on it the poor dead. It is unspeakable, godless, hopeless. I am no longer an artist interested and cautious, I am a messenger who will bring back word from the men' (16 November 1917).

It is clear from these passages that, under the stress of this emotion, Nash was also realising the object more precisely. He was clarifying the mystery in concrete terms. To those for whom all visual language becomes unintelligible the moment it transcends the diagram, Nash's first war drawings seemed eccentric, fantastic and unreal. That was why Nash had begged Rothenstein to make Buchan understand the value of his work as 'records'. 'As you know', he went on, 'I draw very frankly what I see, so that altho' my subject is, I suppose, coloured by my imagination it remains credible and real to other eyes' [1917 c. August].

Herbert Read, on his return from the front, found that to be so. 'I was immediately convinced . . . because there was someone who could convey, as no other artist, the phantasmagoric atmosphere of No Man's Land.'[1] I must add my witness. In the same circumstances

---

[1] *Nash: Read.* Sir Herbert Read has assembled all his writings on Nash into one long essay in *The Philosophy of Modern Art*, Faber 1952. The relevant passage is on p. 177.

they were to me the only true war pictures. They *were* the war, equivalents for the war and not reports on it. They were the soldier's experience and not the journalist's or the touring artist's.

I have already said that it is a mistake to treat Nash as the painter of an uninhabited world. It is demonstrably so in connection with his war work. Sir John Rothenstein, for example, has written: 'No artist ever showed a slighter awareness of his fellow men than Paul Nash: a summary, formal figure or two appears occasionally in his drawings of the Western Front, but hardly anywhere else, so far as I can recall.'[1] But of the sixty war pictures which I have been able to re-examine, though many of them only in photographs, twenty-nine contain figures—almost exactly half. Ten are primarily figure subjects. I would, however, agree that these are the least good: indeed some are positively bad. The figures are most effective in *Leaving the Trenches*, but perhaps that is because except for the three nearest men we only see tin-hats above the zig-zagging communication trench. The effect is to evoke with peculiar vividness, even at this distance of time, the memory of those files of men wriggling their way through the earth.

But it is not this visible presence of figures in so many of the drawings that matters. That is not the important point: the important point is that *all* the drawings are expressions of an intense 'awareness' of man, not in his person but in his effects, in the presence of the absent. This war landscape was entirely made by man. Have we no 'awareness' of a bird when we only hear its song? Or of a shell when it has only torn our flesh? In Nash's most desolate landscapes we are, on the contrary, made tragically aware of man by the mark of his passage—his terrible footprint. But we are also aware of him because he is still there. That is the centre of Nash's truth about the war landscape: that man's presence in it was something we could never forget precisely because we could not see him. 'In the midst of this strange country . . . men are living in their narrow ditches.'

As the gentle Nash had been roused to attack cruelty at school with his fists, so now he attacked the cruelty of war with his pencil and brush. It was as if, dreaming in the quiet pastures of his imagination, he had suffered the blow of conversion, had heard a call to prophecy, to 'bring back word from the men'. Most of the other war artists only saw an explosion; but the explosion took place inside Nash. It wounded him where he was most sensitive—in his love of nature, of the earth which his family had worked for so many genera-

[1] *Nash: Eates*, p. 20.

tions and out of which he, too, had resolved to get his living as a landscape painter.[1] His feeling was Edmund Blunden's:

> *I have seen a green country, useful to the race,*
> *Knocked silly with guns and mines, its villages vanished,*
> *Even the last rat and last kestrel banished—*
> *God bless us all, this was peculiar grace.*[2]

Nash was not to forget that. From now on he was a dedicated messenger. The message about war was soon given, and it was not to be repeated in the next war; but there was to be another 'message' about the invisible inhabitants. I do not mean anything occult or even precisely supernatural, but news of the reality which Rilke saw just behind the hoardings:

> *... O aber gleich darüber hinaus,*
> *hinter der letzten Planke, beklebt mit Plakaten des 'Todlos',*
> *jenes bitteren Biers, das den Trinkenden süss scheint,*
> *wenn sie immer dazu frische Zerstreuungen kaun ...,*
> *gleich im Rücken der Planke, gleich dahinter, ists wirklich.*[3]

I do not mean by 'message' any kind of philosophical or religious precisions, and certainly not any moral lessons. I mean only, as I think he meant in using the word, that news which is the business of any artist who is not a mere recorder of masks.

The bulk of Nash's war pictures consists of the twenty drawings exhibited at the Goupil; and the fifty-six paintings, drawings and lithographs exhibited at the Leicester. The only important additions are *The Menin Road* and *A Night Bombardment*. This, with two or three unexhibited drawings, makes all but eighty—a very substantial output. The majority roughly fall into three groups. The first, which is Nash's most original contribution, is of still and brooding desolation, of a useless land of broken trees, mud and wire. At least nine of them are nothing but 'close-ups' of the mud, the shell holes and craters, the writhing earth itself, naked grey or decked with weeds of sumptuous colour, a beggared earth in royal finery. With a foretaste of such later titles as *Stone Sea* or *Stone Forest*, which announce the metaphysical transformation of matter, he called one *Caterpillar Crater*. The suggestion of movement has not only a metaphysical sense: it was in cold fact an unstable landscape, and we crossed its mud insecurely; and when the smoke cleared away we saw the changed forms that were still the same—the caterpillars that had only shifted from one place

---

[1] See *Outline*, p. 123.   [2] *Report on Experience*.   [3] *Die Zehnte Elegie*.

to another. The pictures of the second group show this change happening in violent action, the earth flung up and falling; and the pictures of the third emphasize the litter of battle, the twisted metal, broken duckboards and dead bodies.

All these are landscapes seen over the parapet. There are only some half-dozen trench 'interiors'. There are even fewer pictures of any sort in which the ruins of buildings appear. Nash expressed what man was doing to man and his works, through what he was doing to the soil which feeds him.

There are certain images which recur frequently throughout—transformations of his earlier images and transitions to his later. The comfortable trees of Iver Heath have turned into the stark pointers that were to culminate in the wooden fingers of the second *Wood on the Hill*, that of 1937. The face in the sky, circled with stars, has become the aircraft, circled with the bursts of fire, that was to become the aerial flower and the symbol of death. The peculiar frequency of aircraft, which were not such a common feature of the first-war sky, belongs, I think, to his constant pursuit of the inhabited sky. So does his intensely personal treatment of the sun as a huge and alarming personality, which projects its rays, like harsh searchlights, and soaks the sky in blood. But he was to come to terms with it later and make it the benevolent protagonist of his last vision.

One other image, for which he was to have little further use, was of the thin relentless tracers of the rain. The rain does not fall: it strikes. It has not the sweetness of useful rain: it is not a nourishment but a further cruelty, like the rain in *Lear* or in Dame Edith Sitwell's *Still Falls the Rain*. It was the rain which made the mud and bent us in total submission to its unbeatable and pitiless attack.

Hartley Ramsden has drawn attention to one curious and immediate effect which his new vision had on the shape of Nash's pictures. From being predominantly vertical, they became during this period almost exclusively horizontal—'presumably', Ramsden says, 'because few verticals remained to show where the old landmarks of the country had been'.[1] But nothing has ever been more vertical than the leafless and branchless trees or the chimney that stood alone. There must be some other explanation, and perhaps the key to it is in the exceptions: the figure subjects are usually vertical. The men are directed by the constraint of the roadside trees in *Marching at Night*, by the trenches in *British Trenches* or *Stand-To*, by the tunnel in *In the Tunnels*. But the war landscape was the same whichever way the eye

[1] *Nash: Eates*, p. 26.

turned. The view over the parapet had no direction. There is nothing more remarkable in the small landscape drawings—and some of them are very small indeed—than their extraordinary power to convey a world that goes on and on, stretching all ways to the rain-blurred or shell-blasted horizons.

But this horizontality was not the only formal change which took place. Nash's whole technique was revolutionized. There was no time for patient searching after the subtleties of form. The urgent note had to be made with a jab of the pencil, as it were. 'Meet it is I set it down. . . . So, uncle, there you are.' The Verey light soared and bent over and fell and left the world dark again. Its harsh Grecoesque light had to be snatched—in *Verey Lights* and *Night in Ypres the Salient*, for example. I do not mean, of course, that he literally drew like that; we know in what tranquillity these drawings were in fact completed. But the feel of that urgency was preserved in his massive outlines and in the steely hatching with which he netted his darkest tones. He frequently used rough brown paper. He drew the heaving forms of the mud in black chalk, then touched in with white their glistening tops and the pools between. He drew the wire coiling over them in rusty brown and the distant hills in blue. He streaked the sky with blood-red. It was a simple and direct technique imposed by necessity. I am thinking here of such drawings as *Sunrise*: *Inverness Copse* (Plate 3) or *Dawn*: *Sanctuary Wood* or *Landscape*: *Year of Our Lord 1917*. It was perhaps in these sombre and stagnant landscapes that Nash was at his best.

In another type of drawing, he evolved extraordinary technical resources for distinguishing the textures among the chaos, so that sometimes, as in *Hill 60*, the terror of the impact is weakened because the texture is too sensuously beautiful and too subtly varied. Nash was also less successful when he tried to convey the exotic colour of rank vegetation—the persistence of spring on the old battlefields. It was not until his last years that he could manage such strong colours. *Ruined Country*, *Vimy* or *Air Fight at Wytschaete* or *Sunset*: *Ruin of the Hospice*, *Wytschaete* are not among his best drawings. On the other hand, he did occasionally, as in *Crater Pools under Hill 60*, introduce variety of colour without losing the feel of desolation; but they were not exotic colours. In other cases, such as *Hill 60 from the Cutting*, he avoided charm by stiffening the delicate colour with sharp lines in pen and ink.

It is more difficult to estimate the success of the 'violent' works. They are mostly oils. It seems as if it were not until he had left the scene and was using the more deliberate medium that he felt able to face the greater complexities involved. Perhaps, too, the unfamiliarity of the medium made it easier for him to break with his habitual quietness. One of the most sensational is *The Mule Track*. The landscape for this was taken from a quiet water-colour, *Dunbarton Lakes*, in which there are neither figures nor explosions. It has a predominantly humping caterpillar movement but there is a suggestion here and there of an angular rhythm particularly in the duckboards which zig-zag into the distance. In the later painting Nash so developed this suggestion that it became a strident jagged discord which echoed all the thrusts and sweeps of the explosions. The sombre olive-green, which is the dominant colour of both pictures, is similarly jagged in the painting with flashes of orange and gleams of white.

This is rivalled in sensationalism by *Void*, the most popular of Nash's works at the time. The wreckage of battle is scattered over the landscape in hideous chaos and I do not feel that there is a full resolution into design. But I say this tentatively. I have not seen the original, which is in Canada, since 1918. Perhaps the most artistically effective of the 'violent' pictures is *After the Battle*, and perhaps that is because the violence itself is over. The jagged rhythm is built of duckboards, the stakes of barbed wire, the rain and the formalized clouds. Across this the mud and the wire writhe and coil, and the whole is a complicated and troubled pattern; but there is a pattern. The dominant colour is the grey of death, only varied with the rust or gleam of metal. The rust is repeated in the sky and on the face of the body to the right. The horror of this face without features and the huddled posture of the body in the centre are among the most expressive of all his figures. They are observed and felt and not, as in many cases, mere signs for men.

I have made the most casual mention of oil painting. But Nash had himself passed to that medium almost as casually. He was to be most particular in later years about quality of paper and precise and clean statement. But he had not begun like that. Bottomley had tasked him more than once with his slovenliness, and an answer he made in 1912 is very much to the point here:

'I have an unhappy thirst for bad paper I always do my best drawings on bad paper, Im positively superstitious about it. . . . As soon as I begin a design on a pure white Whatman sheet I feel uneasy and invariably shave it and bathroom tap it to a state of emaciated collapse. . . . But with regard to my mixed methods and muddled mediums I know I am rather a crawler. . . . I feel tho' it

all points to beginning oils I *want* to and I *ought* to, so I shall'
(21 August).

But he did not. I do not know why. Nor do I know why he now
suddenly did: he has left no hint. He simply wrote to Bottomley: 'Oils
for me were a complete experiment you know—a piece of towering
audacity I suppose as I had never painted before and the first three I
did were purchased two for the Nation and the other (*Void*) for
Canada' (16 July 1918).

There were five in the Leicester Gallery Exhibition, of which only
We are Making a New World can be ranked high among Nash's works;
and that can be ranked very high. It is a development of the drawing
called *Sunrise: Inverness Copse* (Plate 3), which it follows closely.
There is only one very marked change and it is an astonishing invention. In the drawing the sun is white against a pale blue sky and
its lower edge rests on a mass of brown cloud that reaches down to the
horizon. In the painting the whiteness of the sun and paleness of the
sky are repeated but the mass of cloud is red, as if the very source of
life has spilt all its blood. Yet it rises, and may even yet regenerate the
waste.

The two principal oils painted after the Exhibition were *The Menin
Road* and *A Night Bombardment*. The latter was a large picture commissioned for the Canadian War Records in 1919.[1] If I may judge
from a photograph of a picture which I have forgotten, it was singularly unsuccessful. Nash's intuitive impulse seems to have died down
and the result is little more than conscious pattern-making.

The Menin Road, on the other hand, is the most elaborated as
well as the physically largest expression of his whole war experience.
'I think I can say, by far the best thing I have yet done,' he told
Bottomley [April 1919]. It is indeed a remarkable achievement in the
organization of many complex elements, a very full and deliberate
statement, but I cannot feel that it has the intensity of the best drawings. Beside them it seems a little laboured, but it remains massively
impressive and its order is imposed with authority.

The Menin Road has recently been the subject of a poem by a young
poet, A. J. Bell.[2] His theme is the hope which springs from the possibility of that order. The artist who finds design in chaos is reflecting
the purposes of God.

> *Here everything is dead, must die.*
> *Only, beheaded, still the trees*

[1] See Rothenstein's *Men and Memories*, Vol. II, p. 350.
[2] *Poems in Pamphlet III*, Hand & Flower Press, 1952, p. 64.

WAR PICTURES

Live, pointing the finger of God
From earth to sky . . .

The miracle of design is in the Divine geometry 'shafted from the sky'.

Nash was now to move on and find that miracle in many other manifestations. Far from exploiting his success as a war artist, he could, as early as 1919, look back on his war pictures as no more than a stage in his development. In a letter to Rothenstein he wrote:

'I am pleased to have done them but I should have liked to have done them again! Only a few seem to me (looking back at them from the standard I have reached since) to be adequate aesthetic statements however telling they may seem at first glance as statements of certain violent emotional experiences' (2 September 1919). And, ten years later, writing to a lecturer who asked if he might use one of Nash's war pictures as a slide, he said:

'Of course the trouble is that the chaps who painted away from the battles seem to have made such much better pictures. What *is* interesting about some of our Great War paintings is, I suppose, the record of "atmosphere"—mood. I don't know—it's a long while ago and I am painting something else' (2 April 1929).

V

Whiteleaf and Dymchurch
1919-1925

i. Chronicle

In *Outline: Notes* Nash described his state in the period immediately following the first war, as: 'Struggles of a war artist without a war'; and in a letter of 1942 to Richard Smart, he said: 'I didn't quite know where I was and hadnt got into my stride' [September]. His difficulties were increased by the fact that not only did he not know what to paint, but he also did not know how to live. His army pay had stopped and a new life had to be built.

For nearly two years the Nashes were unsettled. They began at Judd Street but the flat was much too small for a permanent home and they did not want to live in London. In those first few months he was exceedingly active in a miscellaneous way. He had pictures to prepare for the Friday Club and London Group exhibitions. He edited a book of nonsense verse by Lance Sieveking,[1] and he began to write art criticism for the *New Witness* from the issue of the twenty-fifth of April 1919, using the name of Robert Derriman. This led to the one incident I have to record where his integrity failed and, in his own phrase, he fell below his standard. Under this assumed name he gave a very favourable review to the book of nonsense verse.[2] He described two books that he had himself illustrated as 'perhaps his [the publisher's] happiest effort',[3] and he consistently praised the work of his brother and his close friends and at least twice drew favourable attention to his own.[4]

[1] See Bibliography 25.
[2] *New Witness*, 19 September 1919.
[3] *Idem*, 17 October 1919.
[4] *Idem*, 9 May and 1 August 1919.

These 'indiscretions' became known, and a worse was to follow. Nash was invited to prepare a supplement of eight contemporary drawings for *Illustration*. He wrote an introduction signed with his own name and *Notes on the Artists* signed R.D. The Notes began: 'Mr. Nash, in his introduction . . .' This, of course, clearly implied that 'Mr. Nash' was not 'R.D.'. In one Note he wrote of his own 'extremely personal vision' and of his brother as 'perhaps one of the most able and original water-colourists since the old English masters', and of them both that their 'understanding of landscape . . . is penetrating and large'.[1]

This was really too much, and Frank Rutter revealed the whole affair in the *Arts Gazette*. His protest appeared on the twenty-seventh of December 1919, and in the correspondence columns of the issue for the seventeenth of January 1920 Nash wrote a frank admission and apology, to which he added that his brother had not seen the article before it was printed.

Later in the year Nash wrote a long account of the whole affair to Bottomley, which contains the following passage:

'It was a ridiculous piece of wrongheadedness on my part and of course I had to stand the racket. . . . What a sordid tale, but I am too fond of you, and believe you to have too much affection for me, to be indifferent to what you might feel. If a man does something below his standard and below his friends' opinion of his standard I think he owes them at least an explanation—after all I did feel I had let myself down and I felt, as acutely, I had let down my friends. . . . It has quite seriously taught me a lesson . . . in regard to myself who, I discovered to be far less reliable than I had imagined. I suppose that's always happening thro' life' [1920 c. July].

In the meantime the Nashes had stayed for some weeks from the beginning of July 1919 at the Red Lion at Whiteleaf in the Chiltern Hills. There were to be many visits there and many pictures painted of that countryside. Its general character attracted Nash, but the antique mystery of the cross cut in the hill had its special significance for him, for itself and because Wittenham Clumps can be seen from it.

John Nash and his wife now lived near by and the party was often joined by Eric Daglish, who was Paul's pupil in woodcutting, his wife Alice, Barbara Nash and Rupert Lee. Alice Daglish has described those visits—the long walks on the Chilterns with Nash

---

[1] *Illustration*, Vol. IV, No. 5, ed. by Gerard Meynell. House organ of the Sun Engraving Co.

stopping to draw whenever he felt inclined, the immense supper and the evenings of drawing, reading aloud and music. Nash had an extraordinary gift for working through such occasions without being detached from the company. He would look up, perhaps, and comment on the music or the reading, sometimes rather acidly. He could do this with a twinkle in his eye and almost—but not quite—a smile on his pursed lips, which robbed his comments of all power to hurt, without removing their piquancy. If he wanted to cut, he could cut sharply; but then the tone and look were quite different and displayed the intention.

At some time during this year Nash paid a visit to Dymchurch on the Kent coast between Rye and Folkestone. The exact date and duration of this most pregnant visit cannot be fixed, but the circumstances can. The French singer and diseuse, Raymonde Collignon, had commissioned Nash to design a cover for a song-book and suggested that he should visit her at Dymchurch to discuss it. The visit may have been very short but it made its impression: the seed for an important period of his work was sown.

In the November Nash held an exhibition in a large studio at 9 Fitzroy Street, Bloomsbury, which Wyndham Tryon had lent him. The Nashes lived there until their return to Judd Street in early 1920. In that year Nash became involved in two activities which distracted him from 'free' picture-making—designs for the theatre and for mural decoration at Leeds. I shall discuss the theatre work in a later section, and I need say little about the Leeds scheme. It has already been recounted in at least two books,[1] and an even fuller version will be given in the late Kenneth Romney Towndrow's forthcoming life of William Rothenstein, who was in charge of it.

Nash made two designs, *The Quarry* and *The Canal*; but he was not happy about them as drawings, although he believed in them as designs for execution in another medium. He explained to Rothenstein the cause of his dissatisfaction:

'It was my first experience of preparing a *show* design in one medium for a design, infinitely larger in scale, to be executed in another medium and I have been terribly oppressed most of the time... I think one reason for my failure is that I never make detailed drawings for a large painting both *The Menin Road* and the Canadian picture you saw practically grew on the canvas.... I must persevere in a new system' [1920 *c*. August].

[1] *Men and Memories. Recollections of William Rothenstein 1900–1922*, Faber 1932, pp. 348–9. *Michael Ernest Sadler. A Memoir by his Son*, Constable 1949, pp. 319–27.

The whole scheme, however, unhappily petered out. There was violent opposition from the local 'art' pundits, a controversy in the press and even a law case. Nash never again had an opportunity to design for work on such a scale.

During the spring and summer of 1920 the Nashes wandered again. Their movements cannot be exactly plotted, but they included visits with the Daglishes to Whiteleaf and Dymchurch, where they found a theatrical circle—Athene Seyler, Claud and Grace Lovat-Fraser, Sybil and Russell Thorndyke—and to Bertram Buchanan, a retired colonel who was farming and, with his wife, practising various arts, at Oxenbridge Farm, Iden, near Rye in East Sussex. The Buchanans were to remain life-long friends and later to be neighbours. Nash described the farm to Alice Daglish:

'This is an enchanting place—a more ideal farm I defy you to discover—of course we are all fearfully hot and collapsable except Bunty [Margaret Nash] who dances about like a gnat—a gnat who is putting on weight one might say too—however—As I was saying this farm is perfect. . . . There are calves and ricks and hens and cows and sheep and a cat and two kittens and two lovely ponds with pines and willows and poplars and a moorhen with chicks. Then we have scalded cream and lots of home cured ham and eggs . . . and we bathe in the river at the bottom of the hill every day' [1920].

The 'lovely ponds' in particular and the Iden countryside in general were to be the material of a later phase in his work. And he loved, though he does not mention it, the great beauty of the house itself—a long low whitewashed building, which carries its antiquity with a most distinguished reticence.

In this year, 1920, Nash also began an activity which was to recur intermittently for many years. He described it to Bottomley:

'In October I begin my first teaching! Albert R[utherston] has a school at Oxford[1] in the centre of the crusted culture of University home life—sons of dons and daughters of professors as material Albert and I are visiting pedagogues—distinguished artists from London—and in fortnightly parts—I am to ground the pupils in wood engraving Rather an excitement dont you think? and capable of much development' [1920 c. July].

This work continued until the end of the summer term of 1923, when Rutherston handed over the school to Sydney Carline. After the summer wanderings of 1920, the Nashes were in Fitzroy Street until the following February, except for a short visit to Paris. Then they were

[1] The Cornmarket School of Drawing and Painting.

again at Whiteleaf and in May at 2 Rose Cottages, Dymchurch. From there, Nash wrote a letter to his brother from which I want to quote a long extract as an example of his most spontaneous letter-writing:

'My poor old Victim what the hell are you doing with flu and this time of the year. . . . Of course this weather is a little too much. At 9.30 this morning having finished breakfast . . .[1] we strolled out into the most perfect sunshine. Ten minutes later a strange darkness came over and a sneaking wind, in a quarter of an hour it was raining and damn me if it hasnt rained ever since. Really my heart bleeds for the masses—and this wet Whitsun and all the poor little profiteers down here peeping thro their lace curtains at the rain and the restaurant sharks and all the bloody little tradespeople like so many baffled spiders whetting their beaks or sawing the air with their antennae or whatever it is that spiders do and scarce ever a fly. . . .

'It is really delightful here and I have no intention of going away. This room is about 20 × 15 × 12 with a huge window also we have a pleasant bedroom and there is a spare room to put you up. . . . There is much good stuff or material here tho' I'm not sure how it would strike you personally I am much excited by the various possibilities it grows slowly on one and wants a little probink. Our walks about are full of adventure now a sheep to be pulled out of a dyke—immensely swollen and stupid—now a larks nest in the grass or suspicious behaviour of unknown bird in the rushes again some peculiar flower— my dove surprised I do not know its name (happy thought: make it up) or yet again while walking the coast a dead seagull or horrific crab. If it isnt one thing its another—if it isnt a starfish it's a sea mouse or a dog fish or a sea mew or hog fish. Marsh or shore each is fascinating I have several plans for the future one of which is to open a class for the better sort of young lady in Folkestone where she may learn to sketch a little or something of that kind anyway I shall endevour to live here for the present by some means or other.

'Coma, the coma of Sunday and Whit Sunday at that, the coma of a meal done justice to and of slowly suffocating afternoon oozing towards another meal also to be done justice to I have no doubt (what am I to Do I cant get away it is raining outside—here I am cooped up here—I shall have to face it—to face it. Coma I say creeps upon me. And I have written many letters.

'My jetty sends fond love. I append a note to your breakwater' [15 May 1921].

In June the Nashes were again joined by the Daglishes and the

[1] No omission.

Lovat-Frasers, but the promise of as pleasant a summer as the last was suddenly broken by Lovat-Fraser being taken seriously ill. He was hurried to hospital for an operation, but died shortly afterwards. Nash, who was just recovering from his post-war disorientation, the Derriman incidents and certain resulting quarrels, was deeply disturbed by this sudden intrusion of death and by a duty that he felt it necessary to undertake, for he accompanied Grace Lovat-Fraser to break the news to her husband's parents. However, the effect of all this strain was not immediate, and he launched on one of his largest pictures, *Chestnut Waters*. But Margaret Nash was continually unwell and things were going badly, and then a second shock followed. While staying at Hillingdon in September, Nash went to visit his father, who had not been well. He found him lying unconscious on the floor and at first thought that he was dead. Very soon after this, he was himself hit by a strange illness which he described in *Outline: Notes* in two bare sentences: 'I get up in the night and fall down. Black out.' He remained unconscious for a week. In this condition, he was taken to a London Hospital for Nervous Diseases, where his state was diagnosed as suppressed war strain aggravated by his recent strain and shocks.

At first it seemed that Nash would be unable to work for some time and his friends rallied to his financial aid, particularly Rothenstein and Eddie Marsh. But he made a much more rapid recovery than had been expected, and by November he could write to Bottomley that he was in 'a state only just short of "The pink".' He had returned to Dymchurch and soon afterwards Bottomley was able to visit him there, one of the rare meetings in that long friendship.

And now the time of difficulties and unsettlement was at last over. Dymchurch had got its hold on Nash and he went forward with a new confidence. This was justified by many signs of his growing reputation and by increasing sales. One of his purchasers was T. E. Lawrence, who bought the very early Dymchurch painting, *Coast Scene*, to hang in his room at the Colonial Office. 'It will make, inshallah, a great difference to the Colonial Office,' he wrote.[1] But when Lawrence was leaving in March 1922, he wanted the picture taken away, because he did not feel it could survive his departure, although the fact that it had survived so long showed that it was 'pretty powerful'. 'Nothing else decent lives there', he said; and he had no room for it in his attic.

[1] Nash's letters from Lawrence were sold and the owner cannot be traced. The phrases I quote are from copies.

In September Nash wrote to Bottomley:

'Lawrence of Arabia is writing a book on his campaign and all sorts of artists are providing him with drawings to illustrate it. To me he has offered the task of providing the landscape part of the book —all to be designs made from his photographs. It sounds awful but having seen the photographs and reading Doughty's "Arabia" I think its going to be great fun—what a place! Petra the city of the Dead! O what a dream! Lawrence is of the salt of the earth and I know he's doing much of this simply to help painters who find a difficulty in *affording* to paint' [12 September 1922].

Lawrence had told Nash that he wanted him to translate the photographs 'into life', and that he saw no more harm in doing so than in 'painting the execution of Mary Queen of Scots—from a printed description'. Then follows a group of letters about the details and payment. 'Pictures can't be paid for: but painters should live while doing them,' Lawrence said and in January 1924 he acknowledged the drawings with great enthusiasm. The last letter, written in February 1929, agreed to Nash selling the letters. 'These ghouls would publish a man's washing bill, if they could . . .' he wrote. ' If only I could strike a vein of gold for myself: it's like Midas: a gold-producer, but not to his own advantage.'

The Nashes spent 1922 at Dymchurch except for various visits, one of which was to a new friend, Percy Withers, who lived at Souldern Court near Banbury. It was arranged by Bottomley who was staying there at the time. Withers was then a man of about fifty-five, a doctor by profession, but also an extension lecturer in English literature, a writer and a patron of the arts. This was the first of many visits from which Nash was to profit, not only because he sold several pictures to Withers, but also because he made several of Souldern and its neighbourhood.[1]

During the late part of this year the first general book on Nash was being prepared.[2] Albert Rutherston was the editor of a series of short monographs called *Contemporary British Artists*, and he invited me to undertake the volume on Nash. My friendship with him began in this way, and particularly during a long week-end in December at Dymchurch where the Nashes had moved from their lodgings into the minute Pantile Cottage. It was also in this year that Nash published his own first book, *Places*, and proposed his first but abortive organization of artists. I shall treat both these matters later.

[1] The collection of eighty-four letters to Dr. Withers, his wife and their daughter Audrey, now Mrs. Victor Kennett and editress of *Vogue*, is one of the most important.

[2] The earlier volume on war pictures alone has already been mentioned. See p. 96.

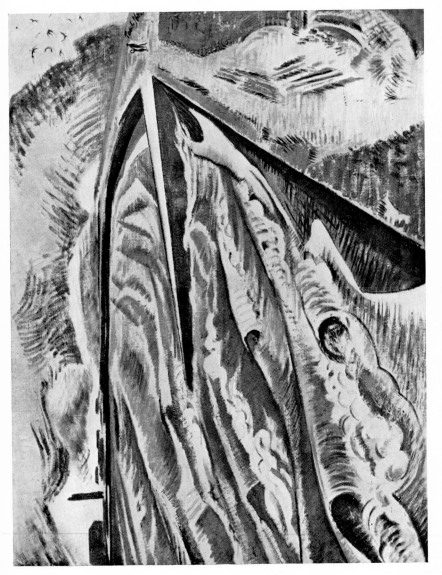

5. Coast Scene. 1921

Oil

6. Berkshire Downs. 1922
Oil

There is little to chronicle in the two following years. At first Nash was working steadily for the exhibition he was to hold at the Leicester Galleries in 1924, which was particularly successful because the majority of sales were to new patrons. He stayed with the Buchanans, with Ben Nicholson in Cumberland and with Withers three times.[1] On the first of September 1924 he was appointed an assistant in the School of Design in the Royal College of Art, where he taught for a day and a half in each week. 'South Kensington is frightfully interesting', he wrote to Audrey Withers, 'and I have a huge studio and an official desk with a tin box for letters and lots of buff envelopes and a tray with 14 pens. I tell you I'm the Hell of a nut' [Autumn 1924].

This light-hearted attitude to his new work was not reflected in the work itself. He was not in the ordinary sense a teacher, but 'a practising artist of great distinction who was willing to treat students as though they too were artists of distinction'. That phrase is taken from a letter of Edward Bawden's in which he gives me his memories of Nash at the Royal College. He goes on:

'In manner he was kind and thoughtful, he regarded everything he saw—whether the work was good, bad or indifferent—with attention and an obvious desire to be helpful. He did not resort to sarcasm, was seldom humorous. But the fact that he did not make the usual remarks common to art teachers which have an air of being profound and yet are evasive, but instead tried only to give his own reaction plainly and clearly gave a real personal value to his teaching. But though his teaching was personal it was always related to what he conceived was individual to each student; in other words he did not hand out propaganda for his own point of view but endeavoured to bring out instead whatever—slight though it might be—seemed unique in the student. He was a first rate teacher.'[2]

Another of his students, Lucy Norton, has sent me her memories. She emphasizes the dynamic effect of Nash's arrival—'like an explosion'. This was because he concentrated on art rather than technique. 'He enlarged our minds,' she says, 'made us aware of beauty.' And this he did partly by extending his students' feeling for art as a whole, particularly for poetry, urging them to read the *Iliad*, Dante, Borrow, Granville-Barker's plays and Yeats. This startling selection is obviously a survival of his own uneven reading; but its very unconventionality was part of his ' focus . . . on new adventures and new ideas'. It was this stirring-up of his students that made him

---

[1] See letter to Bottomley [7 January 1924] for a description of one of these visits.
[2] See also *Edward Bawden* by Robert Harling, Art & Technics, 1950, p. 14.

so successful with the best and so unpopular with the plodders, who only wanted the technical training that would help them to diplomas and teaching posts.

The one weakness which Lucy Norton does remark on was that Nash gave them 'a feeling that art began with the Post-Impressionists'. Margaret Nash assures me that it was his deliberate policy to avoid speaking to his students of the past because he considered that they heard enough of that from other sources, and that he constantly visited art galleries and had many and varied enthusiasms at different times, which included the early Italians, Botticelli, El Greco, archaic Greek and negro sculpture and the paintings of the cave-men, the Mexicans and the twelfth-century Chinese. But in spite of this I retain the impression that he was more interested in contemporary art than in anything that came before. He was certainly not a student of art but an artist who responded here and there to what he happened on, which is perhaps the best way for an artist. And the fact remains that in all his letters and writings there are amazingly few references to any artists before the later nineteenth century.

Just before the Christmas of 1924 the Nashes went to Paris and early in 1925 on to Cros-de-Cagnes, which Lance Sieveking had recommended to them as Nash country and Nash colouring in particular. The following extracts from three letters describe his reaction to it. The first is to his brother:

'This would be a jolly place with a spot more sun. . . . The natives swear that never, never have they known such bloody awful weather —in French of course but attribute it to invasion of the English who are about in great numbers—I cannot write with that nib—alors— However when the sun shines its very pleasant. . . . I have had agreeable surprises For instance the colour of things instead of being hot and hard as the pictures of certain visitors to the Cote d'Azur lead one to suppose is exquisitely subtle bright and pale. Lovely grey blues, pinks, grey greens infinite gradations of tones of yellows creams and whites especially in the buildings. The buildings excite me no end. Old Cagnes just behind on the hill is a complete Troubadour town utterly mediaeval in colour tone and smell. . . .

'Our quarters here [Pension de la Plage] are very agreeable. A bedroom just large enough to work in looking over the sea with a tiny balcony outside the window where if it were only warm one might sit shrouded by pines and mimosa branches the pebbly shore is thick with gay coloured boats the plage with odd shaped dogs and fishermen playing a sort of bowls with flat stones off the beach. The villas and houses are most amusing in colour with quaint decorations in pale tints on the walls. Sometimes the side of a house will have only one "practical" window all the others being painted imitations in relief perfectly deceptive at a distance. And sometimes on warm days stout men with nothing to do will lean so long against door posts as to tempt me believe they also are but painted images.' [Early 1925].

The second letter is to Audrey Withers:

'The bay is a miracle of blue when it isn't a shield of silver on a dish of dark, badly polished pewter, but when its blue its blue, its the bluest thing you can fancy. The country inland is hilly not to say mountainous covered by a flashing grin of the Alps startling in their whiteness against the cerulean sky. Oranges burn among the dark hills, mimosa gleams at intervals incredibly yellow. Olives, those cool blessed trees harmonise all these strange notes' [Early 1925].

The last letter is to myself:

'What a country! what people, what a jolly, sane, alive sort of life! Why dont all the people I care for come and join me!

'At first I could do nothing and as it is I feel myself changing under the new influence—partly no doubt due to the fact that here I have time to think, few cares and a sympathetic climate. But as I say to begin with it was too overwhelming and I just sat and goggled at the splendours of the Cote D'Azur. Now I am slowly producing, and I have hopes of something coming out of it all' (2 March 1925).

The Nashes stayed in Cagnes until about the middle of March 1925 and then went on to Genoa, Florence and Siena. Unfortunately I have no letters from Nash describing this tour, which seems to have been curiously unimportant to him. He was not happy in the restrictive atmosphere of Fascism, and although his wife tells me he was particularly attracted by Siena, and even thought of returning to stay there for some time, Italy never 'got' him. They returned to Cagnes for a few days and were back in England by the second week of April.

The day before leaving for this tour, Nash had written to Bottomley: 'Life is almost too full—and so much is irksome and looks like leading nowhere' [20 December 1924]. Soon after his return he wrote to him again:

'In the old days I had leisure and I mean to have leisure again, now I'm driven and it dont suit me a bit. When I was a painter I had the evenings for amusing myself now Im a bit of a painter and a pedagogue and a lecturer and a designer for the theatre and for textiles and a plugging engraver to boot. But it wont do. So Ive quite firmly resigned my usher's job at the Royal College of Art and I'm not going to lecture again if I can possibly afford not to and when my present jobs for books are cleared off Im going to settle down to paint again' (22 April 1925).

In fact he did not leave the Royal College until the summer term, nor was that to be the end of his connection with it, nor was he yet free from the distraction of too many activities. Various 'jobs' were to go on for several years; but a period of his painting had come to an end.

ii. Writings

In 1922, Nash told Bottomley that the theatre remained his only connection—as a painter—with literature.[1] It was not factually true: he was still illustrating books and was to do so for some years. But it was emotionally true. He wanted to believe himself in line with the current purist attitude, a visual artist with no taint of the 'literary'. Of course, this was only 'as a painter': he did not deny his interest in literature 'as literature': it was a great time for dissociating activities by the conjunction 'as'. He had quite finished with the Machens and Blackwoods of pre-war days, and we find him soon after the war wanting to discuss with Bottomley the work of the Sitwells, Robert Nichols, Edward Shanks, T. S. Eliot, Aldous Huxley, Richard Aldington, Wyndham Lewis and James Joyce—a list which shows that he was alert to contemporary writing. But he adds: 'I find no poet who has sprung since quite so good as dear old [Edward] Thomas. He seems to give us something peculiar and rare, something perfectly distinguished and necessary to English poetry. I had a long talk with [Ralph] Hodgson about him and his work the other day. Hodgson is a man of decided opinions' (1 December 1919).

This fidelity to the Georgians probably derived from his love of the English country, which was also reflected in *The Sun Calendar* for 1920, which he edited. It contained an illustration and a poem for each month. The illustrations were by himself, his brother and Rupert Lee. The poems were not entirely his free choice because of a limit on copyright material, but allowing for that, the choice may be taken as reflecting his tastes at the time. The poets included are Blake, Herrick, Walt Whitman, Sacheverell and Edith Sitwell, Edward Thomas, Aldous Huxley, Drinkwater and Landor. They are almost all concerned with the country and the seasons—landscape poems.

On the other hand, the article in the disastrous *Illustration* supplement was an argument against naturalism. The style is condescend-

[1] For the whole passage, see p. 128.

ing and pompous, and quite unlike Nash's mature writing. Its matter now reads as a series of commonplaces, but it was not everybody in 1919 who accepted even the mild 'distortions' of the work reproduced. Its interest is that it shows Nash at that time accepting the fashionable doctrines of Roger Fry and Clive Bell.

Nash's criticisms for the *New Witness* are also of little value, perhaps because of the unreal presence of 'Robert Derriman', who set up as a hard-headed business man and could use the very language of the Philistine. 'In these days when one sees so many examples of hysteria and extravagance in an effort to advertise and astonish. . . .'[1] That is not very decent in the circumstances, because in the same article he says: 'The artist who comes into the market to fight for his living must advertise his work'. Indeed he writes frequently on the problems of marketing.[2]

The most unhappy passage in these articles is a denial of his poetic self:

'I think that poets on the whole possess rather deplorable ideas about pictures; their tendency being to approach them from a sentimental rather than an aesthetic standpoint. They come to them with their minds clouded by peculiar prejudices, a little dim with the shadow of their intellects, and, wiping the mist from horn-rimmed spectacles proceed to utter curiously irrelevant remarks. . . .

'The most tiresome form of attack upon a picture . . . is that known to artists as "Find the old man's face", where the poet, overcome with childish curiosity persists in discovering old mens' faces in the trees, giants and elephants in the sky, serpents in brooks and something unintentional in everything.'[3]

That passage was signed with his own name, as if 'Derriman's' attitude seemed perfectly respectable to him, who had been ready to 'cry like a kid' if he could even hear himself called a poet and was later to find monsters in trees. I can only see it all as an assumed attitude, a deliberate attempt to purge himself and his work of the last hang-over from his early second-hand and largely second-rate poetastery.

But the paradox is that within three years of his defence of a 'pure' visual art, of his attack on the poet and of another on limited editions,[4] Nash was to publish *Places*. It was his most complete attempt at 'the dual expression' he had admired in Rossetti and Blake, a strictly

---

[1] *New Witness*, 25 April 1919.
[2] *Idem*, 23 May and 20 June 1919, for example.
[3] *Idem*, 22 August 1919.
[4] *Idem*, 17 October 1919.

limited edition and impregnated through and through with the literary and 'poetic' element he was supposed to be discarding. The production was clearly inspired by Blake's practice. Nash made the whole book except that he did not print it. But he designed the cover, cut the seven wood-engravings and the lettering, and wrote the texts. The title-page describes these as 'illustrations in prose', a deliberate transposition to suggest that the primary expression is visual; but only in that phrase is there any suggestion of that primacy.

Nash was not happy about the texts. 'I have been trying to write sort of prose poems . . .' he told Bottomley, 'and am feeling uneasy over 'em' (*c.* 12 September 1922), and later he wrote: 'Ford Madox Hueffer[1] has already told me what *he* thinks of the prose pieces and I confess I quite agree with him. But if they are largely nonsense they are more or less decorative nonsense and as their original use was for a decorative purpose they have this excuse' (31 December 1922). But visually the book is very beautiful. Its title recalls his feeling for the *genius loci*; but it is an unusual feature at this period that that is embodied in a figure in all but one of the cuts. This elongated female figure, with its cascade of hair, haunting the secret lakes among the woods or following the paths through them, and also, in other designs, flitting along the sea-wall at Dymchurch, is never a complete human being. It is almost as if the absent presence were succeeding in being thinly embodied, so thinly that it is sometimes transparent. It is most successful here in *Winter Wood*, altogether the best of the woodcuts, which also uses two of Nash's persistent symbols most effectively. The fence across the foreground would shut us off altogether from the secrecy of this dark place, but for the gate; and through that gate the insubstantial figure has passed and moves forward along the path through the wood which penetrates to its end. We can follow only in our imagination. We are too material for that company or that Place.

The woodland pool, too, which is another recurrent symbol at this period, has its moonlit bather in *Dark Lake*. The figure has assumed more substance here, in this quite unapproachable centre; and the fence guards it like a palisade. There is again a path through the wood, but again we cannot take it. Again the Place is not for us to enter, only to contemplate.

In addition to the seven full-page blocks, there is a small tailpiece which was called *Farewell* in separate prints. The fence is now closed

---

[1] This is, of course, the earlier name of Ford Madox Ford, for whom he was illustrating a book.

right across our front. Beyond it, a door is ajar and the figure, a mere black silhouette, has passed through into light. Above her are two birds. If 'Derriman' were to say that to regard all this as symbolism is but the tiresome finding of 'something unintentional in everything', then he would compel us to believe that Nash was so stifling his deepest intentions that they could no longer reach his intellectual consciousness. But the fact is, of course, that 'Derriman' was a fiction and Nash can hardly be held responsible for his opinions or his sins. The whole book is obviously drawn and written in symbols.

iii. Book Illustrations

When Nash first decided to be an artist, he had wished, as we have seen, to be an illustrator. His early efforts to get such employment failed: his early success with pictures perhaps diverted him. In any case it was not until 1918 that he had his first commission; but thereafter he continued to illustrate books regularly, though not extensively, for fourteen years. Excluding his own writings—*Places* and *Dorset*—he did sixteen books,[1] of which nine fall into the period of this chapter. By the end of it he was recognized as an established illustrator by the most critical circles,[2] but only two books are sufficiently important in relation to his whole work for us to examine them here. A third, *A Midsummer Night's Dream*, will be better discussed in the next section.

The first is Ford Madox Ford's *Mr. Bosphorus and the Muses* (1923), a long poem in dramatic form and in various metres, which includes frequent descriptions of visual 'effects' which were particularly suited to the illustrator. Ford was a severe and outspoken critic and his reception of Nash's designs was the highest praise they could get— 'just *exactly* what I had imagined, desired and hoped for ... *nothing could have been more sympathetic*'.[3]

That sympathy was particularly evident in Nash's changes of manner and feeling to parallel similar changes in the text. The frontispiece was admirably 'given' by Ford—'a garret predominantly furnished with shadows. Rain and wet leaves fall upon the skylight. Dusk. . . . Later a tallow dip lights itself'. The visual image is precise and clear and Nash seized it to express mystery—the clarity of mystery. It is one of his most delicate and technically accomplished woodcuts, and its mood of desolation and weariness perfectly corre-

[1] The Bibliography gives particulars of them all.
[2] See *Signature*, No. 15, New Series, 1952, for an account of him as guest speaker to the Double Crown Club.
[3] Letter from Ford to Nash, 21 May 1923.

sponds to the opening of the poem. But when Ford passed into a boisterous parody of Arthurian legend, Nash could not follow him. It is as if Rossetti had laid a rebuking hand on him, so that he produced a lovely woodcut which would be fitter to an edition of the *Morte d'Arthur*. When the fantasy and knock-about of the poem increased Nash changed to a broader, less representational technique. His sympathy here is not so much with the intention of the poet as with his decline, for at this point the book loses grip. Neither recovers until the opening of Act IV, where Mr. Bosphorus and his Southern Muse wander along the road over the bare land beneath the rain. The illusion of their escape to poetry is precisely symbolized in the vivid white of the road and the gay-forlorn figures who move along it, indifferent to the blackness and emptiness and Lear-like rain, which are the reality about them.

Nash was now ready to embark on *Genesis* (1924), his most successful work as illustrator until the final triumph of *Urne Buriall*. He must already have arrived at the view, which he later expressed in a letter to the American poet and critic, John Gould Fletcher, that the illustrator's proper function is not, in fact, to illustrate, but to 'accompany' the text, to find visual equivalents for it [Autumn 1927]. *Genesis* is a great result of such an approach. When Bottomley acclaimed some preliminary prints, which Nash had sent him, as 'works of unadulterated genius which it would be impertinent to criticise' (27 March 1924), Nash answered:

'My dear generous extravagant Gordon you mustn't go off pop like this over your young protegés doings they really are far far short of my aim but it is jolly to set a [illegible word] light to you like this and get covered with golden showers. . . . I have tried perhaps impossible things but I feel the whole lot do hang together pretty well. They came quite easily one after another and I know they are much better engravings technically' [1 April 1924].

It was indeed a most ambitious undertaking, which he had himself proposed; and its challenge raised him higher than he had yet been. We can examine it in some detail because all the plates are easily available in reproduction.[1] There are twelve of them, and they are all of the Creation, and therefore cover only the first chapter of Genesis and the first three verses of the second.

The first plate is of the earth without form and void. It is a black rectangle, except that the top corners are slightly cut off diagonally, as if to prophesy that the formless world will be rounded into form;

---

[1] *Nash: Eates*, Plates 29–32.

and the sides are a little lightened with a delicate white criss-cross, as if to prophesy the coming of light. In the second plate the waves of the dark waters are just visible by the light on their crests and the spirit of God moves across them in the form of a transparent crystal. The light from the sides is stronger and leans in from the base so that it invades the area of darkness.

The visual artist is a maker of images. He cannot dispense with them. The poet may say: 'and the earth was without form and void'; and he may say: 'the spirit of God'. The visual artist can say neither. I do not know any attempt to approach the poet's possibilities in such a theme which so nearly succeeds as these two plates of Nash's, except the *Paradiso* drawings in Botticelli's illustrations to Dante. We are generally expected to accept the Eternal Creator in the image of an old man crowned, or in the isolated hand of early Christian iconography. Even Blake's *Ancient of Days* is not different in kind from his human prophets. Nash's image is, at least, of pure thought, which perhaps is nearer to spirit *as image* than any image of flesh.

In the third plate Nash tackled the tremendous difficulty of the presence of light and darkness before the creation of the sun. The waters are now almost still, only rippling in orderly parallels as if in hushed reception of the mystery. One great plane of darkness falls across them and one of light rises up through it, gleaming at its emergent end, the light penetrating the darkness and the darkness the light. By this Nash symbolized the days of creation which were not of night and day but of evening and morning, 'because the knowledge of the creature, compared to the Creator's, is but a very twilight'.[1]

After the geometrical stillness of this plate, the creation of the firmament and division of the waters from the waters introduces us to the dawn of the urgent and dynamic world. The design is a complex of solid uprights which bend in arcs towards one another to express the huge controlled upheaval. In the next plate, the earth emerges, angular, bare and harsh, and the tumbling waves largely lose their curves and are assimilated to the rock. The whole rhythm is violent. The appearance of vegetation on the third day set a more familiar problem for Nash, who had already acquired his personal stylization of vegetable growth and particularly of trees. They play the major part in this design, but they are promoted into a transcendental language of rising forms that 'shatter into falling masses of

[1] St. Augustine, *De Civitate Dei*, Lib. XI, cap. vii. The whole chapter and the next can be usefully read in conjunction with these plates. I have quoted from John Heeley's translation as modified in the Everyman edition, 1945.

leaves' and demonstrate 'that growth is both upward and downward, both a protection of shade and a reaching up towards the light'.[1]

But if, in this design, Nash depended on his past discoveries, in the creation of the sun and moon he looked forward, rather, to his final work. The design is divided into two wedges. The sun blazes like a sunflower on the top of the right wedge and fills all its area with tremendous rays. It is in the ascendant. In the left bottom corner of the other wedge, the moon hangs, massive and rayless in contrast with the molten and dynamic sun. This contrast is to appear again and again in his last years, but in some pictures the moon is to be in the ascendant.[2]

The stars that had so dominated the night skies of his early work were reduced in this plate to an insignificant sprinkling of the darkness behind the moon, for he was obliged to give the sun and moon an immense mastery. Perhaps because he disliked this inevitable belittling of the stars, he introduced a second plate for the fourth day, where two stars are vast crystalline forms, raying out like star-fish. Another star is dim, another brighter but small and far, another falls trailing its light as a sparkling wake. Above the black sky a scattered irridescence suggests the infinity of stars.

Nash expressed the creation of the birds and the fishes in a semi-abstract pattern of great flocks wheeling over the arrowy fish and the spinning sea. It is a fine plate, if less awful in its impact than its predecessors; but that is as it should be, for these are familiar things. The next plate is the one failure. The beasts of the earth are primeval bovine creatures which are quite unconvincing, and the whole design lacks order and decision. Nor are Adam and Eve satisfactory: they are robot figures.

Nash called the last plate *Contemplation* when he printed it apart from the series, because its position here was facing the words: 'and God saw every thing that he had made and behold it was very good'. It is an abstraction of geometrical forms too complex for verbal description, but dominated by a diamond and a pyramid. They are right but the complexity is wrong. Contemplation, even for man, simplifies by transcending multiplicity and engagement. For God it is the essential act of His supreme simplicity, the celebration of rest.[3]

[1] John Gould Fletcher in *Print Collectors Quarterly*, July 1923, p. 220.
[2] For the symbolism of sun and moon in Nash's work, see pp. 289 et seq.
[3] Mrs. Nash informs me that Nash intended the text for the seventh day to face this design also, but it was carried over to the next page by the printer and so appears with no design facing it.

iv. Designs for the Theatre: 1911–1927

Nash's schoolboy interest in the toy theatre grew into a persistent but spasmodic delight in certain aspects of the living theatre. At times it was in spectacles like Rheinhardt's *Miracle* and excluded acting, so that he could say 'I think actors and actresses are terrible mistakes, Gordon, they spoil everything for me' [1 January 1917]. But before that he had written, also to Bottomley, that he could be 'pleased to shakings of laughter by the vulgar wit of Connie Eedis [Ediss] and Edmund Paine [Payne] and at the same time appreciate every good thing of good acting' (22 November 1911). One form of acting that always pleased him was the music-hall comedian's. He wrote enthusiastically in *Outline* of Dan Leno, Little Tich and Marie Lloyd, and in letters of the radio-comedian, Tommy Handley. This general interest in the stage was stimulated by his meeting Nugent Monck, Gordon Craig and Bottomley. His relations with Monck were ephemeral, and unfortunately I can say little of those with Craig, as I have been unable to see the letters to him[1] and the few from him which Nash preserved give no material; but the Bottomley correspondence fully documents his most important theatrical activity. Indeed this could be considered as beginning with the 1910 drawing to *The Crier by Night*, although that is in no sense a theatre design, but early in 1911 Nash did a drawing for *The Riding to Lithend*,[2] where there is more suggestion of a set. A second drawing for *The Crier* (1914-1922)[3] has a more definitely theatrical character which must be largely attributed to the intervention of Albert Rutherston's influence. Nash later described this in an article:

'My first glimpse behind the scenes of the theatrical workshop was in 1913, when I became acquainted with my friend Albert Rutherston while he was engaged in designing the décor for Bernard Shaw's "Androcles and the Lion". I think I was very thrilled, especially by the exquisite craftsmanship of my new friend in the construction of his models, but it was not until the autumn of last year [1921] that I

---

[1] This is not Mr. Craig's fault. On the contrary, he has been most anxious for me to see them, but circumstances have made it impossible.

[2] The reproduction of this in Bottomley's *A Stage for Poetry* is dated 1913. The evidence of letters and of style show this to be an error. Reproductions of other theatre designs will also be found in this book and in *Poet and Painter*.

[3] The date 1914 appears on the drawing, with 1922 written over in Nash's hand. No doubt he revised it in the latter year, although he speaks of it as if it were new in a letter to Bottomley of *c.* 2 July 1922.

first attempted to build scenes in miniature and realised the possibilities of a new form of expression.'[1]

Nash's first and only production was far from the best opportunity he could have had. He was attracted to plays which dealt with primitive and heroic passions, such as Bottomley had written up to that time—a foretaste of his later obsession with ancient stones and the ways of Druids. Now, in 1920, he found himself commissioned to undertake the setting, costumes and accessories for *The Truth about the Russian Dancers*. It was a fantasy of mime, opera and ballet produced by Gerald du Maurier with music by Arnold Bax, and choreography by Karsavina, who was also the first dancer. But unfortunately there was also the author, J. M. Barrie, and there is a distressing irony in Nash, who loathed the Peter Pannish, having his only practical affair with the theatre in the service of that master of basic whimsy.

The scene was described as: 'One of the stately homes of England, but it has gone a little queer owing to the presence in the house of a disturbing visitor.'

Nash had to conceive his design 'mainly with the tongue in the cheek . . . by positive instructions of the author'.[1] He deliberately imposed the character of Diaghileff's more recent and austerer ballets on the conventional 'stately home' set. The drawing, now in the Victoria and Albert Museum, is an entertaining design and very gay in colour. The costumes of the operatic cast were fantasticated variations on contemporary clothes, while those of the ballet were of contrasting beauty and elegance. But it was all a waste of his powers, though the press was enthusiastic.

His first model was for Bottomley's *King Lear's Wife*. He made it himself and he found great stimulus in the skilful contrivance. The character of the set depended on the lowness of the massive stone walls and the height of the pyramidal roof which appeared to bear down oppressively on the room. The only furniture was a table and a high four-poster. The text justified his giving the bed such consequence. He described it to Bottomley as 'greyish pinky brown with curtains of an orange tint—looking very like leather and the posts and sides painted with a pattern in vermillion. It looked devilish Norse!' [16 December 1921]. The costumes had a barbaric and timeless character, so that the figures could have appeared in the landscape of the megaliths without embarrassment. It is a very personal creation, and yet it does not contradict the principles which Nash

---

[1] 'The Artist Outside the Theatre' in *English Review*, August 1922.

set himself to follow as a stage designer: 'First, to understand the play, next to interpret the play, finally, to heighten its drama.'[1] Bottomley certainly did not feel that Nash had imposed too much of his own personality. 'It is not "just what I want," ' he wrote, 'it will not "do beautifully"; it is exactly what I mean, it is what my inward eye saw ten years ago, I feel it could not be otherwise ... such sympathy is a miracle' (28 December 1921).

Nash's second model was for Bottomley's *Gruach*, where he got the oppressive atmosphere by the opposite method. The bare stone walls rose out of sight, and there was no escape for the eye from the foreboding interior except through a low door to narrow winding steps or out to the snow-covered landscape.

These models were exhibited in January 1922 at the Amsterdam International Exhibition of Theatre Art and Craft which was transferred to the Victoria and Albert Museum in June. Nash was widely praised, notably by Hermon Ould, who described him as the only Englishman 'reaching out towards something new';[2] and by Craig, who said categorically that the best model in the exhibition was Nash's.[3] That is a measure of what the theatre lost through not encouraging him.

Other designs which Nash made during this year were for the Drama League stage[4] and for Hermon Ould's *Black Virgin*.[5] But he was soon disillusioned with the idea of being a free-lance designer for the theatre. 'I think I shall share Craig's satisfaction by working for a theatre of tomorrow' he wrote to Bottomley (4 March 1923), and within a year he told him: 'I remain "the artist outside the theatre" ' [7 January 1924].

Gordon Craig has made the same comment to me—that Nash was not of the theatre, 'but', he adds, 'the compliment of a true artist even wishing to thrust his hand into the wounded body—this is a good deal to me'. In 1930 Nash wrote an article, 'I Look at the Theatre',[6] in which he said: 'It is now more than five years since Gordon Craig urged me to "come into the theatre" and I excused myself on the ground that I wished to be a painter. "But there are so many", argued Craig. Impossible to refute such logic; I turned from

---

[1] 'The Artist Outside the Theatre' in *English Review*, August 1922.

[2] *Manchester Guardian*, 30 January 1922.

[3] *The Times*, 30 January 1922.

[4] Reproduced with a text by Nash in the League's periodical, *Drama*, December 1922.

[5] See *English Review, Theatre Craft Supplement*, ed. Herman Ould, September 1922, for the letters of disagreement between them. Ould did not feel that Nash had interpreted his play correctly.

[6] *Theatre Arts Monthly*, December 1930. The article goes on to blame the audiences as chiefly responsible for the state of the theatre.

that persuasive tongue. I cannot say I have regretted my obstinacy. Yet there was an earlier time when the smallest practical encouragement to develop the keen interest I then had in designing for the stage would have turned all my energies in that direction.'

But he was soon to realize that that 'keen interest' was not enough, that he was the kind of man who is a painter and not the kind who is a designer for the theatre. A year later he could write with more detachment: 'The theatre cannot be blamed for not inviting *painters* to come into the theatre, because painting pictures is one thing and scenic design is quite another. . . .'[1]

His flirtation with the theatre, then, had been no more than an incident. It was now over. Nash broke up his models and Bottomley wrote the postscript: 'The theatre didn't want either of us: but O, Fra Paolo, what fun you and I could have if we had a large room of our own with a bare platform not quite at one end, and could do what we liked without audiences' (2 February 1932).

There is, however, one important and lasting memorial of Nash's connection with the theatre—his 'illustrations' to *A Midsummer Night's Dream* and *King Lear* for the Players' Shakespeare. He began work on *A Midsummer Night's Dream* (1924) by making a scale model of the Coliseum stage, which he knew from his Barrie experience, for these were to be essentially stage-designs, not illustrations. He described his approach in a letter to Bottomley:

'My ambition is to make very rough models for all the scenes and drawings from the models. One thing I am trying to bring off is the Wood from two different points of view A) the Fairies—plants and flowers the sizes of trees etc etc B) the humans normal vision of a wood, and these constantly changing almost imperceptibly as A or B hold the stage' [4 April 1922].

He made nine designs in black and white, and five in colour, one of which is a page of sixteen costumes. There are two sets for the palace of Theseus. In both two columns rise the whole height of the stage, gently broadening up from their bases, while the doors have jambs broadening down from their lintels. The dominant colours in both sets are a blue-grey, a pale olive green and the most exquisite pale pink. Those tapering lines and those delicate colours give lightness to what might otherwise have been too severe a structure for the play; and any risk of weakness in the colour is avoided by the stronger notes of green, orange-red and purple in the costumes. The total

---

[1] 'The Painter and the Stage,' *The Listener*, 23 December 1931. The remainder of the article argues that there is a place for the painter in designing for the ballet.

effect is gracious and noble. In contrast to those civilized palace sets, the wood (Plate 7.a) is fantasticated, yet not so violently as to weaken the interpenetration of the play's two worlds. Bold straight trunks rise like the columns the whole height of the stage, but boughs curve off them to produce a series of half-arches. On a painted dado round their bases, reaching far above the heads of the fairies, is an arching design of undergrowth echoing and varying in little the massive effect of the trees. The whole wood is suffused with the pale green of moonlight.

King Lear (1927) is less successful as a whole, but contains grander individual scenes. The set for Act I, scene i, is very weak, but we turn the page and the terror strikes us. We are in the storm of Act III, scene ii (Plate 7.b). On the stage right are two vast truncated pyramidal towers, symbols of monoliths and of the forbidding gates that Regan has shut. Beyond, painted, one imagines, on a back cloth, are the shafts of crashing rain. In the foreground, barely emerged from the towers, the Fool cowers against the storm; and ahead of him, in the centre, Lear proclaims his frenzied defiance of it with the Homeric gesture of his whole body. Nash has found a near equivalent to the tragedy, not a mere setting for Shakespeare's text and still less an illustration to it. But Lear's arraignment of his daughters in Act III, scene vi, *is* an illustration. The madness and the terror are in the figures only, and it would be the actors, not the scene painters, who would transfer it to the stage, as it would be the lighting director who would have most to do in the blinding of Gloucester. Sinister gleams and great shadows are the emotive forces.

The last plate is almost as disappointing as the first. The avenue of white cone-shaped tents, down which Lear stalks with the dead Cordelia in his arms, is most impressive; but the waiting figures have no tensity, and the tender greens and pinks are utterly foreign to this most terrible moment. Nash's design sinks to prettiness beside the words that face it.

Perhaps this colossal opportunity came too late or too early in Nash's life. What it might have been only appears in the storm scene and, perhaps, the blinding. But in the end we must ask ourselves whether Nash's imaginative world was ever really adaptable to the theatre. It is not a world of dramatic conflict, but of the still presence which holds the potentiality of dramatic conflict: it remains itself essentially pictorial.

Nash was now entering a period of discipline in purely visual expression. He had written to Bottomley:

'The theatre remains my only connection—as a painter—with literature—that is, my only concious connection I have still a certain amount of the literary stuff in my aesthetic system! But once one has begun to find the plastic values all other considerations seem irrelevant' (22 April 1925).

After the discipline he was to resume 'the literary stuff' as thematic material; but he was never again to depend so directly on the literature of others as he had done in the theatre, except in the outstanding case of the *Urne Buriall*.

v. Pictures

During the war Nash had produced no paintings and very few drawings which were not concerned with it. In 1917 he had returned to figure drawings.[1] These included three designs for Blake's *Tiriel*, which have more value as documents in his spiritual history than as works of art. Obviously Nash had been deeply moved by the poem. It had prepared him for *King Lear* and perhaps evoked some of the imagery which he was to use so wonderfully in *Urne Buriall*.

There is a small cluster of landscape drawings, made in 1918 or shortly after, in which violent weather intrudes into Nash's characteristic stillness. They reflect the stress of the war pictures and some even display the same devices, the steely diagonals of the rain, for example, in *Sudden Storm* or the clouds pierced with dramatic shafts in *The Field Path*. Other examples, but of freer handling, are *Wind in the Beeches* and *Tench Pond in a Gale* (1921–1922). Violent weather was to appear at intervals in Nash's work, but always as a disturbing stranger. It does not correspond to his normal contemplative serenity. As a child he had 'listened to a new kind of silence' in his Place in Kensington Gardens. It is there, where the sensory distinctions are fused and the voice of God is heard, which Philo described as 'made to be *seen*'.[2] Nash's way there, like Wordsworth's, led through nature, and he had sometimes to encounter these storms which image the conflict rather than the arrival.

It becomes necessary at this point to consider Nash's attitude to nature and his use of it as a way. We can begin with a statement he made in 1919: 'Art is not primarily concerned with representation. Art is concerned with creation, convention, abstraction and interpretation; not in order or at the same time, but variously and upon

---

[1] In a letter to Bottomley, 28 September 1917, he mentioned seven and 'some heads of Margaret'. *Poet and Painter*, p. 93.
[2] *De Decem. Orac.*, 11.

7*a*. Design for *Midsummer Night's Dream*, II.i. 1924

7*b*. Design for *King Lear*, III.ii. 1927

8. Oxenbridge Pond. *c.* 1928
Oil

different occasions.'[1] It is useless to analyze what *precisely* he meant by these abstract words—representation, creation, convention and so on. He did not use words philosophically, and we must not try to pin him down to any systematic theory of aesthetics. His general meaning is clear enough. In May 1933 he intervened in a controversy on Nature and Art. It had begun with a letter from Tonks attacking *The Times* art critic—an astonishing letter. He interpreted him as having suggested in a recent article that contemporary art is not dependent on Nature; and he therefore warned young artists of the danger of 'thinking too much of "Nothing"', which must for the future form his source of inspiration'. The critic answered by a distinction: that he had not been denying Art's dependence on Nature but its dependence on the representation of Nature; but he failed to challenge the astounding presumption that the only alternative to Nature is Nothing. Tonks made an irrelevant reply, and at that point Nash intervened with a letter, which contained the following paragraph:

'Contemporary expression in painting . . . is by no means concerned with an interpretative art based comfortably upon a "fondness" for Nature. That is not to say, however, that it ignores Nature. It is acutely observant of all phenomena, but with a constructive eye, that imagination may build.[2] Often, it is true, the eye is turned inwards in contemplation (called in common parlance "thinking of nothing"), which Professor Tonks, as an ex-medical man, advises against as being, in his own experience, productive merely of dizziness and a fear of dementia. But many other artists throughout time have tried the experiment with quite different results' (19 May 1933).

It would not have been consistent with the mental atmosphere of the time for Nash to have said what, in fact, that 'experiment' had been—the attempt to find an image for God. What nobody in the controversy pointed out was that while Tonks was perfectly free to be a materialist, he was not free to presume that all artists, or indeed any but a very small minority, were or are materialists. In fact where he pleased to see Nothing the huge majority has seen God, or at least, in Blake's phrase, 'the Permanent Realities of Every Thing which we see reflected in this Vegetable Glass of Nature'.[3] Nature therefore has

---

[1] *New Witness*, 11 July 1919. Writing in his own name.

[2] 'The painter does not look at nature as at a separate thing-in-itself, to be copied or imitated in its external appearances. He looks at nature as at a creative mystery which he tries to imitate in its secret workings and inner ways of operation, and which, by means of poetic intuition, comes through his eyes to the recesses of his own creative subjectivity as a germ or a key of that object which is the work to be produced into existence.' Jacques Maritain in *Creative Intuition in Art and Poetry*, Harvill Press, 1954, p. 129.

[3] *Vision of the Last Judgment.*

served them as a Jacob's ladder by which they climb to the assault of some Form through which they may reveal Him. In this process, representation (not imitation) has, through the *Splendor formae*, its rôle as the manifestation of the *splendor veri*.

This does not mean that Nash, or any other individual artist, is always consciously concerned with Form in this transcendental sense, except in so far as truth cannot exist outside God: but, speaking more loosely, one may say that he is at least always concerned with Form as the image of a relative or 'natural' truth.

Tonks and his like presume that Nature itself is some kind of absolute—that that tree *is* and is wholly knowable objectively. Nash had already made his own view on that point clear when he had defined Nature as 'being simply that which the painters of the day before yesterday made people believe in';[1] and which they had not apprehended by sight alone. 'It is a great mistake' he had said in the same article 'to suppose that pictures appeal only to the eye. The eye is merely the channel or medium of perception, not the perception entire.' Indeed his position was almost exactly Blake's:

'I see Every thing I paint In This World, but Every body does not see alike. . . . The tree which moves some to tears of joy is in the Eyes of others only a Green thing which stands in the way. . . . But to the Eyes of the Man of Imagination, Nature is Imagination itself. As a man is, so he sees.'[2]

The imagination of the painter transforms what his eye sees. A ball may become the sun and the sun, as to Blake, 'an Innumerable company of the Heavenly host crying, "Holy, Holy, Holy is the Lord God Almighty";[3] but, since the painter deals in sense experience, it is the ball he must always keep his eye on. The actuality of his vision depends on it. Hitherto perhaps Nash had been tempted to work from the vision to nature. Now he was entering a period of discipline in which he ran the risk of losing his vision in too intense a concentration on nature, of being distracted from the 'Soul of Nature' as Wordsworth confessed he was on occasion,

> *giving way*
> *To a comparison of scene with scene,*
> *Bent overmuch on superficial things,*
> *Pampering myself with meagre novelties*
> *Of colour and proportion; to the moods*

[1] 'Nature, Life and Art' in *Week-end Review*, 5 December 1931.
[2] Letter to the Rev. Dr. Trusler, 23 August 1799.
[3] *Vision of the Last Judgment.*

PICTURES

Of time and season, to the moral power,
The affections and the spirit of the place,
Insensible.[1]

The risk Nash ran, then, was of entering a dark night of the imagination; but he did not: he discovered nature, or rather *his* nature, which was to be the source of his mature vision. He was to find Form *in* and *through* nature, and to establish 'the fine balance of truth in observing, with the imaginative faculty in modifying the objects observed', which Coleridge attributed to Wordsworth.

Croce has said that a landscape is a state of mind. But it is also a landscape. The artist reveals himself to himself through his contemplation of nature: but he also reveals nature. The man who is not an artist sees no more than a confused reflection in a blurred pool, the reflections of a thousand others overlaying his own. We are now to examine Nash at a period when he was mainly concerned with focusing the pool itself—the object. His early experience of nature had been very properly that of wonder. 'Something about the trees and the light across shorn fields is always making me wonder . . .' he had told Bottomley. 'In fact I do nothing but walk about marvelling at the wonder of the world in general—perhaps I shall paint a picture or write a poem one day' [July 1911].

He was later to give several accounts of how he eventually got down to painting a picture. I shall give two here, and others in their chronological places. He sent the first to one of his dealers, Rex Nan Kivell of the Redfern Gallery: it concerns a picture that is particularly familiar in reproduction:

'With regard to *Wood on the Downs* it was "taken", as people like to say, from a spot near Ivinghoe Beacon in North Bucks. Millions of motorists must have passed the place—it is on the main road on the top of the hill. I have wanted to do something about it for years. The drawing for the painting was made there on the canvas and a separate drawing made with notes on the colour . . . The sketch used to supplement the drawing was afterwards coloured and exhibited at Tooths': Frank Rutter bought it. It differs slightly from the painting which was of course developed quite separately and un-naturalistically nearly a year later according to plan. The painting is simply a synthesis of a scene and mood of nature at a particular time of year—March. The red "foliage" is the effect of massed buds of the beeches before they break. *There!*' (22 December 1931).

[1] *The Prelude*, ed. de Selincourt, p. 431.

The second account concerns *View 2 and View A* (1934). They were drawn from his room in the Hotel des Princes at Nice, where his view was interrupted by the large letters of the word 'Princes', seen, of course, in reverse as in a mirror:

'At first, this vaguely worried me, but gradually I found I did not see the letters, although they stood against the view. Then I began to like the letters individually as pieces of ornament in relation to the scene beyond. But I did not like them *where they were*. It was obvious that if I painted the word or words as these on the balcony with the sea in the distance I should not be able to make either a good combination of the two opposing elements or give the true ornamental or formal value which the letters seemed to me to possess in themselves. ... The problem was solved by detaching the letters I wanted and setting them in a different relationship, when they were on equal terms, so to say, with the rest of the pictorial matter. ... Now it seemed to me I had what I wanted—Actually I had rather more than I first thought of because in the act of imagination necessary to make this state of things, I wanted a certain new dramatic interest and a certain mystery in the meaning of each picture.'[1]

Nash, then, was not an artist to whom nature was everything; but he would have been nothing without it. If in his early days he had been inclined to bully nature into conformity with his 'visionary' preconceptions, he was from now on to observe it with strict accuracy. But he retained his freedom to transform it into the image of his romantic imagination. I am, at the moment, using the word 'romantic' particularly as it is applied to Blake and Wordsworth. Nash never fully understood this use: he was inclined, rather, to associate it with its other senses of fantasy and mediaeval revivalism. When John Piper sent him his *British Romantic Artists*[2] in which he reproduced Nash's *Spring at Fawley Bottom* [1938] Nash wrote to him:

'Romantic art what is that? Alas, I found myself disagreeing with *illustration* of the definition in almost every case. I turned the pages wondering more and more. Romantic? this? that? Constable, Steer, Sickert *Romantic* painters? Finally I came upon my own contribution. ... Well, dear John even armed with your explanation I could not understand the selection. Except for private and personal reasons this might have seemed the least appropriate picture you could have chosen. Therefore it must have for you a *meaning* I have missed and

---

[1] The pictures were lent to C.E.M.A., a war-time cultural organization, for a travelling exhibition called *Pictures to Live with* (1942–3). The text from which I extract this was written by Nash to accompany the exhibition.
[2] 'Britain in Pictures' series, Collins, 1942.

still cannot see as *Romantic* any more than I can find that dubious quality in the picture of a nude under a hat by Steer. . . .

'But when all is said I do not like the word Romantic applied to that which in its best and truest expression in English art should be called Poetic' (12 January 1943).

In his answer Piper defended his choice:

'To me, dreams are *not* as romantic as bits of real experience. To me, similarly, Ernst, Dali, you at your most surrealist are not *ever* as romantic as Rouault, Braque, and you searching with calm excitement for the reality that will clinch the bargain of your vision on the Chiltern slopes or the Dorset Downs. . . .

'On the point of your own picture . . . see my definition . . . at the very opening of the book. "Romantic art deals with the particular." . . . Well, your view from my window deals with a bit of particularity that I know very well, since I look at it every day; and I find it abundantly justified as a bit of vision worthy of English Romantic Art at its best. . . .

'Do I confuse ROMANCE and POETRY?

'Do you confuse ROMANCE and FANTASY?

'Why should either of us call either of them a *confusion*?'

It is perhaps unnecessary to point out how consistently Blake proclaimed the importance of 'particularity'. It recurs several times, for example, in his annotations to Reynolds's *Discourses*; and it would indeed be difficult to call Blake's position anything but romantic.

The small private exhibition of thirty drawings which Nash held at his Fitzroy Street studios in November 1919 assembled the first fruits of his attempt to find his way as 'the war artist without a war'. A letter to Bottomley shows his gathering confidence:

'William Rothenstein visited my show yesterday and, I thought, glanced somewhat askance from his gig lamps. My new work is rather away from his highest ideals, tho' I believe you will find it more to your liking It is decidedly not hard, definite, in the take or leave it sense of the word, or tightly enclosed. Will murmured something about "a visiting card left by genius to say how much could be done if only ——" and then built me up a dizzy structure to emulate of probity, of integrity, of nobility It is sad when old enthusiasts wag their beards and say dear, dear, the lad is turning out rather sadly. But I feel on this occasion that I *knew* and Will had missed my message. I hope this does not read very conceited but my new drawings are dearer to me than almost any work I have yet done, I cannot but help feeling *now*, at last I am rising—I have wings!' (1 December 1919).

He repeated the substance of this in a letter to Rothenstein [December 1919], who assured him that he liked the new work very much, but that he felt Nash had not acquired the same sufficient convention in water-colour which he had in oil, for work 'done away from nature', to which Nash answered:

'But my dear Will, nearly all those drawings were done directly from nature and not touched since I brought them fresh from the fields! The two that you fancied and Charles purchased[1] were among the very few which were carried out quite away from the scene. May be they are preferable in result but they are of a different nature and intention. Nevertheless I am acutely alive to the weakness of my skill. . . .' (26 December 1919).

Certain of these drawings showed the beginning of a distinctive new manner for a particular theme which developed during the period under review. It was a return to the study of trees, and with it mostly to the upright picture; but it was no longer the individual trees that he sought to reveal as 'personages'. The individual trees were adequately differentiated but his theme had become their interplay in an embracing design. He defined less strictly and used a more fluid draughtsmanship and brushwork. Although in some cases— *Wood Interior*, for example—he relied entirely on this interplay for his whole structure, he more often stiffened it with paths, roads or fences, as in *Snow* and *The Corner*; or established a solid landscape for the looser forms of the trees to play against, as in *Windy Hill* (Plate 4) or *At Litlington*; or, from about 1923, used the old device of a window as framework, with curtains, a mirror, a chair or some other such geometrical foreground shapes to contrast with the organic pattern, as in *Mediterranean Window*, *Riviera Window* or *Balcony, Cros de Cagnes*.

Another group, related to this but later developing independently, began with *Backwater*. It was the relation of trees, ponds and canals, for which Nash found his motives in the country behind Dymchurch, in the ponds at Iden when he visited the Buchanans and in Black Park near his father's house at Iver Heath. The wide flat surface of these still waters seems to have suggested the more massive treatment of the surrounding trees, which became very pronounced within a year or so, whether in oil or water-colour—in *The Pond* (1921–4), for example, or *Canal under Lympne*. It shows Nash's interest turning to the sculptural rather than the organic aspect of tree forms, to the woody,

[1] *Red Night* and *Backwater*, both now in the Manchester City Art Gallery.

angular and plastic structure of trunk and boughs. In colour, too, instead of moving lightly from tone to tone, he laid on broader, isolated masses. This type of work culminated in *Sandling Park* (1924), where the cubic mass of a house is conspicuous in the design and we recognize the influence of Cézanne. We recognize that, too, in the large oil, *Chestnut Waters*, which began as *The Lake*,[1] particularly in the treatment of the almost rectangular sheet of water which recedes from the foreground between regimental tree-trunks, and of the foliage which falls from the top corners to meet a little below the centre of the whole composition. The foliage is no longer composed of leaves, but of large solid masses which enhance the minor forms and create an almost abstract design. The second figure which appeared in the wood-engraving of this design, used as the frontispiece to *Places*, did not appear in the 1923 painting, but a nude figure reclined across rather more than half of the foreground. In the final repainting of 1937, she was replaced by the reflection of the foliage, but the picture otherwise remained substantially unchanged. Although it sprang, I suspect, from somebody else's *baigneuse*, it ended as a Paul Nash by the obliteration of the *baigneuse*.

It is curiously difficult to discover when Nash first appreciated the importance of the French Post-Impressionist challenge. We have seen that he exhibited with their English followers in late 1913 but was surprised to find himself in that company. Clearly it was Post-Impressionism which had allowed him to take his own line in the war pictures: he could not have produced them so naturally in the atmosphere of Rossetti, Richmond or Tonks. But it was, I think, *naturally*: nothing appears in his letters to suggest any conscious intellectual conversion, and we know how suspicious he had been of Roger Fry's apostolate. The earliest reference I can give to a definite attitude towards the French was written to Bottomley in 1922:

'I think they can take one in but it is often a complete take in because they are able to create a beauty independent of subject-matter suggestion—which is only another kind of take in—and to charm you not so much by actual manners but the state of harmony which results therefrom, a kind of delicious flattery of the aesthetic susceptibilities' (*c*. Mid-February 1922).

This was by no means a whole-hearted acceptance of the prevalent aesthetic beliefs, but five years later Nash was to be saying to Bottomley: 'a gulf has gaped between us so far as aesthetic sympathies are concerned' [Mid-February 1927], which is the measure of how far he

[1] See p. 78.

had by then moved in theory as well as practice. It was far enough to cause a certain, though not lasting, break in that remarkable friendship. A letter of 1930 underlines the break not only between Nash and Bottomley, but also between Nash and the romantic subject. He refers to a long delay in writing and then goes on:

'There can be no doubt something odd happened in my head which seems to have shut the Gate of Smaragdus[1] which leads to You and Yours and then lost the key. I have positive recollections of peeping through the bars from time to time, even of rather irritably shaking them but a kind of complex-inhibition or one of those states of mind one can pick up for nothing these days—prevented me from hunting for the key with any diligence' (11 January 1930).

As it happened, it was about that time that Nash was, in fact, finding the key of the gate again, for *Northern Adventure* had been painted the year before; but probably he did not immediately recognize it, and besides it was by then entirely his own gate. But at no time did Nash's work completely lose its English character, though we are now considering a phase which could be labelled the French Excursion.

But parallel with this interest in volume, Nash was also developing his characteristic linear treatment. Its new form began with such water-colours as *Landscape at Fulmer* (1919), but rapidly developed in the next two years into a series of oils such as *Whiteleaf Woods* and *March Woods*, where the emphatic and writhing trellis-work of bare trees produces a restless intensity that suggests the influence of Van Gogh; but Nash did not pursue this. On the other hand, certain pen and ink drawings of 1921 to 1923 like *Long Down* and *The Hills*, and certain contemporary oils like *Whiteleaf Cross*[2] and *Berkshire Downs* (Plate 6) concentrated on the massive wave-like interplay of hills, leaving the trees to a relatively subordinate rôle. We can associate with them the rare cases where groups of buildings also appeared in relation to hills and trees, as in *Behind the Inn* and *Whiteleaf Village*.

The variety of these experiments in landscape witnesses to his restless search for a formal equivalent to Nature; and yet all of them are in his 'handwriting'. Indeed a Paul Nash is always immediately recognizable in spite of his untiring experimental curiosity, although at times his poetic direction is almost lost in too many 'manners'. But I have now to examine a series of pictures in which there is complete consistency of poetry with manner. I mean the Dymchurch Series.

[1] Reference to Bottomley's volume of poems with that title, published in 1904.
[2] Not to be confused with the 1932 version of this subject.

Just before his return to England in 1925 Nash wrote to me about it. He already saw it in perspective as a separate theme for critical treatment and suggested I should write on 'the drawings and paintings [he] made of the Dymchurch coast ... a place like that and its effect on one—ones effect upon it'. And he added: 'I shall never work there any more, but its a curious record formally and psychologically when you see the whole set of designs together' (2 March 1925).

So far as I can determine there were some twenty to twenty-five drawings and paintings, but it is difficult to establish the exact 'set' because titles have been confused and nothing is remembered of one or two of the earliest drawings; but I believe the important works to be those which I shall now discuss.

Their theme is given in the title of one—*Wall against the Sea* (1922). The first problem was formal: how to relate the rigid geometry of the wall to the unstable organic forms of the sea. In the very first oil, *Coast Scene* (1920–21) (Plate 5) Nash solved this by several effective devices. The large rollers of the sea on the left—the sea is always on the left—are slightly formalized and their crests are defined by lines so that they become, as it were, rounded walls advancing to the assault. On the other hand, the rigidity of the wall on the right is broken by vegetation and varied texture, and it thrusts a long ramp into the water across the centre of the picture which interlocks the two elements and the two sides of the picture. (It is not irrelevant that in traditional iconography, left is the side of evil and right of good.) Moreover, the wall sweeps round in the far distance to embrace the sea, and there on the extreme left a building and tower make sharp vertical accents to re-state geometry, as it were, on the sea's side of the composition. They are balanced on the extreme right by two minute agitated figures on the wall. 'The two little black people on the top of the land are real sportsmen and women. Very good', T. E. Lawrence wrote when he was negotiating for the picture (10 June 1921). It *was* sporting of them: they have dared to walk on this land that is under attack—much more sporting than the presence of that cloaked transparent form which paces the wall in *Night Tide* (1922). Hers is no risky intrusion: she belongs there. No wind moves her cloak though the waves roll in heavily and break up against the ramp in aggressive claws. Probably they had caught her many years before, and her ghost brings no comfort to the scene. The figure in *Promenade* [1922–3] is more substantial. She is simply out for a walk, because the situation is easy in this exceptional picture. The sea is reduced to a very narrow band on the far left and for once we see much of the solid land beyond the wall on the right. Indeed in this case the theme is different. Running diagonally from right foreground to left distance of the picture, and diminishing in perspective, a line of telegraph poles also promenades. It is a picture of the wall *in length*, a thing to walk along, not a rampart facing the sea.

In *Wall against the Sea*, the oil which probably followed *Coast Scene*, Nash introduced another element which immensely helped its formal design and reappears in most of the series—the steps from the wall to the shore. They establish parallels on the wall side which can be naturally related to the parallels of the waves. These steps are particularly useful in two very lovely water-colours, *Dymchurch Strand* (1922)[1] and *Dymchurch Wall* [1923]. The long steps of the receding wall are echoed by the quiet edge of the sea, small and tame on the far left. Between them is the broad expanse of the sand, crossed by a long series of parallel breakwaters—yet another linking device. Along the horizon the buildings are clearly silhouetted against the fading sky. The tide is out: the wind has dropped: it is the time of peace. Considered apart from the series, they do not pose the problem of conflict: considered in relation to it, they solve the problem.

This new serenity of the ebb-tide persists in most of the pictures which follow, and is most perfectly and completely expressed in the very beautiful Leeds painting, *The Shore* (1923). There are no waves in the sea and therefore no insistent parallels. Nash can afford to be without the steps and can reduce the breakwaters in number and emphasis. The ramp slopes confidently down to the sand, not thrusting into a turbulent enemy, but reconciling the three curving bands of the wall, the sand and the sea's edge. There are no buildings on the horizon, only a fusion of the bands. The tender mauves, blues, whites and yellows might have been weak but for the strong blacks which define the geometric forms, the wall's edge and the side of the ramp. Tenderness and strength are resolved in serenity. But we must not be charmed out of apprehension. In another oil of the same year, *The Sea*, the assaulting water again laps the wall and its menacing swing is repeated in the cloud forms; but the wall's edge is unbroken. It is the simplest of the designs; it images the conflict in the barest terms, with no other elements but the sea, the wall and the sky.

In a very small group, which includes *End of the Steps* [1922], *Dymchurch Steps* and *The Wall* [1924], another element asserts itself as

[1] In *Nash: A.B.* this was reproduced as *The Shore* on Nash's authority, but it is quite unlike the oil now known as *The Shore*.

dominant—a huge block of masonry, a fort, as it were. But this does not change the theme: it is clearly only another image for the defence.

Nash began *Dymchurch Steps* in 1923 or 1924, but it was twenty years before he could tell Dudley Tooth[1] that he had found the way 'to solve the equation of that damned block house and the curve of the steps and the curve of the sky' (14 October 1944).[2] Presumably it was one of the 'unfinished canvi' he spoke of in a letter to Bottomley. 'I am painting all day and every day now and have just cut out about half my unfinished canvi as they seem behind the point I have reached. You'll see some strange developments dear Gordon in the next two or three years' (17 February 1923). *Nostalgic Landscape* was another of these interrupted pictures, dated 1923-38 in *Nash: Penguin*, presumably on his authority. It is a composite work, combining, as its title conveys, a number of elements from Nash's life as an artist. The setting is Dymchurch. Near the foreground are the steps, but they cross the front of a strange building which has taken the place of the aggressive closed block house. It is a pale yellow tower, with cornice and quoins in pale blue.[3] An arched doorway opens into a passage of immense perspective, which is independent of the perspective of the wall and sea outside. Above this door is a red circular 'window': above the far horizon over the sea is a red sun, weighty and important as the suns of his latest works. The sky is red as in the war pictures of 1918. Obviously the whole design is more tense with the mystery of interpenetration, of worlds within worlds, than any other of the 'twenties. It is an exciting picture, but one whose place in the pattern of Nash's imaginative history cannot be exactly determined since we cannot disentangle the elements of 1923 from those of 1938.

There is the same difficulty with *Winter Sea*—perhaps the finest product of Dymchurch. It is dated 1925–37. It seems to be unique among the Dymchurch pictures in being of the sea alone, though the wall is suggested, as a presence of the absent, in a diagonal across the foreground and the ramp in a deep blue-grey triangular shape in the centre. A series of transverse waves roll slowly and desolately towards us. Diagonals in perspective narrow to the horizon, suggesting the reflected path of the moon's light; but no moon is visible. It is subdued in colour: all in brown, brown-green, green-white and blue-grey. The forms of the waves, although observed with perfect accu-

---

[1] A director of Messrs. Tooths Gallery.

[2] The painting is clearly dated 1924-44, but in the same letter Nash calls it 'a 1923 affair'. Neither can be relied on as the dating seems to have been added in 1944.

[3] Mrs. Nash tells me it was based on a water-tower between Hythe and Dymchurch.

racy, are almost formalized into abstractions. It is the geometry of the sea, terrible, relentless and holding all its drama absolutely still and, as it were, off-stage, almost Greek in its detachment but for the romantic emotion of its sombre colour.[1]

A question must be asked: what did Nash mean by speaking of these Dymchurch pictures as 'a curious record psychologically'? I suspect him of referring to the old theme of *The Pyramids in the Sea* which had come to him so unexpectedly ten years before. At Dymchurch he found the same interpenetration occurring *naturally*. I shall discuss this theme more fully when I come to those later works in which he again symbolized it more explicitly in subject, as he had done in *The Pyramids*. In the Dymchurch series it is only implicit in the formal expression because at this time he was more closely tied to Nature. His imagination was not working independently of natural events. He was not prepared to transform the sea into the wall, or vice versa, as he was later to transform broken aircraft into the sea, clouds into flowers or the sunflower into the sun. But perhaps he had another consideration in mind when he used that word 'psychologically'—the wall which he himself was building against a too exuberant, visionary imagination, the discipline he was imposing on his own nature, taking a ruler, as it were, to slap the romantic into obedience. Or was it, perhaps, a wall he was building against the emotional pressure of the war and his strange illness?

[1] Hartley Ramsden has made an interesting comparison of it with Turner's *Storm off a Rocky Coast* (*World Review*, September 1946).

VI

Iden
1925-1930

⇒⟩⟩⟩⟩◊⟨⟨⟨⟨⇐

i. Chronicle

Nash's return from France was not to be immediately followed by the contemplative and productive period he had hoped for in his new home. 'We've had a shattered summer with a peck of trouble' he wrote to Audrey Withers in the autumn of 1925; and in another letter: 'From the moment I set foot once more in this country I've been hounded and driven out of all my wits and finally moving down here and settling into a new home our first real home—has pretty well finished me.'

The peck of troubles began with serious illness—first Mrs. Odeh's and then Margaret Nash's. There was delay in getting possession of the new home, which was at Oxenbridge, a few minutes' walk from the Buchanans, to whom it belonged. Then Nash found it too cold. 'It is a summerhouse, that's all', he wrote to his wife, but he went on:

'Mind you I mean to have a good try to make the place habitable, but I am afraid that I shall be beaten. . . . Life is too short and too complicated . . . and there is so much to do. All this sort of thing was well enough for Robinson Crusoe, but then time hung heavy on his hands and he wasn't an artist. . . . I mean to have a reasonably good life with my Dove and my work. I adore my Dove more and more and find her such a comfort and such a companion. I feel too ever increasing faith in my work, gradually improving, very gradually, but I think surely' [October or early November 1925].

The house was eventually to delight Nash. It was 'both a garden house and a ship to live in' he was to tell Bottomley, 'full of sun and wind' [1 January 1927].

The period began uneventfully except that in 1927 Nash held an exhibition of water-colours at the Warren Gallery in Madox Street and paid so many visits that he was away half the year. One of these was to a Riviera friend, Mrs. Hilda Felce, who lived at Lambourn near Savernake Forest where he found material for several pictures.

At the end of the year, Nash wrote a letter from Iver Heath to Raymonde Collignon in Paris which first sounds a note of nostalgia that was to become very characteristic, though he passes into an admirable piece of his equally characteristic nonsense:

'You are so far away and the news we get of you so scarce that we lose touch. It is sad. We so often miss you and speaking of old times grieve for our loss of you. . . . How we have longed for the South this Winter—it has been quite pitiless our charming climate, the rain only ceases to give way to blizzards and frosts and Treacherous silver-Thaws when hundreds and thousands of people break their skulls and bones, the country is like a battlefield—hospitals overflowing, postmen frozen dead in snowdrifts, old men petrified, old ladies sliding to destruction in all directions, the air resounding with the crack of snapping legs, arms spines walking sticks and umbrellas—Quite awful' [1927 c. December].

But in spite of the wanderings during these first years at Iden, Nash had found a new interest there which was to continue for the rest of his life—his garden. By May 1926 he was already writing to his wife with enthusiasm:

'The garden is simply a riot of colour, as the journalists would say, a little too like a Matthew Smith perhaps, because about nine tenths of the flowers have come out red, but there is a deal of pink and the canters bulk up with a good deal of mauve and some white. . . . It was so delicious arriving in the moonlit garden, smelling of flowers and hay. Its too incredibly lovely down here now and by the time you come it will be even more perfect, for all the canters will be ringing their bells and the honeysuckle will have burst into bloom.'

It is appropriate to Nash's love of Sir Thomas Browne to use his words, and most appropriate to his method of gardening. He 'wisely ordered' his 'vegetable delights' and constructed a 'garden contrivance' and 'elegant ordination of vegetables'. He also ordinated his friends in aid. 'Jack [Nash] came in July', he wrote to Withers, 'and built me a very pretty gentleman's rock garden which now absorbs my interest—there are several flats to let! Most of all I want herbacious stuff and *Pinks*, I am making a wattle garden and enclosed by hurdles, it needs stocking with bushy bright flowers on its sloping banks. . . . I should be most grateful for any throwouts' [October 1927].

At the beginning of 1928 Margaret Nash's mother died and the problem of her father's future immediately posed itself, but was not immediately faced. Indeed, Margaret Nash was ill again, and when she recovered she went to convalesce with Ruth Clark in Normandy, where Nash joined them for a few days in late June. Through all this he continued to work, and was able to hold an exhibition of wood engravings at the Redfern Gallery in July and another of oils and water-colours at the Leicester in November.

I shall have so much to record of illnesses, worries and deaths, that I fear Nash's natural gaiety and sense of fun may be lost sight of. That is why I give, at this point, the following account of what seems to have been his first experience of listening to a broadcast, that of a play by Lance Sieveking called *Kaleidoscope* in September of this year. It was to him he wrote it:

'Let me explain. Bunty . . . had a bright idea of listening in from St Pancras Hotel. Believe me or believe me not they had no loud speaker and they told us no one ever used the wireless now. After a little fussing an electrician appeared and knocked the useless box about a bit then the night porter turned out the cloak-room and dug up a pair of headphones and we were assured all would be in readiness by 9.45 with coffee in the Reading Room. At 9.40 we arrived. First we re-ordered coffee from a man who said yes sir very intelligently and kept the secret to himself We then sat down and listened. A great silence reigned except for the hotel band and the L.M.S. goods traffic. As you know my understanding of wireless is less than any other inhabitant of these islands but I got up and punched a knob which stuck out of a box. More silence. Perhaps it was a lever. I pulled it out and pushed it to one side. No. to the other side. No. Pushed-it-in-and-pulled-it-out. Pumped it. Ten oclock. Went out for the waiter's blood. Coffee sir? certainly sir, really sir? very sorry sir, wont it work sir etc etc. Fuss, sarcasm, night porter, bell ringing, telephoning—electrician appears. Ten minutes experimenting taking plugs from right of fireplace putting it on left. Sorry sir battery's gone, new battery. Plugging by the right. Plugging by the left. All right now sir? No. Hear anything *now* sir. *Nothing whatever*. Very sorry madam. No one ever uses it now. Well sir afraid the 'ead phones are gone.

'I dont know what this bright fellow did but eventually (10.15) we were accomodated with a little listener of some sort apiece and teed up together in a corner of the room like a couple of copulating dogs We drank the most poisonous coffee Ive ever tasted and bewildered ourselves for three quarters of an hour. . . .[1]

'We crashed in on a swimming episode—very fine effect of water "clopping". Someone said "I'll race you" someone else said Right ho! Apparently they were both run down by a steamer for there was a long unending siren lasting ten minutes. They were next shot at by a Lewis gun and didn't come up for a long time Later someone said "I feel so slack" I suppose he was convalescent. Then he must have had a relapse or anyhow something happened to induce the playing of the National Anthem. Then I imagine he went to Heaven because very faintly I heard angelic choirs singing the Old Hundredth. The rest was silence.'

It is one of our greatest losses that none of Nash's letters to his father were preserved. The affection between these two men, of such very different characters and interests, was deep and persistent. His father's letters, many of which Nash did preserve, reflect in their stiff, old-fashioned language, his pleasure and pride in his son's success in a world so strange to him. The following example is an extract from one about the Leicester Gallery exhibition:

'Very pleasant reading the catalogue you sent, for which very best thanks, made; and, we gloated over your markings of sales and prices, both of which even without the last week whatever that may produce are remarkably good; our heartiest congratulations to you, Margaret also. More striking perhaps than the number sold is the prices obtained, one wonders how those who fixed them were so daring, but they were right in their estimate of what high prices people will now give for your pictures. Excellent both as regards guests and cuisine was your luncheon, a fitting prelude [to] the show, we most thoroughly enjoyed your gathering and hope you had not to pay over-much for giving us all so much pleasure; we got back quite comfortably, having tea at Paddington Station on the way' (18 November 1928).

A letter from Nash to Audrey Withers, which must have been written about this time, contains the latest account I have of him with his father:

'I am staying with my Parent. Most of today I spent . . . sitting on my croquet mallet in the rain, watching my Father romping slowly round the lawn. There is no more acid test of man's patience and

[1] No omission.

9. Dead Spring. 1928–1929
Oil

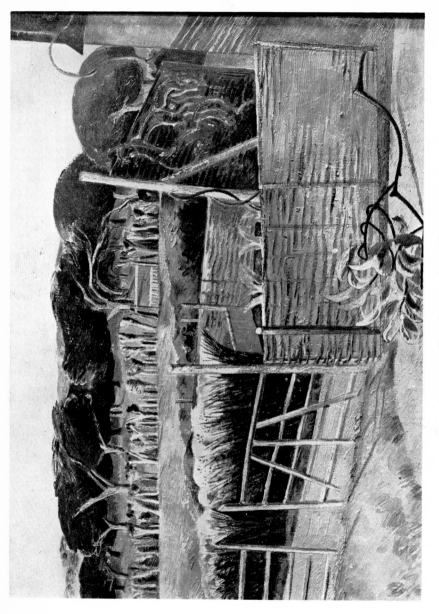

10. Landscape. [1929]

temper than the game of croquet. To be playing badly and getting worse and worse and watching ones opponent playing well and getting better— in a drizzle on a full size lawn 35 × 28 where no birds sing worms do writhe (hey ding a ding a ding) is very trying. Yesterday I played rather well and was only beaten on the post after a fierce struggle lasting 3 hours. I can't get any work done because my dear old Father is so disappointed if I don't play and he's such a pet and 78 which seems fabulous, so there you are.

'I'm not quite comfortable here yet because there still clings about me an air of punctuality, a kind of alacrity for meal times, acquired in your clockwork household. Here one has only to ring a gong for everyone to either stroll out into the garden or retire upstairs to their rooms. After twenty minutes they will return but by then the dinner is colder by twenty minutes waiting. Lunch is at 2 tea 5.30 to 5.45 (according to the croquet position) dinner 8.30 to 8.45. True one has ample time for the things of the spirit as Percy would say and one need never be either anxious or agitated. Nor are the servants in the least perturbed, when they tire of hitting gongs and pealing bells they just sit down and meditate till someone wanders in to eat. My step Mother is the most perversely unpunctual of all and sometimes we sit round the table and have discussions till she appears but no one breaks bread until then.'

Almost exactly three months after that luncheon to celebrate the Leicester Gallery exhibition, Nash and his wife were sent for urgently to Iver Heath. The Dad, as he was always called in the family, was seriously ill with pneumonia. He died on the twenty-seventh of February 1929.

Margaret Nash has told me that nothing in their whole married life so profoundly affected her husband as his father's death. I have seen no letter expressing that grief at its first impact; but in a long letter to Bottomley at the end of this 'grim disastrous year' he speaks of it. 'He died full of years—having passed 80—and to the end was vigourous and clear in his mind. One is grateful for that but the loss is there—it leaves a void. Apart from personal loss I felt acutely the pathos of my father's death.—Do you think I shall see the Spring he said.' Nash went on to speak of how he subsequently 'floundered about in strange waters'—selling Iver Heath and settling business and legal affairs—and received ' "coup sur coup"—not quite the bludgeonings of Fate but some pretty shrewd taps from the jade', which included the serious illness of Ruth Clark and the slighter illnesses of himself and his wife. But on the other hand, he has raised his prices and is selling better, although he had, he says, 'failed to conform to the average collectors conception of me—the label on my back—by experimenting in new directions'; and he was able to continue cheerfully:

'I sold two of my paintings out of my group at the Carnegie International Ex[1] and was awarded a peculiar prize of 300 dollars which is given annually by the Alleg[h]eny County Club for the best painting of Flowers or a Garden. And this was presented to my picture of a bowl-full of dead sea holly! . . .

'I have just had an ecstatic letter from Percy—there surely never was quite such an inditer as the Mutual' [27 December 1929].

Nash had inherited about £3000 from his father, which, with his improved earnings, justified another foreign tour. The Nashes started in the last week of February 1930. A letter to Percy Withers gives a full account of their tour except the exact chronology, and that I cannot establish.

'Our party was rather ambitious. We took a great friend of ours,[2] who had been very ill—just escaped alive through a mastoid operation—I don't think either of us realised quite how little her nerves had recovered from the shock. To make an even number we took along Edward Burra, a young painter who lives at Rye, an eccentric talented delicate creature, extremely amusing. Well, its the easiest, most natural thing in life to say lets all go to the Riviera or the Isle of Man or anywhere else, but I have learnt now that it's far better to open your mouth and let out any other sort of exclamation. The thing to do is to plot very quietly what you want to do and then sneak away taking with you as few people and as little baggage as possible. Just a wife and a suitcase or a trunk and a mistress or a rucksack and an old and well tried friend. Jamais plus, jamais plus, my dear Percy, will I go abroad in a circus. Of course *every*one wanted something different, we ricochetted round the Cote d'Azure like a demented game of billiards. Incidentally quite often we enjoyed many things but it was not really the holiday of our dreams, in fact it was much more like a funny story by Gerome K. Gerome [Jerome] than anything I can think of.

'We went first to Paris for a few days, where I started my series of Cafe drawings, which continued throughout the trip, terminating with an austere design suggested by the Refreshment Room in Dover

---

[1] *The Sea*, bought by Edward Duff Balken for £50 and *Sea Holly*, bought by Albert Lehman. The latter was the prize-winning picture.
[2] Ruth Clark.

platform. You must see this one day. From Paris we travelled South to Toulon where we put up in a strange hotel on the Quai with a comprehensive view of the Port. The view was about all there was to it, though the people were quite pleasant.[1]

'We intended living en pension, but one meal settled that question and afterwards we combed the town for restaurants. But Toulon is quite famous for bad or indifferent cooking, unless you can afford more than you ought to have to pay, so it became rather a bore hunting hungrily up and down smelly streets for new cheap restaurants which weren't too nasty.

'Otherwise Toulon is full of charm. Nothing can be pleasanter than sitting on the Rade in the sun slowly enlarging ones liver with too much coffee and gazing out into the port. Of course the boats are lovely—every sort of boat, from battleships to fishing smacks. I drew valiantly from my window every day, baffled and desperate in my ignorance, tangled up in unsuitable rigging, bewildered yet fascinated by the strange architecture of ships.

'The evenings we spent in sailors' bars or went to the Cinema. I enjoyed Toulon as much as any part of the trip. But, alas, it didn't agree with everyone and it was not very warm so we sailed across the Bay to Tamaris,[2] which is supposed to be a millionaires' paradise and where a Pacha or an ex-Sultan or something like that, once built himself a palace. Actually we lived in a pension called Les Lys, les Roses for 25 francs a day for everything including a most awful lurking smell which we never quite fathomed. . . .

'All the country is a wild tangle of pink marble rocks scented bushes and pine trees, with Napoleons old fort on top. This time those who liked Toulon—not excluding me—disliked Tamaris and vice versa—the sun disappeared and it became wet and stifling. Then reports began to reach us that at Nice people were sitting about in cotton frocks and panama hats. So everyone said, lets go to Nice. So we went to Nice. We had only one address at Nice and when we got to this we nearly fell down with laughing. It was just the nicest sort of genteel hotel ever conceived for the comfort and catering of South Kensington abroad—just a home from home. Ed Burra swore he wouldn't stay another night and the guest room at the back, specially commissioned for Ruth turned out to be just overlooking the demolition of a building which started like a bombardment punctually at six o'clock each morning.

[1] Hotel du Port, Quai Cronstadt.
[2] About the middle of March.

'So after two days we all packed up again—much to the chagrin of M and me who had a sunny room with every comfort—and drifted round the corner to rather a drab hotel which was not at all bad and just half the price. The sun went in. Then we all grumbled and everyone said we really should have gone to several other places. Then the sun came out very strong and we visited our old Cros de Cagnes and Ruth said, This was where she would have come if she'd only known —having always sworn nothing would induce her to go to Cros because she knew she'd hate it.

'Another day we motored to Eze in the mountains and Margaret said of course that was where *she* would have come to if she'd had a chance. Another day we went to St. Paul and Ruth said if only we could have spent all the time we'd wasted in Cafes in this glorious quiet country. Ed Burra said he wished he had gone to Marseilles. So nobody seemed to be where they wanted to be and by that time Ruth had to go back to England. The rest of us stayed on for a week at Nice where I got a chill and felt miserable. Finally we spent four days in Paris up in Montparnasse which we all rather enjoyed. We arrived in England on the coldest greyest day I ever wish to see but since then the sun has returned and the loveliness of an English Spring strikes us as the loveliest thing in the world' (11 April 1930).

At the end of the year the Nashes left Iden. The loss of a home that had seemed to promise them so much, was linked with other losses long after in Nash's memory when he wrote in *Outline: Notes*: 'Father dies in his eightieth year. Bird garden. No country peace any more, troubles pile up. We lose three homes.' They were Iver Heath, Iden and Mr. Odeh's at Hillingdon.

ii. Book Illustrations and Bindings

During the years covered by this chapter, Nash completed his work as an illustrator except for *Urne Buriall*. It included the *King Lear*, which we have already considered, and *Saint Hercules and Other Stories* by Martin Armstrong. Nash had been very impressed by his novel, *Desert*, and asked him if he had any idea for a story in which they could collaborate. Armstrong sent him an outline proposal and his rejection of it is illuminating. I give it in full except for the politenesses at each end:

'It distresses me to think you have written me four pages to describe a story which I cannot believe will interest me in the least! I am afraid I see no scope at all for what I want to do and I would not willingly undertake to collaborate upon such—to me unpromising material. I will take a step further—beyond my province, and say I am grieved that the author of the *Desert* should spend time on this psychological expressionist junk! But as you will retort at once—that is not my affair.

'Let me tell you what I feel equal to tackling—romance—not romantic realism. mystery, terror, legend, fantasy—Im no good at all at village life and as to your theme I cant see how decorations could possibly enhance it. Remember I dont care for human nature except sublimated or as puppets, monsters, masses formally related to Nature. My anathema is the human "close up", I speak chiefly as an artist—apart from that even I'm not much more tolerant.

'What interested me about *Desert* was the imaginative beauty of its drawing searching out so intensely the form of your vision but then it was concerned with vast and primitive things not petty human affairs—True the postmistress not posting a letter and the old lady deciding about a stamp can be made—and I have no doubt *will* be made important but in the province of literature far better than in drawing—it is too long and complex to discuss in writing we must talk some day' (20 August 1926).

Perhaps that was written in 'a mood', but even so it remains surprising that in 1926 he could give such free expression to his romanticism and his taste for the 'Gothick'. He was then being tremendously unfashionable. But that it was an extreme statement of his views appears in a more objective and balanced opinion on a later novel of Armstrong's:

'You asked me to say frankly what I thought of *The Stepson*, well quite frankly I think its a work of art. The whole thing seems to me to begin, proceed and finish with perfect harmony of design and to contain therein a living creation of the imagination. . . . The psychology I have no words to praise enough it strikes me as being so true without any fashionable analysis junk and so little impressed on one which is a relief. I dont know anything about literature but I suppose if one has any sense of values at all one is able to roughly judge not simply good from bad but very good from just good. To me your piece of work here is very good' [18 February 1928].

Nash did immensely like the stories Armstrong eventually produced and he enjoyed illustrating them—or at least the first two—but he found it difficult. 'I sweated agony on that job' he wrote to Percy Withers. 'I am so absorbed now by painting that I have got out of the habit and inclination which produces such work as this.

149

Again and again I redrew the blasted things until at last the rather spontaneous(!)-looking designs you admire grudgingly evolved' [Late October 1927].

The frontispiece for *Saint Hercules* illustrates the episode when Hercules set up a lamp in his cell and called on God to light it as a sign of pardon. But Nash does not depict the episode: he does not show Hercules, but only the altar and the lamp burning white on it between two great palm leaves raised like angels' wings to meet at the top in the image of praying hands. It is a symbol of mystical and contemplative stillness, where the presence of the divine absent is tremendously evoked. A smaller drawing illustrates Hercules and his companion plodding back from the city to their cells. They are most successful figures. Strange pyramidal rocks are, in Armstrong's phrase, 'heaved above the sand, like the summits of a sunken city'— or like Pyramids in the Sea. Nash seems to be feeling ahead to his later engagement with ancient and overwhelmed civilizations.

The frontispiece to the second story, *The Widow of Ephesus*, based on Petronius, is one of Nash's most awful designs. It is the graveyard scene, drawn heavily in ink and washed with grey and grey-blue but leaving patches of startling white like bleached bones. In the centre at the back, on a domed hill, the five gibbets are as crowded together as the trees of Wittenham Clumps. The third tale, *Sombrero*, seems to have moved Nash less or he was tiring. The two small drawings are mechanical.

It is not necessary to discuss the other books which Nash illustrated until we come to *Urne Buriall*, but I must at least mention the remarkable accumulation in A.E.'s *Dark Weeping* of certain images which were more importantly developed in other works—the sea below, the opening door, the stars, and the convolvulus and ladder which climb to them.

It remains to speak shortly of his three designs for binding. The first was for Lermontov's *A Song about Tsar Ivan Vasilyevitch* (Aquila Press, 1929), which Nash also illustrated. The binding is in red leather with rules in blind tooling and inlay in black and white. It is severely rectangular and without lettering. The tall shape of the book gives it a certain elegance but the design is not expressive and the violent contrast of black and white breaks the plane unduly.[1] The second was *Signature* (Curwen Press, 1935-6), an exercise of extreme rectangular severity but with lettering on the spine in a very beautiful variation on his own script. The third was for *Shaw Gives Himself Away*

[1] Nash reproduced it in *Room and Book*, p. 57.

(Gregynog Press, 1939), in which he experimented with curves, using the initials G.B.S. as the basis of his pattern.[1]

iii. Wood Engravings: 1919–1930

In July 1928 the Redfern Gallery held an exhibition of forty-nine of Nash's wood engravings and the *Print Collectors Quarterly*[2] published a catalogue of them, with a critical article by John Gould Fletcher. In effect, this celebrated the end of the activity, for Nash was to produce very few more. I have already discussed many of them as illustrations, notably for *Places* and *Genesis*; and indeed forty-six out of the eighty-four listed in the catalogue were illustrations. This is the only obvious place to say something of the others.

Nash began wood-engraving in the first half of 1919. From the start he used it as a means of direct expression and even when he was working from a design which already existed in oil or water-colour, he 'translated' it into an entirely different and more decorative rhythm. He felt this as so distinctive a characteristic of the medium, that when he wrote of it some eight years later, he put it first:

'With the revival of wood engraving in recent times, artists have instinctively explored the decorative possibilities of the art. . . . The woodcut re-seen as an end in itself . . . discovers itself as a very pure form of art, with its sculptural character, its simple expression in black and white, its direct technique and straightforward application. Of all the arts which are crafts it is the most autobiographical. . . . But there is always the dangerous seduction of skilfulness to be taken into account. Hitherto this has been a temptation mainly for the craftsman. To-day it is likely to prove the artist's snare.

'Because . . . I fear such a danger invading the art I practise I have become lately more interested in woodcut patterns than in woodcut pictures. It is always a relief to be rid of the responsibility of representation.'[3]

Nash went on to speak of being solely concerned with 'the problem of formal relationships' in a passage which I shall discuss later,[4] and concluded with a valuable comment on his reaction to wood:

'Wood seems to yield to the evolution of an abstract design or a decorative arabesque as stone excites the sculptor to the creation of

---

[1] Reproduced in the *Architectural Review*, September 1947, p. 80.
[2] Vol. 15, No. 3, July 1928.
[3] 'Woodcut Patterns' in *The Woodcut. An Annual*. No. 1, ed. by Herbert Furst, Fleuron Ltd., 1927.
[4] See p. 158.

pure form. For it is the glyptic character of engraving on wood which is its peculiar charm, so that the more the engraver cuts into his block —I do not mean literally in point of depth, in fractions of an inch— the greater his sense of contact with the reality of his expression.'

No book has been published reproducing his collected wood-engravings and it will therefore be convenient to confine my comments to eight plates in the *Print Collectors Quarterly* catalogue,[1] especially as these may be taken as his own selection of representative blocks. The first, *Promenade* (1920), has a Dymchurch theme, but it has nothing of the typical Dymchurch recession, the long journey to the horizon which the eye takes in the drawings and paintings. On the contrary, the wall and the sea rise to the top of the design and create an arabesque pattern. But there is a certain overall depth as of bas-relief: one *feels* the cuts into the surface. Secondly, the whole treatment is more angular: one feels that the cuts are into wood. The pattern is sharp almost to starkness, and the long shadows combine with this to produce the drama of moonlight.

In another Dymchurch scene, *The Bay* (1922), the rhythms are so agitated that even the wall is broken into angular waves. Nothing could be more foolish than to consider this design as concerned solely with 'the problem of formal relationships'. It positively explodes with romanticism and its agitated lines 'swing the whole picture out into infinity'. That is Fletcher's phrase and it leads him to a comment of more general application to Nash's work:

'In this use of arabesque line we reach the transcendental side, one might almost say the Northern and Gothic side of Nash's art; for this arabesque is used to heighten the mood of storm and mystery that pervade the block . . . a fusion is achieved between oriental inner rhythm and occidental objectivity. Such a fashion was achieved in the great Gothic art of the Middle Ages; and since it reappears in Nash's work, it is not amiss to call him a Gothic artist.'

In *The Dyke by the Road* (1922), although the tonal transitions are sharp, the general distribution of black and white is more even and yet it is also romantically dramatic.[2] Even in *Still Life No. 1* (1924) Nash was dramatic: the clash of black and white in the technique seems to have stimulated this characteristic. Again, *Arches* (1926), although an abstract pattern related to his textile design of that name, evokes the drama of a great empty Gothic church in the evening gloom. It was in fact suggested by a postcard of a crypt which

[1] There are twelve, but the other four are book-illustrations already discussed.
[2] A water-colour version is reproduced in *Nash: AB*, p. 23.

Ruth Clark sent him from Germany. However much he might protest in words about his exclusive interest in 'formal relationships', he knew that it was not exclusive nor even predominant, for he wrote of Fletcher's article, which freely interprets: 'In England the critics are divided into the journalists on the one hand and the aesthetes on the other. Your writing stands clear of both giving one the just measure of critical analysis and poetic emotion' (17 July 1928).

It is tempting to suggest that during this period Nash was expressing his true self in his wood-engravings while in his drawings and paintings he was pursuing his discipline of formal purification. When it was over and he felt free to pursue that expression in his principal mediums, he abandoned a technique that was perhaps too rigid for him. Or it may simply have been discouragement, because his engravings did not sell. After the Redfern exhibition, he wrote to the director, Rex Nan Kivell: 'Our score for the show is indeed moderate shall we never get away with these bloody woodcuts?' (31 July 1928).

iv. Pictures

It is particularly difficult to group the works of this very rich period. Old subjects continued, some recent ones developed, and others began. Some old subjects took new forms, some new subjects first stirred in the old forms. Of course it is rarely of any critical value to group an artist's works by subject. The same subject may recur throughout the life of an artist, independently of his artistic development—the Madonna, for example, in the long life of Giovanni Bellini, or the bull in Picasso's. But with Nash there was usually a close interplay between subject and aesthetic phase. It was not a matter of one setting the other going but of a simultaneous apprehension of a new subject and a new phase as 'fitting'. He had chosen Dymchurch because it offered the sort of raw material he wanted at the moment; and what he wanted was precipitated by the discovery of Dymchurch. But in the period we are now considering, this relationship is less clearly marked: there are overlaps and mergences. If we are to find our way about, it may be useful to draw a sketch-map to begin with.

The subject of pond-and-trees continued up to about 1928 in two distinct manners, the geometrical and the organic. Flowers in vases appeared as a new subject and was fully explored, again in two manners. The more formal made use of a rigid framework, usually a window, which itself grew into an independent subject and became the basis for abstract designs. Two main tendencies ran through all these: the one, to concentrate on geometric structure leading to abstraction; the other to release a romantic emotional symbolism, leading to a modified surrealism. We must now fill in this sketch-map.

The first pond-and-trees pictures in these years must have been done soon after he arrived at Iden, including *The Willow Pond* which being dated 1925 gives us a date-key to one water-colour manner. It is related to other independent drawings of trees and to the oil *Pond in the Field*.[1] The trees are given a particular swinging rhythm, which is characteristic of their growth but also of Nash—a variant of that he had used before the war, but less laboured. Under Cézanne's influence, he is now contented to indicate the major accents and to leave much expressive white paper. There are several drawings of about 1925 similar to that called *Study of the End of the Canal* and the dated drawing, *The River*,[2] where the linear character of the swinging rhythm is replaced by a more cloud-like massing of foliage. This is contrasted with the solid verticals of the tree trunks and the horizontal plane of the water into which, of course, the tree forms break by reflection. In all these Nash is primarily studying the appearances of nature; they are organic designs. But in other cases he submitted the pond-and-trees subject to a geometric treatment. *Frozen Lake* (1928) is a particularly interesting example to study because we can compare it to the early drawing of the same subject, *Lake in a Wood*.[3] The comparison poses a problem: is the similarity between these two drawings the result of his returning to the same place—we know how strongly places influenced him—or did he return there because he was looking for a place which would stimulate certain formal reactions which he was now in need of? And why should he expect the lake to do this? The early drawing seems to be the first in which he had forced nature into a geometric pattern. Across the foreground is a fence of pointed palings, behind which the lake recedes to an obtuse angle. The tree tops on its far bank are stylized into pyramids, which on the left are jagged into points like the top of the fence. The tree trunks on the right are almost replicas of the palings. Nash was very busy here with formal relationships, but the severity of the drawing is relieved by the rich greens and blues of the colouring.

The 1928 drawing is almost identical in general plan, but the

[1] The dating of this as 1927 in *Nash: Eates* seems to be speculative. Reproductions published in Nash's life-time give 1925 and 1926.

[2] Not *River*, a distinctive drawing with swings in the foreground. There has been unusual confusion over the titles of drawings in this group in various catalogues and reproductions.

[3] See p. 83.

geometry is suggested rather than asserted, evolved from nature, not imposed on it. Moreover, the curvilinear branches of a fir tree intrude from the left, and perhaps more than anything else make the design appear far less intellectual than the first. If we can judge from a pencil sketch also of 1928, *The Lake, Black Park*, which shows the viewpoint from the other side of the lake, there were no such horizontal branches in nature; and we must conclude that Nash introduced them to break the rigid angular pattern of the first design. Indeed, he had already softened it in a pen and ink variant which appeared in the *Sun Calendar*.

Angularity and the ruled line never came easily to Nash. It is most conspicuous in his work at times when his intellect took control and drilled his intuition. He used the ruler in a conscious determination to design; his instinct was to uncover the design he felt in nature or in his free imaginative creations.

We can, then, reconstruct the history illustrated by these two drawings. First we see Nash making an initial attack on geometrical structure and going to an extreme which was far from natural to him at the time. Then, in 1928, after a close study of organic structures, we see him return to the same place with the same purpose; but the new geometry is modified by his new respect for nature and knowledge of her forms.

This comparison leads us to the three celebrated oils in which the research into natural forms reached its culmination, and overlapped with the new research into geometric forms—*The Pond, Iden, Oxenbridge Pond* (Plate 8) and *Sussex Landscape*. It will be enough to consider one of them—*Sussex Landscape*. Nash discovered the complex of fences, trees and stacks of hop-poles in nature. In the preliminary water-colour sketch he substantially revealed the composition, but in the oil, to emphasize and isolate this, he sharpened all the angles, simplified the tree forms into approximate cylinders and turned the stacks into cones. The final pattern is geometric, but embodies the organic forms. The scene remains completely 'recognizable', although its structure is exposed so that we see the skeleton without losing sight of the flesh. Nash has not rendered the brief and unrepeatable moment of seeing the landscape, but the lasting still reflection of its reality in the mirror of his contemplative imagination. It is not, as in the early poetic landscapes, a mood of place which is fixed but an apprehension of form.

There are several other contemporary landscapes, which need not detain us. They are painted in a heavy impasto and are clearly the outcome of the French Excursion. Some indeed were based on studies made during the literal excursion, many of which were tinted pencil drawings of a new exquisiteness, so faint, some of them, as to be no more than fragile notes; but from them he made the massive *Mimosa Wood, French Farm, Riviera Landscape* and so on. Perhaps the finest of the English developments from this manner is *Savernake* [1927], his most important expression of the 'path through the wood'. But no figure explores it and the symbolic character is not underlined. Certainly the most familiar of them is *Wood on the Downs* [1929]. We have seen that it was made from a place by a frequented road but Nash has given these bare downs, only traversed by the empty paths and the belt of trees, a high and deserted air like a memory of Wittenham Clumps. But it is a record of forms in rhythm, not an evocation of what the Clumps stood for.

Nash at this period generally took his material from what he found to hand. It was as if his Muse were saying to him: 'look in thy garden and paint'. Wittenham Clumps were far off; but mystery grew in his garden, where he was to plant his sunflower that was to mount to the sun. There is also a phrase of Sidney's for this noble aim, which applies without adaptation: 'Who shoots at the mid-day sun, though he be sure he shall never hit the mark; yet as sure he is he shall shoot higher than who aims but at a bush.'[1] We are now in the period when his conscious aim was at a bush; but his arrow flew beyond.

First there were pictures of his own house and garden—the *Interior* [1925] of the Dymchurch bedroom, the *Garden Gate* [1926] at Iden and John Nash's *Garden* [1926] at Meadle, in which the sunflower was conspicuous. Then, between 1925 and 1928, there were pictures of the morning-room window at Iver Heath looking on to Bird Garden, such as the three drawings, *Canary, Window of the Morning Room*[2] and *Bird*, and the oil, *Window*. They are not about Bird Garden but about the shapes of the window itself, about a corner cupboard on the sill, and vases on it, and in two cases about a canary in a cage. The garden appears through the window, but it is now without personality. There are no birds in the sky. There are no free birds at all.

Perhaps it is not too far-fetched to interpret this as an *unconscious* expression of his natural revolt against the ruler, the straight bars of the cage in which at this time he was enclosing his genius. He was certainly producing most admirable work, and there is no question

[1] *The Arcadia*, bk. ii, ch. 6.
[2] Reproduced in *Nash: Bertram* as *Still Life*, pl. 8.

of an irksome discipline imposed from without. It was a necessity of his genius at this stage of his roundabout journey—the furthest from his parish—that it should be barred in. But his latest, like his earliest practice, establishes that for him the bird is a symbol which should naturally inhabit the sky. Writing of this canary some ten years later, Nash said:

'There is a difference between real and surreal birds, of course. But, somewhere in between must come my stepmother's canary which has a forked tail like a Kite or Puttock. I have had the honour of drawing this bird now for perhaps fifteen years. When last I drew him I noticed he had got into the sky. His cage depended from a cirrus cloud. Below, a dark sun suffused the upper air with a roseate film. The cage seemed rather to fly than to be hanging there. With its criss-cross slender bars and perches it looked like a Kite. And then, the other day, I heard the bird had gone blind. Poor bird, he cannot see the sun.'[1]

We must now consider the flowers, the new image which was later to become indentified with the free bird and mount to the sky. He was himself to identify that flight of the aerial flowers with death and the beginning of freedom.

Perhaps his earliest flower drawing was *Magnolia Study* (1923), but it is not the great flower of *Flight of the Magnolia* which he painted twenty years later. The interest is not in the living flower nor in any symbolism, but in 'formal relationships'. The big batch of flower pictures was produced in 1926, 1927 and 1928. I have examined, although sometimes only in photograph, some fifteen drawings and paintings in all of which the flowers are in vases except for *Canterbury Bells*. In most of them some device is employed to bring straight lines into relation with the organic forms of the flowers. Even *Canterbury Bells* has a rectilinear stiffening from the square pink bed in which it grows and the pink-white framework behind it, suggested perhaps by a pergola. When Lance Sieveking bought it, Nash wrote to him: 'It is a queer painting and by no means everyones I had secretly hoped it would be bought by a friend who would know what was meant by it ... if you put the wrong frame on, it just goes out like turning off a light' [19 November 1927]. I think the key to what he meant by it is given in that image; for the flower, burning like a still white candle flame, extraordinarily delicate and luminous against the heavy greens, lives its own intense self-centred, self-consuming life.

This is not so in most of the others, where the flowers take their

[1] *The Painter's Object*, ed. by Myfanwy Evans, Gerald Howe, 1937, p. 39.

place in a general pattern. Sometimes this is almost two-dimensional, as in *Cyclamen* where the organic forms of the flowers and the garden beyond, and the curve of the bowl echoed by the curve of the chair-back, contrast with the strong horizontals and verticals of the window and window-sill. But sometimes Nash used a more elaborate three-dimensional scheme, as in *Sea Holly* or *Bog Cotton*. In *Still Life in Winter* an octagonal vase corresponds with the folds of a screen and in *St. Pancras Lilies*, the Gothic flowers echo the related forms of the station. *Autumn Crocus*, although it contains the flower, is 'felt' abstractly, and *Coronilla* is almost wholly abstract. It can only be described as an opening, defined by massive blocks, through which the distance recedes under arches formed by the stalks of a climbing plant whose tendrils play in little spirals all over this geometrical complexity. Window and garden have quite disappeared.

But in one picture, perhaps unconsciously, he seems to revolt against this invading geometry. It is *Dead Spring* (Plate 9). The weak stalks of a plant are prisoned between three stakes, joined by a triangle of string. A set-square dominates the composition. A ruler stands by it. Outside the window is a scaffolding of verticals and diagonals. All these bars have been the death of the spring flower.

Nash was freezing the organic life out of his flowers, that their forms might have another life in that other world of geometry. They were to have their revenge in their later astonishing life in the sky. But for the moment he was pleased if they would remain quite still, and I fancy this accounts for the frequency in these pictures of such 'lifeless' vegetation as bog-cotton, sea holly, bulrushes and dried grasses.

Probably Nash did not paint any completely abstract pictures during the period now under review, but he was already so clearly moving in that direction that I must at this point discuss his attitude to abstract art—'that bewildering expression' as he later described it to Conrad Aiken (31 January 1935). I am here using the word 'abstract' to mean 'non-representational' or 'non-figurative' art, as it is commonly used. But none of these words is satisfactory, and their inadequacy is reflected in Nash's own confusion over them. One of his earliest statements on abstraction occurs in the essay on *Woodcut Patterns*[1]:

'To concern oneself solely with the problem of formal relationships is to escape into a new world. Here one is in touch with pure reality, and the business of make-believe gives place to other considerations in many ways infinitely more satisfying. I would maintain this about all forms of plastic art.'

[1] See p. 151.

It is, of course, quite untenable to suggest that where there is representation there is necessarily 'make-believe': it is to confuse representation with mimicry, Piero della Francesca with Alma-Tadema. It is also to overlook the fact that whatever the nature of 'pure reality', an 'abstract' design is as much an image of it as a representational design—in fact, *represents* it.

Nash was aware of the immense semantic difficulties which this problem presents. In 1932 he again became involved in a controversy, this time with D. S. MacColl. It began from an article of Nash's on *The Pictorial Subject*[1] illustrated with abstract pictures by Edward Wadsworth and John Bigge, of which he wrote:

'They are neither portraits of objects nor pictorial anecdotes. Their drama makes no appeal through association, but depends solely upon the relationship of certain forms and directions, the opposition of planes and the adjustment of mass to space, the suggestion of muscular movement and delicate poise. If we can admit this purpose to be simply the creation of formal harmony, it is not too much to claim that a new incentive is beginning to manifest itself.'

In the last article of the controversy, *Abstract Art*,[2] Nash modified this so profoundly as to change his whole position. First he discussed the meaning of 'representation':

'Representation means exactly the presentation of something *again*; the placing *before*, *again*, of something else, and the implication is, that this refers to the *re*-presentation of a known thing, the intelligible counterpart, in fact, of a recognisable object. Where this representation is absent, or representation, obviously, is not the intention of the painter, the picture is referred to as non-representational, and whether such a picture can be twisted and twiddled into having, in some sense, a representational appeal, does not matter.'

But indeed it does matter: it matters enormously. It involves the whole question of whether the artist can *in fact* concern himself solely with the problem of formal relationships and have, as his purpose, 'simply the creation of formal harmony'. It is the very hinge on which the old controversy over art for art's sake turns. Nash had been misled and had misled himself; and he knew it. He was defending a doctrine he had adopted but did not *feel*. He ended this article with a flat denial of what he had maintained in the first passage I quoted:

'In my original article I claimed that the pictorial drama of certain abstract pictures made no appeal through association. In so far

[1] *The Listener*, 17 February 1932.
[2] *The Listener*, 17 August, 1932.

as the *intention* manifest in these pictures is concerned, I maintain that is true. But I think the expression was misleading, for, in a certain degree, all art, whether realistic or abstract, must have an associative appeal. It is a question of degree and of kind. A representational picture makes a direct appeal to our consciousness, our calculated knowledge and experience; but an abstract picture appeals in more devious and subtler ways, and to a possibly less conscious understanding, a more remote, perhaps unknown, experience.'

In other words, a so-called 'non-representational' picture may not represent a concrete object, but it does represent something outside itself—the transcendental Something which Nash had previously attacked Tonks for calling Nothing.

In his early work Nash had 'represented' this transcendental reality by familiar symbols—angels and devils or pyramids in the sea —which he had represented, in the popular sense of the word, more or less naturalistically; though why a winged human form should be considered to 'represent' an angel more than, say, a triangle would, is difficult to see. Then he had turned to the study of nature itself, but he had soon found that this did not satisfy his profound need to express the transcendental, and he 'abstracted' from nature the essential forms by which he could, *through* ordering them into formal harmony, express (or 'represent') the order and hierarchy of 'a more remote, perhaps unknown experience'. This was not a romantic process, nor were his forms at that time romantic, so that R. H. Wilenski could write of his 'austere and classic purity' and of his inviting us 'in each work to contemplate a completed temple with a foundation, a structure and a roof'.[1] But we may suspect that his choice of the word 'temple' reveals his awareness of Nash's persistent metaphysical urge. It was no more than a Classic Excursion. 'The metaphysician is obscured for a moment in the student of form who builds with cones and globes' John Armstrong wrote in a particularly penetrating examination of this transitional period of Nash's work, and he went on: 'The word "metaphysical", used in regard to his work and himself as an artist, means simply a preoccupation with a perceived relationship between his shapes and colours *over and above their physical relationship*. . . . The relationship itself is inexpressible in other terms than paint, but the expressed result is significant of *more than itself as painting*, and may be explained to some extent by other means' [my italics].[2]

[1] 'Carpaccio and Paul Nash' in *The Studio*, December 1930.
[2] 'The Present Tendency of Paul Nash', *Apollo*, 1933.

11. Night Piece: Toulon. [1930]
Water-colour

12. Nest of the Siren. 1930 or 1931
Oil

In this Armstrong showed a prophetic understanding by speaking of the metaphysician in Nash as 'obscured for the moment'. He spoke also of his possible return to representation. That was to happen, and the represented object was to have an unobscured metaphysical content. Within a very short time Nash himself was to explain the reasons for this:

'What we all do more or less, as Jean Hélion says, is a piece of world, an isolated object. I find my piece of world cannot be expressed within the restrictions of a non-figurative idiom; not by reason of its expanse, so much as by reason of its character. I have known this from the afternoon in Paris ten years ago when I listened with awe to Albert Gleizes' eloquent spate of aesthetic and philosophic theory, to the last time I turned the pages of *Abstraction—Creation*, and marvelled at the beauty of their immaculate monotony. Apart from the world of "pure" invention free from association with recognizable objects, I have no doubt, that the infinite variations of nature may be resolved with an equally incalculable number of complete abstractions. Yet I find I still need partially organic features to make my fixed conceptual image. I discern among natural phenomena a thousand forms which might, with advantage, be dissolved in the crucible of abstract transfiguration; but the hard cold stone, the rasping grass, the intricate architecture of trees and waves, or the brittle sculpture of a dead leaf—I cannot translate altogether beyond their own image, without suffering in spirit. My aim in symbolical representation *and* abstraction, although governed by a purpose with a formal ideal in view, seeks always to give life to a conception within the formal shell. But when I am at liberty to change my mood, and can turn to the geometrical planning of a textile or other form of industrial design, I fancy that I gain something in the release from all representational problems; and it is during these occasional periods, that I find non-figurative painting a pure, unhindered joy.'[1]

This digression on Nash's attitude to abstract art, has led us beyond the period of this chapter. What we have to consider now is the preliminary discipline of the ruler. It will help us to understand this if we recall his own mature definition of the quarry he pursued in art —'the mystery of clarity'.[2] In that phrase, mystery and clarity are identified, for Nash has reversed what seems to be the logical order. It is the clarity of mystery that is the ultimate vision of the mystic, but since in that vision there is also the apprehension of unity, logic

---

[1] 'For, but not With', *Axis*, No. 1, January 1935.
[2] See p. 80.

is superseded and the mystery of clarity remains. In his first discipline, then, Nash explored nature that he might find the mystery. In his formal discipline, he explored clarity. He defined by line, by 'the bounding line' which distinguishes one existence from another.

In a letter to Bottomley (*c.* 25 June 1941) he said that he intended to start *Outline* with a quotation from Blake, which in fact he did not use. I shall give it as Blake wrote it and not as Nash cut and misquoted it:

'How do we distinguish the oak from the beech, the horse from the ox, but by the bounding outline? How do we distinguish one face or countenance from another, but by the bounding line and its infinite inflexions and movements? What is it that builds a house and plants a garden, but the definite and determinate? What is it that distinguishes honesty from knavery, but the hard and wiry line of rectitude and certainty in the actions and intentions? Leave out this line, and you leave out life itself; all is chaos again, and the line of the almighty must be drawn out upon it before man or beast can exist.'[1]

The metaphysical and even moral value that Blake here gives to the line—the concept of rectitude, in particular—corresponds precisely to Nash's attitude to the line in the phase which begins in the years under discussion. It was with an austere, almost puritanical acceptance of this idea that he practically gave rectitude its literal meaning and submitted his vision to a dominant straight line. It is this which I call the discipline of the ruler.

It was by the line that the mystery was to be clarified; but even when he almost abandoned it in later life he did not allow the mystery to retreat into a confusion of shadows. He held its clarity in his lucid colour, which has pre-eminently that quality which St. Thomas Aquinas called *claritas*.[2] He associated it with nitid colour. Surely the primary meanings of *nitidus*—bright, brilliant, shining, glittering—largely suit Nash's colour; and even the secondary meanings are apt enough—elegant, refined, polished, cultivated. That is exactly what Herbert Read found in his 'bright images' when he applied to them Nash's own definition of a particularly English quality—'a peculiar bright delicacy in choice of colours—somewhat cold, but radiant and sharp in key'.[3] There are, of course, those who fancy that the height of mystery must necessarily be plunged in the depths of obscurity. It

[1] *A Descriptive Catalogue*, etc., 1809, Number XV.
[2] See p. 80. But for a profounder interpretation of the word, see Maritain's *Creative Intuition in Art and Poetry*, Harvill Press, 1954, p. 161.
[3] See *Nash: Eates*, pp. 8, 9 and 10. The Nash quotation is from *Unit One*. Its context is given here on p. 183.

was there that Burke and Reynolds looked for the sublime. But surely it is found rather in the shining mosaics of Ravenna or the nitid frescoes of Fra Angelico.

When I entered this digression, I had arrived at Nash's tendency to treat windows and flowers as elements in an almost abstract design. It would be logical to pick up the thread with such a picture as *Lares* [1929], which is again almost, though not quite, abstract; but it is an unsatisfactory work, and I prefer to discuss a group of pictures in which his Iden garden is represented and yet treated in the spirit of abstraction. In one of them, *Month of March* [1929], a window-frame frames three sides of the picture-plane. An open casement establishing a diagonal in depth, links it with the garden. Outside is a tall ladder with converging uprights and therefore diminishing rungs. The garden beyond is rectangularly divided by fences, hurdles and screens, and the perspective is sharply defined by an avenue of bare fruit trees and a high hedge. The distance is closed. Clouds, completely formalized as white bars diminishing in perspective, carry this geometry into the sky. It would be difficult to find a more completely abstract *design*, in which however each element except the clouds is strictly represented; but we do find it in the familiar *Landscape at Iden* (1928). The 'stage' is similarly divided by fences, hurdles and screens, but the orchard runs across the picture, parallel to the hills which close the distance. In place of the ladder, a pile of cylindrical logs, seen almost end on, provides a similar, but broader based triangle, where the rungs are replaced by the horizontal layers of circles. In two paintings, both called *Landscape* and both of 1929 or 1930, in the collections of Miss Macaw (Plate 10) and the Mayor Gallery, there is a similar division with hurdles and fences, but it is less rigid and it is varied with curvilinear organic forms.

A related group of interiors makes use of easels, canvases, rulers and walls to interplay in imaginative geometry. *Token* [1930–1] is a good example, but *Studio* (1929) is even more effective in its masterly ordering of an elaborate complex of rectangular planes. It is again a pure cubist design of represented objects, a conceptual design of percepts. There is a further related group of pictures where Nash has taken over a geometrical skeleton intact from a seen object, as in *The Diving Stage* [1928] and in the very important *Northern Adventure*, begun in 1929 and finished in 1941.

Nash's flat in Alexandra Mansions was high up and faced St. Pancras station across a vacant lot, now built on. Sometimes the fantastic pinnacles were silhouetted against the moonlit sky, and lighted windows here and there broke the black façade. Down below, the lights of cars traced their ways on the curved ramp, along the terrace and through the arches. Nash once said to me: 'Rather too Arabian Nights, don't you think?'—or something like that. It was the possibility of that romantic vision he was brooding on. Soon after, they began to build hoardings on the vacant lot: they made a skeleton. These are the elements of *Northern Adventure*, a picture which, if we may judge from its frequent reproduction, makes a particularly wide appeal. In *Outline: Notes*, Nash wrote: 'Making a name. Achievement and success. A new vision and a new style. The change begins. *Northern Adventure* and other adventures.' The adventure was the release of his imagination from the bonds of 'formal relationships' which was about to take place. The caged bird was setting off for its parish in the sky. But *Northern Adventure* was no more than a harbinger. Nash was to continue his study of 'abstract' problems of design, and indeed it was not until after it that he painted or drew pure abstractions; but the visionary wind was rising, finally to lift him to the knowledge of aerial flowers and the Mansions of the Dead.

In *Northern Adventure* Nash made an intellectual statement through the geometry of the foreground scaffolding which shines out in clear pale yellow as the skeleton of thought. But he dressed St. Pancras in heavier tones, a variety of purples; and he sobered it by removing all ornament and rounding its pointed arches to conform with the slow sweep of the steps and the approach road. The axis of the picture is geometrically defined, both in height and depth, from an upright in the scaffolding by a pillar above and beyond, and through the shadow of an arch above and beyond that, to a square of blue which is at the summit and furthest point of the design. The adventure travels from thought to the sky. All this is no more than adaptation, a simplifying and organizing of the object: but there is a dramatic and most conspicuous event which disturbs so modest a process and wholly destroys the record of fact, transforming it into the record of experience. A window has come down from the invisible upper stories; it touches the road and inclines towards the arch. Through this window, against all factual possibility—for its background is the purple wall—we see the sky, the brightest colour in the whole composition. The symbolism here is supremely successful. The adventure is lifted from any mere journey to the North: it is into the blue. And the blue has come down to us: it shines through the façade of St. Pancras station, like a ladder pitched between Heaven and Charing Cross. But Nash, of course, did not mean anything so precise as Francis

Thompson. All I am trying to suggest is that the invitation is not to grouse-shooting on the Moors or even rock-climbing in the Lakes.

There is a slightly earlier picture which must be considered here—*Swan Song* [1927 or 1928]. The fact that Nash used such a title at this date is surely of particular interest. It was a long time since he had pursued the 'dual expression'. He had ceased to write verse: he had not yet arrived at the imaginative prose of later years. But *Swan Song* marks the beginning of an important literary accompaniment to his pictures. Again and again from now onwards, the title is to provide a key to the picture's symbolism. It is not a comment like *We are making a New World* nor a description like *Landscape* or *Elms*: it is a parallel creation, evocative in itself, having a poetic content of its own. It is part of Nash's expression and cannot be ignored even by those purists who disapprove.

Swan Song is not simply an Autumn Scene, the sensuously splendid decay of vegetation, but a symbol of all defiant deaths. The huge fungus in the centre blazes with a clear scarlet and like Iago's wife plays the swan and dies in music. All round it are the sad browns and purples and greys but the clouded sky above is broken by a pure pale blue. The general composition of the picture is remarkably like that of Botticelli's *Birth of Venus*.[1] When Eric Newton pointed this out to Nash, he recognized its truth, which he had not apparently noticed before. It seems to be another indication of that sympathy which bound Dante, Botticelli, Blake and Rossetti together, a circle which Nash touched at many points. It is not necessary to labour the obvious similarity between Nash's colour and Botticelli's; but there is perhaps a profounder and subtler similarity—the interpenetration of joy and sadness in the work of both painters, the birth in autumnal melancholy, the death in exultation.

I have spoken of *Pyramids in the Sea* as 'an image of the interpenetration of images'. It now becomes necessary to be a little more precise about this without attempting to unravel all its intricacies. We shall be helped, I think, by considering Hulme's discussion of the intensive manifold. The process of analysis, as he pointed out, involves explanation, which 'means *ex plane*, that is to say, the opening out of things on a plain surface'. Anything which can be so separated is called an extensive manifold. Hulme proposed to call the inextricably interpenetrated, that which cannot be analyzed, an intensive manifold;

---

[1] This was first noted by F. E. Halliday, who intended to discuss it in his *Five Arts*, but was prevented by a muddle over copyright. I must thank him for drawing my attention to it.

and that is what we are now considering. The pure intellect cannot properly understand such a concept because 'it persists in forming a diagram, and in a diagram each part is separated from every other part'. An intensive manifold does not exist in space, and therefore cannot be diagrammatically represented. But Bergson has said that although indescribable, it is knowable by intuition. Hulme concludes that 'the simplest way of describing it would be to say that you had a complex feeling about the matter, were not "feeling" such a dangerous word to use in this connection'.[1] But there is no need to be afraid of it. It is precisely a 'feeling' which the artist experiences in his intuition of such an idea; and although he cannot make any image of it as a 'reality', he can and does make an image of the images of its inseparable parts. But we must *see* them in space and *describe* them in time, and so artificially separate them.

At Marseilles and Toulon in 1930 Nash seems to have had a vivid experience of this interpenetration, which exactly contradicts the philosophy of the bounding line, and he expressed it in various drawings done at the time or worked up later. Perhaps the most striking example is *Harbour and Room*. The room is complete except for the far wall. It has a fireplace and a large gilt mirror and striped wall-paper. But half the floor is the sea, which washes up to the terrace of a café on the right, as it might at Dymchurch up to the wall. This café is on a much smaller scale than the room—not so high as the fireplace— and the right wall towers above it like a cliff. Just within the room, a steamer sails from right to left; and beyond it, through the opening where the far wall is missing, the sea runs out to the harbour in the distance.

The physical origin of this and several related drawings such as *Night Piece: Toulon* (Plate 11) was the experience of sitting in a café where a large mirror faced the window. Nash was fascinated by the confusion of objects seen directly and in reflection, of 'reality' and image, of inside and out. He translated it into a new reality from which he often omitted the cause, the window and reflecting mirror. The mirror in *Harbour and Room* is not the cause of the phenomena we see: it only prosaically reflects the opposite wall of the room, but it is a suggestion of the cause.

Hartley Ramsden described this adventure in Nash's work as 'the fused image'[2] and introduced the passage with a quotation from

---

[1] I have been summarizing and quoting from 'The Philosophy of Intensive Manifolds' in T. E. Hulme's *Speculations*, Routledge, 2nd ed., 1936.
[2] *Nash: Eates*, p. 33.

André Breton—'the final unification of the interior reality and exterior reality is the supreme aim of surrealism'. But we must be careful of the meaning we give to 'unification'. These pictures are images of a manifold, an interpenetration in which each element retains its unique identity, and which is therefore analogous to the mystic union; for 'interpenetration and absorption are words which belong to the category of space, and are only metaphors and symbols of the relation of the soul to God'.[1] It may be possible to go further, and say that all symbols are analogous to the Holy Trinity, as Jung suggests in less positive terms: 'Interpenetration of qualities and contents are typical of symbols. We find this, also, in the Christian Trinity.'[2]

But there is another aspect of interpenetration which must be considered in connection with Nash's pursuit in these and much earlier and much later pictures. He was acutely aware of the astonishing behaviour of space and time in our consciousness. As the past can become entangled in the present in uncoordinated fragments, and the future only appears to us as the expression of past and present, since we have no other knowledge of it; so space behaves erratically and objects in one space are liable to find themselves jostled into another. He tried to use these behaviours as symbols for whatever it was he was after, which might be defined as the interpenetration of spirit and matter, where ultimate reality is perceived through the soul and the senses simultaneously and inextricably.

There is a painting from the last year of this period, the *Nest of the Siren* (Plate 12), which presents this interpenetration in a rather different way. Before a window, heavily framed in forest-green pilasters and cornices picked out in scarlet, is a white toy bird on an ornate stand, which is all the gay colours of the fair. The bird has a human head and hair but no features.[3] Behind it, evergreens grow in a window-box, and in them is a nest. There is only blackness beyond.

This siren-bird is obviously not the bird he had previously pursued into the sky. It is an alluring but dangerous imitation, the harlot's imitation of love. The foreground is pebbled: it is the shore of the siren's island but also perhaps the cobbled street where the harlot walks; as the house itself is the nest of the siren but also an expensive brothel. But the picture is not an illustration to the *Odyssey* nor a moral tract: it is a symbol of all siren attractions and dangers that may prevent a man ever returning to his own parish in Ithaca. The

[1] *Christian Mysticism* by W. R. Inge, Methuen, 1899, p. 340.
[2] *Psychology and Religion*, Yale U.P. and O.U.P., 1938, p. 89.
[3] The 'sitter' was a decoration on some huxter's cart which Nash happened on in Caen and immediately drew.

interpenetration lies in the nature of this image which makes the temptation of the flesh symbolize temptation to the more disastrous whoring of the spirit.[1]

But it was not only by such work that Nash was saved from *his* temptation—to the retreat into intellect and the caging of his imagination. He also entered on another pursuit, letting his imagination loose after fantasy and dream. There is a painting also conceived in the last year of this period which exemplifies the beginning of this— *The Archer*. Here the colour is unusually nitid even for Nash. All is gay and full of sunshine with the brightest blue shadows. The Archer itself is a white almond-shaped object, the target a white disc with wind-blown 'rays' and a blue bull's-eye, which a shadow from the Archer pierces, not the shadow *of* the Archer. This startling appearance is in the geometric garden of screens, fences and orchard, but it blows up all the geometry of reason.

The dating of this picture and its companion *Archer Overthrown* is inextricably involved. Nash authorized *The Archer* to be dated '1930–37–42'.[2] The companion was first exhibited at the Leicester Gallery exhibition of 1938. In a letter to Richard Smart in 1942, about November, Nash gave a most muddled account of this mere historical question, but threw far more light on the significance of the pictures:

'This painting [*Archer Overthrown*] has a mixed history. In the first place it is the second of its kind; the sequel to a picture called *The Archer*. . . . The only way I can describe the subject is to call it a private fairy tale of my own invention. But its origin was the object called *The Archer*, a photograph of which you will find in *Surrealism* edited by Herbert Read. Having created this "personage" I began to set it in motion, as it were, and used it like a puppet in two different environments or scenes. In each case the scenes were painted some years ago when I lived at Iden. . . .

'But both canvases remained unfinished—scenes without dramas, and were stored away. The coming to life of The Archer, as object-personage, suggested the picture *Archer Overthrown*. I did not paint *The Archer* until three years later.

'The Archer himself—I *think* he is masculine—is more mischievous than menacing. Also, he is heavily handicapped by being only effective as a shadow shooter. That is to say, he can only score bulls and

---

[1] Cf. Richard Seddon's related but different interpretation in *The Studio*, March 1948, p. 72.
[2] *Nash: Penguin*, pl. 21.

groups, or wound or kill with a *cast shadow*. And he is generally after some rapidly revolving thing like the object in the picture.

'But his real "headache", as you might say, is a counter-menacing *shadow* in the form of a woman with long flying hair! She is always on his track. Nothing but her shadow is ever visible but that is quite enough for the Archer and sometimes, too much—as in the picture *Archer Overthrown*' [November 1945].

I should be inclined to take the Archer as Apollo and his overthrow as a forerunner of the *Eclipse of the Sunflower*, did not the target suggest the revolving sunflower of *Solstice of the Sunflower*. Obviously Apollo casts shadows but that is by no means the only way in which he is effective. Indeed, the symbolism cannot be precisely interpreted and it is better left as a dream adumbration to the more positive and transcendental statement of the two great last paintings.[1] But it is at least clear that at the close of this period Nash's imagination was reaching out towards its latest and highest pursuit, that of a myth to hold his deep religious intuition. It was here that he necessarily failed to achieve the clarity of mystery. His religious beliefs remained without dogmatic structure and this forced him into Romanticism, which Hulme so brilliantly, though incompletely, defined as 'spilt religion'.[2] This is, of course, to use 'romanticism' in the very sense which Nash did not understand—the romanticism of Wordsworth. But it did not so much affect Nash's rendering of nature as his invention of myth and use of symbol; and it is clear that this is what Hulme had in mind from his further statement, which applies so particularly to Nash, that 'you might say if you wished that the whole of the romantic attitude seems to crystallise . . . round metaphors of flight'.[3]

[1] Michelangelo's drawing *The Archers*, where there are no weapons, is notoriously difficult to interpret. See Erwin Panofsky's *Studies in Iconology*, O.U.P., pp. 225 et seq.

[2] *Loc cit.*, p. 118.

[3] *Loc.* cit., p. 120.

VII

Rye
1931-July 1933

―――――○‿○❦○‿○―――――

i. Chronicle

The Nashes settled in their new home at Rye in the December
of 1930. It was large enough to give quarters for Mr. Odeh and
a studio for Nash[1] and had many physical comforts as well as
a view over the Marsh and the sea, and a terraced garden running
down the cliff. But the Nashes were not without desperate moments
of wishing themselves back in their cottage.[2]

It was, of course, necessary to find the right technique for living
with Mr. Odeh, but that was not because he was 'difficult'. Nash had
only recently described him to me as 'one of the few practising Chris-
tians I know and extraordinary good to the old and sick and all
that' [1928 or 1929]. But he was of another generation and a third
person in their household. It was not an easy time. They were all ill
during the winter and Nash had to make more money for their
larger establishment. But he liked Rye, where he had many acquaintances, including Una, Lady Troubridge; the novelists, Radclyffe
Hall, E. F. Benson and Sheila Kaye Smith; the poet Robert Nichols;
and Yeats Brown, a soldier who at that time had some celebrity as a
writer and yogi.

But his increasing intimacy with Edward Burra and his meeting
with the American poet, Conrad Aiken, who was then living at Rye,
were far more important in Nash's growth than all these. It was Aiken's
influence, so far as it was anything external, that turned Nash back

―――――――――――――――――――――――――――――

[1] The decoration of this studio was described in *Vogue*, 1 November 1933.
[2] See letter to Bottomley [1930 *c*. 28 December].

to a poetic attitude. In his disguised autobiography *Ushant*[1] Aiken describes his life at Rye, under the name 'Saltings', from which it appears that he gained as much from Nash as he gave him. Writing of him as 'Paul' and of a 'Nicholas' who is easily recognized, he says that they had provided him with 'two more windows from which to view the wonders of the invisible world'. In another passage he speaks of Nash's 'love of beauty that was oddly both animal and mineral, and could be as soft as a cobweb (as in his drawing for the *Garden of Cyrus*), or the flesh of a woman, or as hard as one of the flints in his *Nest of Wild Stones*'.

In September 1931, Nash went to the United States on the invitation of the Carnegie Institute of Pittsburgh, Pennsylvania. Since about 1900, this Institute has held an annual international exhibition when certain prizes are awarded by a jury of Americans and Europeans. The Institute had invited him to serve on this in 1929, when he had been too busy to accept, but now in 1931 he accepted.

The Nashes sailed on the twelfth of September with the French and Italian jurors. It was a stately journey but Nash in *Outline: Notes* says simply: 'The pleasant voyage. The lonely birds. Ship architecture.' He has left no record of how New York impressed him and I can only quote from an interview in the *Herald-Tribune* (19 September 1931):

'[The skyscrapers'] very preciseness, their extremely subtle color harmony, the variety of straight lines, broken by jets of steam and by penthouses and parks—to me they mean that through this space, balance, stress and contrast New York is in search of harmony. It is trying to find beauty in solidity. . . . This aspect of New York indicates the passing of sentimentalism. It indicates that New York is attempting to face nature and its future alone. . . . Nonetheless the link with the human desire—with superstitions—is so strong that you have not yet developed the courage to completely let go. How else am I to explain those skyscrapers which begin with such marvelous logical simplicity yet which are spoiled by atrocious gothic ornamentation at the top?'

The next day a luncheon was given for the European jurors. James Thurber has sent me an account of this and subsequent New York entertainments:

'Paul had written one or two pieces[2] . . . that dealt with some American comic artists. There was no one in England, or anywhere

---

[1] Duell, Sloan & Pearce, New York, 1952.
[2] 'American Humorous Draughtsmen' in *Week-end Review*, 8 August 1931.

else outside the States, who knew our comic art so well, or appreciated it so heartily.... He became interested in my work extraordinarily early.... When the Pittsburgh gallery had cabled him saying there would be a luncheon in his honor at the dignified old Century Club in New York and asking him whom he would especially like to have present, he amazed and disturbed them by cabling back "Milt Gross, Mrs. Carl Van Vechten and James Thurber". Mrs. Van Vechten was Fania Marinoff, the actress, and I never did find out his special interest in her. I was living in Connecticut at the time, and some official in charge of the luncheon phoned me long distance, beseeching me not to fail to show up at the lunch. Even now I do not know much about art, American or otherwise, and then I knew very little, except the names of a few famous painters. At least twenty were on hand when I arrived at the Century Club, and I recognized the names of Jonas Lie, Burchfield, and four or five others. Paul was a little late, and when he did get there, we all lined up to greet him, like the front file of a platoon. He wandered slowly down the line, shaking hands, smiling, and obviously ignorant of most of the names that were mentioned. When he came to me, he embarrassed the hell out of me, stopping to talk, while the other men shifted uneasily and there was a lot of nervous coughing. He insisted that I sit on his right, and I began to get extremely restless and afraid. Across from us sat one of the most formidable figures I ever saw, an enormous man with flashing dark eyes and a great spade beard. Paul looked at him and said, "Do you know how I could get in touch with Milt Gross?" The gentleman, probably the director of a gallery or editor of a recondite art magazine, replied gruffly, "I am sure I wouldn't have the faintest idea". Paul stared at him. "He is one of your great artists," he said, and I kicked him under the table. They had only given us one drink of Scotch, and we decided to hook the bottle on the sideboard, and did. I needed more drinks to get through that amazing lunch. When we finally left, I said to him, "You didn't seem to realize that you were in the midst of the forefront of American art, and that none of those men ever heard of me or Milt Gross". He looked at me and said, "From what I know of their work, they are bringing up the rear of French Modernism".

'I told him I had not met Gross, but would arrange a meeting, and the next day I took him to see the short, fat, jolly newspaper comic artist, who shared a studio, high up in the Chrysler Building, with H. T. Webster, cartoonist of the *New York Herald Tribune*. Gross had got out at least two of his hilarious "small novels", done in his fantastic slapdash cartoons, and Paul had one with him. Milt is a genial friendly man and he instantly began calling us Paul and Jim. "What is your wife's name, Paul?" he asked, and the delighted Nash told him it was Margaret. So Gross wrote in the book "To Paul and Margaret, with love". Nash did not know Webster's work, because it was not in his area of delight, being a straightforward, realistic daily cartoon of middle-class life in the home.

'My wife and I arranged a cocktail party for Nash and asked several of *The New Yorker* cartoonists he wanted to meet. Twenty minutes before Paul arrived at our hotel apartment, I had started to take a bath, turned on the hot water full force and filled the bathroom with steam. It was too hot there for me to turn off the water, and when Paul arrived—we had left the hall door open—the living room was dense with steam. The hotel engineer had to turn off the water for a while in the whole building. Paul, of course, loved this incident, and especially the fact that, when the fog had cleared, there was Otto Soglow sitting on a chair. Soglow is scarcely more than five feet tall, and was one of the men Nash admired for his "Little King" drawings and the rest. But Otto is a man of moods, and he said nothing but monosyllables until Paul rose to go and then suddenly burst into a flow of amusing talk. Again Nash was delighted and sat down for another hour. . . .

'Nash seemed to know everything about the United States, as he did about the British Isles, and he was eager to meet Harold Ross, the fabulous editor of *The New Yorker*, especially after I told him that Ross knew nothing about art, or music and, as Alexander Woollcott once said, he had the utmost contempt for anything he didn't understand. I took Nash to his office and introduced him, and Ross began by saying "Nash, there are only two phoney arts, music and painting". Once more Nash was delighted. I know he must have been capable of anger and temper because he was a fine artist, but they never arose out of anything like that. His utter absorption in the unique and the unusual overcame all other emotions, and he thought Ross was one of the great sights of New York.'

The jury went on to Pittsburgh, but it is difficult to see exactly when they found time to do their work. There was a colossal programme. The main entertainment was the official dinner where fifty-five distinguished citizens dined among ferns and ascension lilies, 'banked crotans', 'mounds of achevaria', 'urns of gladioli' and 'crystal candalabra bearing sunlit colored tapers'—a series of vivid phrases which I have taken from the local newspapers. It is not surprising that one of them carried the headline: Jurors are Feted like Debutantes. Among the guests was Elizabeth Demarest, Professor of the History of Civilization at the Carnegie Institute of Technology, who also went on to a private party where she talked to Nash. At her death it was found that she had left her large estate to be set up as a trust. The proceeds were to be paid to the Director of the College of Fine Arts and on his death to Paul Nash. He must have made a remarkable impression on her to produce such an effect, or rather such an intention, for Nash died a year before the Director.

After similar festivities and sight-seeing in Washington and Philadelphia, Nash returned to New York where he and his wife stayed on for some days as private guests. They left the States on the ninth of October. In *Outline: Notes* Nash said: 'It all comes to an end. We sail humbly[1] and slowly home, singing the Blues.'

Shortly after his return to England, Nash held a retrospective exhibition of work in various mediums at the Oxford Arts Club and another of his original illustrations and stage designs at the Batsford Gallery. They made eleven guineas between them, which, with an attack of influenza, accounted for Nash's starting 1932 in some gloom. 'No servants and no money and all that sort of thing' he wrote, 'but we are picking up a bit now and hoping for better days' [1932 *c*. January].[2]

He spent most of the year working quietly at Rye, except for visits to Whiteleaf and his brother, and, of course, to London. Some of these were connected with a display at the Zwemmer Gallery in March and April of furniture, textiles, pottery, paintings and sculpture by the most vital artists in each medium, which was held to illustrate Nash's recently published *Room and Book*. Others were connected with a very successful exhibition of his water-colours at the Leicester Gallery in November; yet others with his election as President and Chairman of Council by the Society of Industrial Artists. He was to be re-elected in the two following years, but as his health was preventing him from even attending meetings, he declined further election. In spite of this responsibility coming to him at such an unfortunate time, his terms of office were not fruitless. I am assured by Milner Gray, one of the most eminent of contemporary

---

[1] So that his wife might accompany him, Nash had foregone the first-class journey home.
[2] Letter to the Hon. Arnold Palmer, English representative of the Carnegie Institute.

industrial artists, that the prestige of Nash's name to the Society and to the status of the industrial artist at that time was of great value.

The busy but even flow of life at Rye in 1932 was broken by the sudden death of Mr. Odeh in August, and was to be interrupted even more seriously for Nash early in the following year. On the New Year's Eve, the Nashes had dined at the Gourmet with the Gerald Bullets, my wife and myself. We had then joined Charles Laughton and Elsa Lanchester for supper at the Café Royal, and finished at the Laughtons' flat. It had been a memorable party; but it had un-happy results for Nash. He caught influenza which developed into something more serious. 'Bronchial asthma has been my recent trouble but it is supposed to have been caused by tummy,' he told Sieveking, 'a long boring story but apparently a serious one, so I've got to listen' (26 March 1933). As a result he spent April and May in Tunbridge Wells where he attended a clinic for daily treatment.

Although there had already been slight alarms, this illness must be taken as the real beginning of the fight which was only to end with his death. There were to be periods of respite but the attacks were to return with growing frequency; and the fight to become literally for breath. He would be carried to the edge of suffocation and left utterly exhausted. It was because he maintained this fight and in the intervals produced his most important work, that his doctor has described him to me as 'one of the bravest men I ever knew'.

Now that Mr. Odeh was dead, the Nashes decided to sell the house at Rye. They soon found a purchaser but she wanted possession by the first of August, and Ruth Clark was called in to help with the packing. She has described the strange and uncharacteristic condi-tion in which she found Nash:

'Paul was looking forward to going to France and Spain in the autumn, but he had no reserve of strength to bring to the arduous task of sorting his innumerable papers, magazines, cuttings, books and working materials, piled up in the bookshelves and cupboards of the delightful Rye studio.

'Two or three times he made attempts to direct me in a compli-cated "sortage" only to turn away tired and disheartened. He could not decide what to discard, what to store—and the pile of "I'd better have those with me" grew disconcertingly. He eyed it with alarm. Margaret, who rarely protested at his accumulating habits, was stern—he must "travel light" during the next few months for there would be little room in the London flat or in their trunks. His in-decision at what to throw away, what to keep, what he would need

with him, discouraged him—he who usually worked out with delibera-
tion what would be necessary and brought it down to workmanlike
proportions. Now he would turn rather listlessly aside and saunter
over to sit in the wide window looking far out over the landscape.'

It was therefore decided that Nash should go away in Ruth
Clark's care and leave his wife to concentrate on the packing. He
chose Marlborough for no more precise reason than a vague wish to
revisit Savernake Forest. It was not until he was there, that he
realized how close it was to Avebury. With the vision of the stones of
Avebury a new and most significant phase in his art begins; but it
does not belong here and I therefore reserve Ruth Clark's account of
this visit to the next chapter.

During his last weeks at Rye Nash had announced in a letter to
The Times that a new organization of artists had been founded.[1] This
was Unit One. He had conceived the idea of it from an exhibition
called 'Recent Tendencies in British Painting', which had been held
at Tooth's galleries in October 1931. Nash wrote of this later:

'For the first time it was possible to see, collected together, the
pictures of artists who had been working out, apart, ideas which,
either by conception or the idiom of their expression, or often because
of both qualities, were separated from the main trend of contemporary English art. For the first time, and at once, it was clear that,
however diverse in their ways and means, the majority of these
artists were somehow allied in purpose.'[2]

While Nash was brooding on the possibility of forming a group
which should put 'new life and impetus' into this purpose, he had a
long talk with the architect, Wells Coates. They concluded that a
grouping of architects with painters and sculptors would best serve
the purpose, and that to include industrial and commercial artists
would extend the range unmanageably.

Unit One was born from these considerations by the beginning of
1933. The name was adopted because 'though as persons, each artist
is a *unit*, in the social structure they must, to the extent of their common interests, be *one*'.[3] The majority of the members would be established artists and although their individual artistic views might vary,
they would stand as a group 'for the expression of a truly contem-

[1] 12 June 1933. Reprinted in *Unit One*, p. 10.
[2] 'Unit One' in *The Listener*, 5 July 1933.
[3] Sir Herbert Read in *Unit One*, p. 12.

porary spirit, for that thing which is recognized as peculiarly *of today* in painting, sculpture and architecture'.[1]

That was the hope, but the artistic views of the members were far too disparate for it to be fulfilled. They were the painters Edward Wadsworth, Ben Nicholson, Tristram Hillier, Edward Burra, John Bigge, John Armstrong and Paul Nash; the sculptors Henry Moore and Barbara Hepworth; the architects Wells Coates and Colin Lucas.

The history of the Unit can be very shortly summarized. In April 1934, Cassells published *Unit One*, which was edited and introduced by Herbert Read, and contained statements of their aims by the members, reproductions of their work, and photographs of them, their hands and their studios. In the same month, the Mayor Gallery, which was planned to be the permanent headquarters of the Unit, held an exhibition of their work that was subsequently shown in Liverpool, Manchester, Hanley, Derby, Swansea and Belfast. The press reacted conspicuously, if not always favourably. Indeed, the whole affair was a great success as publicity, and that had been acknowledged as at least one of its aims.[2] But in spite of this, the Unit immediately began to break up from within, and at the beginning of 1935, Nash reported to Conrad Aiken:

'The group has tested itself after a year's life, and is now in the process of re-construction—sloughing off old members and electing new ones. What really happened is rather funny. . . . A narrow majority was found to support the test of a unanimous vote (by secret ballot). My own feelings did not agree with such drastic logic —but other counsels prevailed. The result surprised everyone, I think. Only Henry Moore and myself received the unanimous vote! We quickly invited Wells Coates to join us and so saved our faces by presenting a base representing the three arts on which to build up again. So far nothing more has happened' (31 January 1935).

And nothing more was to happen.

ii. *Publications and Opinions. 1930–1934*

When at Iden Nash had written very little but when at Rye and in the following year or so he was at his most prolific. In the Decem-

---

[1] Nash's letter to *The Times*, 12 June 1933.

[2] In addition to *Unit One* the following long illustrated articles may be consulted: 'Unit One' by Herbert Read, *Architectural Review*, October 1933 (substantially the text of his introduction to the book); 'The Painter Speaks' by Hugh Gordon Porteous, *The Listener*, 4 April 1933; 'Selling Pictures. An Organization and a Gallery' by Anthony Bertram, *Design for Today*, May 1934.

ber of 1930 he became art critic to the *Week-end Review*,[1] and in the following April to the *Listener*, where he alternated with Herbert Read.

I shall not discuss all these articles, most of which were occasional. Their chief value today is in what they reveal of Nash's general interests and attitude. Fortunately he was not tied down by either of his editors to the drudgery of 'reporting' on current exhibitions and art books, but was free to use them as excuses for wider discussions. Even so, his articles were, on the whole, no more than journalism; but they were good journalism, and a notable advance on his work for the *New Witness*. He began to discover that writer's sensibility to words as 'objects' which was to make his later essays and *Outline* works of art. In one instance he brought this into the open. He described 'caricature' as 'an encouraging word, suggesting something amusing and easy to understand at a glance . . . a pleasant, chatty noise'; but 'cartoon' as sounding like 'a sort of doom, the doom of any further easiness in the play of the word caricature'.[2]

One of the most illuminating of the *Listener* articles was in a series called 'What I like in Art', to which various people were invited to contribute. The choice of subject was obviously quite free. Nash was shocked to discover that none of his predecessors—he was the fifteenth contributor—had chosen any modern work; but he was more shocked to discover that he could not do so himself. The only condition attached to the writer's choice was that the picture could be easily seen; and Nash could not find any 'considerable work of art' later than the Post-Impressionists in any London public collection. He chose El Greco's *Laocoon*, which was at the time on loan to the National Gallery, not only because it was 'what he liked' but also, he said, 'because of all pictures within range, it seems to come nearest to those examples of abstract pictorial drama which I had in mind to discuss'.

He had already referred to El Greco as 'the one master who seems to hold in his hands the secrets of the past and future of painting,'[3] and in this article he tried to bring that supreme mystical painter into the company of formalists:

'El Greco may be said to be, primarily, a designer. When he sets out to illustrate a theme, the subject-drama, whatever it may be—

---

[1] Founded March 1930 by Sir Gerald Barry, later editor of the *News Chronicle* and in 1951 Director-General of the Festival of Britain. It was absorbed into the *New Statesman* in January 1934.
[2] 'Caricature' in *Week-end Review*, 24 December 1932.
[3] 'Back to the Sources' in *Week-end Review*, 7 February 1931.

"The Agony in the Garden" or the torture of Laocoon—is not left to appeal by virtue of its own descriptive message. It is infused and animated by an extraordinary force pursuing no seemingly reasonable explanatory course to convey its story but rather seeking to brand the imagination with a series of indestructible images, the true significance of which lies in their *formal* symbolism. This method tends to change the nature of pictorial appeal, so that the unsophisticated or uneducated spectator, instead of asking himself, "What is this *about?*" is inclined to exclaim, "What *is* this?" The natural curiosity in subject is overcome by a startled interest in *object*. In fact, the immediate appeal of such pictures is that of, virtually, abstract values in form and colour alone. . . .'[1]

But the sensitive spectator asks: What does this *mean?* Greco was passionately concerned with expressing his meaning. Like every genuine artist he used 'significant form' to convey it; but of what value is 'significant form' if we do not feel what it signifies? What is signified in 'abstract values of form and colour alone' may be very important, but it is emphatically not what Greco was *primarily* concerned with. But if Nash had omitted the word 'primarily' from his first sentence, it would have been the barest statement of the obvious. All artists are designers and convey their meaning *through* design.

Nash then goes on to make a penetrating analysis of the picture's design, but he fails to enlarge on its symbolism, although he ends by saying that it is 'the outcome of an effort not simply to describe an imagined scene, but to create, by means of formal symbols, a compelling drama of abstract beauty'. But nobody has ever seriously thought that the function of art ever was 'simply to describe'; whereas clearly the function of symbols is to express the artist's theme. The theme is not the subject, but even so Nash cannot really have believed that El Greco chose his terrible subject, still less his *Agony in the Garden*, merely as a means of creating 'abstract beauty'.

Nash was more successful in an article on Picasso. He had been upset by a remark he had overheard at an exhibition that 'although Picasso *can*, he doesn't seem to *want* to paint'. This led him to attack what he calls 'the paint prejudice'. Nash himself had been sometimes criticized for not being 'painty', and therefore I shall quote his defence of Picasso because it was partly a defence of his own practice.

'If an artist creates abstractions he is said to be abandoning painting "as understood". It is a fixed impression that abstraction is a kind of hybrid, an intellectual exercise, a design which could be accepted

[1] *The Listener*, 3 October 1934.

if it was on the floor, but a painting, no, not as "understood". What is understood by paint, of course, is a lot of paint. . . . The old story of Turner revives in one's mind. "Mr. Turner, what do you mix your colours with?" "My brains, madam"—or words to that effect. And so with Picasso. His pictures are not examples of what a painter can do with paint, but what he can do with brains—and yet be a painter. Take, for example, *Le Corsage Jaune* . . . it is a purely plastic creation literally built out of paint, not with a juicy, oleaginous mess, but by a dry luminous substance applied with unerring strokes and layers. The whole picture vibrates with colour and light.'[1]

Although Nash was himself best equipped to write of the painting as object, rather than as symbol, he recognized that another and more important treatment is possible. In discussing Robert Byron's *Birth of Western Painting*[2] he praised Roger Fry, Clive Bell, Herbert Read and others for their 'brilliant explanatory treatises' but said that 'it has been left for a much younger writer, however, to lift the art of aesthetic analysis above the level of subtle criticism or ingenious argument to the plane of creative thought. . . . Mr. Byron is not afraid to approach his subject as a philosopher'. And this led him later in the article to an important confession of faith: 'To perceive through the images and monuments of man some glimmering of an ordered plan, some movement of a rhythm animating the universe, this must be the impulse of the modern writer upon Art who is not content to remain a critic.'

But although Nash might praise 'explanatory treatises' he had little sympathy for the public that needed explanation, or indeed for 'the public' at all. This gave him the occasion for some of his wittiest writing, for example in an article called *The Artist as Sportsman*:

'Epstein is the average man's ideal of what an artist should be. . . . The public like Epstein because he puts up a great show, because he draws a crowd which forces them into a queue, and when they are in a queue they know where they are. What happens after that may be exasperating, even revolting, but it will not be dull. . . . Moreover, there is sure to be a great deal of indignation about. . . . No other sympathy so quickly unites. When the footballer charges his opponent in the back or the boxer hits low, the crowd as one voice shouts "Dirty!" and feels the better for it. Each man rises a point in his self-esteem; he has detected an expert in a fault, he has given judgment. . . .

[1] *Week-end Review*, 27 June 1931.
[2] 'Back to the Sources', *Idem*, 7 February 1931.

'When an artist's work has moved people to this degree they would admit it was justified. It is now within their reach—everyone knows a woman doesn't look like that. Play the game! Dirty! All the same, there was that other thing of his. Clever. Tricky with his hands. Once the public can think of an artist in these terms they have got him where they want him. Now he can take his place with the other public performers—cricketers, boxers, dirt-track racers and dogs. He is a sort of "sportsman", too, with his funny ways.'[1]

Nash's articles were not confined to painting and sculpture. They were also on photography, the cinema, the theatre and industrial design. I shall make use of these in appropriate places. Nash himself made use of some of them to compile *Room and Book*, which he published in 1932. I must have criticized its lack of coherence, for he wrote me a letter which explains its origin and purpose:

'I conceived a book which should be divided into two parts—each holding a group of essays insisting upon various aspects of the two subjects—the room, the book. I then . . . wrote an introduction which seemed to me to explain the nature of the whole—the result of occasional inquisitive concentration—which is precisely what each essay represents. So in a sense you are right. The whole was never planned as a book from the beginning out of nothing. It was built out of material half of which already existed, the other half (most of part 1) being adapted to accomodate the material in hand' [April 1932].

But the book not only suffers from being composed of existing independent essays. The two subjects are viewed from quite different angles, book-design from the technical and room-design from the aesthetic. It is not what Nash calls it in the introduction—'a collection of essays upon aesthetic values'—but rather what the journalist would call a 'timely book', and much of it, therefore, is now stale. His attack on the fake antique and fake modern, and his advocacy of certain principles of good design have now become commonplaces; but they were pioneer contributions to the renaissance of design in the inter-war years.

It will be more appropriate to discuss his views on the relations between art and industry in the next section, but I must touch here on a larger view—that good design might reform the world. He ended the first part of *Room and Book* with the sentence: 'It occurs to

---

[1] *Week-end Review*, 18 April 1931. Sir Jacob Epstein did not like this article. Those who wish to rake up an old squabble can do so in his *Let there be Sculpture* (Michael Joseph, 1940), p. 229, and the correspondence in the *Week-end Review*, 25 April, 2 and 9 May 1931.

me that above all things to-day man needs to create, in however small a compass, a harmonious world to inhabit, where, even for a short space of time, he may enjoy the forgotten luxury of contemplation'. But contemplation is not a luxury: it is a necessity. Without it a 'harmonious world' cannot be created. The world cannot be set in order, by setting our house in order, except in a metaphysical sense. In fact, he seems to be putting the cart before the horse.

But in the meantime, in his pictures, he could make satisfactory worlds, although at this period he wavered between making them imaginative expressions of an abstract intellectual order and making them embody his intuitions. He saw his predicament as that of the artist moved by 'the contemporary spirit', which he defined in an article on Unit One:

'It is the adventure, the research, the pursuit in modern life, and, as these are evident in other activities of thought and action, so they are the impulse of modern art. But the pursuit is not vaguely directed. It seems today to have two definite objects for the mind and hand of the artist. First, the pursuit of form; the expression of the structural purpose in search of beauty in formal interaction and relations apart from representation. This is typified by abstract art. Second, the pursuit of the soul, the attempt to trace the "psyche" in its devious flight, a psychological research on the part of the artist parallel to the experiments of the great analysts. This is represented by the movement known as Surréalisme.'[1]

It was between those pursuits that he was wavering, but neither of them in fact was the way back to his parish. We have already seen that he could not be satisfied with abstraction and that he had no liking for psychology. The 'soul' that was his real quarry had not the psychologist's meaning but God's. How little he understood himself at this time is made ludicrously clear in a passage of his letter to *The Times* on *Unit One*:

'What they [the artists] stand for is decidedly at variance with the great Unconscious School of Painting, also they seem to be lacking in reverence for Nature as such. These facts are frequently pointed out to them. Their answer is that they are interested in other matters which seem to them more engrossing, more immediate. Design, for instance—considered as a structural pursuit; imagination, explored apart from literature or metaphysics.'

If Nash considered himself to be among these artists, and obviously he did, he was amazingly deluded about himself, and about at least

[1] *The Listener*, 5 July 1933.

John Armstrong and Burra among the others. He had recently illustrated *Urne Buriall*, which could not possibly be considered apart from either literature or metaphysics; he included *Northern Adventure* and *Mansions of the Dead*[1] among the works he reproduced in this very book, and they are both highly literary and metaphysical; he had never lacked reverence for nature and he was soon to be openly associated with the most 'unconscious' of all schools of painting—the Surrealists. Surely no artist has ever made a statement which so completely misrepresented his own deepest imaginative pursuit.

The confusion into which Nash had fallen was the result of his intellectual acceptance of a foreign creed. His intellect and his intuition were at odds, for it is the great commonplace about Nash that he was 'essentially English'. Critic after critic has reiterated this,[2] but there are not many who have been courageous enough to define precisely what they mean. Nash himself modestly attempted the task in his contribution to *Unit One*, of all occasions. He beautifully contradicted the passages I have been quoting and flew straight up to his own Gothic pinnacle.

'English art has always shown particular tendencies which recur throughout its history. A pronounced linear method in design, no doubt traceable to sources in Celtic ornament, or to a predilection for the Gothic idiom. A peculiar bright delicacy in choice of colours —somewhat cold but radiant and sharp in key. A concentration, too, in the practice of portraiture; as though everything must be a likeness rather than an equivalent. . . .

'But such characterisation will not help to explain what I have in mind. There seems to exist, behind the frank expressions of portrait and scene, an imprisoned spirit: yet this spirit is the source, the motive power which animates this art. These pictures are the vehicles of this spirit but, somehow, they are inadequate, being only echoes and reflections of familiar images (in portrait and scene). If I were asked to describe this spirit I would say it is of the land; *genius loci* is indeed almost its conception. If its expression could be designated I would say it is almost entirely lyrical. Further, I dare not go.'

But he did, in fact. He spoke of those Englishmen who transcended the 'familiar images', of Blake, whose mythical Albion was the symbol for what his 'inward eye' perceived as England; and of Turner who

---

[1] Perhaps in the unconscious hope of masking his inconsistency from himself, he called it *Aerial Composition*, but he later gave it back its proper title. See p. 195.

[2] See, for examples, Herbert Read and Hartley Ramsden in *Nash: Eates*, pp. 9 and 22 respectively; William Gaunt in 'Paul Nash' in *Drawing and Design*, October 1926; J. G. Fletcher in 'Paul Nash' in *The Arts* (U.S.A.), October 1928.

'sought to break through the deceptive mirage which he could depict with such ease, to a reality more real, in his imagination'. In an article published two years earlier he had said: 'Turner's eye alone saw Nature with a great distraught vision changing the gentle order of the countryside in a grandiose distortion.'[1]

What Nash was really doing in this essay was to explain to himself what was happening to himself, that he was returning to his own language of symbols. 'We, to-day' he went on 'must find new symbols to express our reaction to environment. In some cases this will take the form of an abstract art, in others we may look for some different nature of imaginative research. But in whatever form, it will be a subjective art.'

And that, of course, disposes of 'the picture as object' and proclaims design, not as a 'structural pursuit' but as a symbol. In pursuing that, Nash turned from the classic discipline of the ruler to the *Northern Adventure*.

iii. *The Useful Arts*

In one way or another, though with greatly varying frequency, Nash was active in those Arts which are not 'Liberal' but for which we have no entirely satisfactory name, but call variously 'Applied', 'Useful' and 'Servile'. Although 'Servile' is the best description, it has fallen into disrepute because the word itself has degenerated in other connections. I therefore adopt 'Useful' in spite of its implication that the Liberal Arts are useless.

I have postponed discussing this activity of Nash's until now because this is the period of its greatest intensity and because, in relation to his pictures, it was not of sufficient importance to justify detailed treatment period by period. After the middle of the nineteen thirties he did little more and made no further experiments in new mediums.

It is neither possible nor profitable to consider all his designs. Many were only of ephemeral interest; most are no longer on the market and can only be seen in reproduction by searching old periodicals. I shall discuss some examples, but I prefer, for the most part, to treat this activity broadly and to display his attitude towards the Useful Arts in general.

That attitude was widespread at the time and led many people into

[1] 'The Pictorial Subject' in *The Listener*, 17 February 1932.

aesthetic heresy.[1] In its essence, it was an attempt to break down the hierarchy of the arts, with its old distinction *in value* between the Liberal and Useful Arts. Perhaps Eric Gill's is the most extreme statement of it: 'I say that to make a drain pipe is as much the work of an artist as to make paintings or poems ... It is a different art, that is all.'[2] A more defensible position was adopted by many writers and designers, who insisted on the presence of the aesthetic intention in a work of art; but they based their distinctions not on the value of the idea expressed but only on the value of the expression. This was approximately Nash's position, but it will emerge more precisely as we go on.

Nash was not attracted to the 'arts and crafts' movement, but rather to activities within the modern industrial system. They genuinely excited him, and although some of them were undertaken primarily to earn money, he never lowered his standards. If he had to make something, even if it were not precisely what he would have wished to make at the moment, he did it with all the feeling and skill he could command. The task itself stimulated him and served as a further discipline; and the social character of industrial art and the variety and range of human relationships in which it involved him checked his tendency to social 'disengagement'. They could not do so completely since he was by nature a contemplative artist, but he had less inclination to a recluse life than one might have expected. He generally lived a little withdrawn from the busy centre but he was always delighted to visit and be visited. And yet he wrote to Eddie Marsh of his friends: 'I think I should be afraid to see any one of them *every* day for a week. I like to do with my friends what I ought to do with my clothes—be careful not to wear them too often, put them away for a week, folded and brushed (up the right way)' [*c.* 1914].

Nash was interested in personality, not in the social group. But there were two groups which were exceptions: Englishmen and artists. The English artists' was the one party to which he could belong. When it came to their organizations, Nash was ready enough to join and in some cases to promote them, as we have seen in the case of Unit One. He was at various times a member of at least twelve such organizations: the New English Art Club, the London Group, the Modern English Water-colour Society, the Society of

---

[1] I must intrude here to confess that I was one of them and proclaimed this heresy in various books and articles. What criticism I make of it now, is a criticism of my own discarded beliefs.

[2] *Art,* John Lane, the Bodley Head, 1934, p. 4.

Wood Engravers, the London Artists Association, Unit One, the Council for Art and Industry, the Society of Industrial Artists, the Imperial Arts League, the Artists International Association in which he was a member of the Advisory Council, the Society of Mural Painters of which he was a Founder Member, and the Oxford Art Society.

In about 1922 he had made his first, but abortive, attempt to found an organization of artists working 'within applied design' but 'outside the mystical circle of arts and crafts'. The process, at least to begin with, was to be for members to undertake designs to be applied to existing commercial productions.[1] On this, and on other occasions, Nash wasted a good deal of his time and energy discussing such affairs. He fancied himself as an organizer, but none of his projects materialized except the short-lived Unit One. He was, in fact, an intense individualist but he had a social conscience where art was concerned, and this extended to the relation between art and industry. In the first place, he did not wish the painter to enter industry as a painter. 'I am not advocating that the artist should be turned loose with his eternal brushes and paint', he wrote, 'rather he should be relieved of them by the manservant in the hall.'[2]   In this context, he criticized the Omega Workshop with which he had been connected in 1914:

'In ideals and principles it represented the Morris movement over again with this somewhat melancholy difference—Morris and his workers were both artists and craftsmen; Mr. Fry and his workmen were just artists and painters. The result was that everything, except the textiles which were printed in France or woven in the Midlands, was painted. Chairs, tables, bowls, stools, candlesticks and couches all were animated by a fluid caligraphy of Post-Impressionist design and then varnished or glazed. But painting did not stop there . . . painting invaded not only the furniture but the walls and even ceilings of the house.'[3]

What he did advocate was that the artist should invade the house as designer in 'stone, paper, glass, steel, wood, cardboard, rubber, leather, fabrics and endless synthetic and artificial patent compositions'.[2] But it was industry, of course, that was to do the courting. 'The great mistake is to believe that industry has only to hold out its arms for art to fall into them. . . . If the artist is to have the honour

[1] I quote from Colonel Buchanan's copy of the unpublished syllabus.
[2] 'The Artist in the House' in *The Listener*, 16 March 1932.
[3] *Room and Book*, p. 24.

of being useful, it is likely to be upon his own terms.'[1] And it was industry, of course, that needed to be educated. 'The most usual plea among wholesale firms and manufacturers', he wrote, 'is that they are doing their best to educate the public. . . . In most instances it is the manufacturer who first needs to be educated.'[2] But this did not mean that the artist had nothing to learn. If at times Nash showed little patience with the public and the industrialists, he showed none with the designer who does not understand the processes for which he is designing.

But Nash's relations with the business man were not always easy. John Gloag, who was professionally concerned in some of them, has written to me that keeping the peace between Nash and the client was one of the most harassing jobs he had ever undertaken. Nash held that the business man should know his humble place. 'I have no objection to manufacturers so long as they are inclined to behave decently,' he wrote to Elspeth Little[3] on one occasion; and on another: 'These business chappies must exercise some sort of manners' (c. 1927 and 28 January 1928). And he told Richard Smart: 'Business men amaze me more and more. There is no truer and more enigmatical saying than Business is Business for so far as I can see it is, certainly, nothing else' (March 1941). Nash simply refused to hold his hat in his hand to the business man, whom he considered his inferior. He did not accept the tyranny of commerce nor respect its priests because his values were aristocratic rather than twentieth-century. 'It is no use allowing people to choose,' he wrote, 'give them what you believe in. No artist should ever take the slightest notice of what the public wants or is supposed to want.'[4]

That was written, of course, from the artist's point of view; but when he looked at the position from the buyer's he was equally prepared to argue *his* right of choice and to expect the same integrity on *his* side. The following extract from a letter to Audrey Withers shows him inculcating this principle in the young:

'My dear Baby Elephant,

'Mind where you're galloping I may be devoid of false shame but I have a little false pride. I did not write you because I wished to induce you to buy one of my pictures but because I wanted you to come to my show. And bear this in mind, if you are setting out to buy your first picture, put aside *all* ulterior motives and do not buy

[1] 'The Artist and Industry', *Week-end Review*, 24 September 1932.
[2] 'Modern English Textiles, II, *The Listener*, 15 June 1932.
[3] See p. 191.
[4] 'Personal View' in *Manchester Evening News*, 12 February 1937.

pictures because they are in the fashion or out of charity or because your father's collection hasn't got a specimen or for any other good female reason, but because the thing you see moves you and you long to possess it. If I suspected you of buying anything of mine for a lower reason it would hurt me very much' [October or November 1925].

But this high standard of values must not be taken to suggest that his attitude to industrial art was priggish or dilletante. It was the precise opposite. When he had to deal with a business man who was also an artist—a typographer like Oliver Simon of the Curwen Press, for example—he gave him all the respect and friendship which was his due. Simon has himself described his attitude:

'His qualities and position as an artist on the one hand, and his attitude towards the printed book and the world of business on the other, were unique. He was himself a good man of business and he had a most persuasive almost feminine way of getting what he wanted. But his own way was in the end a realization of his poetic vision, untrammelled by commercial expediency. It was always an exciting and unpredictable adventure to work with him and sometimes exhausting for he was wonderfully particular.'[1]

Although it may seem to us that Nash unduly dispersed his creative energies in the Useful Arts, it did not seem so to him when he looked back at this work in 1943:

'From the point of view of a designer making a critical retrospect, it becomes obvious that the two occupations, picture making and applied design . . . do not work eccentrically but in close sympathy. Although the latter occupation is often referred to as a "side line" it cannot be regarded as a branch line or siding, but rather an integral part of the main system, the lines merging together or seemingly diverging at times, but always moving forward in the same purpose and direction.'[2]

Nash's work in the Useful Arts began, as we have seen, with book-plates, book illustrations and stage designs. In the very early nineteen twenties he began to design book-jackets, an activity which continued until 1941, though late examples are very rare. His general practice was to make a formalized representation of the book's theme rather

[1] 'West End—East End' in *Signature*, No. 15, New Series, 1952.
[2] Introduction to C.E.M.A. Exhibition of his applied design, 1943. Reprinted in full in *Nash: Eates*, p. 57.

than an illustration of any incident in it, but sometimes he made purely abstract designs.

We can associate all his publicity work with these jackets because it is primarily pictorial in expression. It may be remembered that as early as 1910 he had submitted a poster-design for Rothenstein's criticism. In 1913 he had painted a signboard[1] for his second exhibition, a light-hearted picture of himself in large hat and high heels dancing through fields with his future wife, his brother, Rupert Lee and others. Wittenham Clumps are in the background. It certainly has the characteristics of a good sign, as he defined them many years later: 'It must be a bold affair but not bald. It can be crude, but it must be winning in a come-hither sort of way, with an invitation intimate, humorous, strange or even sinister; but, *it must not be respectable.*'[2] In 1918 he had made a lithographic poster for his exhibition of war paintings.[3] But his first public commission for a poster was not, I believe, until 1926 or early 1927 when he wrote to Audrey Withers:

'My next opus is a very large poster concerned with Market Gardening—something to do with this Empire Marketing nonsense. I have been a little nervous of it but now I have a scheme and yesterday I rooted about in a market garden gathering material. It's really a charming world, the veg world with wonderful queer formal properties and a range of most subtle colours—especially in greens and whites, the studio will look like the prize tent of a Flower Show within a week' [1926 or 1927].

In spite of his having to deal with an official who took him for a partner in Messrs. P. & J. Nash Ltd., publicity agents, and lunched him in 'the worst restaurant in Soho' where he 'simply *smacked* his lips over the jaded dishes'[4] Nash produced a most effective, gay and ingenious design of baskets filled with vegetables, a crate, seed boxes and a watering-can formally arranged against a background of garden and greenhouses. It was not a 'view' but an epitome—an expression of the *idea* of a market garden, abstract in design but representational in its elements.

In 1932 he was commissioned to do a poster for the London & North Eastern Railway. Again he plunged himself into his kind of research—getting to know the forms. He spent hours in the York Railway Museum wandering about in amazed delight at the 'mon-

---

[1] Now in the collection of Mrs. Nash.
[2] 'Signs' in *The Listener*, 11 November 1936.
[3] Reproduced in *War Posters Issued by Belligerent and Neutral Nations*, ed. by Martin Hardie, Black, 1920.
[4] Letter to Sieveking [19 November 1927].

sters' he found there. He showed a childlike wonder at their shapes without the least childish wish to see the wheels go round. But he did not allow the intimacy he gained with detail, in this way, to deflect him from the broad treatment necessary to a poster. His engine is convincing as engine, without being in the least photographic. It runs at us—this new monster—straight out of the ruined past which, with a pleasing disregard of the area served by the L.N.E.R., he symbolized by Corfe Castle; but we shall see that Corfe had a special significance for him.

Naturally he was involved in the adventure of Jack Beddington's advertising campaign for Shell in the inter-war years.[1] He designed a poster in each of the two series known as Preferences and Follies. In *Footballers Prefer Shell* (1936) a football and a formalized goal with its netting were set against an abstract suggestion of the tiers of seats; but there were no footballers and no spectators. It was broadly coloured in three browns, white and a most delicate powder blue, and stiffened with sharp notes of black. His Folly (1937) was more pictorial and more personal. He chose Kimmeridge Folly, in that part of the Dorset coast which was so significant for him at that time. He made the conspicuous sun throw its solid white shafts as in his first war work, and the sea advance in long parallels as at Dymchurch. The foreground was the tumble of rock and seaweed in which he was seeing 'ghosts'. This late poster was the work of a Nash who had returned to his 'visions', and whom we have not yet discussed. Footballers belonged to his rationalizing foolishness: Folly to his new visionary wisdom which released him from the bars of the ruler.

From then on, Nash could no longer toe the line. A drawing he did for an I.C.I. advertisement in 1941 was not used because, they said, the public would not have understood it. It was his last attempt, I believe, at any design except for 'picture-making'.

The work mentioned so far is all clearly related to book-illustration; but the pattern-papers and textiles which we must now consider pose an altogether different problem to the designer and one which was quite new to Nash—the invention of repetitive designs which neither illustrate an existing idea nor advertise an existing product. It is because of this freedom, perhaps, that Nash was almost invariably successful with them. No doubt his good understanding with Oliver Simon helped him to make the four excellent pattern papers for the Curwen Press. Three are wholly abstract designs and

---

[1] Nash paid his tribute to this in 'The Artist and the Community' in *The Listener*, 20 January 1932.

in the fourth, a crocus, itself highly formalized, is related to abstract shapes. They all suggest a limited third dimension, which enriches the pattern by an effect of low relief.

Nash's first designs for textiles had been made at the instigation of Lovat Fraser in about 1920, but they were not printed until 1925, when they were issued by Mrs. Eric Kennington's workshop, known as 'Footprints'. They were shortly afterwards taken over by 'Modern Textiles', a producing and selling enterprise launched by Elspeth Little. Nash became involved with this in other directions: he painted a signboard for the shop and designed the note-paper heading. The bad printing of this produced a characteristic protest:

'I did not remember my drawing to have these marks on it. . . . I have written asking for my original again to make sure I myself am not in fault but in any case no printer should pass a thing like this without referring back to the designer. It really is wicked. In the meantime I must absolutely insist upon these sheets being destroyed. If I am in any way to blame I will stand the expense' [c. 1927].

In no circumstances would he pass imperfect workmanship, even if he had to lose money by his firmness. Nor would he become too closely involved in this business. 'I think I had better not be definitely associated with *any* party, I prefer to be on my own entirely', he wrote about the same date. And when Elspeth Little reported that a commercial manufacturer was 'interested' in his designs, his answer showed the same artistic integrity and independence. 'I am excited about the manufacturer', he said, 'because it looks like a courageous move in the right direction. I cannot however allow anyone to alter my designs . . . but I am willing to consider his scheme for rearranging this motif, work upon it and submit it to him again. . . . *But* I must be sure of what sort of juggling this gent thinks of doing. . . . If I can agree we will come to terms, otherwise—I fear not.' Nothing seems to have happened about this proposal, but in 1929 Cresta Silks undertook the marketing of Nash's designs. It is enlightening to read the bulky file of their correspondence. It shows, letter by letter, Nash's tireless struggle for perfection. Nothing could ever be passed as 'good enough'. He even insisted on having a say in the advertising of anything he was concerned with, to ensure that it had 'dignity, order and distinction'. The directors were immensely patient and co-operative. 'Your whole outlook', one of them wrote, 'is delightfully uncommercial, yet there is a logic about your suggestions which makes them very helpful to me.' However, the advertising specialist did point out to him that women who were attracted by good design for dresses, had not necessarily as lively a sense of good prose or as intellectual an attitude towards design as he seemed to think. Not a detail escaped him. He protested against a phrase in one circular, that they were employing 'artists like Paul Nash' and against the use of display cards on dresses marked: Design by Paul Nash. There are, he pointed out, no artists like Paul Nash and the *dresses* were not designed by him.

I have preferred to give this space to Nash's dealings as a textile designer rather than to his designs, because abstract designs cannot be discussed by description.[1] Most of his were abstract, although some, like *Cherry Orchard*, *Arches* and *Bird-Cage* were formalized representations.

In later years, Nash designed furnishing textiles for the Old Bleach Linen Company and the Calico Printers' Association, and upholstery for the London Passenger Transport Board. He also designed rugs for the architect, Robert Symonds, which were executed by the Edinburgh Weavers. This is not a complete list, but it is enough to indicate how active and successful he was in textile design. Moreover, he showed his interest in the designs of others by writing of their work and giving it generous but discriminating praise.[2]

About 1931 Nash made his first experiment in designing glass. Chance Brothers launched a series of decorative sheets for the use of the architect and interior designer. When Nash was invited to design one, he studied the whole process of production at the works, making thumbnail sketches all the time for technical criticism. When his design was approved, he guided the craftsman who was cutting one unit direct on to the steel roller. The result, which was called *Coptic*, was not a success either financially or artistically, but that does not affect the picture of Nash's careful co-operation with an unfamiliar industrial process.[3]

Shortly after this, he designed two sherry sets, called *Spots* and *Swirl*, for Stuart & Sons. They were artistically most successful but too modern for the traditional buyer and too discreet for the 'jazz'. His only other work in glass was a bathroom for the dancer, Tilly Losch, which her husband commissioned in 1934 for their house at 35 Wimpole Street.[4] The walls and ceiling were covered with an elaborate

---

[1] Reproductions of some of Nash's textiles will be found in 'The Textile Designs of Paul Nash' by Darcy Bradell, *Architectural Review*, Supplement, October 1928; *Art and Industry* by Herbert Read, Faber, 1934, p. 118; *Design and Decoration in the Home* by Noel Carrington, Country Life, 1938, p. 85; *Architectural Review*, September 1947, p. 80; *Room and Book*, p. 50; *The Cabinet Maker and Complete House Furnisher*, 10 June 1933.

[2] 'Modern English Textiles, I and II', *The Listener*, 27 April and 15 June 1932.

[3] The glass was reproduced in John Gloag's *Industrial Art Explained*, Allen & Unwin, 1934, Pl. X, and in *Design for Today*, July 1933, p. 108.

[4] It was dismantled when the house was converted into flats, but the glass is preserved.

13. Salome. [1931]
Oil

14. Mansions of the Dead. 1932
Illustration to 'Urne Buriall'

mosaic of varied glasses in rectangles of varied sizes. The dominant colour was dark blue-grey, in plain, mottled and reeded glass, varied with black marmorate glass and rose and white mirrors and occasional cutting and sand-blasting. But Nash felt that the main decoration should be supplied by the reflections of Tilly Losch. To give these greater possibilities, he supplied a vertical ladder in chromiumed-steel from floor to ceiling. This startling design gained considerable celebrity and was frequently reproduced.[1]

A second experiment was in ceramics. In 1933 Nash designed four tea-sets for the manufacturers of Foley china, who had commissioned designs from artists of different aesthetic allegiance, which they exhibited with the original designs at Harrods Stores in November 1934.[2] Nash's designs were not outstandingly successful, but they had more of his real quality than he had been able to get into glass. I cannot find that he did any other ceramic designs that were carried out, but he showed sketches for faïence ware at the Curwen Press exhibition of 1937.

A third experiment was in wood. In the spring of 1936 the Timber Development Association held an exhibition at Charing Cross Underground station of photographs illustrating the theme of 'Timber Through the Ages'. Nash was invited to design a mural, twenty feet long by ten high. In an article which he wrote for *Wood* (April 1936) he described his first interest in wood—'the study of tree anatomy . . . a research which gradually brought me closer and closer to the tree, the wood itself'. He went on to express his dislike of highly polished wood and his horror of those marquetry 'pictures' where the grains are unnaturally contrived to imitate something else, like 'animal humiliations at the circus'. 'It was against the parade "quiff" on the one hand', he said, 'and the buffoonery of pictorial wood naturalism on the other, that I wished to oppose a method of using veneers which could be considered at once natural and classical'. He therefore composed in simple panels—all rectangles except one oval—so that the main effect was left to the eight grains and colours of the woods, which ranged from pale blue-grey through yellow and ochre to russet browns and chestnut reds. It illustrates his resolve to design *in* a material rather than *for* it, that he worked out his design on a small scale in the actual veneers.

[1] For example, in the *Studio Year Book of Decorative Art*, 1934, p. 120, and *Design for Today*, October 1934, p. 364.

[2] An account of this interesting experiment with many illustrations was published in *Design for Today*, December 1934, p. 461. An example of Nash's work is reproduced by John Gloag, *loc. cit.*, Pl. XV.

iv. 'Urne Buriall' and 'The Garden of Cyrus'

Nash's finest illustrations were for a one-volume edition of Sir Thomas Browne's *Urne Buriall* and *The Garden of Cyrus*, which he had himself chosen. It was issued by Cassells in 1932. At the time, Oliver Simon, to whom the printing had been entrusted, wrote to Nash that he felt it would 'enter the small category of magnificent and monumental books', and later Herbert Read was to describe it as 'one of the loveliest achievements of contemporary English art'.[1]

The binding, which Nash also designed, is in ivory vellum, lettered in gold on the spine only. On the front a large rectangle of warm brown morocco, set up to the right top corner, occupies most of the area. In the centre of this a quincunx is tooled in gold and inlaid with vellum. This motif is repeated on the vellum back with the morocco inlaid.

Nash first made a drawing for the illustrations in hard black chalk from which collotypes were prepared. He then painted these in watercolour, and stencils were cut from them, which were used by the Curwen Press craftsmen under Nash's supervision to hand-colour the plates. These were by no means illustrations in the conventional sense, but the sources of their formal and imaginative inventions are to be found scattered through the text. They were closely linked to it by innumerable little nerves, so that most of them do not belong exclusively to any one passage. In this way they are visual equivalents of Browne's whole imaginative attitude and not diagrams to correspond with the progress of his thought. They correspond, that is, to the artist, rather than to the scientist in him, but also to the close and curious observer, for Nash was that too. In the frontispiece[2] Nash drew the Urne to make a pattern with a wall and a wine-dark sea and sky, and twining worms. He read the phrase: 'water hath proved the smartest grave' and he drew the skull and the bones on the sea-bed among queer anemones and fish; and he read a passing reference to the Phoenix and drew it rising triumphantly—a bird, his old symbol —and beside it a snake, its head stemming into the sun and its body coiled like a nest.[3] He was later to paint *Nest of the Phoenix* (Plate 21), where the nest was almost the same shape, and the water-colour

---

[1] *Philosophy of Modern Art*, Faber, 1952, p. 180.

[2] As very few readers will be able to follow this with the original edition, I give references to those drawings which are reproduced in *Nash: Eates*. This is Pl. 63a.

[3] These are drawings in the text. I shall distinguish full-page drawings by using the word 'plate'.

Landscape of the Megaliths, almost identical with Plate 18, where the snake that twines round the twining convolvulus carries its head against the white moon, so that at first glance it seems to be a seeding dandelion—the little sunflower. The old Nash symbols and those to come are gathering together.

In the second plate, which he called *Token*, Nash set the mementos of the dead, described by Browne, to make their pattern among the worms, and he added two birds. He read of 'the Gemme or Berill Ring upon the finger of *Cynthia*' that her lover Propertius saw when 'her Ghost appeared unto him': and he next drew a bone and a worm wearing rings. He read: 'We conceive not these Urnes to have descended thus naked as they appear, or to have entred their graves without the old habit of flowers': and in his third plate he showed the urns twined about with convolvulus and briar roses such as he had drawn in his Pre-Raphaelite days, and he added worms. He read: 'some drew provocatives of mirth from Anatomies, and Juglers shewed tricks with Skeletons': and he drew a head that balances two bones on its chin and a bone supporting a skull on its forehead.[1]

He followed with the plate of the funeral pyre, a recurrent and essential theme of the text but one of the least effective of the drawings. He read: 'teeth, bones, and hair, give the most lasting defiance to corruption': and he drew a skeleton in a coffin with long faded gold hair to where the waist had been. (I have no evidence that he ever read Donne's poems.) He read: 'Before *Plato* could speak, the soul had wings in *Homer*, which fell not, but flew out of the body into the mansions of the dead': and he drew the plate called *The Mansions of the Dead* (Plate 14).

At this point, I must stop glancing through the book and examine one of Nash's most remarkable works and its other versions, which he described in a letter to Hartley Ramsden. After speaking of this first version, he went on:

'Later I made a large version [in] water colour of the design.[2] . . . I then made a new and different version for a painting. This was on tracing paper and was exactly enlarged to scale onto a canvas 30 × 20. The painting was shewn at the Art Now Exn. at The Mayor Gallery 1934? under the title *Aerial Composition*. . . . Later, when I became interested in Surrealism I gave it back its proper title which expressed the original idea of the *Mansions of the Dead*. . . . But it was only the other day that it occurred to me that Sir Thomas Browne

---

[1] *Nash: Eates*, Pl. 63b.
[2] There is also a small water-colour version in the collection of Rex Nan Kivell.

must have been thinking of tombs *under the earth* when he wrote of "The Soul visiting the mansions of the Dead". To me that suggested only aerial habitations where the soul like a bird or some such aerial creature roamed at will perching now and then on these convenient structures in the clouds or in the pure upper air' (4 June 1941).

Obviously Nash had not turned up the phrase in Browne although he was thinking so much of it, for he repeated his introduction of the word 'visiting' in *Aerial Flowers*. Browne says nothing about 'visiting': he is talking about death and lasting habitations. The letter I have just quoted shows that 'visiting' had got into Nash's mind by 1941, but I can find no catalogue or reproduction where it is included in the title until the Penguin book of 1944. In these later years Nash had the sense of such possible visitings, and we shall even find him speaking of his own visit to 'the other side'. It seems that although he had no wish to die, he yet felt the fascination of death, he felt the call, as it were, to visit but not to stay; and gradually the idea lodged in his imagination that this design had been, not of death, but of visiting. He must have come to talk of the design in that way and so, after his death, it appears in *Nash: Eates* as *The Soul visiting the Mansions of the Dead*.[1] Moreover, if he had turned up the phrase in Browne he would have seen that it fully justified his aerial mansions and creatures— 'the soul had wings and flew out of the body'.

The fact that Nash made several versions of this design shows that he recognized its importance to him, although not so completely as we can, who see to what final inhabited skies it pointed.

The form of the mansions was suggested by the divisions of an egg-box. The problem was to find some visual image that would suggest both 'mansions' and the airy habitations that cannot be drawn. They had to be habitations that were not prisons or cages or burrows, not even houses with their limited doors and windows; and yet they must define space. The visual artist cannot avoid compromise: he must work through a concrete object because he cannot project the insubstantial straight into our imaginations as the poet can. It is the same with the upper structure, the great corridor, the avenue, the path through the wood that has become the path through the sky. It must be drawn, it must be defined somehow; but it must have none of the horror which belongs to the tunnel from which the traveller cannot

---

[1] Miss Eates did not know Nash until these later days, and Mrs. Nash may well have been conditioned by Nash's own changed attitude into inventing this title with its significant innovation.

escape. Nash, it may be remembered, had dreamt of this in child-hood. In *Mansions of the Dead* he celebrated his escape from it into the blue freedom. This aerial corridor shows a way, it *is* a way, but it does not compel the traveller to take it.

Mansions of the Dead is succeeded in *Urne Buriall* by a plate which Nash called *Ghosts*. The word 'ghosts' recurs frequently in the text of Chapter IV, where it is set. In this design, there is a complete inter-penetration of water, sky and earthly mansions. It is true that the surface of the water is at the bottom, but strange marine creatures float above it—domed jelly fish like fungi from which long streamers depend so that altogether they are disturbingly like parachutes; and yet the parachute, the Rose of Death, could not at that date have invaded Nash's world of images. A spirit tree that suggests a one-armed headless figure grows out of the water and beside it a convoca-tion of worms circles in the ambiguous element. Out of a series of Gothic arches at the back, a male figure floats down a flight of stairs visiting the underworld or it may be Nash himself, for there are two ghosts there from his own past. The 'face in the sky', the face of Sybil with its streaming hair almost exactly as it appeared in *Vision at Even-ing* over twenty years earlier, floats in the centre; and from a cloud in an area that is more sky than sea, though the ghost of a crab is above it, appear two hands—the 'silver hands'. This design is peculiarly open to the multiple interpretation of all symbols. The survival of the soul in this world of ghosts is also the survival of Nash's own youth in his adult imagination. Therefore we are surprised, on turning two pages, not that we find the Pyramids, but that they stand prosaically in the desert. When Nash had set them in the sea he may have had some intuition of them as life-symbols,[1] but he is using them here simply in Browne's terms as marks of man's vanity, for 'to subsist in bones, and be but Pyramidally extant, is a fallacy in duration . . . that duration, which maketh Pyramids pillars of snow'.

But in the next drawing Nash returned to the personal image, the tree, a giant wide-spreading oak which stands beyond a grave. We see both through a circle inscribed in a square, whose common centre is a smaller circle containing the letter H. Obviously these are the symbols of life and death. In *Urne Buriall* Browne says: 'Circles and right lines limit and close all bodies, and the mortall right-lined circle, must conclude and shut up all'. But Nash must have transposed the H from a passage in the *Garden of Cyrus*: 'The same number [Five] in

---

[1] According to H. F. Dunbar's *Symbolism in Medieval Thought* (Yale University Press, 1929) they stood for the sun in its threefold character as giver of heat, light and life.

the Hebrew mysteries and Cabalistic accounts was the character of Generation; declared by the Letter *He*, the fifth in their Alphabet; According to that Cabalisticall *Dogma*: If *Abram* had not had this Letter added unto his Name he had remained fruitlesse, and without the power of generation.' I can see no other explanation of it.

The last plate[1] in *Urne Buriall* is of three broken columns on the shore. Over the sea beyond them a sexless human figure flies towards the sun, from a tall insubstantial wall of darkness. 'Darknesse and light divide the course of time, and oblivion shares with memory.' Nash has embodied memory in the broken columns, the funeral urns and wreath, the mask and the branch of evergreen in the foreground. The book concludes with an abstract design of interpenetrating light and darkness, which incorporates suggestions of the sea, the shore, the rock, and the word *Finis*.[2]

In *Urne Buriall*, Nash was inevitably most concerned with symbols, and I have therefore confined myself to indicating them; but since he was an artist, it can be taken for granted that he ordered them into design. In *The Garden of Cyrus* the design, the order itself, becomes the symbol, because its theme is that 'all things began in order, so shall they end, and so shall they begin again; according to the ordainer of order and mysticall Mathematicks of the City of Heaven'.

After a diagram of the Quincunx itself, which closely follows the plate in the earlier editions, Nash drew 'the vegetable creation' as frontispiece, remembering in its design his wood-engraving for *Genesis*. It is followed by a small design of 'the Pensill or hanging gardens of *Babylon*', whose form is much like the rocks in the desert of *St. Hercules*, that were themselves 'like the summit of a sunken city'— of Babylon. The subject of the next plate derives from a phrase in the dedicatory letter—'Plantations of venemous Vegetables'—and its form from the Nash theme of a vase of flowers before a window, but it holds a heavier significance. Through a rectangular opening we see a plantation that rises in steep perspective to two domed hills. On a table before it are a vase of poisonous plants, red berries, an *arum maculatum*, an hour-glass and a tumbler of purple liquid. The drawing is dark with the presence of an absent Death.

The next plate is *The Quincunx Artificially Considered*.[3] Here Nash directly tackles the form which is at the centre of the whole theme— the network of lozenges *Quid Quincunce speciosius, qui, in quam cunque*

---

[1] *Nash: Eates*, Pl. 64.
[2] *Nash: Eates*, Pl. 66b.
[3] *Nash: Eates*, Pl. 65.

partem spectaveris, rectus est. The reticulation is found in many and varied forms, mostly derived from the text, such as the laurel wreath on the bust, the ruin pierced by a diamond-paned window, the terrace paved with lozenges and the fishing nets. But these are draped from baskets of reticulated weave, for which there is no hint in the text, and there is none for the diamonds he found in the moonlit ripples of the sea. Out of that sea rise two rocks, one in the form of a torso, the other of a pyramid.

In the next small design, Nash further artificially considered the quincunx in a number of objects—the folds of linen round the mummy, the cross-legged table, the cut gem and the scissors—for all of which he had found authority scattered in the text, so that these two designs particularly demonstrate how closely he followed it as a whole, though without confining himself to illustrating any one passage. It is the same with the next plate, *The Quincunx Naturally Considered*,[1] where most of the examples again have their origin in the text—the catkins, the teazle, the cone, the acorn and the sunflower, the sunflower which was to have such significance for him, 'the noble flower of the Sunne. Wherein in Lozenge figured boxes nature shuts up the seeds, and balsame which is about them'. Nash pursued the same theme in two further designs. In the first it was in corn and leaf, in the shadowed intersection of boughs, in lightning and in '*Jupiters* beard, or houseleek; which old superstition set on the tops of houses, as a defensative against lightening, and thunder'.[2] In the second it was the pineapple, the scales of fish and a snake which twines up the stem of the fruit-stand like a convolvulus. The next drawing is one of the strangest, most lovely and most suggestive of them all. A convolvulus twines up a post and lifts its trumpets to the sun, and the sun answers with two brilliant diagonal rays. Beside the convolvulus is a figure in which vegetable and human nature interpenetrate. Its legs twine like the convolvulus and its shoulders break into leaf and flower.[3]

But this extremely organic design is followed by the violent contrast of *The Quincunx Mystically Considered*, an abstract geometrical composition which is almost identical with the water-colour called *Poised Objects*.[4] At the summit is a sphere with a human eye at its centre—the one element that is not geometrical—from which a cone of light radiates horizontally to the edge of the design. The eye is

[1] *Nash: Eates*, Pl. 66a.
[2] *Nash: Eates*, Pl. 67, gives an oil based on this.
[3] Nash also made an oil version of this.
[4] *Nash: Eates*, Pl. 68, and *Axis*, Early Winter 1937, p. 12. There are slight differences between these reproductions. Nash may have modified the drawing, as Mrs. Nash is certain there were never two versions.

clearly a symbol for the sun. From its sides depend two figures. Each is a lozenge in outline, but one is constructed of pink and yellow pyramids and the other of pink and yellow cones. Another sphere is spiked on the lower point of the double pyramid, which is exactly accommodated in the upper half of an X inscribed on it. 'The geniall spirits of both worlds, do trace their way in ascending and descending Pyramids, mystically apprehended in the Letter X.'[1] The lower section of the double-cone is enclosed in an incomplete cylinder, which in turn penetrates a tilted square, whose lowest point is vertically below the eye. The best commentary on this design is in the last seven paragraphs of Browne's Chapter IV.

After this, Nash returns to representation with a haunted scene of columns and arches among a tumble of rocks, where a full moon lets down a beam solid as a plank, a gangway from Heaven to the ruins of Babylon; and the tree of vegetable life lies prone and dead.

At the head of Chapter V there is a difficult design, in which a hand, whose *five* fingers are 'the first rest and pause of numeration', rests its finger-tips on a sheet of paper marked with the alchemical sign of Mercury ☿—the signs of sun and moon united by the plus of the cross, which 'hath had the honour to characterize and notifie our blessed Saviour'. Beside this paper is a nest full of eggs, which recalls to our memory the birds-nesting boy who loved his grandfather's eggs at Langley, and the alchemical significance of the egg which I shall discuss in the next section.

The last plate is *The Order of Five*, a pattern made of many objects, all botanical but for two star fish and all illustrating the 'Quincuntiall Ordination'. The last design in the text is one of the most beautifully strange and evocative. It is divided into four parts by straight lines. In the left top quarter is the starry sky, and below it is the calm sea. In the right top quarter is an interpenetration of sky and sea, and below it is the upper part of a face with closed eyes—'a penthouse over the eye' that 'maketh a quiet vision'. We see this right half through a lattice and 'meet with abstrusities of no ready resolution.'

I have not discussed the symbolic significance of the Five on which all these designs to the *Garden of Cyrus* were necessarily based because Nash's source was the book itself, which can be easily consulted. But I want to give two other sources that offer important links to Nash's general symbolism, which were probably unknown to him. The first is quoted by Bayley[2] from Plutarch but without exact reference: 'The

---

[1] This X is omitted from the water-colour.
[2] *The Lost Language of Symbolism* by Harold Bayley, Williams & Norgate, 1912, p. 108.

ancients regarded the number five as sacred to the God of Light, and the attributes of Deity were held to consist of *five*, namely, Being, Sameness, Diversity, Motion and Rest'. The God of Light is, of course, figured by the Sun and the Sun by the Sunflower. The second is quoted from Ludwig Keller[1] by Silberer.[2] He has been discussing how the number Five came naturally to symbolize the five-leaved plants and then comes the startling quotation which links so many of Nash's symbols for us:

'The flowers, however, and the garden in which they grow, early served as symbols of the Fields of the Blessed or the "better country" in which dwell the souls passing through death to life; in antithesis to the terrestrial house of God, the temple built with hands, which was represented by the rectangle ⬜, the holy number 5 denoted the celestial abodes of the souls that had attained perfection, and therefore represented both the house of eternity or the City of God and the Heavenly Jerusalem. The holy pentagram in the form of a rose, not only in the ancient but in the early Christian world, decorated the graves of the dead, that in their turn symbolised the gardens of the blessed.'

I can imagine the circles of amused astonishment which Nash's eyes and mouth would have made at reading that. He would not have taken it solemnly—I think his sense of humour must be recalled at this point—but he would have taken it seriously, though perhaps with some such mocking but credulous phrase as: 'I *say*, the Rose does get about, doesn't it?'

In this long examination of one product of Nash's art, I have started many hares; and now I must pursue them a little more closely. This is the crisis of Nash's artistic life, for in his illustrations to these two books the essentially symbolic character of his work finally emerges and all his symbols are present or foreshadowed.

v. Symbolism and Nash's Symbols

I have hitherto used the word 'symbol' without comment. I must now try to remedy that. The word has many meanings, some of which overlap while others are mutually exclusive. The symbol *in art* must involve the artifact, which is an image. We have, therefore, nothing whatever to do with its use in mathematics or symbolic logic,

---

[1] *Geschichte der Bauhütten und der Hüttengeheimnisse*, Leipzig, 1898.
[2] *Problems of Mysticism and its Symbolism* by Herbert Silberer. Trans. S. E. Jelliffe, Moffat, Yard, N.Y., 1917.

for example, where no image exists and the choice of symbol is arbitrary. The conventional sign, such as the crown or the cross, is not as easily disposed of. Such a phrase as 'the power of the crown' has no meaning in relation to the artifact itself, but only in relation to what it 'stands for'. The artifact itself is not intrinsically symbolic: it is not an image of power or royalty. It can be comfortably replaced by 'sceptre' and no change takes place in the idea signified. On the other hand, the artist can and does employ such signs in a way which it is difficult not to call symbolic. When the Byzantine artists represented Christ on the cross, crowned and robed as the Emperor, they were surely raising the sign to symbol because they were working at one remove. The idea of Emperor *is* imaged, and becomes therefore the symbol for the divine power. The symbol is not intrinsic to the crown and robes but to the power they image by conventional association. But the cross is neither an image of power nor redemption: it remains a pure sign. If Christ had been beheaded, the axe would have served exactly the same purpose. But the crucified Emperor, as a whole, does, I think, become symbolic by association.

The cross, on the other hand, outside Christianity, is an image of quaternity, in the same way that, within Christianity, the equilateral triangle is an image of the Trinity. But these images cannot be called symbols in art because they are not emotive, though they may be emotively used. We may therefore advance a step by modifying our first statement: the symbol in art must involve an *emotive* image.

But because the conventional sign can be used symbolically in art, this does not alter the fact that it is not in itself a symbol. The same, I think, is true of the object which the alchemist, the psychologist or the mythologist considers, for his purposes, as symbolic. The alchemist made use of many signs that were no more images than the mathematician's, but it seems now to be established that his whole system was symbolic. The psychologist makes use of the alchemist's 'symbols', for *his* purposes, not alchemically. He may also make use of a work of art, but not artistically. It is the same with the mythologist. We have here then a group of people—and there are others, of course—who may use the word 'symbol' of an emotive image, of any image or of a mere sign; but they are only concerned to use it as 'standing for' something else in their own field of study. The symbol in art, therefore, may contain the alchemist's or the psychologist's or the mythologist's 'symbol', but it is not that which gives it an artistically symbolic character.

A further problem is offered by the images of allegory and emblem, but again, although these may be used by the artist, their nature is to be signs. They are images which 'stand for' something else: there is only an 'external union', as Croce says, '*this* image must represent *that* concept . . . thought remains thought and image image in this juxtaposition.'[1]

It is clear, then, that while several uses of the word 'symbol' may involve the use of an image, and even of an emotive image, it is primarily as a sign; and the interpretation of the 'symbol' is only concerned with what it 'stands for', which can exist without it. Our interpretation, when we are considering the work of art as work of art, is as much concerned with the image—that painted sunflower, for example—as with what it 'stands for', because what it is and what it 'stands for' are *identical*.

The process by which the symbol in art is arrived at, is of the image drawing closer and closer to what it images until there is complete fusion. It begins with a simple 'likeness'. The fall of the leaf, for example, is like man's decline into death. The likeness is physical: the leaf also is dying. My love, for another example, is like the red, red rose. Here the likeness is not direct but by transference of certain qualities—beauty, softness, delicacy, sweet perfume, and so on; and of certain associations—the pleasantness and desirability of spring, sunshine, warmth, and so on. These are similes. They may be raised to metaphor by dropping the term of comparison. Macbeth's way of life falls into the sere, the yellow leaf: it is not merely like it. Love *is* a rose. In the final stage we have 'metaphors detached from their subjects'.[2] The falling leaf or the Rose appear unexplained, as in Nash's *Swan Song* or Yeats's 'far off, most secret and inviolate Rose'.

Through this process of intensification and union, the symbol tends to universalize and exalt the original idea. The love who is merely *like* a red, red rose, remains a girl. For Yeats, the Rose had become 'a symbol of spiritual love and supreme beauty'. Coleridge described the symbol as characterized 'above all by the translucence of the eternal through and in the temporal' and Goethe as 'a vivid instantaneous revelation of the inscrutable'.[3]

But although the nature of the symbol in art resides in this metaphor detached from its subject, we are not excluded from also interpreting it in terms of other uses of the word, provided they involve

---

[1] *Essence of Aesthetic*, Heinemann, 1921, p. 26.
[2] Edmund Wilson, 'Axel's Castle', Scribner's, N.Y., 1935, p. 21.
[3] I owe these three quotations to Louis Macneice (*The Poetry of W. B. Yeats*, O.U.P., 1941, p. 65); Sir Maurice Bowra (*The Romantic Imagination*, 1950, p. 67); and Dean Inge (*Christian Mysticism*, Methuen, 1899, p. 251).

images. I have already spoken of what are so often, but so unsatis-
factorily, described as its 'layers' of significance.[1] The symbol in fact
is polyvalent:[2] it can be subjected to multiple interpretation, which
partly reconciles certain of those other uses which we began by separating. This was better understood by mediaeval man than it is today,
and he reduced it to a system which was expressed in the mnemonic:

> *Littera gesta docet,*
> *Quid credas allegoria*
> *Moralis quid agas,*
> *Quo tendas anagogia.*

A statement, in any form, was held to be open to four interpretations, one literal and three 'symbolic'—the allegorical, the tropo-
logical and the anagogical. These three are explained by Dunbar[3] as
being truths in relation to humanity as a whole, including Christ as
the head of humanity, truths concerning the moral lesson which may
be learned from any statement, and ultimate truths, belonging
neither to time nor space.

We are little inclined today, however, to interpret a symbol
allegorically, although we may recognize it as having an allegorical
element; nor shall we often interpret it morally. But we do take necessary notice of the two extremes: the literal and anagogic significances.
The painted sunflower is an image of the literal sunflower and that
is fused with its anagogic significance. But to that anagogic significance itself, we may apply multiple interpretation: it is neither
precise nor unique.

It is not precise primarily because it is an image of a spiritual or
'mystical' apprehension, of which no concrete image can be properly
made. But the word 'mystical' is commonly applied to the works of
such artists as Dante and Blake and not uncommonly to that of Nash.
Herbert Read has said that Nash was 'not in any true sense of the
word a mystical painter—he was not a visionary like Blake or
Palmer'.[4] That implies that there can be mystical painters and at
least suggests that 'visionary' and 'mystic' mean the same. But it is
open to question whether either is true. Of course there can be
artists who are also mystics. St. John of the Cross is the obvious

---

[1] See p. 60.
[2] See, for example, *God and the Unconscious* by Fr. Victor White, O.P., Harvill Press, 1952, p. 221; and Jacques Maritain, *Creative Intuition in Art and Poetry*, Harvill Press, 1954, p. 128.
[3] *Symbolism in Mediaeval Thought and its Consummation in the Divine Comedy*, by H. Flanders Dunbar, Yale U.P., 1929, p. 19.
[4] *Nash: Eates*, p. 11.

example, but it does not follow that his poetry is itself mystical. The same question lies at the centre of both difficulties. Is the presence of an image, in vision or work of art, compatible with the mystical state? It will be enough to say that so eminent an authority as Abbot Butler in his *Western Mysticism* is consistently suspicious of all psycho-physical manifestations, while Dean Inge in his *Christian Mysticism* seems to agree but causes confusion by speaking of 'ecstacy or vision' as differing from hallucination or poetical inspiration 'because the imagination is passive'.[1] But surely without active imagination there can be no vision. A vision *is* an image, but it is not to be identified with ecstacy.

Both authorities give many definitions of mysticism and accounts of the mystical experience, most of which emphatically deny the presence of any image in it. There is the same consensus of opinion in the many passages quoted in support of this view by Père Poulain, S.J., in his standard work on mystical theology.[2] It is also the conclusion reached by William James in his *Varieties of Religious Experience*. If, then, there is no image present in the mystical experience, the aesthetic experience cannot be mystical, for it depends on the image.

But there is a contrary view. St. Augustine, in the famous seventeenth chapter of his *Confessions*, after speaking of that surely mystical experience when his mind *pervenit ad Id quod est in ictu trepidantis aspectus*, went on to say how he saw clearly the invisible things of God 'which are understood by the things that are made'.[3] This seems to let in art, at least as means to mystical understanding. St. Thomas Aquinas goes further. 'Human contemplation at present cannot function without images. . . . In its present condition the mind cannot actually understand anything except by reference to images. . . . Even God is known through the images of his effects.'[4] But St. Thomas of course, was an extremist in this matter—*Nihil in intellectu quod non prius in sensu*—and Dante followed him when he asked the imagination what could move it if the senses offered nothing—*chi move te, se 'l senso non ti porge?*[5]

It seems, therefore, that two distinct levels of mystical experience are recognized, and that in the lower, which Dean Inge distinguishes as 'objective or symbolic mysticism',[6] sensory images do occur and

[1] p. 14.
[2] *Des Graces d'Oraison*, 7th ed. 1909, pp. 126–39.
[3] *Confessions*: VII, 17.
[4] These quotations come from three different sources. See *St. Thomas Aquinas: Philosophical Texts*, ed. Fr. Thomas Gilby, O.P., O.U.P., 1951, p. 234.
[5] *Purgatorio*, XVII, 16.
[6] *loc. cit.*, p. 340.

take the form of symbols. But finally I would quote an important passage in which, for other and profounder reasons, Jacques Maritain distinguishes between the aesthetic experience (or poetic experience, as he prefers to call it) and the mystical.

'Poetic experience and mystical experience are distinct in nature: poetic experience is concerned with the created world and the enigmatic and innumerable relations of beings with each other; mystical experience with the principle of things in its own incomprehensible and supermundane unity. . . . Poetic experience is from the very start oriented towards expression, and terminates in a word uttered, or a work produced; while mystical experience tends towards silence, and terminates in an immanent fruition of the absolute.

'But different in nature as they may be, poetic experience and mystical experience are born near one another, and near the centre of the soul, in the living springs of the preconceptual or supraconceptual vitality of the spirit. It is not surprising that they intercross and communicate with one another in an infinity of ways.'[1]

It is, then, only on the lower level of the doubtful 'objective or symbolic mysticism', and by affinity, that we can possibly speak of any work of art as 'mystical'. We must now enquire whether Nash's symbols can be called mystical in this limited sense.

In 1941 Bottomley called Nash a mystic, and Nash answered: 'I liked enormously being called a mystic' (Early August). But what did he think it meant? He had used the word ten years before, when he had spoken of English art as 'developing through mystical and imaginative qualities into the abstract form',[2] and we have recently seen that when he considered the quincunx mystically, he made an abstract design. This would suggest that he was at least inclined at one time to use 'mystic' as meaning unattached to natural objects; but in fact, in his own work, he is nearest to mysticism when he uses natural objects symbolically. This is not surprising because the effect of nature on him had an affinity to mysticism. He speaks of this in *Outline*: 'Whatever happened to me there throughout my life, I was conscious always of the influence of the place at work upon my nerves—but never in any sinister degree, rather with a force gentle but insistent, charged with sweetness beyond physical experience, the promise of a joy utterly unreal'.

In 1934 Nash was invited to contribute to a symposium called *Sermons by Artists*, published by the Golden Cockerel Press. He began

---

[1] *Creative Intuition in Art and Poetry*, Harvill Press, 1954, p. 234.
[2] Reported in *The Art Digest* (U.S.A.), 1 October 1931, p. 6.

by describing his own 'religious' upbringing. I have already said enough of that, I think, to explain why it alienated him from 'established religion and the observance of the Sabbath'. It was a purely aesthetic and emotional reaction and quite unrealistic: he never seems to have examined the doctrines of Christianity or the claims of the Church, but simply to have dismissed them as 'dogmas and creeds' which he took for enemies of the spirit. But he tells us that he had made what he calls 'a simple discovery', which we must accept as the nearest we shall get to a positive statement of his belief.

'There seemed to be two indestructible realities which neither doubt nor cynicism could affect; which, whether one believed in a personal or an impersonal God, or could not believe at all, remained accessible, unchanged. These were the philosophy of Christ's teaching and the poetry of the Bible.'

We have no means of knowing what he meant by the philosophy of Christ, but clearly, without a belief in a personal God, it could not imply belief in the Incarnation, which is fundamental to Christianity. But this was a general statement and did not commit Nash himself to belief in a God—personal or otherwise. Margaret Nash is convinced that, in later life at least, he did believe in a personal God. Nash went on to say that he then examined himself on the Bible at that moment of writing, and found that three verses surged up into his memory. The first was: 'Lift up your heads, O ye gates, and be ye lift up, ye everlasting doors: and the King of Glory shall come in'; and the second: 'Why leap ye, ye high hills?' on which he commented:

'In both a power of movement is ascribed to inanimate things; no human or even angelic agency is called upon. . . . Such understanding strongly appealed to me; these things seemed right, although I could not reason why. Again, both images, as they stood, were independent of meaning, apart from themselves. As I see them today they possess something of the character of abstract paintings.'

The third verse was: 'Wherefore seeing we also are compassed about with so great a cloud of witnesses, let us lay aside every weight, and the sin which doth so easily beset us, and let us run with patience the race that is set before us'; but it first arrived in his memory only in the isolated words 'a cloud of witnesses', and on this he commented:

'For some time I conscientiously searched the back areas of memory for a form, but the image remained vague, unsubstantial; I was aware only of a gentle wheeling, aerial movement as of birds in circling flocks. . . . A mystical suggestion which threatened me, I put aside.'

I wish he had not done so, but perhaps we see what it was when we consider his last inhabited sky and the cloud of witnesses in the form of aircraft and flowers, the sun and moon.

Nash then traced the words in his Bible and found that in the previous chapter St. Paul had written of 'the substance of things hoped for, the evidence of things not seen', and he then commented on the image St. Paul employed: 'Instead of referring to the prophets as an *army* of witnesses, which would have left them on the ground, he floats them in the air, thus appealing to an ancient conception of the spirits of the dead, that they roam the skies.'

It was these dead witnesses that he was to fly up to, to meet and converse with in his latest work, 'visiting' their mansions; but in 1934 he shied away and at this point his essay collapsed. He interpreted what he had discovered as an allegory of the artist in the modern world, an interpretation that was so forced and clumsy that we can only take it as a witness that Nash avoided the issue he had raised. I know of no other written source which can help our enquiry, and this has certainly not helped very much. We must now look for help to the symbols he employed in his painting.

These were not private, except in their accidents; nor were they consciously adopted to clothe his ideas. They *were* his ideas, and we have seen that most of them appeared, though sometimes only in embryo, in his childish dreams, his 'visions' and his earliest works. They were *his* ideas, but he had 'inherited' them in Jung's sense, not physically, of course, nor even by tradition, but biologically; because his 'unconscious mind has worked along the same line of thought which has manifested itself, time and again, within the last two thousand years ... regenerating the same or at least similar ideas'.[1] That is, of course, to say that Nash's symbols were archetypal. I shall not however attempt to relate them to any system of symbols because it is my business to relate them to him; but I shall from time to time draw attention to their frequent correspondence with such systems as the alchemists' or that which scholarship has deduced from myth and folk tales.[2]

It will be convenient to examine Nash's symbols in the pattern of myth, for Yeats could have said of Nash, as he said of Blake: 'He was a man crying out for a mythology, and trying to make one because he did not find one to his hand. Had he been a Catholic of Dante's

---

[1] *Psychology and Religion*, Yale U.P. and O.U.P., 1938, p. 111.
[2] See, for example, the list of names for the *prima materia* given by Silberer, *loc. cit.*, p. 123, and the typical folk-tale pattern described in *The Golden Well: An Anatomy of Symbols*, by Dorothy Donnelly, Sheed & Ward, 1950.

15. Path. 1932
Water-colour

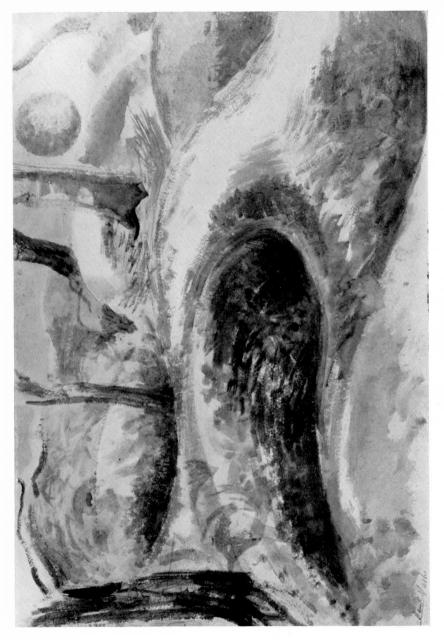

16. Landscape at Pen Pits. [1934]

time he would have been content with Mary and the Angels.'[1] The pattern of myth is usually vertical, but Nash did not begin at the bottom. He never looked into the dark caves under the earth where man lives in complete materialism, for even the mole's habitation in the *Earth Home* is brought to the surface and its apertures admit the light. Nash's darkest cave is no darker than Plato's. At least there are shadows of reality to be seen—illusion, perhaps, but not Nothing. But when we rise to the waters we at once meet a typical Nash symbol. It recurs constantly, as we have seen, in the sea, in ponds, pools, rivers and canals. Its significance is complicated and may at first seem self-contradictory. On the one hand, the sea is the sterile, the uncultivated: on the other, water is the fountain of life, even life itself, and the patristic writers often used it for the Holy Ghost, the life-giving Spirit.[2]

The sea also symbolizes the passions of man, and thereby becomes a principle of death because they destroy him if they are not controlled. In Nash they are controlled by Dymchurch wall. So in pre-Christian mythology, the river of life is also the *Flumen Mortis*, which Nash drew so early in his career; it is the mystical abode of the unborn and of the dead. But this duality may be resolved by recalling that the sterile can be cultivated with the aid of itself, the waste land by the water, which is itself waste. Nash, however, avoided these difficulties by separating the symbolic functions of water. In the stagnant pools of the first war pictures, it is pure sterility: in the seas of Dymchurch and Dorset it is the destructive force of passion but sometimes it lies so disciplined and harmless that it passes over into the creative function: in the canals and ponds it is the wholly beneficent fertilizer. This was the golden well of legend which must be guarded: and he guarded it with willow trees, to whom its water gives life.

In the pattern of myth man next passes to his trials and encounters. His way is across the sterile and pathless desert or sea, or through the dark forest. Nash was never lost on the way, nor ever caught in the labyrinth: there is always a path through his forest. Perhaps this confidence sprang from only facing the problem of the Way in its images.

The typical trials and encounters of man in myth are to find the tree or fountain of life, to guard the well, to capture the Golden Bird, to defeat the Monster. At the point in his work which we have reached, Nash had already found the tree, which, as we have seen, was never for him a mere vegetable growth, although in his early

---

[1] *Essays*, London, 1924, p. 140.
[2] Jung quotes many examples in *Psychology and Religion*, p. 129.

years he had not heard of the Golden Bough on the tree at Nemi that was to fascinate him later. He had already found the still ponds and set his willows to guard them. He had already captured the bird, but it was not yet the golden bird which he was to find in the shape of the sunflower and the sun, as he was to encounter the Monster in the shape of the *dead* tree. I do not try to disentangle this. Nash was not painting in allegory, which must be self-consistent, but in symbols where there must be the inherent contradictions of reality as we imperfectly apprehend and interpret it.

In the vertical pattern, the advancing man must next ascend his hill to where its shoulder meets the light.

> *Ma poi ch'i' fui al piè d'un colle giunto,*
> *là dove terminava quella valle*
> *che m'avea di paura il cor compunto,*
> *guardai in alto, e vidi le sue spalle*
> *vestite già de' raggi del pianeta*
> *che mena dritto altrui per ogni calle.*[1]

I need not enlarge on the familiar symbolism of the high places, the sacred places of Transfiguration; nor on how persistently Nash's imagination had been occupied with them. Wittenham Clumps rose out of the land towards the sky, as his pyramids rose out of the sea. We have also seen the ladder in his work, which is the next step up, because it may reach above the highest hills to be a way for the traffic of Jacob's angels and which again, of course, Dante saw:

> *di color d'oro in che raggio traluce*
> *vid'io uno scaleo eretto in suso*
> *tanto, che nol seguiva la mia luce.*[2]

The ladder was a common symbol in mediaeval teaching for the contemplative life: and Nash was a contemplative artist.

After the journey through the forest and the trials and encounters and the climb, questing man normally arrives in myth at the *Pratum Felicitatis*, which is also called the Celestial Garden, the Garden of Peace or of the Blessed and the Mountain of Joy. Today we know it best, I suppose, at the end of Dante's *Purgatorio*. This was, as we have seen,[3] foreshadowed in Nash's early Bird Garden, and he was to 'return to his parish' in many gardens, culminating in that at Oxford

---

[1] Dante, *Inferno*, I, 13.
[2] *Paradiso*, XXI, 28.
[3] See p. 81.

where he grew the sunflower and another on Boar's Hill, from which he saw Wittenham Clumps and the matter of a whole series of paintings concerned with the Sun and Moon. From this garden—which is the return to the parish of Eden, Paradise regained, Beatrice re-met, the symbol of earthly blessedness—the way up is flight, the final stage of the journey; and it is here that we come to the group of symbols which Nash most fully developed and best understood. The whole literature of spiritual aspiration is so full of the images of flight that there is no need to illustrate them, but I want to quote one example for a certain special relevance to Nash. St. Teresa, commenting on David's cry for the wings of a dove, said: 'It is plain that this is the flight of the spirit upwards above all created things, and chiefly above itself: but it is a sweet flight, a delicious flight—a flight without noise.'[1] In *Aerial Flowers* Nash complained that mechanical flight was fundamentally unsatisfying because the apparatus was heavier than air and immensely noisy 'whereas the essence of the virtue of flying was the escape into vast lonely spaces in complete freedom of bodily action and, above everything, in silence'.

The symbol of flight naturally leads to the bird, and we have seen how large a part the bird played in his early life, wheeling about the skies of his childhood and adolescence. In the first war pictures, the noisy aircraft took its place; and then, during the years of concern with the forest, the sterile waters and, as we shall see, the Monster, it is almost entirely absent. But we have already seen the first signs of its return in *Mansions of the Dead* in a form which, again, is described by St. Teresa: 'this little bird of the spirit seems to have escaped out of this wretchedness of the flesh, out of the prison of this body.'[2] In *Aerial Flowers*, Nash called this bird 'the emblem of the soul'; but in *Mansions of the Dead* it is more than this, for it is in a circle or egg. The bird in the circle is the old symbol of the Holy Ghost. The circle is the symbol of All, and with a point at its centre, it is the symbol of God, centre of All; this is the nearest the *visual* symbol can get to the famous image of God: *Totum intra omnia, et totum extra: ac per hoc est sphaera intelligibilis, cuius centrum est ubique, et circumferentia nusquam.*[3] The circle had many other related significances, of course, in other religions and philosophies; and it is particularly noticeable, in connection with Nash, that the circle with a point at its centre was the

---

[1] *Life of St Teresa of Jesus written by Herself.* Trans. by David Lewis. Ed. Benedict Zimmerman, O.C.D., Barker, London, 1932.
[2] *Loc. cit.*
[3] Quoted in the *Roman de la Rose* and St. Bonaventura's *Itinerarius Mentis in Deum* from an unknown source.

alchemist's symbol for the sun and for gold. The connection of all this with Nash's later work will become clear when we consider it.

We can make the easy transition from the circle to the egg by way of a strange quotation, given by Damon[1] from the sixteenth century philosopher, Robert Fludd:

Mundi circularis centrum est terra; humana vero rotunditas punctum centrale est secundum quosdam in umbilico; sed nos potius illud circum genitalia ponendum esse putamus, si quidem ut in mundo centro semina rerum reconduntur, sic etiam juxta hominis testiculos delitescit virtus eius seminalis.

The egg was the natural symbol of fertility and the perfect shape of the egg was the circle; therefore the circle was the symbol of perfect fertility, the divine creator. The alchemists treated the egg as identical with the *rotundum*, but the receptacle in which the *magnum opus* was to be accomplished was egg-shaped.[2] It has no significance that millions of schoolboys collect eggs, as Nash did; but surely it has some when the form recurs with peculiar persistence in an artist's work, as it did in Nash's.

It is also an easy transition from the circle to the serpent, which also occurs frequently in Nash's work. It is found devouring its tail or in a series of coils in ancient Egyptian, Chinese, Aztec and Indian art and in many other works of primitive religion.[3] Bridges commented on this in *The Testament of Beauty*:

> Reality appeareth in forms to man's thought
> as several links interdependent of a chain
> that circling returneth upon itself, as doth
> the coil'd snake that in art figureth eternity.

It first appeared in Nash's work as early as the *Book of Verses*[4] and I imagine that the part it plays in Blake is most likely to have caught his attention, which may have been revived by meeting its use as an image of death in Conrad Aiken's *John Deth*.

With the circle, of course, and its related symbols, we have been dealing with an inhabitant of the sky—the sun itself, symbol of God Himself. We know that God exists outside place—*cuius centrum est ubique*—but man has persistently localized Him symbolically in the sky. It was certainly Blake who first stimulated Nash to look consciously to the sky and it was there he found his first visions—the

---

[1] *William Blake, His Philosophy and Symbols* by S. Foster Damon. Constable, 1924, p. 103.
[2] See Silberer, *loc. cit.*, p. 116; and, for another aspect of the egg's symbolism, *Piero della Francesca* by Sir Kenneth Clark, Phaidon Press, 1951, pp. 49 and 210.
[3] See Panofsky's treatment of it as an attribute of the Time-Saturn figure in *Studies in Iconology*, O.U.P., 1939, Chapter III, and specially p. 74, n. 12.
[4] See p. 63.

silver hands, the face in the sky and the cloud 'in the shape of a great rose'. Apart from these more visionary inhabitants, he had peopled it with birds—'the white merle', for example, and the hawk, and with the sun and moon and stars.

It may be well at this point, when we are about to consider Nash's maturity, to recall to our memory the boy who could write to Mercia:

'Last night about half an hour after sunset or rather sooner when the clouds were changing rosy to dun there suddenly flashed in a clear space of sky—the evening star . . . very pale and liquid and trembling under the edge of a cloud. Not to be described in any words but with its sudden beauty suggesting all sensitive brilliant fragrant things—white roses, shimmering lakes white merles and silvery sounds a mystery of other world' [c. April 1912].

What we have now to watch is the recovery of that vision in mature and personal terms; but as there are many stages to be traced and many other images to be recovered, I shall postpone what I have to say of the last inhabitants of his symbolic world. Then, at the end, we shall consider his last symbols, the mystic rose, the sun and moon and sunflower.

But we have yet to answer the question as to whether Nash could, in any sense, be called a mystical artist. We have seen that the symbols which recur most persistently in his work were all, by biological inheritance, those used by man in many times and places to express intuitions of God and the mysteries of spirit. In particular, we have found his concentration on flight and the symbols related to it. If this expressed his desire for what St. Gregory called 'the flight of contemplation', away from all earthly plagueings and inadequate images, then clearly it was mystical. But if, as I believe, he was satisfied with what he found *in* the images, then, in Maritain's phrases, we can speak only of his poetic, not of his mystic experience. We can only allow him to be 'mystical' on the lower level and by affinity. His flight had no determined goal but was only the symbol of the Way.

vi. Pictures

I have already mentioned a letter Nash wrote to Cecil Collins in 1944,[1] where he indicated the sections into which he considered his work could be divided. He chose to enlarge on one of them, which almost exactly coincides with the period now under review.

'Paintings, drawings, applied design 1930–33

[1] See p. 54.

'Abstract and "near" abstract forms and patterns, groups of paintings and drawings of like tendencies, designs for glass mural, designs in bookbinding, book jackets and certain typographical ornaments etc. etc. The work here comes along from *Northern Adventure* and *Dead Spring*. . . . 1929 through a period of architectonic design expressed in various ways. It includes the *Urne Buriall* book and reaches the point of the *Mansions of the Dead* drawings and painting. This section shows the break from "interpretive" landscape and still life painting to the experiments in non-figurative design or "near" abstract which coincided practically with so called "Surrealist" content. *Northern Adventure* is one of the first (I suppose this would be one of the most important sections).'

Nash was right. It is the crisis of his artistic life; but it turns, I believe, on *Urne Buriall* rather than on paintings. Indeed, there are not many of them. The period was cut into by his activity in other arts and by his American journey and his illness. Most of the pictures are abstract or 'near' abstract, but a few suggest the symbolic representation which was only fully explicit in *Urne Buriall*. *Opening* (1931) is one of these, and one of his best paintings, and one of his last and most formalized uses of the window theme; but it has become a symbolic opening rather than a window. In the original drawing the treatment is entirely abstract, but in the painting Nash felt the need to support it with some representation—the hints of stonework, the sea-shore and the sea. The whole effect is quiet, clear and assured, as if Nash were calmly at ease, having reached the satisfactory end of a particular exploration.

Salome (Plate 13), which he painted about the same time, can be associated with it. There is no opening but the folds of a screen are disposed like the related planes of window-frame and open casement. In place of the vase of flowers on a table which we have so often seen, there is a bowl containing an egg-shaped form which symbolizes St. John's head. It stands on a book which bears one word: Salome. St. John announced the Lamb: the egg announces the bird. Two coils of raffia that hang from the screen suggest Salome's hair. But Nash gives these references as witty comments, so to speak, on what is primarily a still-life design, and the significance is not deeply felt.

Pure abstractions, such as *Kinetic Feature* (1931), are rare, but even the series of representational drawings done on his Atlantic journeys or worked up later—*Atlantic, Voyage, Liner, Ship Interior* and so on— have an abstract quality in that Nash has accepted the mechanical forms of the ship with which to build a pattern of straight lines and circles, in the extreme manner of the 'ruler' discipline. In one of them, *Voyage*, there were sea gulls, but even these were removed. The whole series is completely uninhabited and undramatic, but for *Ship Interior* (1932), in which something else is happening. In the foreground is a table surrounded by chairs, as the ship is surrounded by sea. We are made to feel this strongly by a direct view of the sea through a window, and an indirect view of it through a window reflected in a mirror—the device we have already met in the Toulon drawings. The geometric form of the ship is islanded in the organic forms of the sea, like the *Pyramids in the Sea*, as the geometric table is islanded, and 'the presence of the absent' suggested, by the disposition of the chairs about it, whose rhythm echoes that of the sea.

There are several other drawings in which Nash made his last statements of geometrical structure. One of them, *Skeleton* (1932), is a view from above of the curved tracks of a scenic railway set into play with the verticals and diagonals of its supports. Another is *Circus* [1931] where we see the ring in perspective as an almond shape, framed by the uprights of the big top; and we also see a most astonishing apparition in the ring—a horse, the only horse, I believe, in all the work of this landscape painter, a riderless horse. A third is *River*, where swings hang empty and motionless from the rectangular framework in the foreground, set against the S curves of a river, which winds to the far horizon. In all these, Nash was studying geometrical structures which he found out of doors; but he also found them indoors, as in the excellent *Studio at New House, Rye* [1932].

At the same time, however, Nash was studying organic structures, which he treated in the more fluid manner of earlier and later work, as in the drawings *Hudson* and *Path* (1932) (Plate 15) and the oils *Forest* [1932] and a second *Whiteleaf Cross*. But none of this work justifies special comment; nor do the various studies in the woodyard at Rye, the best of which is probably *Totems*, where the pile of gateposts suggested the title.

There is only one drawing which seems to foreshadow a new development. I mean *Group for a Sculptor*, whose title has no other significance than that it was made for Henry Moore. It is an arrangement of two leaves, a piece of lichenous wood, a burr and a tennis ball—a formal pattern of organic objects but also a 'strange encounter'. I postpone the discussion of that theme until it emerges more importantly; but if the date of 1931, which has been suggested for this drawing, is correct, then it showed that Nash was already ripe for new adventures.

VIII

Swanage and Hampstead
1933-1939

≈≈≈◆≈≈≈

i. Chronicle

I broke off my chronicle where Nash left Rye in July 1933 for a
holiday at Marlborough with Ruth Clark. She has written how
for a few days they wandered idly about the town and Savernake
Forest; and how one day they took a local bus to Avebury and what
happened then:

'Suddenly we saw on the left great Stones standing up in the field.
Paul was excited and fascinated. We spent long hours on the great
grass banks entranced at the sight of the stones below in the large
green enclosure—great "personalities" erect, or lying prone or built
into the structure of houses by indifferent generations of dwellers in
Avebury. His response was to the drama of the Stones themselves in
this quiet setting. His sensitiveness to magic and the sinister beauty of
monsters was stirred, and he long contemplated the great mass of
their forms, their aloofness, their majesty, the shadows they cast on
the green, the loveliness of their harsh surfaces and the tenderness of
their colouring. He seemed to have found renewed vitality in this
countryside and in these ancient symbols. At this point of time—at
this point of change in his life—they gave to an English painter virtue
and inspiration.

'For the lull had ended. Not only was Paul better able to walk and
to work without fatigue—he was now charged with purpose. His
strength was equal to the quest he was minded to follow. I felt a glow
of satisfaction as I returned from a long ramble to the top of Silbery
Hill ("Why do you always want to get to the top of things—people

216

are so odd about wanting to climb things") to find Paul had been drawing and painting all the time, working intently, sitting cross-legged in the stubble, and on his knees was not just a notebook but a full sheet of drawing paper.'

'If anything will preserve my interest in landscape from a painter's point of view,' Nash wrote to his wife, 'it will be this country', and he suggested that they should consider it for their new home. But wherever that was to be, they must settle, they must avoid another move for many years. But it did not work out like that. The holiday was followed by a period of wanderings and temporary homes which began with three months at Judd Street, interrupted by various country visits. About the middle of November they set off abroad with no planned route or time-table, but generally making for Malaga.

A letter to Ruth Clark from Nice, begun on New Year's Eve, describes their journey up to that date:

'It's almost amusing how we have been defeated on this journey—nobody's fault, particularly, just an inconsequent conspiracy of events. . . . In Paris . . . we became involved in seeing people and things and I, believing myself rid altogether of my trouble, more or less eat and drank what came along which included some vilainous champagne at the Bal Tabarin. No doubt too we went to bed too late so that by the time we left Paris, I'd done myself just no good at all.

'Ah well, we thought, a nice quiet time in Provence away from the fog and cold and noise will soon put us right and, at the great inconvenience of my suitcase I remembered I had packed my new light suit because it would be *warm* in Avignon! was it warm in Avignon? Dunt esk.[1] We arrived about 7 a.m. in a cold rain. At dawn I looked out brightly on a country entirely waterlogged—acres of flooded fields. Yes, dear, this was the warm midi where the autumn sun would still be shining. But of course there were consolations.

'A charming town en fete with stalls and booths and fairs all over the place. We turned in to the Crillon which was really too expensive but was very comfortable and seemed to have superlative cooking. After all it was only for a few days—we stayed three weeks. . . .

'I don't know the first cause of my starting to cough and wheeze again but I put our premier view of Roman remains as a very probable one. The theatre at Orange was illuminated by a shallow sunlight just sufficient . . . for me to take two very interesting photographs. On the other hand, the first row of the stalls where I was

[1] The title of a book by Milt Gross. See p. 224.

standing was raked by a draught from the emergency exit. . . . We had the misfortune to take an autobus in quite the wrong direction for Avignon owing to the Mouse trusting to information received. This was silly because we had long ago decided that information with the French is a sort of abstract thing, it has no *necessary* relation to facts. . . . Well that was a long coldish unnecessary drive. . . .

'No sooner were we decided to cross into Spain than Spain broke out into the most frightful racket. Then of course we simply hung on waiting for news from North and South. Then of course the Mistral travelling down the Rhone at incredible speed hit the town like a tornado from hell—supposing Hell to be the coldest known spot. Also alas it seized me by the throat and that, on top of all, gave me back most of what I'd spent nearly a year getting rid of.

'So there we were again. I simply incarcerated until the Mistral stopped. The streets were glacial, fat Frenchmen skidded about in all directions. The fountains were frozen stiff and the hotel chauffage declined naturally to meet the emergency. At last we were able to escape. By then Spain was indefinitely postponed and it seemed evident that Nice and an English doctor was the first consideration' [31 December 1933–2 January 1934].

Another letter to Ruth Clark is from the Hotel des Princes at Nice:

'Now we have another setback. I must have got a cold off someone after my last treatment for I suddenly went frankly bronchial and frightened the poor Mouse into fits by exactly reproducing my worst performance at Tunbridge Wells only rather more intense.

'I dont mind admitting I got the wind up. Do you know I just put up a desperate prayer a real old-fashioned prayer to le Bon Dieu and I believe it got picked up somehow for the very next day I was a different chap. . . . I'm stuffed and sick of myself, loathe eating and can't yet work but I'm sure I'm shaking it off. . . .

'Of course all this means we can't leave Nice before the end of February. But it's very pleasant here in this large room overlooking the Bay,[1] where I can paint and we can live a restful life—given a spot of health to go on with. . . .

'2 days elapse—

'I have felt dreadfully lazy and just read tecs I hope I get out to-morrow the strain is telling on the Dove and she's hopping with nerves. I suppose the English winter would have knocked me out but I often sit and wonder why the Hell I'm here—a tiresome invalid, profitable to no one but the bloody french—of all the laughable

---

[1] The room from which he painted *View 2* and *View A*. See p. 132.

fiascos! Still there is the sun—we make a lot of the sun and then there is something about the twilight over the bay with palm trees silhouetted against the sky which recalls childish days in Egypt to our Mouse. . . . I wish we knew a few people. . . . Nobody comes to this mountebanks paradise now only *very* rich invalids can afford to be so expensively bored. . . . Monstrous dago nancys with flashing oily hair, leading repulsive dogs, give a barbaric touch, but it's not the place it was' [January 1934].

Using letters to carry forward the story of one's subject makes him appear as only concerned with himself. But that was not so with Nash: it is I who am always concerned with him and therefore make only those extracts which are about him. The next letter, again to Ruth Clark, opens at length about her affairs and only then goes on to speak of himself:

'I am now painting every day and working at drawings or writings most evenings. The next step is exam by French nose specialist followed by treatment according to report. But no ops for me. . . . Mouse is improving too. She's all sweetness and light and hardly ever gets wild or irritated. There was a moment however last week when doctors were on the carpet in some general denunciation of medical chicanery and the Mouse was suddenly going to *devote her life* to exposing their iniquity—you wait, stormed the Mouse I'll raise such a mare's nest for them. . . . I call that a good one practically in the first class. I suppose "raising a hornet's nest" was the key to it but I had a wild vision of dreadful crazy cart horses hatched on to [?into] Harley Street. A fearful Webster fantasmagora.'

The letter went on to describe how the carnival cars passed in front of his hotel on their way to the festivities:

'They were unlit except by the rays of the street lamps they passed, which cast queer lights and monstrous shadows on the immense grotesque figures as they went nodding along against the dark sea. . . . Actually the carnavalistic imagination is not very happy; it runs to silliness and vulgarity, but these piled up groups of nonsense only half discernible, awful bloated forms in crude colours swaying and doddering about as high as the palm trees with the black waves breaking on a ghostly shore beyond, had a nightmare dignity which I found fascinating' (6 February 1934).

The English doctor, having now improved Nash's general health, took him to a French ear, nose and throat specialist for treatment of the local centre of trouble. Nash announced the result of the consultation in a postcard to Burra:

'Did you know I had at least a dozen polipi more or less the size of small haricots in my unfortunate nose, no? Nor did I, but they've removed eleven to date. Its quite a well known affair in France—ah, les Polypes, le vegetation—mais, oui' [30 March 1934].

In the second half of April the Nashes went to Marseilles for about a week, and from there to Gibraltar where they were held up by a return of his bronchial trouble. But he recovered sufficiently to visit Algeciras and Ronda and then to sail from Gibraltar to Ceuta and go on by omnibus to Tetuan, where his health greatly improved. Unfortunately I have no letters from which to give any account of all this. Indeed, Nash wrote a postcard to Desmond Flower in which he said: 'Since I left Nice I've written to no one—too busy being amused by a new country and *what* a country it is' [25 May 1934]. This was written on their return from North Africa to Gibraltar. From there, after being abroad something over six months, they returned to a cold English June and their cramped flat. Neither suited Nash and they unwisely escaped to Romney Marsh, where after a short stay at Owley they moved into a cottage called 'Cullens', near Small Hythe. It was isolated, bat-haunted and damp, but there were compensations for Nash. One was that it was there he first met Clare and Charles Neilson, who were to be among his best patrons and friends. His first letter to Clare described other compensations and disadvantages:

'The great joy is the landscape which is everlastingly lovely. It is peopled with numerous birds of different kinds which I watch through the glasses. I saw a very serious looking heron catch an eel in the most jaunty nonchalant way. Snipes go tearing round the sky in a dement fashion God knows what for. . . . Yesterday I found a superb piece of wood sculpture (salvaged from the stream) like a very fine Henry Moore it is now dominating the sitting room waiting for a bright sun to be photographed. Dear Clare, this room is getting intolerably fuggy, if I open a window a host of mosquitos is waiting outside to pounce; my eyelids shut up like a roll top desk, they feel like locking' [6 August 1934].

The object was that which became known as *Marsh Personage*. It was to be exhibited in the Surrealist Exhibition of 1936 and afterwards to accompany Nash to Oxford, where it survives. There are drawings and photographs of it.[1]

The following extracts from a long letter to Ruth Clark give the last news from Romney Marsh:

[1] See *Fertile Image*, Pl. 59, and 'Object and Landscape' by P. M. Shand, *Country Life*, 3 June 1939.

'We may come back to town earlier than we meant to as this place doesnt seem to agree with us. . . . Yesterday we went to see a famous local quack who has cured asthma. . . . He has a panacea he plugs you with—according to him it's all a matter of senile decay. So jolly! . . .

'As to . . . plans I can say nothing until I know whether I am taking on this crazy job. This crazy job is to decorate several hundred of feet of wall at the end of the Dance Hall at the ——!¹ Of course they want it done in a hurry and I expect they want it done cheap but in that case I don't bite.

'It is rather an opportunity to have some fun but somehow I feel they don't really want a serious piece of work—only a bit of smart aleck harlotry.

'Still I may be mistaken and of course if they accept my terms it doesn't matter, I shall do what I want. . . .

'The poet [Conrad Aiken] . . . is a changed man—it would seem for the better—a wholesome-looking, pipe smoking poet, open and cheery as the blue sky and so *patient* it is quite uncanny. . . . Our Conrad is expecting to be made London correspondent of the New Yorker. . . . He is torn between the enchanting prospect of jaunts to town with a well-lined pocket and dread of being invited out to dine and having to wear evening dress.

'Which somehow reminds me of a lovely story he told of Ed's [Burra] arrival in New York. Conrad met him at the Customs displaying the most awful mess of Woolworth underwear mixed up with paints and French and Spanish novelettes which was passed by the Customs officer, an enormous Irish Yank. But as Ed stooped to close up his bag a large *bulge* in his hip pocket betrayed a considerable bottle of whisky. The officer leant over and without a word tapped the bottle with a pencil. Conrad began to feel anxious and I'm sure did a lot of scratching behind his ear. But Ed didn't even straighten up, he leered round at the cop and said in that withering voice *it's a growth*. Conrad said the chap was completely broken, he just got very red and wandered away looking at other things!' [1934. July or August].

Nash's note for *Outline* on the Swanage period, which we now enter, stresses the feeling of a new start: 'Finding new friends . . . finding new forms; a new world opening.' Mrs. Hilda Felce² lent the Nashes her house called Whitecliff on Ballard Down, the headland that

---

¹ A famous London hotel. Nothing came of the proposal.
² See p. 142.

divides Studland Bay from Swanage Bay. They arrived there on the eighth of October 1934 but their visit began badly. First Nash was ill and then his wife. But I shall not continue to record each incident of illness in their lives. From now on there is hardly a letter of Nash's that does not mention that one or the other or both of them are ill. For the moment, however, Nash was able to stave off the worst attacks on his breathing with a new inhalant; he could live and work more or less normally but only with care and constant awareness of the lurking enemy.

Nash rapidly expanded in the imaginative atmosphere of Dorset and, oddly enough, particularly in that of Swanage, which for a time stimulated his interest in the lighter, more 'amusing' aspect of sur-realism. He described this in *Swanage or Seaside Surrealism*.[1] He passed the autumn uneventfully in the enthusiasm of his new forms and new friends. The chief of these was Archibald Russell, then Lancaster Herald,[2] who lives on the hill above the town in a house full of beautiful objects, where Nash could enjoy good talk and good wine. Russell played a large part in keeping the Nashes in Swanage, and when they had to leave Whitecliff at the beginning of February, they took lodgings at 2 The Parade.

Nash was soon widely extending his knowledge of Dorset while preparing his volume on that county for the series of Shell Guides which the editor, John Betjeman, had asked him to undertake. It appeared in 1936 and was dedicated to 'the Landowners of Dorset, the Council for the Preservation of Rural England, the Society for the Protection of Ancient Buildings and all those courageous enemies of "development" to whom we owe what is left of England'. But in the text his eye was fixed on older inhabitants than the builders, on the stones and the fossils, the earthworks and the legends of Druidic peoples. It is really a guide to Nash's new imaginative world for which Dorset offered so much material, and his treatment is entirely subjective. His symbols crowd into the description of Badbury Rings, for example:

'It is round rather than oval, and has the dread peculiarity of a crown of dense trees planted in concentric circles. I have read of enchanted places, and at rare times come upon them, but I remember nothing so beautifully haunted as the wood in Badbury Rings. . . . Beyond the outer plateau the rings heave up and round in waves

---

[1] Reprinted in *Outline*, but without his excellent photographs which illustrated it originally in *The Architectural Review*, April 1936.
[2] He was appointed Clarenceux King of Arms in 1954.

40 feet high. A magic bird in a haunted wood, an ancient cliff washed by a sea changed into earth.'

One of the water-colours which he contributed to the Guide is of this characteristic Place. Another is of Corfe Castle, in which the mound, bearing its ruins as Badbury or Wittenham bear their woods, stands like a pyramid among uncultivated wave-like hills. The dark antiquity of Dorset, he said, can be too easily dispersed by sunshine or crumpets, but 'Corfe, alone, is implacable. No mood of nature or human intrusion can affect that terrific personality. It dominates the county like a calvary, a symbol never less than its history'.

His account concentrates particularly on the coast of the Isle of Purbeck, and is full of his new enthusiasm for stones. In his symbolism the natural stones were now taking the place of the constructed Dymchurch wall. 'The coast is an iron wall' he said of the Kimmeridge area 'seeming to be literally built of huge grey-black blocks. The seas are vicious here, and there is no more bitter war between land and water than is fought along Winspit Cliff and Dancing Ledge.'

While Nash was at work on this publication, he held an exhibition of water-colours at the Redfern Gallery, whose remarkable success, he told Percy Withers, made him feel 'a little bewildered and slightly suspicious!' [1935 c. June]. The Nashes were in London for this and afterwards in Buckinghamshire, but by the middle of June they were back in Swanage, full of a scheme for building near Archibald Russell's. But this fell through because the place was too exposed. Then they began to pay visits away from Swanage while still ostensibly looking for a house there. But really Swanage had begun to pall and by the autumn Nash was writing to Ruth Clark that it was 'unbearably vulgar'. 'The people who live there, my God,' he went on, 'the people who come there on the buses and steamers—beyond belief. Somehow they come from the North I don't know why but they somehow seep in from the more savage suburbs of our great industrial cities' [1935 c. November]. But they lingered on for two or three months and then moved to an hotel in Hampstead, where they had now decided to look for a house. They soon bought 3 Eldon Grove and were settled in by the autumn.

In the meantime, the International Surrealist Exhibition had been held in London. It was organized by a distinguished committee of which Nash was a member. The influence of Surrealism on his work will be discussed later. It is enough to say here that he never accepted the whole creed although the *Bystander* labelled him 'English Surrealist-in-Chief'. But René Magritte, the leading Belgian Surrealist, gave him the more suitable title of 'The Master of the Object', which he described years later to Hartley Ramsden as 'rather a nice title like the Master of the Amsterdam Cabinet and other half mythical personages' (12 November 1945).

It is at this point that Nash's notes for the continuation of *Outline* come to an end with the phrase: 'Pause to look round—back and ahead. Life at 3 Eldon Grove and so on.' But in fact there was no break in his work at this time, and therefore I shall not break my chronicle. Hampstead was not a Place: his move there was not an event in his imaginative life. It was only his body which lived there and it was a burden to him. He was always obliged to work slowly, and often with his brush in one hand and his inhaler in the other. But he was able to prepare a large exhibition which was held at the Redfern Gallery in late April 1937. By August he could write to Burra: 'I still have my asthma thanks a lot, only its not so much on top.'

Nash would not let it get on top. He fought it with his courage, his humour and above all his passion for work. But by the end of that month he had to go into a clinic in Hertfordshire, which he described to his wife partly in the language of Milt Gross's *Dunt Esk*, which he had frequently used ever since he had discovered it just before going to America.

De Bin

wit

de Cloinic

wit

de Maternity Home ...

'Dollinck Dove

'Iss diss place glifful mit sweetness und loight, dunt esk. Is it beyoind biluff wot de dreams is made from, no kidding. Does one get a kick outa de vegetarium cooking mit Kellog shavings mit de bare faced carrot mit de potato in de straight jacket mit de boigns mitt roll a la Viennese. Yes baby, a kick from de pents ...

'The Buckman Boys are here. They are taking their holiday here, I ask you, and are they having fun? But they won't worry me, they are very cliquey. I live in another world. But the first thing I read on the Inner Book of the Words was—If you have any habits injurious to health, lay them aside at once. The use of tea, coffee and tobacco is a harmful luxury, etc. etc. (and that goes for gin too). . . . So what! . . . It looked like no tea this afternoon. That's too much. And I just

17. Paul Nash. c. 1936
Photograph by Gerty Simon

18 Landscape of the Megaliths [1927]

ordered it up to my room and I'll have it if it costs me another seven shillings or go into the Maternity Home or go nuts, or run away to sea. Please send me twenty Waverley. . . .

'Tomorrow's stummick business at 8.30, takes four hours but they give you breakfast, its part of the fun. I swallow two feet of tubing it seems. . . .

'Send me all letters, packets, etc, to make me look busy and keep me clear of all these frightful people' [31 August 1937].

Nash never gave in to his illness. He was ready to try any treatments that offered hope, but perhaps he did not give his doctors a chance. There was an alarming succession of them, interspersed with quacks, in each of which he put unfailing but short-lived faith.

After the Hertfordshire ordeal, he paid visits in Dorset where he was happy and at peace, and on his return home he prepared an exhibition of industrial designs and book-illustrations which opened on the sixth of October at the Curwen Press.

It was about this time that James Thurber was in England and saw a good deal of Nash. In the letter from which I have already quoted, he wrote:

'I was always impressed by that little smile of his, and his keen eyes that looked at you so steadily and seemed to be expecting everything they saw to be interesting, amusing and different. He was a remarkable observer, one of the best I ever knew. . . . In his study, in the house on Hampstead Heath, where I met Conrad Aiken for the first and only time, I was enchanted by the wonderful litter of paintings, lithographs, collages, montages, and all kinds of constructions and arrangements. . . . I did not think his surrealistic stuff was as good as some of the rest, but he was vastly interested in everything, and it was wonderful to see his eyes light up when he showed you around. . . .

'He used to say that no comic artist, not even the Americans, had ever succeeded in making death funny. He had an intense hatred of death. . . . And, as you know, he was able to face the awful and too early discontinuance of his vital life, largely by persuading himself that the experience of death was akin to flowers aerially borne, a kind of eternity of fragrant and gentle drifting, which seems as good to me as anything else . . .

'He said that the common drawing of a man falling from a building and speaking to someone on the way down did not represent death, since the man was forever poised in the air, and it was Paul who said of my drawing *Touché!* "that the man whose head had been cut off was not actually dead, because he could obviously put it back on again". This line has been widely quoted in America, usually without credit.'

In January 1938 Nash resumed teaching at the Royal College of Art for two periods a week as Assistant in the School of Design, a post which he relinquished when the College was evacuated in 1940. Rothenstein's successor, P. H. Jowett, has written to me enthusiastically of Nash as a teacher in this second period, beloved by his students and never sparing himself. But one student has spoken of him as 'cold and aloof but very impressive', indifferent to poor work and often reducing his girl students to tears. Her husband, who was her fellow-student but not a pupil of Nash's, has described how he would occasionally meet him on the stairs or in a corridor when 'one knew', he said, 'that this was a great person, but the great person did not seem aware that one existed as one squeezed back to let him pass'.

Nash was also busy in early 1938 with writing *Outline* and with preparing for an exhibition of oils and water-colours at the Leicester Galleries, which opened in May. His oils were now fetching up to a hundred and fifty guineas, and his reputation had grown to such proportions that the Venice International Biennale of this year included a retrospective exhibition of his work—sixteen oils and eleven water-colours.

At the end of June he paid his first visit to Madams, a name which was to occur in the title of many pictures. It is the Neilsens' house near Newent in Gloucestershire, a lovely and retired place in a wood. Today the garden is of great and individual beauty but at the time of his visit it was hardly begun, for the Neilsens had only moved in at Easter. During this visit Nash designed the rock garden, enjoying himself enormously because for once he could command lavish materials.

The natural beauty, the admirable house and food and wines, the collection of rare books and above all the hospitality and charm of the owners, were to make his visits to Madams a special happiness for Nash during the years of war and advancing death. A remarkable collection of his works now hangs in the house; and his taste and sense of fun survive in the things he planted and the names he gave to places about the garden and the woods. Perhaps it is the kind of home he would have made for himself if circumstances had been kinder, but I am not sure. He loved the country, but he never lived right in it, but rather in little towns or their neighbourhood, in places where there was company to his taste. He loved his homes, but yet he was always moving on.

CHRONICLE

There is little to say of the last months before the Nashes left Hampstead. In March 1939 they were in Bristol for a holiday, when he made several water-colours of Clifton Suspension bridge and gathered material for his essay called *Giant's Stride*.[1] The bridge fascinated him. 'It had an unhappy air like the dream of an ambitious mind, never quite realised. What dream was walled up in this impressive travesty? . . .' he wrote. 'Strange forces had been at work in the Avon Gorge, I felt convinced, not those alone of honest engineering'.

After his return to London he held a small exhibition at Tooths' Gallery—they had now become his sole agents—and a larger one at the Gordon Fraser Gallery in Cambridge. But one has a sense of suspended activities during these waiting months, although Nash continued to work, writing *Outline* in the early hours before breakfast, painting or gardening.

An old friend visited him often—Alice Daglish. She would drop in to find him among his plants or in his studio, where her portrait hung that had been painted nearly twenty years before in the peace of Dymchurch. 'Paul said he wanted me to have it', she has written, 'if we could find someone with a car . . . but we didn't seem to find anyone.' The helpless little incident is heavy with the pressure of the time.

Nash could leave London without embarrassment. Ill as he was, he would, it seemed, be useless to the war if it came, though he was not to be; and the war would be uselessly dangerous to him. There was something valuable he might preserve by leaving London, and on the nineteenth of August the Nashes went to Oxford where they stayed in the Randolph Hotel. He described what happened soon afterwards in a letter to Clare Neilson:

'Margaret had a sudden hunch and we decided to empty the house as far as possible. We went up from here and nearly killed ourselves packing. We managed to get a local carrier before the exodus started and we ourselves returned here more dead than alive a week ago by the last train. . . . Now the house is almost bare. We watched our lovely home break up and vanish under our eyes. We were left sitting about on odd bits of furniture, just crying. Not only have we lost what all that meant to us—and you know what it was—but all Margaret's money and what was left of mine. We have enough to live for a while and a year's supply of my drug.

'But you know it is rather exhilerating beginning again. I dont think either of us minds a damn if only we can keep well. . . .

[1] *Architectural Review*, September 1939. Reprinted in *Outline* without the illustrations.

'After some futile searches we have got some delightful rooms a few doors from here in Beaumont Street.[1] Two poor young things a few months married—just as Margaret and I were at the beginning of the last war, only we weren't actually married—have fallen into our care. He will be snatched up into something but she is taking one of the rooms with us and contributing a little to the rather expensive total. . . . Our idea is to be near the hub of things and see if I cant pick up a job. . . . Incipit vita nuova [nova]. . . .

'I do not look very far ahead. I think we can only live now like certain creatures who in the scheme of Nature have a limited span. It is not true that butterflies live only for a day as people believe but I believe they're rather short-lived and they always seem very gay, except maybe the Large Meadow Brown' (2 September 1939).

ii. Photography

Nash did not take photographs only in the years covered by this chapter, but it is convenient to consider all his photography in one section. He began seriously in 1931[2] with the simple camera his wife gave him for their American journey and which he used to the end of his life.

Nash did not make the usual records of his travels or his friends. His photographs are part of the same imaginative activity as his picture-making, although he wrote that 'photography may not be termed an art, but there are certainly artists in the medium of photography'.[3] He meant by that, I think, that the choice or arrangement of subject is an artistic activity but the mechanical recording of it merely one of skill because nothing is added to the imaginative perception by the act of photographing.

And, indeed, Nash did not profess to use photography as an artistic medium but as what he called 'a complementary science'. 'Its importance', he wrote, 'lies, surely, in the wealth of matter it places at the disposal of the modern sculptor or painter.'[4] He had two distinct uses for it. The first was as an aid to study. 'Photographing has enormously widened my picture vision', he wrote to Ruth Clark, 'so that when I begin on a period of painting I believe I shall feel the benefit, as they say' [1934 c. July]. The second was as a sub-

[1] It was at number seven.
[2] He had taken some photographs years before, for example, the conventional portrait of his wife reproduced in *Outline*, p. 125, and there attributed to 1912, before he had met her.
[3] 'Art and Photography' in *The Listener*, 18 November 1931.
[4] 'Photography and Modern Art' in *The Listener*, 27 July 1932.

stitute for the documentary function of the sketch. His illness made it more and more difficult for him to work out of doors. The camera's record became a way of taking notes. He published one document which shows us the process at work, *Monster Field*, in which he reproduced his photographs of the object, and the water-colours and paintings which he subsequently executed with their help.

At the exhibition of Nash's photographs held by the Arts Council in November 1951, a selection of water-colours was similarly shown with their related photographs. We were able to see how closely Nash adhered to the object as recorded by the camera when he made his water-colour, and yet how entirely free that water-colour is from any photographic quality. The painter's eye entirely superseded the camera's, but the transition was possible and easy because it was the painter's eye which had set the camera to work. In fact the beauty of his photographs is that they 'impart to us his way of looking at things' as James Laver wrote in his introduction to *Fertile Image*, a selection of Nash's photographs which was published at the same time as the exhibition.

It is not necessary to discuss his photographs at any length precisely because they are so closely linked to his paintings, and I shall confine myself to a brief commentary on that selection. It was primarily made by its editor, Margaret Nash, to show his photographs as records of found objects. The first are of the rhythmic and textural relationships of rocks on the Dorset coast, often in parallel or contrast to the movement and texture of the sea (Plate 19.a). The next are of stones cut by man and laid in a wall or set up as a gatepost. It is characteristic that worked stones only interested him for his art when they were old enough for the natural stoniness to have reasserted itself, lichened and irregular.

The second group of photographs is of wood, and here we become aware of a startling change which has taken place. We have seen that trees had fascinated Nash from childhood as living things, as 'personalities'; but most of these photographs are of dead trees or are close-ups of bark. It is the long-lasting skeleton of the tree which now seemed to absorb him rather than its transient foliage. I cannot dissociate this from his pursuit of a symbol for death; and indeed he also found the simplest of all, the human skeletons which he photographed during the excavations at Maiden Castle. But they were more than common skeletons, for they belonged to those ancient beings whose memory inhabited so much of his later imaginative world. Nash described the effect of them on him:

'I was not particularly interested in the archaeological significance of the discovery. But the scene in its dramatic elements had, indeed, an awful beauty. The sun beat down on the glinting white bones which were disposed in elegant clusters and sprays of blanched sprigs and branches. Or some seemed to be the nests of giant birds; the gleaming skulls like clutches of monstrous eggs. It was a place, with these scattered groups of fantastic nests and long raised ledges on the open hills, resembling a bird sanctuary. A sanctuary for moas.'[1]

The innocent radiance of his Bird Garden had changed into this charnel vision of a sanctuary for extinct birds; and in the photographs of the vegetable world which follow, the frail flowers of his earlier work are replaced by plants whose prickly forms or leathery foliage have least suggestion of life. They expose their structures and are vegetable skeletons.

iii. Pictures, Objects and Collages

We are now entering the most important period of Nash's work. After the long study of the natural appearances of objects and of their physical structure, and of structure itself in his abstract or near-abstract works, he is returning to the imaginative and enigmatic world from which he began. The work of mere seeing is done and he turns now to what Rilke called 'heart work', to the release of the pictures secretly germinated within him,

> Denn des Anschauns, siehe, ist eine Grenze,
> Und die geschautere Welt
> Will in der Liebe gedeihn.
> Werk des Gesichts ist getan,
> Tue nun Herzwerk
> An Bildern in dir, jenen gefangenen.[2]

Twenty years earlier he had had that advice from Bottomley which I quoted at the end of my first chapter: 'Our own parish is the only place we need when we would find subjects for our art; but we have to go round the world and enter our own parish anew from the other side before we can see those subjects.' In 1937 or 1938 he must have told Bottomley what was happening, for although the letter is missing we have Bottomley's answer: 'You tell me to take heart because you

---

[1] 'Unseen Landscapes' in *Country Life*, 21 May 1938.
[2] 'Wendung' in *Späte Gedichte*.

are now on the short way home (to the kingdom in which we first met)' (17 January 1938).

Just before his death Nash wrote to Richard Smart that at Swanage he was in his kingdom.[1] But, indeed, his kingdom is not on the map. It was simply that he happened to be living at Swanage when he recognized where he was returning, and began to see clearly the new symbols in which he would describe it. They would no longer be borrowed from Rossetti or Blake, Machen or Blackwood, but discovered for himself, as Yeats described how he had 'worked out with the excitement of discovery things known in [his] youth, as though one forgot and rediscovered oneself'.[2]

The process began at Marlborough, but without immediate result in pictures. Nash produced very little during his subsequent tour abroad, and it is not of particular significance in his development. But a letter he wrote to me from Nice showed in one passage the new direction he was to take:

'I feel I am beginning now to find my way between the claims of 'Abstractions' and pure interpretation. As you know, I am far too interested in the character of landscape and natural forms generally —from a pictorial point of view—ever to abandon painting *after* Nature of some kind or other. But I want a wider aspect, a different angle of vision as it were. This I am beginning to find through symbolism and in the power of association—not the rather freakish unlikely association of objects, so much as the *right* association as I feel it to be . . . I desire to penetrate further—or if you like fling my net wider to include a relationship of spiritual personality—only I suppose I must find another word for spiritual, or be misunderstood. I confess I have not yet reached a very articulate stage but perhaps you see my drift' (14 April 1934).

Here is the germ of the coming development, except that it was not to be a way between abstractions and symbolism but a way clear off from abstractions in the sense of geometrical design. The ruler was to be thrown away: he was from now on to use almost exclusively natural forms, from which he was to abstract their spiritual significance. *That* abstraction he was to go after at full boost. It might seem that the aircraft of 1940 were to be an important exception, and certainly he needed the ruler for them, but he was to use it in a wholly different mode—to abstract the life of these 'aerial creatures',

---

[1] Quoted in full on p. 306.
[2] Quoted without reference in the introduction to *W. B. Yeats: Letters to Katherine Tynan*, Clonmore and Reynolds, 1953.

their personalities as symbols of living forces and not to record their shapes as mechanical contrivances. One other comment must be made on the passage: he was not wholly to escape the 'freakish unlikely association', but sometimes to force, instead of finding, the entity which is created by meetings.

I do not want what I have just said to suggest that abstract art, in the sense of non-representational art, is necessarily without spiritual significance. That would be absurd. I mean it only in relation to Nash, to whom it was really foreign: it was the organic forms of nature that stirred his deepest intuitions. They symbolized for him the mystery of interpenetration and eternal flux, which appears as his view of the universe:

'So life runs on, not cut and dried like some horrible tobacco the Padre smokes, or locked away in an abstract like a fly in amber. But flowing backwards and forwards and throughout; a complex maze of associations which keep the mind guessing, and imagination hovering like that gay summer monster which suggests a nightmare trinity, the elephant-hawk-moth with his inveterate tongue.'[1]

This vision was to dominate his future work. Its surface paradox is that while he was imaginatively conscious of the personality of each being, animate and inanimate, he could imagine them as so completely interpenetrated that they lost personal identity and could even change places, and yet not lose their 'personal' characters. This may be logically nonsense, but Nash was not a logician. The absurdity only comes of trying to put an imaginative vision into logical statements: its 'truth' can only be perceived by the intuitive reason.

It will simplify our discussion of his new development if I begin with the exceptions. For the remainder of his life Nash was to work in the service of his imaginative symbolic pictures; but since his symbols were drawn from nature, he constantly needed to refresh himself at the source. We find him therefore working on two planes. On the lower he simply noted appearances in rapid water-colour sketches. But even these were not mere topographical records: Nash was incapable of such 'scientific' statements. He charged the least sketch with his intuitive experience of the object, through all those qualities which distinguish the work of art from the diagram. These drawings express Nash when he is acting 'naturally' and not sacramentally, not changing the substance of the object into symbol. But none the less, because he always felt symbolically, they suggest the *hidden* symbol. Although we may only see the shell of the egg, we are aware

[1] *The Painter's Object*, a symposium edited by Myfanwy Evans, Gerald Howe 1937, p. 38.

of the potential bird. I shall give instances of these drawings which were later used for overt symbolic expression, but there are others, of course, which were never developed, such, for example, as *Gregynog* and *Road in Wales*, which he made on an excursion from Bristol.

There is another group of such drawings made at Hampstead, where Nash was mostly content to use his physical eye. The 'visionary' was resting and the skilful hand was simply translating appearances into a bright pattern, for though they were mostly made in winter, they are not wintry but gay and vivid in colour. Those, however, which included his grotto—the water-colour *Grotto in the Snow* and the Tate Gallery oil—are symbolic. The grotto, I suppose, is the nest, the safe home, the refuge from the cold and the bare trees. But they are also gay, because the winter is not dangerous: there *is* a nest. All these have that lyric quality which Nash had recognized as essentially English, but now we must turn to those which could more properly be called epic—the creation of his myth.

In his introduction to the catalogue of the Redfern exhibition (1937)[1] Nash made a statement about his new vision, which he seems to have recognized rather as a return to his youthful vision in new terms, because he included some very early work in the exhibition—the *Falling Stars*, for example, of 1912. He did not yet see that he should have included even earlier work:

'Ever since the discovery that pictorially, for me at least, the forms of natural objects and the features of landscape were sufficient without the intrusion of human beings, or even animals, I have pursued a diverse research in land and by the sea, interpreting the phenomena of Nature without ever missing men or women from the scene.

'Gradually, however, the landscape, as a scene, ceased to be absorbing. Some drama of beings, after all, seemed to be necessary. A few attempts to escape into the refuge of abstract design proved me unsuited. But at this point I began to discover the significance of the so-called inanimate object. Henceforth Nature became endowed for me with new life. The landscape, too, seemed now possessed of a different animation. To contemplate the personal beauty of stone and leaf, bark and shell, and to exalt them to be the principals of imaginary happenings, became a new interest.'

It now becomes necessary to consider what part Surrealism played in this. Apparently Nash first became interested in it some seven years after the first Surrealist Manifesto. In 1931 he wrote an article on

[1] Reprinted in *Nash: Eates*, p. 53.

Chirico[1] in which he particularly noted *La Petite Fille au Cerceau*. In *Outline* he described an event in Kensington Gardens which he had seen as a child. A hoop moved by itself across an open luminous space. A child, who had been hidden by a tree, soon emerged; but for a moment that isolated hoop had imaged very precisely the presence of the absent. The presence of the child was *more acute* in its absence. The memory of this must surely have played its part in his strong reaction to Chirico's rather different but related event. 'This picture', he wrote, 'is the record of an experience outside the normal consciousness'; and he went on to describe Chirico in terms which could be applied to his new self: 'Chirico must be seen simply as a creative artist in two senses of pictorial drama—the subject drama and the aesthetic drama. He has, in his best moments, an extraordinary power to make things *happen* in a picture. . . . They happen with all the startling event of a vision or a dream.'

He saw what all this might contribute to his own art, but he feared 'the dangerous charms of Surrealism'.[2] In 1933 he wrote enthusiastically about Max Ernst[3] and again he seized on the material of interpenetration that existed also in his own imaginative life—'the disconcerting association of birds and flowers, suns and forests—suns which look like targets, forests which more resemble seas'. But he insisted that it was disconcerting and still feared it, for if we want to understand Ernst we must 'abandon' ourselves to his vision and that, he added 'is not to say it is wise for your soul but, if you can follow the sublime or dangerous explorations of Ernst's mind, you will encounter new experiences; and you must face evil as well as good'. But he was not, like so many Surrealists, attracted by evil, nor did he ever accept or even bother about all the ethical and political nonsense in the official Surrealist programme. Still less did he share their pessimism. 'Their space is black to hide its emptiness; his space, transparently empty, remains blue', John Armstrong said at the time.[4] The triumph of Nash's optimism is that in his last period, the blue was inhabited by flowers.

But he did not wholly escape the 'trimmings' of Surrealism. He sometimes indulged in the 'amusing' game of *putting* the sewing-machine and the umbrella on the dissecting table; whereas, of course, the essence of Lautréamont's classic phrase, the sacred text of Surrealism, lay in accident—*la rencontre fortuite*. When Lawrence Gowing,

[1] *The Listener*, 29 April 1931.
[2] 'Contemporary American Painting' in *The Listener*, 4 November 1931.
[3] 'Art and the English Press' in *Week-end Review*, 17 June 1933.
[4] 'The Present Tendency of Paul Nash' in *Apollo*, Vol. XVI, No. 95, November 1932.

an admiring but not idolizing young artist, met Nash in 1942, he went home and noted these diversions with regret:

'He is now, as he said "involved" with the surrealists, has an enormous collection of amusing cuttings and photographs, he calls them his monsters and passes them round after dinner. One of Lady Oxford talking to two soldiers—"Margot is the monster here," he said. I feel that this vein is hopelessly at war with the talents for which I respected him.'

But although Nash played with this forced Surrealism in scrapbooks and objects, he gave it little scope in his pictures. And he did not even play with the Surrealist belief in the value of automatic painting or writing: he never repudiated the part which conscious control must exercise in art. He made this plain in a letter to Hartley Ramsden, who had recently discussed his work in an article called 'Paul Nash: Surrealism in Landscape':[1]

'Of course aside from the emotional content there is a very definite insistence on design—on form and colour. And there is too, what is not so Surrealist (with a large S) a feeling for painting itself—I mean quality of paint. I would have it understood that all these are vital matters to me in making a picture and my preoccupation with them is perhaps the chief point of departure from the "automatic" painting of the surrealists. Of course I am not alone here; from Picasso sideways you have painters working under the Surrealist idea who are both painters and designers. But this is not always made clear to the uneducated' (20 February 1941).

In the same way, we find that his attitude towards the dream element in Surrealism was strictly that of the conscious artist:

'The problem of the dream world for the artist is, like that of any other world which lies before him, to determine its pictorial value, and although this particular world may seem at first inscrutable and too alarming even to begin to define, already a vast amount of material has been drawn up from the quarried wastes and hewn into new forms and meanings for the uses of art and literature.'[2]

Nash, then, was never a Surrealist but he was influenced by Surrealism, which primarily meant for him 'the release of imprisoned thoughts, of poetry and fantasy',[3] which was the release also from the puritan and formalist discipline through which he had been passing. 'The constipated negativism of our dismal Mandarins', he wrote, with

[1] *Country Life*, 2 January 1942.
[2] 'Surrealism in Interior Decoration' in *Decoration*, June 1936.
[3] 'Personal View' in *Manchester Evening News*, 12 February 1937.

an eye on Roger Fry, 'has set up such a neurosis in the often timid minds of English painters and writers that they dare not freely express their true selves, their real selves, their surreal selves.'[1]

Probably the specific element in Surrealism which was most useful to Nash was the evocation of disquietude in the 'strange encounters', the meeting with a footprint that signals the presence of the absent.

We find man's footprint, as I have said, in nearly all Nash's work. Untamed and uninhabited nature held little significance for him. In his work the field was always bounded by hedge or fence; the sea faced by a wall; the forest traversed by a path; the garden framed by a window. The very sky was inhabited by birds or aircraft, the personal sun or moon, man's self or man's symbol. He contemplated man at a remove; and by an inverted perspective, he saw him bigger, more awful and disquieting, the further he was in time and space from his footprint. Nash's landscape was inhabited by an immense absence rather than with the petty presence of a poor, bare, forked animal. Human nature was not for him a 'punctual presence', but, as for Wordsworth:

> *a spirit*
> *Diffused through time and space, with aid derived*
> *Of evidence from monuments, erect,*
> *Prostrate, or leaning towards their common rest*
> *In earth, the widely scattered wreck sublime*
> *Of vanished nations.*[2]

But Nash not only virtually expelled man's body from the world of his work, but he broke the boundaries of his personal identity as man, interfusing him with vegetable nature and the inhabitants of the sky. He found personality more tremendous when he had imaginatively transposed it into stone or tree or sun. He *knew* of course that these things are not persons, but he found the marks of personality in their 'character' as experienced by persons or in their shape as modified by persons. He was himself mirrored in the tree he contemplated. He found the long-dead Briton resurrected in the monolith: the child moving in its hoop through the luminous space: the soul living as a bird in the mansions of the dead. It was a vision of being without distinction, but symbolized in the distinct and closely observed mark,

---

[1] 'Surrealism and the Illustrated Book' in *Signature*, March 1937.
[2] *The Prelude* (1850), VIII, 610.

to which he transferred personality. It was also a vision of being without hierarchy. In his pursuit of the 'nightmare trinity', the elephant-hawk-moth, he was compelled to diminish the rôle of the human being precisely because it might 'steal the scene' *and he knew it*. He could only persuade himself and us that the stone or tree had personality by isolating it from the competition of human personality. But, of course, his whole imaginative procedure here reasserted it, for the personality he projected into the stone or tree *was* a human personality: his own. And he reasserted the hierarchy in which man is supreme among created terrestrial existences: he reasserted himself as the image of the Creator by his own act of creating stone or tree in his own likeness.

But at the same time, by his removal of man from immediate presence and presentness, he could find the footprint to be a closer image of the immortal soul than the Academy portrait of yesterday's mayor; and if Man Friday had been dead a thousand years and his footprint a fossil, he would have found the image so much the closer.

One of his earliest drawings—it was shown in his first exhibition—was called *Their Hill*. It was of a Berkshire hill cut into lynchets. The owner of the hill, Lord Henry Bentinck, asked him why he had given it that title. He answered: 'I felt it was the sort of hill which could not belong to anyone in particular, but to an ancient people perhaps, or to fairies even.'[1] This had nothing to do with archaeology which he angrily disliked. 'He has no interest in the past as *past*', Myfanwy Evans wrote, 'but [in] the accumulated intenseness of the past as *present*.'[2] He felt that the past should be left alone in its *natural* presentness, neither preserved nor destroyed. When he revisited Avebury after the archaeologist had been at work, he wrote that the 'primal magic of the stones' appearance was lost'[3] and when he revisited Stonehenge he felt that anyone 'airing archiological small talk should be fined five shillings and hustled into the highway with the utmost ignominy conceivable'.[4]

Many of his pictures show the marks of the absent in the landscape itself, in the earth they shaped. *Silbury Hill* [1938?] is probably the best known example because of its commercial reproduction. The hill stands like a pyramid in the wave-like fields, and beyond it is a domed hill crowned with trees, the image of Wittenham Clumps which from now on recurred in his work with growing insistence. It

[1] *Outline*, p. 128.
[2] *Axis*. Early winter 1937.
[3] *Picture-History*. See p. 239.
[4] Letter to Audrey Withers [Autumn 1927].

appears in the almost contemporary drawing, *Landscape: West Dorset*, which he made for the Shell Guide, where we have already noted *Badbury Rings* and the castled hill of Corfe.

In a group of landscapes made in 1934 or 1935, which includes *Maiden Castle*, *Hill Architecture* and *Landscape at Pen Pits* (Plate XVI), Nash proclaimed the continuing life in the earth by the wave-like movement he gave it; and since those waves were the handiwork of ancient man, he thereby proclaimed that he still inhabited it. *Pen Pits* is also inhabited by the sun, a solid and aggressive globe, a very old sun whose original flamboyance has withered to the colour of dry mustard, which here and there touches the crests of the swirling blue and purple land. And yet perhaps it is not proper to call this an 'inhabited landscape', in the sense in which Nash used the phrase. He generally meant that man had left an Object in the landscape or that an Object had invaded it or somehow taken charge of it; and therefore, we must examine what the Object meant to Nash before we can consider the true 'inhabited landscapes'.

I use the capital to distinguish between the object as merely perceived and the Object as invested with personality. By force of contemplation, Nash projected himself into the object; which is only a way of saying the opposite—that he absorbed the object into himself, giving it a new subjective reality. This had nothing to do with animism. Nash did not *believe* that the objects he became fascinated with, that he collected round him, photographed, grouped into constructions and even introduced into his paintings—he did not believe that they were personages, conscious living beings, any more than he had believed in his personification of trees.[1] He perfectly well understood what he was doing. He was assuming the ancient right of the poet and of the folk in myth and fable to animate inanimate objects. He said so in an essay on 'The Life of the Inanimate Object',[2] where he claimed as precedents the imagery of the Psalms in which 'floods clap their hands, hills leap and break into song'. But indeed the precedents are in all poetry. Nash, being a poet whose most intense experiences were visual, made his images not in words but in objects. The Object in fact was a metaphor. It remained itself—a piece of wood, a stone, a fungus, a doll's head—but it also became a person whose existence only had 'reality' as an emanation of Nash's existence.

I speak as if this were peculiar to Nash, but of course it is not. It is

[1] See what was previously said on this, p. 81.
[2] *Country Life*, 1 May 1937.

only peculiar to the artistic experience and distinguishes it from the scientific. The scientist *tries* to see objects objectively; the artist *knows* them subjectively. The peculiarity of Nash's attitude is that he gave a twist to the process by imagining that these Objects, subjectively animated, were in fact alive objectively; and that of course was 'alarming'.

But Nash was only quite serious about the Object when he introduced it to pictures. The Objects he constructed or assembled were largely play, and it will be enough to mention three of them: *Goodness How Sad*, where a sea-worn brick supported a piece of coral shaped roughly like the human head and shoulders, and two ivory back-scratchers projected on either side in an attitude of despair; *Victorian Paradox*, where a bone joined to an ivory hand lay up against a wooden upright surmounted by a spindle-shaped object; and *Desert Bird*, where a stone, that was like a headless bird, was poised on another stone.

But it is not with such fabricated meetings that we are concerned in the inhabited landscapes, but rather with the apparition of Objects of more awful personality in natural circumstances. But first I wish to consider the stones, which preceded them.

In the autumn of 1943, at Dudley Tooth's suggestion, Nash began a short survey of his artistic development. He began with the pictures of that year and worked backwards, but only a few fragments were written, and it is only now that I can begin to make use of them. After 1943, he added further fragments on current work. I shall refer to all these by the title Nash used: *Picture History*.[1] The first quotation I want to make concerns the stones:

'The preoccupation of the stones has always been a separate pursuit and interest aside from that of object-personages. My interest began with the discovery of the Avebury megaliths when I was staying at Marlborough in the Summer of 1933. The great stones were then in their wild state, so to speak. Some were half covered by the grass, others stood up in the cornfields were entangled and overgrown in the copses, some were buried under the turf. But they were always wonderful and disquieting, and, as I saw them then, I shall always remember them. . . .

'Their colouring and pattern, their patina of golden lichen, all enhanced their strange forms and mystical significance. Thereafter, I hunted stones, by the sea shore, on the downs, in the furrows.

'In most instances, the pictures coming out of this preoccupation

---

[1] Unfortunately the manuscripts are missing in most cases, and I shall be obliged to use typed and printed copies. Where the manuscript has survived, there are discrepancies between it and the copies, but as those may have been Nash's corrections, I shall use the copies.

were concerned with stones seen solely as objects in relation to landscape, as in the *Landscape of the Megaliths* Series, or as stone objects related to other objects, or groups of objects. But later certain stone personages evolved, such as the stone birds in the *Nest of Wild Stones* and the more "abstract" forms in *Encounter in the Afternoon*.[1] In the later, larger compositions—*Circle of the Monoliths* and *Nocturnal Landscape* the stones have a character influenced by the conditions of Dream.'

Like Bottomley's Goneril in *Lear's Wife*, Nash might have said: 'I lost myself before the giant stones.' But in losing himself, he found himself; he found his own mythology, which would grow from these places where he believed the sun had been worshipped to the sun itself and the sunflower. I am told by Alexander Keiller, the archaeologist who reinstated Avebury, that 'we are ignorant of any "religious" significance of Avebury'; but of course the artist is not bound by such scientific ignorance. What Nash *felt* about these places was religious.

The title *Landscape of the Megaliths* has been given to four pictures— one oil, a lithograph and two water-colours. One of these watercolours I do not know: the other is very like the familiar lithograph (Plate 18), of which Nash wrote:

'Avebury may rise again under the tireless hand of Mr. Keiller, but it will be an archaeological monument, as dead as a mammoth skeleton in the Natural History Museum. . . . Yet it is odd to consider that in my design I, too, have tried to restore the Avenue. The reconstruction is quite unreliable, it is wholly out of scale, the landscape is geographically and agriculturally unsound. The stones seem to be moving rather than to be deep-rooted in the earth.'[2]

Indeed the stones advance diagonally at us from the far distance across a stubble field whose lines parallel their march, growing rapidly larger like the powers that come at one in dreams. In the distance are a domed hill with earthworks and a pyramid hill set in the wave-like movements of the earth. In the left foreground a snake or a snake-like stalk, intertwined with a convolvulus whose flower points at the sun, rears up its head to lie against it. But however complex the symbolism, the design is grandly simple: a quincunx made by the diagonals of the stones and stubble crossing with those of the cast shadows. This is the answer to the closing passage of Nash's contribution to the *Unit One* book:

[1] The oil, not Plate 23 here. See p. 242.
[2] 'Landscape of the Megaliths' in *Art and Education*, March 1939.

19*a*. The Flats
Photograph by Paul Nash

19*b*. Environment of Two Objects. [1937]
Oil

20. Wood on the Hill. [1937]
Water-colour

'Last summer, I walked in a field near Avebury where two rough monoliths stand up, sixteen feet high, miraculously patterned with black and orange lichen, remnants of the avenue of stones which led to the Great Circle. A mile away, a green pyramid casts a gigantic shadow. In the hedge at hand, the white trumpet of a convolvulus turns from its spiral stem, following the sun. In my art I would solve such an equation.'

The oil with the same title is quite different. Two stones occupy the foreground, and the sun has intruded into one of them. They are flanked by domed hills crowned with trees, seen almost in plan. One is contoured with lines of stubble, the other is crossed by curving tracks like the sewing of a tennis ball.

Nash has himself described in *Picture History* another important work associated with this:

'*Circle of the Monoliths* [1938] is a picture of the kind of dream that might come to a sleeper who had lately spent hours on the shore of Swanage Bay where the cliffs are like these cliffs. And not long before the dreamer had walked in a field near Avebury and wondered at the strangely patterned megaliths that stood up here and there between the hedges. Perhaps each place made a very deep impression, deeper than he knew. But in the dream the sea invades the fields, the hedges take the place of breakwaters, the great monoliths and their pools of shadow seem to reappear in the form of needles of white chalk, another kind of monolith. And to complete the magic circle, a spout of water rises from the sea in a narrow cone.

'I do not say I dreamed the picture. It is simply a painting concerned with two landscapes or a landscape and a seascape of particular character and peculiar beauty with whose appearance I was intimate, even enchanted. The paralogism of dream frees me to paint a picture where the two images are fused.'

The same familiar symbolism appears in *Nocturnal Landscape* [1938] where the stones have merged into vegetable growths and stone-birds, which seem ready to fly off the earth to the night sky, so that we are not surprised to find the 'egg-box' from the *Mansions of the Dead* in the left distance. In the right distance, below the green sea and the ragged moon, are the two monoliths and the pierced circular stone of Men-an-Tol near Lanyon. Nash never saw this strange Cornish monument, but he must have seen photographs or drawings and been impressed by the similarity of the circular stone to the Archer's target.

All these pictures are in some degree images of interpenetration—snakes with stalks, breakwaters with hedges, stones with vegetation and birds, and so on—but that theme has been incidental. It becomes the protagonist of the drama in such works as *Stone Tree* [*c.* 1938], where the texture of a monolith merges into bark, or *Stone Sea* (1937), where walls of flat stones break across the landscape like estuaries of the invading tide. In *The Nest of the Wild Stones* [1937] two angular flints, like arrow heads, and two round pebbles are arranged in a hollow in a desolate rolling landscape. Nash wrote of this:

'If I broke all the shells of all my wild stones I should find that precious yolk which is like precious stones, the black core of the flint.

'If stones are eggs they are birds, too. . . . Sculptors knock birds out of stones. By the time they have done with them they are neither birds nor stones. Except Brancusi's. But the stone birds of the field are always both. They do not insist. Perhaps, when they are lying on the ground they are stones, and when they stand up they are birds, but, thank God, they never look like stone birds.'[1]

When he had fondled the eggs at his grandfather's Nash had thought only of their forms: now he is seeing the egg as the symbol of fertility, and the precious life within it as a precious stone. This seems to involve the idea of the philosopher's stone, whose function was to turn the baser metal to gold, to make the sick well—that is, precious—to free man from suffering and to give him back his youth. By its power man would rise again like the phoenix. About the same time Nash painted *The Nest of the Phoenix* (Plate 21). The bird, with human breasts, rises diagonally from a nest shaped like a coiled snake, and beside it indeed is a coiled snake which raises its head parallel to the bird and once again meets the sun. I need not enlarge on the symbolism of this tremendous event, but only recall that Shakespeare wrote: 'Death is now the phoenix's nest.' The Phoenix itself escapes out of death to the inhabited sky: it is the traditional *figura resurrectionis*.

But for the present, I must indicate further inhabitants of the earth. There are the white bird-stones in *Encounter in the Afternoon* (1936), who inhabit a dream world in which the artificial and natural interpenetrate. The foreground 'shore' is a pale blue pavement latticed with white lines which also invade the black 'water' beyond, whose darker blue 'icebergs' also invade the brown hills on the far horizon. And there are the assertive geometrical inhabitants of *Equivalents of the Megaliths*, *Rotary Composition* and *Objects in Relation*, all painted about 1935. Nash explained the intention of these

[1] *The Painter's Object*, p. 38.

242

pictures in a letter to Lance Sieveking, who had bought *Equivalents*. He described Avebury and then went on:

'These groups are impressive as forms opposed to their surroundings, both by virtue of their actual composition of lines and masses and planes, directions and volume; and in the irrational sense, their suggestion of a super-reality. They are dramatic, also, however, as symbols of their antiquity, as hallowed remnants of an almost unknown civilization. In designing the picture I wished to avoid the very powerful influence of this antiquarian suggestion, and to insist only upon the dramatic qualities of a composition of shapes equivalent to the prone or upright stones simply as upright or prone, or leaning masses, grouped together in a scene of open fields and hills. Beyond that resolve the picture cannot be traced, logically. It developed inevitably in its own way' [4 May 1937].

Nash, I think, was beginning to apprehend a larger and older footprint than that of pre-historic man, a footprint in all stones, that was larger and older than even the operations of nature:

> Among these rocks and stones, methinks, *I see*
> More than the heedless impress that belongs
> To lonely nature's casual work: they bear
> A semblance strange of power intelligent,
> And of design not wholly worn away.[1]

These equivalents, on this interpretation, are symbols for the first design in the pure conceptual forms of geometry, and therefore they are symbols for God.

As the megaliths could be replaced by other things, so could the trees. We can see this particularly in three closely related pictures. The first is *Wood on the Hill* [1937] (Plate 20), an expression in more mature and personal language of the same experience which informed its early predecessor with the same title. This picture also derives emotionally from Wittenham Clumps, but the wood is transposed into sections of a glove-stretcher.[2] These bare finger-trees point at the sun which blazes at the central summit of the picture and like spires declare its power, for they are not crowded together into impenetrable darkness but so widely spaced that the circle inside them catches the sun's light, as the chalice catches the precious blood in early Crucifixions.

The second picture is *Wood of the Nightmares Tails* (1937), where

[1] Wordsworth, *The Excursion*, III, 80.
[2] Also used in the Object called *Forest*.

the 'trees' are those plants called Great Horse-tails (Equisetum Telmateia Ehrh.) which are known from fossils to have grown in the carboniferous swamps over two hundred million years ago. Here, on the sea's edge under the moon, are the footprints of life long before man. In the third picture, *Stone Forest*, the 'trees' are bare petrified poles, which startle the imagination with a memory of the trees Nash painted in the dead landscape of the first war, and reiterate how persistent and interfused and interpenetrated his images were. That is emphasized by the huge 'socket' of a 'tree' which lies in the foreground, in the shape of the Phoenix's nest.

Wood, or equivalents for wood, appear in many other pictures, as, for example, the logs that pile up into waves in *Wood Sea* (1937); or the dead trunks that are adrift in the rotting landscape of *Strange Coast* [*c.* 1934] or the gnarled and weathered roots or fragments of bark such as that which lies beside the slow featureless sea in *Andante* [*c.* 1935]. Perhaps the most important of these relics is the stump which meets a tennis ball in *Event on the Downs* [1934]. This is a natural event. Anybody might chance upon the stump and the lost tennis ball on the huge downs, and taking the stump for a wicket and a walking stick for a bat, let his friends bowl the ball at him; but Nash did no such thing. He contemplated the strange meeting and so enlarged the ball that it became the sun fallen and blanched, or perhaps the moon, and he related the curves of its sewing to the tracks over the hills, over the round world. He has left an image that, but for accidents, will survive until the cricketer's bones are found by another Nash to serve as Objects in another image. For bones, also, washed up on the shore, inhabited his world. For example, I take for bone that strange object that stands in an undulating shell on the edge of the quiet sea in *Ballard Phantom* (1935) where the background is the sleeping mass of the headland against a dull orange sky. It is the same Object that appears, with stone and egg, in *Landscape of Bleached Objects* [1933] which Nash took as an example of what he meant by 'unseen landscapes'. These are, he said, 'not part of the unseen world in a psychic sense, nor are they part of the Unconscious. They belong to the world that lies, visibly, about us. They are unseen merely because they are not perceived'.[1]

Nash now largely gave himself to noticing what is generally unnoticed. He combed the beach for jetsam, but the treasures he looked for had neither historical nor market value, nor were they of any use

[1] 'Unseen Landscapes' in *Country Life*, 21 May 1938, reprinted in *Outline* without its illustrations.

21. Nest of the Phoenix. [1937]
Oil

22. Paul Nash in his Studio. 1940

to the police. An oddment of seaweed lies stranded across the fore-ground of *Sunset at Worth Matravers* (1937). Beyond it is an earthwork or perhaps the lynchets of *Their Hill*. The sun, half sunk below the horizon, has splashed the sky and the sea; but its colour is now of dried blood. The sun is dying and the seaweed Object is a stranded sea beast and the men who shaped the hill are invisible. These are the mysteries of time and death in the jetsam on the shores of memory. Sometimes Nash gathered 'jetsam' from the land, a leafy twig or cones and needles blown to the neutral shore, and combined them with the sea's contribution of bark or cork or seaweed into trophies for all powers that detach and scatter. Such are *Object on the Sands* (1935). One of the strangest meetings happens in *Environment of Two Objects* [1937] (Plate 19.b). The Objects are a doll's head, pink and white with glossy black hair, and a half-burnt wooden thing, some piece of turnery, whose origin and purpose are lost. The en-vironment is the smooth black shale of Kimmeridge Bay from which the Britons made bracelets before the Romans came. The pretty trivial toy that a child lost yesterday, now staring aimlessly at the sea, the relic of a burnt ship meets in tragic irony on the platform of a clay, that is bituminous and burns and poisons the air with vapours of sulphurated hydrogen.

There are, of course, many other types of Object and environment in Nash's landscape of this period, such as the vegetable creatures and the slag heap like a pyramid in the *Denizens of the Forest of Dean* [1939] or the fungus that floats on the sea before Ballard Down in *Voyage of the Fungus* [1937] or explodes in a plain, where the trees are cut down to stumps, in *Landscape of the Death Watch* [1938]. But I want to consider more particularly the apparition of the Monster in several pictures of 1938 and 1939. Nash has given a full account of this in *Monster Field*.[1] The Monster Field, in so far as it was anywhere, was in the neighbourhood of Madams.[2] It contained two dead trees 'bleached to a ghastly pallor'. Nash explained his attitude to them in this passage:

'We are not studying two fallen trees that look like animals, but two monster objects outside the plan of natural phenomena. What reference they have to life should not be considered in relation to their past—therein they are dead—they now excite our interest on another plane, they have "passed on" as people say. These now inanimate

---

[1] Originally published in *The Architectural Review*; reprinted as a pamphlet by Counter-point Publications, 1946; and in *Outline* without illustrations, but with errors. I quote from the pamphlet which Nash presumably corrected.
[2] See letter to Clare Neilson, p. 305.

natural objects are alive in quite another world; but, instead of being invisible like so many of that huge community, or only made visible by the complicated machinery of spiritualism, they are so much with us that I was able to photograph them in full sunlight.'[1]

He identified one of them with Blake's horse in *Pity*, but as the sightless courier of the air after it has crashed to earth and fused 'its image with the rigid tree'. This is surely most significant. It was a *flying* monster by nature: an inhabitant of the sky he was soon to enter. He was inclined to identify the other with Picasso's bull in *Guernica* but felt that it was not male—the cow, perhaps, to that bull but 'as mysterious and as dire'. This relation to Picasso's bull also appears in two water-colours, *Monster Pond* (Plate 24) and *Minotaur*, 'a stump by a pool which bore a disquieting resemblance to the Monster'.[2] This is indeed very different from the attitude of 'Robert Derriman', who had so strongly condemned 'the poet' who persisted in finding 'old mens' faces in the trees, . . . serpents in brooks', and so on.[3]

Nash made two water-colours and an oil called *Monster Field* and he also painted an associated picture, *Monster Shore*, in which one of the Monsters appears in a different setting. He began this later, and only finished it after the war had broken out. It is a particularly illuminating example of how he combined observed elements to make his imagined scene. The landscape is almost exactly that of the 'straight' water-colour called *The Severn Bore*, but he has introduced a doorstep into the foreground. This is disquieting indeed and might seem wholly fanciful; but in fact he had come upon and photographed such a doorstep isolated in a field near Swanage, a relic of some destroyed building. He had then used it in a montage with a harp, in obvious reference to Psalm cxxxvii. Now, by the waters of Severn, the steps give on to no Sion but only on to desolation—only on to the flood and the patches of earth it has not invaded where there is nothing but three tree stumps and the Monster. The house and the trees are present in absence: only the Monster is fully *there*.

It was also near Swanage that Nash came upon a three-sided roofless shelter, probably for sheep, which he used in the water-colour called *Inhabited Landscape* [1937]. It stands in an empty and dreary land and shelters an Object like a head and shoulders. The drawing is related to all those in which Nash used the symbol of the Nest,

---

[1] See p. 229.
[2] *Picture History.*
[3] See p. 117 for the whole passage.

which I shall discuss in connection with the series of Bomber Lairs; but I must draw attention here to *Earth Home or The Fortress*. Nash said that this was based on 'the miraculous design of the fortress of the mole',[1] but he set it on the surface of the landscape so that it became also the labyrinth—'one of the oldest symbols of the haunt of the enigma'.[2] But the symbolism has a particular and temporal meaning. Man at that time—it was drawn in 1939—was in prospect of insufficient shelters. Even the Underground Railway, a labyrinth which had left its Minotaur in the sky, was vulnerable to that flying Monster. This *exposed* shelter, this inadequate mole's fortress, has all the implications of the burrow in Kafka's tale.

The concept of interpenetration, at least implicit in all the works we have recently discussed, is explicit and dominant in a small group of pictures where Nash returns to the image he had discovered in the café at Toulon, the double mirror reflecting 'reality' and reflecting reflections, in a symbol of infinity. It occurs, for example, in the Tate Gallery oil *Voyages of the Moon* (1934), where a moon, which is an electric light fitting, travels far down an endless corridor of these self-reflecting reflections; and in *Metamorphosis* [*c.* 1937], where we follow a long corridor of reflections to the track of the sun's reflection in water to the sun itself just above a far horizon which, of course, in 'reality' is behind us through the café window. It occurs also in a simpler form in *The Different Skies* [1939]. An attic window at Madams is half open, and through the opening is a calm and summer landscape, but a stormy sky, rent with lightning, a terrible and dangerous sky, is reflected in the window-pane. We may interpret this on the surface as an image of the threat of war, but it is also of other and more universal threats.

The last picture I wish to speak of in this chapter is one of Nash's most remarkable and most enigmatic works, the Tate Gallery oil *Landscape from a Dream* [1938].[3] A great deal of Nash symbolism is combined here. The scene is on the Downs above Swanage. A folding glass screen runs diagonally into the picture from the right, but soon meets an immense square mirror set parallel to the picture-plane. The hawk stands at the meeting place, with its back to us. Through the screen are the blue bay and the headland beyond. In the mirror, is the face of the hawk. Beside the hawk is a ball of dried grass, whose

[1] *Bombers' Lair*. See p. 275.
[2] 'Paul Nash 1889–1946' by Richard Seddon, *Studio*, March 1948.
[3] There is also a water-colour of almost exactly the same design. The hawk used in the composition was an Egyptian carving now on Nash's grave. The ball of dried grass derived from a film in which he had seen such things blowing across the prairie.

reflection leads to the sun that touches the horizon of reflected hills. The sky, which is directly seen, is a serene blue, but the reflected sky is blood-red and inhabited by the massive red sun and a flying hawk. Nash was indeed returning to his parish, but it is no longer Spring at the Hawk's Wood.

IX

Oxford
September 1939-July 1946

———✦———

i. Chronicle to January 1945

Nash was deeply moved by the impact of the war in 1939 and not merely irritated by a disturbance as he had been in 1914. He was moved not only by the prospect of man's suffering, which he had learnt to know in 1917, but also by a conviction that this war was necessary, just and of the greatest possible importance to mankind, a crusade not only for the liberty of his country but also for the liberty of thought and of the artist throughout the world. He saw Nazism as the diabolic Monster. There could, of course, be no question this time of his fighting it physically, but he immediately undertook what was in his power.

His first activity was to found the Arts Bureau in Oxford for War Service, a sort of information bureau to help government departments make the best use of artists' special qualifications.[1]

We have seen how the Nashes were sharing rooms in Beaumont Street with a young couple. The husband, Maurice Cardiff, became secretary of the Bureau, and at the beginning of October they opened an office at 62 Holywell, where they also lived. Nash was chairman of the executive committee, which included Lord Berners, Lord David Cecil, John Betjeman, John Piper and Albert Rutherston. Besides this artistically impressive committee there was a Panel of Authorities, as it was called, which ranged from the Vice-Chancellor to Major-Generals and included Sir Kenneth Clark. But in spite of

---

[1] Nash gave a full account of the foundation and early life of the Bureau in 'Letter from Oxford' in *The Listener*, 30 November 1939.

this powerful support the Bureau did little more than prepare the way and supply some material for other organizations. And Nash soon began to feel that he had something more important to do than office work. 'I want to explain [the war]', he wrote to Sieveking. 'I expect I shall find a way, if only the damned asthma would let up a bit. . . . I want to paint and whats more I wanna paint reccuds' (22 November 1939).

In January 1940, the Bureau began to hand over its dossiers to other organizations, and by March it had completed this and ceased to function.

In the meantime Nash had been approached just before the new year to undertake work as an official artist, for which he had been recommended by the War Artists Advisory Committee, and in March 1940 he was appointed to work for the Air Ministry. A medical board refused him permission to fly, but he had every other opportunity of becoming familiar with aircraft. He was to try for permission again in late 1941, but it was again refused and to the end he never flew in the body; and yet he was to convey the feeling of flight better than any other artist. I shall not trace the various visits which Nash paid to Bomber stations, but it may help the dating of his work to mention that he began with Wellingtons and Whitleys and did not meet the Blenheim until late August. At the same time, he was also making studies of crashed German aircraft. There was at least one officer in the Air Ministry who disapproved of these, not on artistic grounds but because, as he expressed it, the hunting man prefers a picture of a horse to one of a dead fox. It was not a point of view that Nash was likely to understand.

Nash soon became absorbed in his work, but all the time he was battling with his asthma and with money difficulties. Towards the end of the year he explained his position to the Chairman of the Committee, Kenneth Clark:

'Please do not think anything would induce me to leave my Air Ministry work, short of positive dismissal or the firing squad. I have never before had such a stimulating adventure as an artist and, of course, its possibilities of development are infinite.

'No, all I want is enough money to keep me and my modest home alive in order to make the most of the opportunity the Air Ministry job gives me. At the moment I am embarrassed by debts which had to be incurred. I have to live in a particular way which is not luxurious but rather soft. I have to buy an expensive drug all the time. At this particular moment when I am most embarrassed my teaching

job folds up—thus depriving me of £120 per ann.[1] All outside sales
suddenly cease, and my salary of £650 is invaded by the income tax
monsters. Actually this salary is worth £520 now. I really can't bore
you with more details but the rigid obstinate fact in front of me is
that I must be able to add to my salary. . . .

'The difficulty is however, that this job is so absorbing that it is
extremely irksome to switch my mind off it at all, and I would so
much prefer any other means of making more money than a different subject matter.

'Let me tell you what I want to do. I am passionately anxious just
to strike a blow on behalf of the R.A.F., apart from any triumph of
art for its own sake. I am acutely conscious of the position I hold and
what I believe to be its responsibility. I want to use what art I have
and what I can make as directly as possible in the character of a
weapon. I have always believed in the power of pictorial art as a
means of propaganda. I think picture leaflets should have been used
if they were not, and a number of other devices directly appealing to
the eye *quickly*, striking and leaving an impression before any power
can prevent the impact.

'Photography is useful, of course, but it is too general, too much
taken for granted. . . .

'So, I feel the artist must come in' (8 November 1940).

In the meantime, in July, the Nashes had moved into a ground-
floor flat at 106 Banbury Road, which was to be his last home. His
studio gave on to what he described to Clare Neilson as 'a huge
garden, all lawn and borders *between red brick walls*. Lovely to develop
if one can think of any future'. And indeed he was to make this grain
of sand—for it was a very modest garden—into a vegetable world of
his own, where the sunflowers were to hold Infinity. For there, in this
back room which he called his ivory basement, he was able to escape
into himself and recover his kingdom. Now the visionary was rising
again, but through many entanglements. His letters show him becoming the victim of moods, growing ever more extreme, blacker and
brighter, as his struggle against his difficulties retreated or advanced.
For the remainder of his life they were written at the oddest hours,
for by now his illness was attacking sleep. Gradually, one feels, time
edged out of the back room at Banbury Road, night merged with day.
The following extracts from the letter to Clare Neilson from which
I have just quoted, will illustrate his rapid alternations:

'What can you think of me. I am quite a case now about not writ-

[1] The Royal College of Art was evacuating to the Lake District.

ing. I write quite often to you and a few chosen, in my head and sometimes may be heard mumbling and intoning to myself as I wander in the College gardens or thread my way through the Oxford streets jostled by the late British Expeditionary Force from France and the more recent female force of expeditionaries from Piccadilly and Leicester Square. . . .

'We have had the most awful time. I get very wretched often and pray for death. What can come out of such madness. I could not have dreamed of such horrid depths of the human mind. Worst of all is the defilement of our own people from the stench of the Boches, what shall we be fighting for soon. Margaret has been very unwell. We are quite miserable often. . . .

'The R.A.F. work is increasingly absorbing and exciting. Now it begins to develop. As an earnest of my intentions I have just had set up in Woburn Place[1] a canvas ten feet by fifteen!' [8 July 1940].

Or here again are passages from a letter to Ruth Clark:

'I suppose we shall all end by dosing ourselves. I well understand the despair which is growing. I do not believe it comes so much because of a sense of terror or defeat as from the inability to believe that this mighty effort of blood and pain and heroism is vain.

'No new, better world will come of it, can you believe—I cannot. On every hand we have the shopkeepers making their profits . . . and the Civil Servants and the politicians whipping up the exhausted people, draining them dry, shouting or simply announcing into their deafened ears You can take it. . . .

'Captain Balfour[2] has written to say how much he likes drawings I have done for them. This rather gives me my Wings!' [1940 c. November].

It therefore came as a surprise to Nash when he learnt later in November that his appointment with the Air Ministry was to be terminated at the end of the year, although at the same time the Ministry of Information invited him to work for them. This was to be far more satisfactory for Nash, but at the moment he protested indignantly. The Air Ministry was within its rights, because it was a fixed policy that artists should be changed from one department to another at intervals of about six months, and Nash's service had already been extended to nine. He had known this but forgotten it, and he was justified in complaining that when he had discussed future plans, they had not reminded him. But his indignation was chiefly because, although he knew that his work had been appreciated by the pilots,

[1] A studio lent to him by the Air Ministry.   [2] Under-Secretary of State for Air.

23. Encounter in the Afternoon. 1940
Water-colour

24. Monster Pond. [1941]

he believed that there were forces working against him in high places at the Ministry, individuals whose 'tailor and cutter' view of art disapproved of the liberties he took with the dimensions of aircraft. But so far as I can ascertain—and I have seen the files—there was only one such individual. In Nash's eyes the whole Ministry had to bear his sins. 'I have ceased to work for the Air Ministry,' he wrote to my wife. 'They engaged me as an official artist but forgot to imagine that being an artist might mean more to me than being an official' [1941 c. January].

The Christmas of 1940 was a failure. What happened at Christmas always mattered a good deal to Nash, for he had the sense of feasts and occasions, and would celebrate them whenever possible. He still gave valentines to his wife. This year, he told Clare Neilson, 'Margaret was sick all day. . . . We were left quite alone: no service to be had. Outside in the cold larder, our goose sat solid and uncooked' (27 December 1940).

But the New Year opened more brightly. Nash began to work for the Ministry of Information on a much freer basis. They had first refusal of all his war work at reduced prices, for which advantage they gave him travelling and maintenance allowances, facilities to visit Air Force and other service establishments and the cost of his materials. What they did not want, he could sell at his own prices. But as it worked out, his large oils of this year, *The Battle of Britain* and *The Defence of Albion*, were definitely commissioned.

In this chronicle of Nash's last years I can use even more letters than hitherto, to render the movement of his inner life, for more have been preserved and they are more revealing. I must print many that are sad and strained, but I must counteract them by others to show that he kept his sense of humour and love of nonsense—trivial letters, perhaps, but necessary to the understanding of his courage. Here, for a first example, is an extract from one to Lance Sieveking—'dear old creature'—who had been staying with them at the beginning of the year, and photographing Nash:

'It was damn bad luck we couldn't do better but I knew I couldn't manage that cold and misty posturing you required. . . .

'Since then we have been ill and busy. We cracked every nerve and muscle preparing for the establishing of a German (Jew) housekeeper who looked and sounded promising . . .

'She is just a poor dumb exasperating termite. Otherwise she is a nice old noodle who is driving Margaret rapidly crackers, nuts, nerts and bugs' . . . [11 February 1941].

253

In early March Nash spent a week in the Acland Home, and it must have been about then that he reopened his correspondence with Bottomley. It had never completely broken, but the letters had thinned out in recent years and there had been none since the war began. Then they simultaneously sent out feelers. Bottomley wrote on the twenty-ninth of March, beginning: 'Would you mind telling me where you are?' and Nash had written a letter which would have crossed Bottomley's, had it not been mislaid. But he found it to enclose with his answer:

'You know Gordon I am now as old as you were when you wrote many of those letters—listen "Your aged friend (I was 53 yesterday—isnt it a damnable business) Gordon."

'I shall be 53 in May! Yet a moment ago I was still thinking of you as the sage and myself as the young artist seeking advice. . . . I seem to have gone on quite inconsiderately considering myself as young. Am I that most trying of all forms of life a peter-pan! God forbid. Be your age! . . .

'You may remember I was trying to write my 'life', I am still trying. . . . The happy, hazy past—yet, not so hazy perhaps I have been living in it considerably lately.' (1941 c. end of March.)

This was followed by a brisk correspondence, as in the early days, but I shall quote little from it as it is available in print, and I have so many other sources for this period which are not. For example, there is a gay letter to Clare Neilson, only a little touched by autumn:

'Time totters on and still no word from the snug wooded hollows of Madams where you live like some lovely wicked monster-insect surrounded by your endless relations. What about the poor male mantis as it were . . . where does he get a look in? He yearns for woods and Nature's Bounty, westering suns and the daft hootings of cuckoo birds. He was never meant for a subub creature and he pines suburbanly. At the same time there is a garden now created here which is no mean effort. . . . Well, anyway give me a ring one evening, I feel rather neglected . . .' (25 April 1941).

Within a month he sent Ruth Clark a deeply depressed letter:

'Forgive such a delay. I can't seem to cope with letters at all. I don't get on with my work, I don't get on with my book I'm just a mental mess. Your letters have been very welcome. It's good to hear nice things about myself I find in my state of insecurity. . . .

'Before we left London Mouse and I crowded in a visit to Cheapside and all that by taxi . . . moving in its queer dismal beauty. Very hard to detach from sentiment. I am quite miserable about it all and now in a sort of despair. . . . Just heard that Tooth's is quite destroyed. I have lost a few drawings one was one of the best I'd done alas—and no photograph. . . .

'Mouse is ill again and complaining terribly. I am worried stiff. . . . Our problem gets steadily more opaque and stinking' (20 May 1941).

But a visit to Madams soon after this was written seems to have cheered Nash. He was soon writing to Richard Smart: 'I am sending you something to amuse you the first fruits of my new "line" of Portable Pictures, a Nash in the hand is worth two in the Blitz. Watercolours for the Wallet and so on' (17 June 1941); and to Hartley Ramsden: 'I am most interested to hear of your swaying about on top of your isolation pinnacle. It is rather disconcerting too because I had just begun to climb painfully up a pinnacle myself, carefully drawing it up after me so that when I got to the top I should be quite free of the earth. However one goes on like this up and down, hither and thither' (20 June 1941). It is precisely that that I am trying to illustrate with these extracts from letters—the vicissitudes of Nash's inner life.

One aspect of it was a return to his interest in Rossetti. He had been particularly moved by seeing his drawings again at Rothenstein's when he had paid him a visit from Madams, and he began to ask Bottomley questions about him because he was planning to write on Kelmscott. He had, he told him, fallen in love with Rossetti all over again and stood 'bare headed before the early water colours' and nearly all the poetry (August 1941). And so it went on through letter after letter—not only an excitedly revived interest in Rossetti but in the whole romantic Pre-Raphaelite world. Bottomley's answers were full of the same enthusiasm and a great deal of information; and they passed to the same shared love of Calvert and Samuel Palmer. It was indeed the old correspondence reviving, the parish being revisited. And a nostalgia was invading him for all the past of his life. Referring to some drawings of Cagnes which he had given to Sieveking he said: 'I'm so glad you like the frail drawings, those whispers from the peaceful happy past of both our lives I'm glad I was able to salvage those last two fragile echos' (29 January 1942). He was listening, too, to these whispers as he continued at intervals to work on *Outline*.

It was in the same pursuit that he revived his friendship with Percy Withers, who now lived at Epwell Mill near Banbury. He mentions a visit to him in an immense and entertaining letter to his brother:

'Ive been trying to get a letter written—this seems a good moment going up in the train. M[argaret] has just got into conversation with two old women and a baby and is giving them all a lot of mixed general information on the war, Russian Sovietism and child well fare. One woman has so far made no contribution. She just stares at M. The baby either stares at me in an abstracted sort of way or goes to sleep with mouth open. The other woman . . . began well with a long rehearsal of last years bombing of Balham and Streatham—(you know the old Regal Cinema in the corner well, its gone, blown flat,) M, out of courtesy I suppose, pretended an intimate knowledge of Balham but I think this was strategic as I now hear only M's voice telling the women, now passive listeners, about the magical properties of tomatoes (against rickets) and fruit juices for everything else. This has been followed by a frightful whispering by old rusty about asthma. Shes noticed my "puffer" but I'm supposed not to hear at the end of the carriage. All I do hear is—"I remember my poor sister just before she died," hiss hiss shiss. She is discouraged on this topic and the baby causes a panic by suddenly smiling. . . .[1]

'Now all have got down into the tubes and deep shelters. M is quoting Lord Horder but I think the women have confused this personality with the Minister of Food. Now M has led her audience into the Moscow shelters where it seems to be so safe and comfortable that I shall leave them. . . .[1]

'I'm sorry to hear about your great boredom. In the Last War I seem to remember a fairly tolerable mixture even in the Mess at Gosport. . . .

'Recently I finished a large canvas on the Battle of Britain—a daring shot rather which I hope has come off. Our K [Kenneth Clark] seems very warm about it and Dicky [E. M. O'R. Dickey] is excited. I reckon myself very fortunate to have found a second time true inspiration in the subject of war. I feel too a sort of responsibility beyond what is naturally owed to myself, as it were, as an artist. I try to make my work strike a blow in that much neglected field—Propaganda—a good picture first but if possible a picture to make you feel good (or, if you're a Nazi, not so good) Well well, there goes the old bore again which makes me think, zip my pants! but you should never be out of line among even Royal Scotch Marines[2] because, damme, look at the variety of things you know about. . . . You're a rummy old cock! Fry my giddy liver we spent a long weekend at Percy's the other day after a lapse of *years*. . . . The Dove hadn't

[1] No omission.
[2] John Nash was now in Scotland as a captain in the Royal Marines.

25. The Vale of the White Blackbird. [1942]
Oil

26. Landscape of the Vernal Equinox. 1943–1944. *Oil*

stayed with them for 18 years. Oh boy. The old packet was in the Acland Home for a week and came in to see us and was in a fine state of emotional hyperbole I'll say. . . . But of course on his own base old Percy hoisted his old colours. . . . He picked on poor M something terrible and when I accidently rang the bell when I went to bed early instead of turning on the light over the bed Percy heard about it and burst out—He must be *Half Witted*. . . .

'I droole on . . .[1] so sorry to have taken so long. . . . Best of luck old dear' [1941. ?November].

From Epwell the Nashes visited Mrs. Michael Asquith at Scarlet-Sub-Edge near Stow-on-the-Wold, and after a short stay in London they returned to Oxford. 'Far away in this Rip van Winkle paradise,'[2] the Nashes gave a modest Christmas Eve dinner to his sister and two other guests. They would not let go of their celebration altogether.

Nash began 1942 with bronchitis, and even by the end of March he could still only report to Clare Neilson that for weeks he had been more or less idle—'just somehow unable to get on, sick with the cold, and worried by Margaret's ill health and the house work' [26 March 1942]. He wanted to get on with a big picture, *The Defence of Albion*, and a series of propaganda designs and the material for an exhibition of water-colours. Everything hung fire, and in an effort to break what seemed the unhappy spell of their driven life at Oxford, they took a short holiday in April at the Three Swans in Hungerford, Berkshire. It was an occasion for being with a very old friend indeed, his cousin Nell Bethell. She was now married, and she and her husband kept this simple and attractive fisherman's hotel.

Soon after his return to Oxford, Nash heard from the Ministry of Information that they would no longer expect him to sell them pictures at reduced prices, but on the other hand would no longer pay his expenses. They only asked for the first refusal of war pictures. He was now free to paint what he liked and sell it at what prices he could get. They did however continue to commission individual pictures, which included *The Defence of Albion*, on which he now resumed work. He delivered it by the first of May.

A letter to Clare Neilson reintroduces the subject of Nash's reading:

'You ingrate! Are my water colour "gems" (water colours for the wallet series) and my inspired monsters specially enlarged photographically and my handsome enlargements specially done for you

[1] No omission.
[2] Letter to E. M. O'R. Dickey, 31 March 1941.

of the Madams sequence (altho not yet complete) are these *nothing*. I know I do not keep dates but I keep faith—Impecunious asthmatical grasshopper that I am I cannot send you worldly gifts. I can but express myself in a few tones and colours on a few bits of paper. But there was a day when I eagerly opened my parcel to find some rare book precious to me not for its costliness so much as its worth in spirit since it was so often not only an inspiration to me—Perspective and the Avebury volumes have both yielded material for pictures—but a charming compliment as expressing your *thought* for my work through myself. Not that I have not treasured the more ephemeral tokens of scarves and jackets but you have a surer taste in books.[1] I cannot help feeling that it no longer amuses you to find me a special book and that saddens me' (8 June 1942).

I could not identify the Perspective book when I examined Nash's library, but the other must have been, I think, *Avebury. A Temple of the British Druids with some others* described by William Stukeley, London, 1743. During these years at Oxford, Nash acquired a number of old books on archaeology and astronomy, whose illustrations he brooded on. We have seen that he was not a steady reader and certainly he did not read these books nor was he in the least troubled at their being out of date. It was not scientific information that he wanted but food for his imagination. This was the sort of books he brooded over: *Cloudland* by Rev. W. Clement Ley, Stamford, 1894; *Organic Remains of a Former World. An Examination of the Mineralised Remains of the Vegetables and Animals of the Antediluvian World generally termed extraneous Fossils* by James Parkinson, Nattali, 1833; *The Gallery of Nature. A Pictorial and Descriptive Tour through Creation* by the Rev. Thomas Milner, Orr, 1849; *Travels in the Air* by James Glaisher etc., Bentley, 1871; *Rude Monuments in all Countries. Their Age and Use* by James Ferguson, Murray, 1872; *Palaeontology or a Systematic Summary of Extinct Animals and their Geological Relations* by Richard Owen, Black, 1861.

On the other hand, he seems to have read Frazer's *Golden Bough*, although he probably never read it through. Indeed, he had only the abridged one-volume edition and odd volumes of the complete work, and they are not all cut.

In June Nash held an exhibition of water-colours at the Redfern Gallery which began successfully. 'But just when all was swinging along we bumped into trouble. Since Tobruk I understand not one has been sold . . .' he told Clare Neilson, writing from Hungerford.

[1] See pp. 47 and 48.

'M and I came here for a small break. M has been and still is in a rotten state of health. I am very worried. . . . Life just gets mingier and mangier—we dwindle, the lights dim, the shadow creep nearer. The only thing to do is to keep ones eye steady on the target' (29 June 1942).

Nash now had a new doctor—yet another one—who refused to believe him incurable, 'which' he told Hartley Ramsden 'is quite a new view' (9 June 1942). It was also, of course, a wrong one. But he was active and lively at Hungerford, I am told by Nell Bethell's daughter, driving about the country with them, sitting alertly in the back seat and making quick sketches of clouds. One of these drives was to the Avebury megaliths, a visit which Nash described in *Picture History*:

'They were altogether changed in appearance collectively. The work of re-instating and ordering the Circles had been completed. Sometimes the effect was immensely impressive. I made a few rapid drawings and took a spool of photographs. Again the spell of these deeply moving monuments began to work upon me. I wanted to study anew their disquieting beauty, to live near them for a time. . . .

'As soon as possible, perhaps this summer I hope to return.'

But it was his last visit to the Stones.

There is that picture; and then there is the desolating picture in a letter he wrote to Burra in September: 'We now live such a dot and carry one existence and are so indescribably falling apart—not from each other but just each one—that the slightest extra effort annhilates us. Its so boring. So often we want to die. I cant explain' [11 September 1942].

In October he retreated to Madams for a week and worked well; and then in November found another and nearer retreat, the house of Hilda Harrisson[1] at Boar's Hill, where he was to paint some of his best late work. In the far distance, over the Bagley Woods, he could see Wittenham Clumps.

The Christmas of 1942 was spent at a London hotel but it was not a success. Margaret Nash was ill and Paul poisoned his thumb, which did not recover fully unil February. 'But with practice I believe' he told Herbert Read[2] 'I could paint L handed. I find that an encouraging thought for my last phase' (26 December 1942). It was a

---

[1] The friend to whom the letters were written which Desmond Macarthy edited as *Henry Herbert Asquith: Letters of the Earl of Oxford and Asquith to a Friend*, 2 vols., Bles, 1933 and 1934.

[2] Unfortunately the many letters from Nash to Read have been mislaid. Two letters, which had become detached from the collection, are all Read has been able to find. This has led to a bad distortion: Read's name should have occurred frequently in this book.

most unlucky interruption. The demand for Nash's work was growing rapidly. In January 1943 Dudley Tooth reported that two buyers for oils and six for water-colours were 'all teed up' and in May that the queue had grown to over thirty.

Now Nash had success indeed, but his illness and his domestic worries prevented him from enjoying it. Nor was he able to get on with painting. First he was distracted by having to prepare a loan exhibition of his industrial designs which the Council for the Encouragement of Music and the Arts held at the Ashmolean Museum, Oxford, in the spring and afterwards toured in the provinces. Then he had to help prepare a retrospective exhibition of paintings at Temple Newsam, Leeds, which he went to see. Then there were visits to Richard Seddon at Sheffield and to Madams.

Back in Oxford in late June, he wrote a quiet, sad letter to Alice Daglish. That portrait of her which somehow, in the pre-war suspense, nobody had found a car to collect, had been exhibited at Leeds. When the exhibition closed, Nash had arranged for it to go direct to her.

'The only thing to do about your sweetest letter is to reply before the day begins to get on top of me and I gradually lag behind and then, in the end, haven't time or mood or energy to write, and then it will be done tomorrow, and tomorrow and tomorrow, with more and more Ms and RRs—because, alas, I'm like that.

'I have often tried to plan for this picture to reach you and then the heaven sent occasion arose with all the machinery suddenly supplied to restore you to yourself, so to speak. . . .

'As you will see from the introduction . . .[1] you are set on record as my only portrait! which is as true as makes no matter. Yes, I too remember that time so well—and the long walk we went down the Icknield Way with Eric. . . .

'I wish I could see you. . . . Yes, life is always a little too much for us now. I am not very energetic and my poor Margaret is worn out working for me. I am so sad to feel I am such a permanent sort of nuisance. . . .

'Well, my very dear, I have come to the end of my sheet and breakfast is just in' [1943 c. June].

Nash was again beset with his inveterate troubles: his ill-health and his wife's, the lack of servants and money, and so on. 'Often it is impossible to ignore these affairs' he wrote to Dudley Tooth; 'often

[1] To the catalogue. It was written by Sir Philip Hendy, then Director of Temple Newsam and now (1955) of the National Gallery.

they invade my thoughts for days. To pursue the sort of work I am engaged upon successfully it is absolutely necessary to paint with the utmost degree of "awareness", so to say: to work mechanically at all is ruinous to the virtue of ones painting' (6 August 1943).

But again I must set a different picture against this frequent depression and lassitude. Nell Bethell's daughter was an undergraduate in this year and she has described how she and her friends would visit the Nashes and sit on the floor listening to him reading Thurber or Milt Gross, or how he would go to their parties and when the air became thick would fight for breath but would not leave. 'Only his extraordinary and wonderful spirit', she says, 'could have engaged ceaselessly with his physical disability'. I was in the army and did not see him after 1940, but that is what I hear from all who met him in those last years.

It was partly this resolve not to give in, I suppose, that made him so restless. He feared the ivory basement. At the beginning of September he was away again at Hungerford. 'It is a sad visit all the same,' he wrote to Sieveking, 'for at this time last year my beloved Nell . . . was our hostess. A few months ago she died of cancer. I saw her in London in hospital—What courage! Now this place seems curiously full of her spirit not like a person so much as an emanation —a warm and kindly influence—encompassing' (1 September 1943). Straight from that visit, the Nashes joined Sieveking for a four-day tour of Dorset. He was on broadcasting business and they had petrol for three hundred miles. They were able to include Swanage.

The Christmas of this year was described to Dudley Tooth:

'I 'fell down' on Christmas hopelessly so far as the outside world was concerned and only managed to carry through my annual part of Father Christmas to my perennial child, which I confess I enjoy. I have now done all that could be reasonably expected of me, including seeing a performance of Charlies Aunt with supper at the Randolph and half a bottle of Sparkling Beaune (not at all bad by the way and a better date on it than the casserole perdrix should have had, but never mind, "half a partridge and a glass of Burgundy" sounds well in the imagination . . .). . . . Our Christmas tree would make you weep for its very beauty. Three years we have been frustrated either too ill or too miserable to make a tree. But this year a benificense reigned in The Banbury Road Parallel—like the chap in the song, "Someone started polishing the Sun", and everything came our way. I may do a painting of the Christmas tree. I nearly always try and always fail' (3 January 1944).

In February 1944 the Nashes lost another home—the house they had left derelict in Hampstead. He wrote of it to Archibald Russell:

'Margaret is greatly set up by the appearance of six good black bottles of that nice friendly claret of St. Emilion. . . . It comes too at an auspicious moment—the occasion of the lifting of an immense burden from our necks—the sale of our beloved but embarrassing house in Hampstead. The final deed is signed today—goodbye for ever to all that I fear. Farewell No. 3 Eldon Grove! Farewell Surrealist and Pre Raphaelite ghosts[1] alike, and many charming happy days and a few dark and disenchanting ones. It was a sad reverse when I had to abandon my studio—the first and only room I have had for work only—because it was too far to climb up. . . .

'Tell Janet I have had the peculiar honour of being bought by the Queen'[2] (10 February 1944).

Shortly after Nash wrote a long letter to Percy Withers, from which I want to make several extracts:

'. . . You must not think I am a lost friend or a fair weather pal or any chap of that sort. I'm simply a rather tired man who has sometimes but not always enough energy to get his work done and has got into the bad habit of evading letter writing even to his nearest and dearest. . . . There's Gordon too on my mind it's almost two years since I owed him a letter and Oh friends out of number. . . . I don't think there is any excuse.

'I suppose I expend about 60% of my energy in coughing and spitting and a great many hours altogether inhaling and so on. My work suffers of course, is slowed down. . . . Tooth's have been wonderfully long-suffering for frequently I have disappointed them, people have been waiting to buy my work—for the first time in my life I have been able to sell almost as soon as the picture is shown. . . . Even so I sell very well now and this year have made quite a lot of money. . . .

'All the money we make and can keep goes towards a wonderful dream. The end of the war, and escape from England, escape from what England has become and I fear must be, escape onto a ship to get to sea and someday to set foot in North Africa and find somewhere to live not far from the Desert where the Atlas mountains stand against the far sky' (9 May 1944).

[1] William Allingham had frequently stayed in the house in 1887 and 1888. See *William Allingham: a Diary*, Macmillan, 1907. Eldon Grove was then Eldon Road.
[2] *The Landscape of the Vernal Equinox*. It is Queen Elizabeth the Queen Mother who is referred to, of course.

With that letter he sent an old drawing of Souldern, which Withers thought he wanted to sell; but Nash answered that it was a gift, but if he did not like to accept it, he could send some wine in return—

> *'Can I achieve the very near divine*
> *By changing watercolour into wine'* (16 May 1944).

His last letter to Percy Withers spoke of Bottomley: 'I got a letter off to Gordon at last. . . . They've been making him a Litt.D., he says he's already a D.Litt., I find that interesting but confusing. He's bringing out an exciting book. He's a wonderful boy' [1944 *c.* June]. And then about a year later he was writing to Bottomley: 'Our Mutual has gone. Poor Percy, he was a long time dying, but went very peacefully' [1945 *c.* July].[1] It could have been written two years later of himself.

In carrying forward to the end of this friendship I have passed over the publication in April of *Paul Nash* in the first batch of the Penguin Modern Painters. He sent a copy to Eddie Marsh—another feeler to an old friend from whom he had also a little drifted away: 'I fear if ever you came to Oxford you would have too many other friends to see but think of me if you have, then, an empty half hour' [1944 *c.* April].

Nash went up to London for the lunch which celebrated the beginning of the Penguin series. I am not, of course, recording all his visits to London. They were fairly frequent, although every fight for a bus or a taxi was a fight for breath; and his fastidiousness made him hate the squalor of war-time London more even than most of us did.

But when the flying bombs came he gave it up. 'Its the "terror that flieth" keeps me away I cant stand being forced into shelters or suddenly falling flat with my glass gadget round my neck', he later wrote to Rex Nan Kivell of the Redfern Gallery [1944 *c.* October]. Tooths immediately suggested that he should draw the flying bomb and Kenneth Clark followed with a proposal for a large oil. Nash told Ruth Clark that he was considering it, but had 'no idea about it beyond horror and worry' [Summer 1944]; but clearly these aerial creatures excited him, and he broke out to Sieveking: 'I *say*, these bloody missiles these "sightless couriers of the air". . . . Now isn't the artist wonderful always a jump ahead of *what happens* with his *whats going to*' [Summer 1944]. However, he did nothing about them. He had passed beyond the phase to which they belonged and could not detach himself from his new adventures.

[1] The passage is cut in the published letters.

Actually, he was feeling curiously happy during the early summer. He had resumed the writing of *Outline* and he was stimulated by the interest in his pictures which was being taken by a group of young artists, who were launching *Counterpoint* in Oxford, which he described later to Eddie Marsh:

'It is the mouthpiece of a scarcely formed or even conscious group representing the younger painters of the Poetic School, shall I say, as opposed to the Euston Road boys, and their ruddy realism. Among other ventures these young blades seem to take a kind of filial interest in me as an English painter on the offside of fifty who, to their eyes, seems to be still alive and standing for a few of the things they are interested in' (24 June 1945).

They proposed to publish a large book on Nash, and he worked at this for some time. It was not completed, but his selection and arrangement were largely the basis of the Memorial Volume.[1]

But this happier mood was not to last. By August, there were signs of returning depression and worse health. We can trace it in three extracts from letters, which I give not in chronological but in emotional sequence. The first is to John Betjeman:

'Is Bath much battered. Stands my Pump Room where it did? I have an Aunt in Bath. I suppose practically everyone has. I am horribly bored in this congested burgh. My only intellectual relief is dining at irregular intervals (because of the Rations) at Christ Church the High Table of which or whom I have had the peculiar honour to be made an hon temp member (also Common Room where I never quite decide to go) So now and then I assume an aesthetical donnish air and sit among my betters sipping Madeira and enjoying it gluttonously' (7 August 1944).

The second letter is to Dudley Tooth:

'I was glad to have your nice sympathetic letter its comforting to feel something firm in my present fluid world where I seem to drown daily. . . . I feel exhausted and witless. And nothing apparently can be done about it. . . . I feel we shall never see the Fall. . . .

'We must have been near the end of the War the other day when those incompetent Generals committed their crowning incompetence?[2] With that cruel, castrated mountebank dumb and dead the whole bloody circus would run gloriously amok and gouge out Goebbels little stoney eyes and rip up Goerings stomach' (10 August) [1944].

---

[1] See Preface to *Nash: Eates*, p. ix.
[2] The bomb attempt on Hitler's life.

It is astonishing to read the violence of that outbreak. Violence is so rare in Nash. He was naturally far too civilized and had too much humour for such ways. He had his dislikes and even his decent hatreds, but he could usually deal with them suavely and ironically. It is a mark of his serious decline in health at this time; and so is the staccato and tired manner of the third extract, which was written to Ruth Clark. The earlier part of the letter had been frequently interrupted:

'*There* I've got to stop again Why? because I must get in some painting *somehow*. . . .[1] Well, here I am again hours and hours later. Some gardening had to be done too. Two ladies with plans for feeding art to the Forces bagged my late afternoon. Had to feed out—too tired to write when I got back—another day gone. Can't get started this morning, bed-making hung up, breakfast plans awry, news depressing. Nerves in the kitchen Mouse at low ebb. Weather heavier than lead. . . . Me I cringe and wilt. . . .

'I am wildly trying to find a hotel somewhere to take us for a few days. Winter is upon us. If only I can make a success of this picture[2] I could be free to go anywhere. But where? I really think our home life is over, the position is hopeless. . . Wherever it is to be from now on it must be more or less hotel life. The garden is my chief happiness it has been and is at this moment lovely. You will come for a day or two won't you? I want you to see the little flowers I got with your present—nearly all have turned out quite large affairs not at all rock garden midgets such as you hate but quite robust "colourful" chaps with hairs on their chests. Well I have covered some paper for you but so much is unworthy wail. All sales have stopped by the way! Luckily we don't want money so much as health—health matters first and last I knew that years ago. And 2 crocks are at least 1 too many if not 2. We both ought to be dead.

'Our love and my love to you sweetheart. Forgive so much squeaking' [July 1944].

Perhaps it may seem that there was too much squeaking. I have felt so, from time to time, as I transcribed these passages, remembering what others were putting up with. Nash, too, felt it. 'Everyone is in the same jam' he had written to Tooth 'and compared with thousands we live on velvet' (3 January 1944). But pain, struggle or even mere inconvenience is not relative to others but to oneself. It is inept to remind a hungry man that others are starving. Nash's life also was

---

[1] No omission.
[2] Probably the *Battle of Germany*.

a battle—a battle to carry on with his art when all that is most against art was against him. And again, of course, depression was part of his illness. He was fighting against that, too, as well as for breath. Not one of those who saw him in these last years has ever suggested that he gave way to self-pity, but all of them have emphatically asserted the contrary. It was his courage they admired and no squeaking they had to forgive. His letters were lonely affairs, cries to his friends out of the centre of his troubles. When he was with them, Nash was stimulated to his habitual gaiety. But that, I cannot recapture.

At any rate, the present crisis landed him in the Acland Home at the beginning of September for five days' rest. He was again there in early October, when his wife joined him with what looked like an alarming illness; but she made a quick recovery. On the twelfth they were able to go for three weeks to the Rising Sun Hotel on Cleeve Hill above Cheltenham, with which a whole series of water-colours is associated. From there he wrote to Seddon:

'This hotel is nearly a thousand feet above the plain. The air that rushes around is very high quality and usually refered to as like champagne or like wine. I need hardly say it is not in the least like either but all air of a curative or invigorating nature is always so described and *always* as if the similitude had only that moment come as an inspiration. The *air* my dear is like CHAMPAGNE! (Did I hear you say champagne, Handley? I dont mind if I do)[1] The landscape is very lovely with far away vistas of far hills and not a few mountains. Most of the time the far views have been blotted out by mists but they too are lovely and gave me a new thing to paint in my best Chinese manner. Sunsets, too, are WONDERFUL. (Mr. Nash *did* you see the sunset this evening. It was *wonderful*, you were eating crumpets in Cheltenham? O, what a pity) And I feel I have let the hotel down. For by now of course it is well known I am an artist if not *the* artist, and indeed when I get excited over one of these sunsets I tend to erupt from the ordered decorum of afternoon tea and go splashing wild colours onto bits of awkward sized paper in the bay window. Painting a sunset is no joke, in spite of our Turner tradition The thing is to make it *out* of a sunset into a picture. But I go on trying' [October 1944].

The holiday indeed was an immense success and by the end of it Nash had made fifteen drawings. But as soon as the Nashes got back to Oxford, domestic troubles started again. They were, however, able to return to Cleeve Hill for Christmas, but for once I have no account

---

[1] A quotation from Tommy Handley's wireless programme, called Itma, to which Nash was devoted.

of how they celebrated the feast, probably because it was eclipsed by the news that Margaret Nash fell down a flight of stairs and broke her wrist two days after it. Nash's delight in certain of his wife's idiosyncracies was part of his devotion to her, and this comes out with particular force in the account he sent Ruth Clark. It ended:

'She has had a lot of pain but of course she has been simply terrific. An airman with a decoration has told her she is a miracle of bravery and above all she is quite serene in spite of all the extremely complicated repercussions that must ensue. . . . Here she is quite happy. . . . She can talk from 2 p.m. to 2 a.m. if you like—or They (in turn or collectively) like. And I must say she stirs 'em all up mixes 'em chaffs the stiff ones eggs on the timid informs the ones who seem to be most informed—but very often aren't! draws out shy Professors comforts agrieved wives advises young lovers and so on. Meanwhile I am free to paint. . . . But oh my darling what a miracle of an escape we've had' [January 1945].

The Nashes were back in Oxford by early February and began a year of which there is little to record but exhibitions and illnesses. There were three exhibitions: the first in March at the Buchholz Gallery in New York, part of which later went on to Chicago; the second in April at Tooths', which consisted of nineteen water-colours he had made at Cleeve Hill; the third in June at the Cheltenham Art Gallery, a retrospective loan exhibition of nearly ninety items including industrial designs and illustrated books, which was so successful that the closing date had to be postponed. The Nashes stayed at Cleeve Hill for the early part of this, and in late August they were in Hungerford again, where Nash finished a long letter to his brother:

'Dear old dearie you know how certain experiences have an odd, tedious, way of repeating themselves, like those recurrent dreams we have or think we have? . . .[1] There is one which in my life recurs every decade, perhaps,—or, is it quite haphazard?—on any given *crowded occasion*, or *should* be "crowded", like one's Private Views, or those of our brother artists? I don't exactly know. But, up it slowly comes to the surface of consciousness and *then*, yes, there is the same little wizened old face at the other end of the room, peering and scowling a little, at me. And, alongside this funny old frigate with the beetling figurehead, is rather a frisky sort of a craft vaguely friggled and steel specsy who now and then looses off a gummy smile on the port side, which just clears the old girls shoulder. On my side I retalliate a bit with a smirk or two, but it gets me nowhere. The little

[1] No omission.

267

old face continues to peer and scowl. Sometimes a little whispering goes on but, always, I feel I am kept in view because, as I move about the room, if I look up and take a long dekko from any point, always about the same distance away as before—practically on the horison, is the watching patrol or the Privateers or whatever they are that have got their $\frac{\text{Tabs}}{\text{eye}}$ on me. Then, quite suddenly, when I am off my guard, the little old face is *quite closé!* bearing down on me with frisky frig fairly grinning in the wake. There is no escape: the little old face opens up and I hear it saying *you don't remember me I expect* (which is quite true) but I hear myself replying from the port gun Oh yes I do ... and after that its just anybody's conversation. ... Miss Frigate ... is an artist *too* and does the most stunning things. Frisky's face becomes tortured with grins. I say oh I didn't know—as if she had two hammer toes too many or something as queer. Then I make a rush for it and remain winded for the rest of the afternoon. ...[1] Well, all this, or as much of it as you can believe, happened the other day at Cheltenham, of all places, where for a few obscure reasons I was holding an exhibition of what I am pleased to call my art for the benefit of whoever cared to look in at the Public Art Gallery and Museum. You know, anything can happen these days and practically no one can do anything about it. But the show turned out rather a satisfactory affair, although it had no means of making any money for us—just a *Prestige* show as they call it. This letter is so much in arrears that I despair of bringing it alongside so to speak. ... My garden has reached a succession of peaks in degrees of beauty. But now is when I approach the doldrums. Roses are blown, jasmine is falling soft fruits are all picked and the pyrotechnics of the rock garden almost all spent. Ours is what Thornit (the gardener) calls a *brashy* soil which sounds wet like a hash but is really dry like a break-fast food. The sun has been breaking it to dust and our tortoishell cat being on heat in *her* way the garden is riddled with toms uttering their satanic cries shivvering their rigid tails and poluting the ground and the air. Rugg Tugg a horrid brute with the face of a Boche thug had the nerve to penetrate *into* the studio in pursuit of our creature who *is* a pretty piece of goods I must say—at that point I was interrupted for about 5 weeks. I get like that—cant finish a thing—just worry over it not being finished and occasionally take it up and look at it but put it down again because I haven't the time to continue the letter. Neurasthenia I suppose. Excuse, please. I am now at the Three

---

[1] No omission.

Swans, Hungerford. . . . We came here by car and I had to take one to London the other day, very pleasant and refreshing but expensive. The London trip was to see Horder[1] who I found was a fan of mine and a most charming chap. He is designing me a new sort of behaviour which I only hope I am able to tolerate. The important thing is that he does not appear to regard me as a hopeless mess which is my usual reading of the average doctors diagnosis. But then Horder is no ordinary doctor' [26 August 1945, but begun July].

A number of stories on the exact nature of Nash's illness have been circulated and some have even appeared in print. I have not tried to investigate the question fully. The Nash habit of switching from doctor to doctor, or even juggling with several at the same time; of mixing them with a sprinkling of quacks and eccentrics; and of generally bedevilling the whole issue, would have made any research a most laborious and delicate undertaking, which would have produced no single answer. I therefore confine myself to printing the opinion which Lord Horder has been good enough to send me: 'He was suffering from a gross form of chronic bronchial catarrh with asthma and a failing heart. I had no reason to attribute these troubles to gassing' (4 May 1951).

I had specifically enquired on this because it has been stated in print, in more than one place, that his illness was due to gas which he had absorbed at Passchendaele. Margaret Nash however states that other specialists definitely told her that part of her husband's illness was due to gassing.

Lord Horder's report on the consultation was somehow delayed, so that when he was at Hungerford Nash did not know that it was an order to lie up for at least a month. When he did learn it, he insisted on finishing a picture and then retired to the Acland Home in early November. By the end of the month he had recovered his vitality. 'I am tired of resting,' he wrote to Hartley Ramsden, 'I find it is so very fatiguing. I have a . . . nurse with the face and mentality of a Brazil nut. She is driven by some queer horse or mule power at a fearful fretful fitful fatuous rate up and down and round about uttering staccato sounds 80% of which resolves into the word *"Yes!"*. Yes she says and yes *Yes*. My defence is quite suddenly to say *No*' [November 1945].

He also wrote to Conrad Aiken, or rather added to a letter which had been begun at Banbury Road. Between the two parts he had had the news that Aiken was in England:

[1] Lord Horder. The consultation was on 25 July.

'You see Ive come undone *again*. Am I who I imagine myself to be or only a posthumous afterthought of Lewis Carrol's. . . . Well, my Conrad, the impossible has happened You're back again before this letter has got finished—*dont* tell me you didnt get my postcard . . .?[1] I dragged all the various beginnings into the Nursing Home thinking *now at last* Ill send a good fat letter and a copy of Penguin (herewith) in case it never reached you before (November 1945).

'Conrad! are you really there old friend? Oh God just in time to catch the mail—here it is . . .[1] can you ever forgive me or explain me —have a heart youre a psychologist some days of the week. Look where I've got to. . . . This is more of a Maternity Home than a Mental one. But if you know your English history very well you may have read somewhere sometime that Lizzie Sidall just before Rossetti did the right thing by her was prescribed for and dosed and nursed up to a better level of life by the great Doctor Acland in Oxford. . . .[1] Well this time the great Doc Horder has ordered (lingering pun involved) me a months complete bed. Too long to explain. Too long coughs and so on. But *hell* I would hate to be here when you come back. Look I cant write a lot. I must see you both if its humanly possible.' (1 December) [1945].

Nash left the Acland about the middle of December, but he was not cured. He described his state to Archibald Russell:

'I am about again but sworn to paint in any but a standing posture. All kinds of mobile, volatile behaviour has been suggested but in the end I expect to become slung from the ceiling like an aggressive sort of Christmas decoration stubbing with fistfulls of brushes at the bewildered canvas.

'We have borne many exasperations recently . . . and above all we long to smell the sea once more before we die! . . . There is no place I have a stronger nostalgia for than Swanage or near by, and to reunite . . . would surely be a lovely thing' (18 January 1945 but clearly 1946).

At this point I break off my chronicle. Little remains to be done except to give an account of his last illness and death. It seems proper that that should be postponed until after we have considered the work of his Oxford years.

[1] No omission.

ii. War Pictures, 1940–1943

In 1943 Nash wrote an article called *Art and War*.[1] It was not a good article, but we must agree with his general conclusion that 'war for all its dramatic incentive has produced singularly few exciting pictures'. There are, however, two passages worth quoting for their relation to his own work. He considered Uccello's *Battle of San Romano* 'the greatest of all war pictures', and he said of it: 'Above all, for me, the most convincing character of reality is the *unreal* quality of this scene. It is like a battle in a dream, fought out among green hills and flowering hedges. I remember the tall grasses and the wild flowers that nodded over the gaping trenches in front of Ypres in 1917.' Then after tracing the growth of the human element to its peak in Goya, he went on: 'With the first gas attack the human element of war pictures began to decline . . . henceforth men often became monsters. Finally, machines, pictorially speaking, took the place of men.'

We know that Nash had never made the 'human element' his primary medium of expression; but this was now less idiosyncratic, more 'natural': it followed inevitably from the changed face of war.

His 'first pictorial comment on the war', as he wrote on the back of a proof for the Penguin Book reproduction, was a collage called *Lebensraum*.[2] He drew a desert landscape on which he imposed leaves and a cut-out of an animal's skull. The skull dominates and death establishes its *Lebensraum* in tragic paradox. There were to be other general 'comments', but he was at first engaged in the particular study which was most fitted to the stage of his artistic development. It was a continuation of his researches into the Monster, which he no longer had to imagine in a dead tree but met face to face in the form of the aircraft, 'dead' or 'living'.

I want to speak first of the 'dead' aircraft, the crashed German bomber, which was a direct continuation of his Inhabited Landscape. Nash gave his own account of this in *Picture History*:

'The fact of their being *out of their element* and being found not among the clouds but in the cornfield or on the moors or stretched across the sands under the cliffs, this had a strong and natural appeal for me. So, for some time, I persisted in my preoccupation of the monster in the fields, although I made other studies of 'planes in flight, but very few quite isolated from the land below.'

[1] *World Review*, May 1943.
[2] But see his reference to *The Rose of Death*, p. 281.

There are about twelve water-colour drawings of individual crashed German aircraft, apart from the studies for *Totes Meer*. They are all specifically related to landscape, but perhaps *Dead March: Dymchurch* is the most significant in this respect. The shore, crossed by break-waters, curves into the distance, as Nash had seen it nearly twenty years before. On the left a huge aircraft lies parallel with it, half sub-merged, but thrusts one wing inshore like a long aggressive breaker. The sea attacks with its dead. *Down in the Channel* and *Raider on the Shore* have backgrounds of cliff which recall Ballard Point; in one, even, there is the form of Old Harry Rock. Nash did not physically see these new events at Dymchurch or Swanage but found them in-vading his already matured imaginative world. This invasion is per-haps most dramatically effective in *Encounter in the Afternoon* (Plate 23) where the bomber lies dead in the fields before Silbury Hill. It is peculiarly flattened so that its forms almost merge into the rolling landscape, as if it had already like Silbury become a memory of life. Man's oldest and newest footprints encounter. *The Raider on the Moors* is also sinking into the forms of the landscape but in other cases the wreckage is still raw. The tail of the aircraft in *East Anglia Heinkel* sticks up like a stiffened limb, and the wheels and propeller blades in *Death of the Dragon* are like the legs of a creature on its back, utterly finished—out for good. The flames and black smoke roll up from it as if from the funeral pyre—unless they are the dragon's last breath. The landscape is desolate and this is a solitary death. In *Bomber in the Wood* the wood that had been so long a part of Nash's most personal landscape is invaded by the great cylindrical fuselage. It is like a crashed tree, and its tail fins are like leaves. In *Under the Cliff* nothing of the bomber is left but the tail and a short length of fuselage, but the fin overlaps the cliffs beyond and its scale becomes that of a monolith or the fragment of some colossus from a lost civilization. In all these water-colours Nash displays a new assurance in the handling of the medium. He floats it on with perfect mastery, defining where necessary with a massiveness as of oil, but for the most part suggesting his forms with a most evocative economy.

These individuals were eventually merged into the comprehensive vision of *Totes Meer*. This picture was based on a large dump of wrecked aircraft at Cowley. Nash described its first effect on him in *Picture History*:

'There lived here in death innumerable vehicles of destruction of different personality once all directed by human agency, some in the character of ships manned by crews, others as closely bound up with

27. Incident at Madams. [1944]
Water-colour

28a. The Rose of Death. [1939]
Collage

28b. Dawn Flowers. [1944]
Water-colour

man as a horse to its rider. A few weeks back, a day or two ago, a few hours even, some of these traversed the skies, one by one they had been hurled to earth and gathered up and scattered here. How could they be so soon quit of their human freight? Was it too fantastic to suppose these things were haunted? I did not care to think of them conventionally so, yet there was a persistent suggestion of a ghostly presence even at this hour of half-past two in the afternoon, in the August sunshine. I do not mean the wraiths of lost pilots or perished crews were hovering near, it was nothing so decidedly human, but a pervasive force baffled yet malign hung in the heavy air.'

Nash took photographs and made sketches of this terrific trophy. They were still records of chaos, but in the painting he imposed order on them. In a letter to Kenneth Clark he described the origin of his vision:

'The thing looked to me suddenly, like a great innundating Sea. You might feel—under certain influences—a moonlight night for instance—this is a vast tide moving across the fields, the breakers rearing up and crashing on the plain. And then, no: nothing moves, it is not water or even ice, it is something static and dead. It is metal piled up, wreckage. It is hundreds and hundreds of flying creatures which invaded these shores. . . . By moonlight, this waning moon, one could swear they began to move and twist and turn as they did in the air. A sort of rigor mortis? No they are quite dead and still. The only moving creature is the white owl flying low over the bodies of the other predatory creatures, raking the shadows for rats and voles' (11 March 1941).

The sea advances with the rhythmic beat of waves to the long diagonal barrier that holds it off like Dymchurch Wall. The Dymchurch experience of conflict finds its last expression in these attacking aircraft piled up to destruction against the strained but holding wall of Albion. I use that name from Blake's mythology because Nash was to use it in a later work. He also saw England as a personality, a being who defeated this sea of monsters. For the sea *is* defeated: the effort is over: the white moon hangs in the green sky over the green skeletons. The night of death replaces the inappropriate day in which he had first seen them. It is night over the battlefield, and for all its physical loveliness the colour is the colour of death and corruption.

What Nash felt about the lost personalities of these 'dead' German aircraft, we learn from his study of the 'living' English. In his essay *The Personality of Planes*[1] he explained his approach very exactly. He

[1] *Vogue*, March 1942. Reprinted in *Outline* without illustrations.

began by speaking of the human forces involved in the war of machines:

'Pictorially, they seemed to me unimportant compared with the personality of the machines they employed as weapons, for, so powerful were these agents of war that, once set in motion they very soon dominated the immense stage. . . . Everywhere one looked, alarming and beautiful monsters appeared . . . all had individual beauty in terms of colour, form and line, but beyond, or was it *behind* that actual appearance these things possessed each a personality, difficult to define and yet undeniable. It was not wholly a matter of mechanistic character. There seemed to be involved some *other* animation, "a life of their own" is the nearest expression I can think of, which often gave them the suggestion of human or animal features.'

What did he mean, at this time, by his frequent use of that word 'pictorially'? In what sense were the human personalities 'unimportant'? We remained ourselves, our *modified* selves, even in the belly of an aircraft, even dangling from a parachute. What he meant, of course, was pictorially *for him*. This was the old vision of the footprint in the new form, the footprint of man's personality in the machines he made and rode. The passage I quoted from *Picture History* shows what was deep in his mind. There is a paradox here, which becomes sharper in a letter to Ruth Clark: 'Over my head in the wide sky sail my strange creatures impersonally with their impersonal crews of light-hearted boys all bent on varieties of murder' [Late 1940 or very early 1941]. The paradox is this: when he remembered the men in the machines, all became impersonal. Only when he was free to concentrate on the machines alone—the footprints—did they live with 'a life of their own', whose reality, as he said of the Uccello picture, lies in the unreality; so that they become symbols of man in his terror, his power and his pitifulness. Pictorially only the symbol lived for him.

He began his search for these symbolized personalities by filling his room with photographs of aircraft. Then he visited the machines and photographed them for himself and made rough line-drawings. He read *Flight* and *The Aeroplane*. He pasted photographs of engines into folders and worked out an equivalent image in water-colour on the opposite page. He was resolved to *know* these unfamiliar models first, to have them fixed in his memory before he worked on them with his imagination. In the end, it was only away from these insistent factual details that he could project them into works of art.

At first he called the whole series of drawings 'Aerial Creatures', but later he grouped them into Studies, Portraits, Bombers in Open and Bomber Lairs. The Lair was a development of a particular symbol which I have left almost without discussion—the Nest. Nash himself described this in an essay, *Bomber's Lair*, printed in *Outline* but not, I believe, published elsewhere. There is one passage which gathers up almost all the examples we have seen so far. He described a Victorian book called *Homes without Hands*, and then went on:

'In the lore of this discreet compendium, I found inspiration for a series of paintings. I began to concentrate on the subject of the nest. Until then I had drawn on Mythology for two ideas—*The Nest of the Siren* and *The Phoenix's Nest*. . . .*[1]* Now in the miraculous design of the "fortress" of the mole and again in the deep poetical implication of the petrel's nest . . . I found wonderful material for new paintings. At another time, the surrealist conception of a nest of wild stones intervened and absorbed my imagination for a while. Perhaps this was a new occasion for such a pre-occupation. Why not a nest of the wild planes? The idea of the nest had become already a feature of the war. There were constant references to machine gun "nests" which, of course, gave no suggestion of rest or snugness but rather of a danger spot like an adder's nest or a hive of hornets. I began to consider the meaning of its application to the airplane.'

That can be left to speak for itself, but a little must be said on Nash's vision of the individual aircraft as a 'personality'. He wrote of this in *The Personality of Planes*, but his characterizations there are not wholly consistent with his drawings or with the aircraft as I knew them. The drawings are 'true', the descriptions partly forced. In particular, it was a weakness that he tried to compare each of them to an animal, although it is true that having compared the Wellington to a killer whale, he went on: 'Even so the Wellington is *not* a whale. It is a Wellington, and for two pins it can look like some other creature. I must insist here that these "resemblances" should not be regarded literally.' This character of the *killer* is particularly underlined in *Wellington Bomber Watching the Skies*. The beast crouches in its hangar, its snout pointing at a strip of sky, waiting to be let out into its hunting field—a killer, but hardly a whale. This sense of expectancy is suggested in such titles as *Wellington about to Fly* or *Wellingtons Waiting*. In *Wellington Bomber Drawn on the Day that Hitler Invaded Belgium*, a tarpaulin hangs over the forward guns as if it were a hooded hawk. It is indeed a Protean machine or like the cloud Hamlet fooled Polonius with; but it is not, as he had said in his essay, 'jolly' or 'on the plump side'.

[1] No omission.

It is equally odd that he should have described the Whitley as 'an intellectual thing . . . cerebral and deadly . . . a queer bird-like creature, reminding [him] of a dove'. But his drawings were faithful to the plodding, senseless, brainless machine, the long ugly box that was called the flying coffin. I cannot tell whether he meant the title *Whitleys at Play* to be as sinister as it appears to me. If it is play to stand about the field and bar the sky with lugubrious indifference, then it is the play of thugs waiting for the next victim.

Nash is hardly more convincing when he writes of Blenheims as reliable characters, friendly and trustworthy; but he is, when he says: 'As to animal equivalents, the short-nose Blenheim is, naturally, enigmatical. You might say it has *no* face—which is true, in a sense, and also terrifying—but I would prefer to say it wears a mask, or that behind a mask it is *growing* a face which, when at last it appears, may eclipse that of all others for its dire beauty. The long-nosed Blenheim, however, has, literally, no end of a face.'

When we look at the drawings, we see only that face, particularly the very aggressive face in *Flying against Germany No. 3* and *The Flare Path: Long-Nosed Blenheim Taxi-ing off*, for Nash seems always to have drawn the front of this machine. He draws it as a vicious and strident character.

Nash's final bomber was the Hampden, for which he could only find an equivalent in pre-history. 'It is plainly', he said, 'some sort of pterodactyl.'

I only know two portraits of it, and neither is such a good 'likeness' as he made of its predecessors *in the drawings*. But they are both beautiful drawings for other reasons. The better known is *Hampdens at Sunset*, and there the presence of the red cloud, like a colossal rose, rather overwhelms the aircraft. The second, *Hampdens: Studies No 2*, also contains elements which distract us from the aircraft—a pyramid, for example. Other symbols were intruding.

Although some of the drawings I have mentioned were of aircraft in the air, they were related to the ground and seen from the ground. They had no feel of flying. But in the drawings *Flying against Germany No 4: Hampden Bomber* and *Moonlight Voyage: Hampden Flying above the Clouds* and the oil *Flying against Germany*, which was a war casualty, we experience being in the sky with a force which is extraordinary when we remember that Nash never flew. We are isolated in the air, with no landscape but that of clouds. It is not so much the height but the detachment, the cutting of all anchorage, which is so remarkably rendered. These pictures hold that silence which lies just under the noise of the engines and is almost within reach, so that a voice in the earphones is never less than a surprise. These are pictures of flying, not merely of aircraft in flight such as the camera can record. We may also notice here the later drawing, *Arrival of the Stirlings*, commissioned in 1943. Nash did not know these aircraft intimately as he had known those of 1940 and 1941. They are impersonal, like the long clouds they move among. This is a skyscape with aircraft. We see the difference at once if we turn to the two bombing watercolours, *Target Area: Whitleys over Berlin* and *Objectives: Blenheims Bombing the Barges at Le Havre*. He was able, by an act of pure imagination, to transport those machines which he had become familiar with on the ground into the dangerous sky where he had never been, to transport them as the personalities he knew. The Whitleys assert their typical harshness as they jab across the far earth, which is seen in plan as if from high above them. It is not a possible view, because they are seen in profile, but the effect is exactly of that confusion between earth and sky, between levels and directions and aspects which comes of anxious flying among swinging searchlights, among explosions above and below and around. In fact there are no searchlights in this drawing, but they are prominent in *Objectives*, where their verticals and diagonals impose a quite different design. Moreover, the brisker Blenheims do not move in the dead march of horizontal bars but fly into the picture or soar and bank in evasive action. There is danger, one feels, for these inhabitants of the sky; but the Whitleys drop their load and themselves plod on unperturbed.

Nash returned to the theme of bomber raids in *Halifax Attack* and *Raid by Lancasters*, both of 1944, but it is not necessary to enlarge on them nor on his few and far less acute portraits of fighters. But there is of course one picture concerned with fighters which I must speak of, the celebrated *Battle of Britain*. Nash began this about July 1941 and finished it in October. He described it in *Picture History*:

'The painting is an attempt to give the sense of an aerial battle in operation over a wide area, and thus summarize England's great aerial victory over Germany. The scene includes certain elements constant during the Battle of Britain—the river winding from the town areas across parched country, down to the sea; beyond, the shores of the continent, above, the mounting cumulus concentrating at sunset after a hot brilliant day, across the spaces of sky, trails of airplanes, smoke tracks of dead or damaged machines falling, floating clouds, parachutes, balloons. Against the approaching twilight new formations of the Luftwaffe, threatening.

'To judge the picture by reference to facts alone will be unjust to the experiment. Facts, here, both of science and nature are used "imaginatively" and respected only in so far as they suggest symbols for the picture plan which itself is viewed as from the air. The moment of battle represents the impact of opposing forces, the squadrons of the R.A.F. sweeping along the coast and breaking up a formation of the Luftwaffe while it is still over the sea.'

When it was delivered to the War Advisory Committee, Kenneth Clark wrote to Nash enthusiastically: 'I think', he said, 'in this and *Totes Meer* you have discovered a new form of allegorical painting. ... You have discovered a way of making the symbols out of the events themselves, which I think very important' (22 October 1941).

In particular I find the symbols in the narrowing of the Channel and in the division by the low line of the continental hills of the Channel and the brown soil of England below from the embattled sky above. And I find them in the intricate pattern of the white exhaust trails and the streamers of black smoke from the plunging bombers. This interplay of white and black—the white for us, the black for the enemy—plots the battle in the sky and renders its speed and concentration. There is an extraordinary beauty, too, in these trails and streamers, fragile and organic like the skeletons of flowers. Only the distant formation of the German second wave introduces a rectilinear and foreign element to the design.

The last picture of aircraft I wish to mention is the *Defence of Albion*, which he finished in the Spring of 1942. Nash described his symbolic intention in an account of the picture which he sent to the Ministry:

'The Sunderland ... becomes in the imagination of the artist a beast as important as the Lion or the Unicorn in relation to Britain; and for this reason its delineation is not confined to a mere accurate representation, certain features are exaggerated more particularly in the tail fin. The action represented, the sinking of a U boat by bombing, takes place off the coast of Portland[1] where the rocks are like Cyclopean walls and the white Portland stone is quarried to rebuild what the Luftwaffe have tried to destroy of Albion' (27 May 1942).

But the picture was not a success. The paint is dry and laboured and the design incoherent. In trying to emphasize the character he gave the Sunderland in *The Personality of Planes*, as 'most animal of all planes, charging along the coast with its great snout thrust out', he

---

[1] Obviously also of private significance for Nash as the Coast he most ardently hoped would be defended.

greatly reduced the span of the wings; but he did not achieve his aim and for once I am on the side of the 'tailor and cutter'. Since it fails imaginatively we must regret that it also fails as a prosaic record.

Nash regarded all these works as propaganda. I have already quoted what he wrote to his brother on this. He enlarges on it in a letter to a Ministry official: 'In all my work I aim at something more than a picture to be exhibited in the N.G. Where-ever possible I should like pictures to be used directly or indirectly as propaganda. . . . Although I know how terrifyingly gay and decorative war and especially war in the air, *can* look, I would like to give a feeling of *dreadful fantasy* something suave but alarming. Its difficult. I know how difficult and I do not flatter myself I have succeeded except now and then. But I would get *inside* this business and frighten someone or bust!' (18 March 1941).

The fact that we have seen Nash forced by circumstances into his ivory basement, preoccupied with his own work and his own vision, his illness and thwarting irritations, must not hide from us his deep distressed anger.[1] It is therefore not surprising that in 1942 he tackled more direct propaganda: the set of three water-colours called *Follow the Führer* for example. In the first, *Above the Clouds*, a monster balloon of fish-like body and cruel fanged face floats in the sky, with aircraft swarming about it. In the second, *Under the Water*, fish-like submarines follow a sea-serpent whose open mouth bellows them on. In the third and most effective, *Over the Snows*, a great sea of skull-like heads rolls forward under a stormy sky following the central and largest head whose mouth also gapes in horrid bellowing. Another example is *Enemy Image*, a folder of black paper into which he pasted photographs in montage which he titled in white ink. On the cover is *Evil Growth*, where the stalk of a fungus blossoms into four heads of Hitler. Inside this is the one word *Look* and facing it two montages of hands and the caption: *Look. The Führer's Magic Finger acts the Dove of Peace Stems the Red Tide*. On the next page the hand points at corpses on the snow and is captioned *Raises the frozen dead*. . . . Facing this, Hitler's hand, fist and face are isolated against the black, and captioned: *Murderer's hand Tyrant's fist Madman's fear Where will they lead you Germany?* It continues in this way, fierce and effective and angry, and one is staggered that it was never used. But this way of hate and violence was not really Nash's. He had a different journey

---

[1] A long minute to the Ministry in the Imperial War Museum archives (GP/55/13 under May 1941) shows that he was following the course of the war in a way which his letters would not lead one to expect.

to take, which he described in *Picture History*, as it started, or rather set off again, from *Battle of Britain*:

'This was my first essay in flight; pictorially, in imagination, my first that is, since painting *Mansions of the Dead*. . . . I do not despair of making convincing aerial pictures without leaving the ground. In fact, everything I am thinking of and imagining now tends towards objects poised, floating or propelled through the middle and upper air, the spaces of the skies and the miraculous cloudscapes that constantly form, change and disappear. But beyond any conditions of the scene and its passing figures, I have become increasingly absorbed in the study of light and the drama of the great luminaries—particularly the moon and her influence upon all nocturnal objects whether on earth or in the heaven. Landscape at night has always fascinated me; my first exhibition of drawings contained four or five night pieces; my first imaginary designs were of nocturnal scenes. *The Combat* (an angel fought a devil), *Pyramids in the Sea*, *Cliff to the North* and others.

'Now I am re-opening my research, renewing the solution of problems of light and dark and half-light.'

iii. Pictures: Landscapes and Symbol

'I am trying to pursue a certain imaginative "idea" which is behind the formal structure of the pictures', Nash wrote to Dudley Tooth. 'It is a somewhat different process to that of Mat Smith, for instance, where "subject" seems not particularly part of a *scheme* as it is with me—*particularly at present*. . . . Even so, there are always a good few drawings which are purely landscape studies' (6 August 1943).

That is the material which now remains to be examined—the works of pure imaginative and symbolic art and the contemporary studies of natural appearances which he produced during the Oxford years. But they interpenetrate, or rather, like parallels in perspective, they converge on the vanishing point of Nash's vision of the invisible. We cannot separate the two 'types', nor should we really separate them from the war pictures. I have only done so for convenience in handling such a large body of work; and to demonstrate that there was no real cleavage, I shall draw attention first to a war picture, or rather collage, *The Rose of Death* [1939] (Plate 18.a). I have quoted Nash's description of *Lebensraum* as his 'first pictorial comment on the war', but he gave this precedence to *The Rose of Death* in his description of its origin in *Aerial Flowers*:

'When the War came, suddenly the sky was upon us all like a huge hawk hovering, threatening. Everyone was searching the sky expecting some terror to fall; I among them scanned the low clouds or tried to penetrate the depths of the blue. I was hunting the sky for what I most dreaded in my own imagining. It was a white flower. Ever since the Spanish war the idea of the *rose of death*, the name the Spaniards gave to the parachute, had haunted my mind so that when war overtook us I strained my eyes always to see that dreadful miracle of the sky blossoming with these floating flowers. The first picture I made of the War was a collage of the *Rose of Death*.'

The centre of the design is the open canopy of a parachute, which has neither cords nor passenger, but exists by itself in its pure flower form. Three almond-shaped sequins in mother-of-pearl are disposed about it, like views of it in perspective. Below it a cloud rests on the top of a semi-circular cut-out from the sky of Bartolommeo Vivarini's *Adoration*, as the clump of trees at Wittenham rests on Sinodun Hill. This is echoed in the Vivarini by the church on the top of a hill, silhouetted against the sky. The sky is inhabited by groups of angels that recede in perspective like aircraft in close formation. This collage is, then, compact of Nash's symbols and although it is not in itself of any great artistic importance, it serves as a link with what we have discussed and a prelude to what we must soon discuss.

During 1940 Nash was so busy with his work for the Air Ministry that he produced little else except some dozen water-colours, made unexpectedly and rapidly while he was staying for a few days in London. They are variations of the view from his room high up in the Cumberland Hotel overlooking Marble Arch and the entrance to Hyde Park. Most of them were never exhibited but rapidly sold and scattered to private collectors. Only the Tate *London: Winter Scene No 2* is in a public collection. I have seen very few and what I now say is mostly based on photographs.

The essential element in these designs is the dashing curves made by the roads, paths and railings which radiate from the park entrance. Sometimes these curves are emphasized by car-tracks in the snow. The goal of these inviting and urgent ways are insubstantial palaces on the horizon, made with geographical freedom from the pinnacles of South Kensington, the spire of the Albert Memorial or the dome of the Albert Hall. It is unmistakably Hyde Park, and yet it is strange, because although the roads and paths have an unaccustomed vitality of their own, it is otherwise uninhabited except for the thinly scattered, slightly indicated figures of *London: Winter Scene No 1*.

But sometimes the sky has other inhabitants: a great hawk in *Bayswater Landscape*; a flock that agitates above the grass and trees and meets dramatic shafts of sunlight in *Gull Field*; a huge and aggressive sun in *Winter Park*, which is ambiguously related to a barrage balloon in *Bayswater Balloon*.

The sick and ageing man sat up in his high temporary lodgings and looked across over the winter landscape to the Palaces by his first Place and parish in Kensington Gardens. In those years—I cannot date it exactly—Nash made what I believe was his only attempt to capture that Place. In the water-colour called *Kensington Gardens* a fence crosses the foreground and beyond is an open space walled with secret trees, a luminous space where a hoop might cross, and no child ever appear to explain it.

But a new Place had become active for him at Madams—the garden and a view over the valley to the Malvern Hills; and new creatures inhabited it—the Madamites. He wrote to his wife from there in June 1941:

'Nature is stepping out a bit at Madams. A huge snake of which alas I was only in time to see the tail, appeared at lunch in the ditch over Charles' [Neilson] wall. . . . Also there is a toad in the rock garden who comes out at dusk and meets another toad, who comes from the pond. Each sits for hours. No one has ever seen them meet and as it is about 12.30 a.m. one would have to strike matches to see what was going on. No-one knows. Owls are about too. But most important of all are the Madamites which I have invented.'

After that visit, he wrote to Clare Neilson: 'Take note the name *Madams* has started on its unknown flight' [18 July 1941]. But I am not clear what the Madamites were. They were certainly primitive: the echo of the name Adam could not have missed Nash's ear. In *Madamite Moon* [1941] the world is peopled only by huge fungi: and in *Garden of the Madamites* (1941) only by stone toad-stools and a pergola that has become massive as a Druid arch. The moon broods over them both. Sometimes the garden was serene, but sometimes, as we have seen, the outer dangers invaded it. It was defended by the *Sea Wall at Madam* [1941], a title which shows that Nash was fully conscious of the connection between this new symbolism and the early symbolism of Dymchurch. Near the end of his life, the snake, like a curling breaker, mounted that wall in *Incident at Madams* [1944] (Plate 27).[1]

---

[1] Cf. the Serpent which invaded the 'Valley of the Princes' in Dante's *Purgatorio*, VIII, 94–108, an incident which Blake illustrated. See *Blake's Illustrations to the Divine Comedy* by A. S. Roe, Princeton U.P., 1953, Pl. 76. Nash cannot have seen this, though.

But the wall was not the only defence: there was also the 'home' wood. But it had its work cut out: in *Wood against the Tide* (1941), for example, it is menaced by the open fields which heave up to its very edge and by a huge snake that glides rapidly to the attack. The snake reappeared in 1943 curving over a hill no bigger than itself and rearing its head into the sky. But in this tragic symbol that head is a hand which waves towards a bright cloud. Nash called the painting *Farewell* (Plate 30). Writing of it about 1945 he described how, before a wood on a hill in the Chilterns in August or September 1939, he had come upon a lichened snake-like bough and soon after had drawn out the design on canvas. The war intervened and he said that when he took it up again:

'One detail only baffled me in the reconstruction of the scene in its pictorial form. The head of my object personage was not a snake's head—which, as you may know, may be a flower—it was a woman's hand waving farewell. It had always been there in the original drawing and it is as much an essential part of the picture now as anything else there but, unlike the rest of the picture, I cannot explain it.'[1]

But beyond the threatened garden was the Vale and beyond again the bastion of the Malvern Hills. Between 1942 and early 1944, Nash painted and drew them again and again. The Vale, in particular, became a secure outer Place. The dangers lay between, the trials and encounters that had to be met before coming to rest in the *Pratum Felicitatis*. One of the earliest of the series was *The Vale of the White Blackbird* [1942] (Plate 25). Clearly this was a return of 'the white merle', although I do not know whether he remembered that romantic name. If he did, he deliberately dropped it. The painting is a 'straight' landscape except that the bird is large in proportion. It is not in the sky but flies along the valley low over the pleasant fields. Perhaps Nash felt that that valley was itself the sky. The bird reappears in almost exactly the same position in one of the last of the series—*March Landscape: Landscape of the Vale* [1944]—but otherwise the valley is uninhabited. Even when the sun or moon appear they are not very assertive: perhaps again that is because they were at home.

Most of these pictures were water-colours, in which Nash displayed an astonishing mastery, a sensitive, suggestive economy for which there are few parallels in Western art. They recall, rather, the work of the twelfth-century Chinese water-colourists, particularly in such tender and evocative drawings as *Landscape of the Vale: Dawn* [1943]

---

[1] *Transformation*, ed. by Stefan Schmanski and Henry Treece. No. 3, n.d., *c*. 1945, p. 133.

and *Sunset over the Malverns* (1944). Nash knew this. At some time in the second half of 1944 he wrote to Richard Seddon: 'I have just had a moving experience Margaret has given me a superb book on Early Chinese Painting[s][1] I found in the Turl Bookshop. Marvellous colour plates but beyond all a thing I have been searching for, a treatment I feel can just do for me something I have been groping after.'

The floating cloudy unstable images of the inscrutable, which Nash was now to pursue, needed a more fluid technique than the 'bounding line' of his early work. It must have been chiefly in three or four of the later Plates that he found what he had been groping after—the power of omission, of the spaces *between* the stated forms in which form continues a life of its own, but *invisibly*. The veiled presence of a tree with no leaves defined, of a hill that floats like a cloud, of fields that may be water, or rippling water that may be plough, which we find in most of his late landscapes, express the absent not by association—the ball left on the hill—but by the absence of the substantial hill itself. The titles alone evoke this mystery as of a world behind the pattern of frost on a window—*The Landscape after Frost*; *Hill, Plain and Clouds; Landscape Emerging; Landscape under Mist and Frost*. Now fades the glimmering landscape. . . . Nash has become the painter of the ghost of landscape where in the solemn stillness we wait for the event. The clarity of mystery now emerges, not in the 'ruled' symbol, but in the image of the mystery itself. Emergence and fading are now the same thing: it simply depends on which side of the window one is on. Only a sharp dark tone, here or there, holds these fragile forms on the paper.

The material for these late landscapes, mostly of 1944 and 1945, was gathered on his various visits, but worked up or developed in oil at Banbury Road. There is a seeming paradox here. At Madams or in hotels, there was tranquillity, for there were no unmade beds; and yet there—perversely, it might seem—he looked out over the Vale; whereas at Banbury Road, where the troubles most pestered him, he could build his inner tranquillity, his positive silence. But the paradox does not go deep. Perhaps we can destroy it by assuming that Nash was one of those who need the pressure of distraction to build their most solid works, who are stimulated by what they most complain of and relaxed by comfort. At Banbury Road he looked *in*. Certainly, we can destroy the paradox by remembering that, at this time particularly, Nash's inner and outer worlds were not distinct. The double vision transcended such arbitrary divisions as inside and out. Con-

[1] By Osvald Sirén, Chiswick Press, 1938.

sider, for example, the two late drawings *Moonrise: Cleeve Hill* (1945) and *The Bluff* (1946). They both represent bare hills like heaving but never breaking seas. Stone walls crawl right across them and here and there bony trees stick up gauntly. They are terrible drawings, images of a sterile land and a comfortless sky; and they perfectly illustrate the definition of landscape as a state of mind. It is difficult to see any other sense in which they can be called 'pure landscapes'. Indeed, there are very few pictures of these later years which can be considered as no more than renderings of physical impressions on his eye. That eye itself, still accurate, alert and observant, was also a filter coloured with his imaginative vision. But certainly there are a few drawings which could be called what he described in *Picture History* as 'studies and reportings of new country usually drawn or painted direct from the scene'. They were made at Madams, at Hungerford, in the Cotswolds, in Derbyshire,[1] in Dorset, at Cleeve Hill—wherever he visited. But very few at Oxford, where he lived. And yet he had once intended to use Oxford. In 1913 he had planned a series of lithographs 'to reveal something of that wonderful place Oxford—the poetry of it'.[2] Then again, in 1930, he had planned a series of drawings. But now he lived in Oxford and loved it, he found nothing in its beauties which could serve him as well as the sunflowers of his suburban back garden.

We must now examine the successive groups of work which could in no sense be called 'pure landscapes'. Nash gave an account of the first in *Picture History*:

'By the end of 1940 I had to a great degree exhausted my interest in the personality of airplanes. . . . Also I was beginning to lose interest in the monster type of object-personage pertaining to 'civil life' as it were. . . . Now I was looking round for a new form and character of object-personage. This came to me eventually in a round-about way through studying a book on palaeontology. Looking at the engraved plates of fossil impressions, it seemed to me these delicate, evocative forms could be revitalised in a particular way. I made a series of drawings of ghost personages, which showed them in the environment they naturally occupied in pre-history. The ghost of the shale in the Black Cliff of Kimmeridge clay. The turtle on the Dorset Shore, the gigantic ghost of Megacerous Hibernicus (Irish Elk), in the moonlight forest.[3] . . . These water-colours were not

---

[1] He had visited this county during his stay with Seddon at Sheffield.
[2] Letter to his wife (24 September 1913).
[3] *Ghost of the Megacerous Hibernicus* [1942]. The other drawings are discussed later.

merely romantic conceptions, each was constructed in a formal plan, the character of the personage being subtly echoed in the features of the surroundings.'

These drawings, then, were conceived and executed long after he had left Dorset, taking their images from his memory and his photographs. One Place was particularly active—Kimmeridge Bay, on the Dorset coast about midway between St. Aldhelms Head and Lulworth Cove. It is remarkable for its geological formation and its fossils. One of these is the Pliosaurus Grandis whose head, seven feet long, is in the Dorchester Museum. In Nash's drawing, *Kimmeridgian Ghost* [1942], it is restored to its setting and lies along the cliff face, a stratum among the geological strata.

On the Kimmeridge shore the tumbled rectangular blocks of stone are interrupted by smooth platforms of black shale. One of these in particular, on the east shore of the bay, appeared in the photograph called *The Flats* (Plate 19.a) and was the setting for *Environment of Two Objects* (Plate 19.b). In that picture Nash put the two Objects there. Now, in *Ghost of the Turtle* [1942], he found an Object which naturally appeared there, a form like the flakes of shale, a creature whose fossil he might have found. These ghosts are a new kind of personage in that they are not imaginatively contrived but imaginatively evoked, worked out of the shale as the British craftsmen worked out their bracelets.

Writing to Seddon about 1944, Nash said, 'this ghost business is too profound and queer to go into here'. I hope that I have said enough of Nash's imaginative life to excuse me also from discussing it. He was pursuing the absent back to the dim beginnings of animal life, to long before man left his megaliths and earthworks as 'footprints'; and he was no longer content with 'footprints' but used the very form of the absent, the petrified being itself. He could come closer to it, because it had been so long dead.

In November 1942 he flushed another quarry and, as usual, it was also closely linked with a Place—the garden of Hilda Harrisson's house at Boar's Hill. Again, Nash himself supplied the best 'explanation' of it in *Picture History* at the point where he began in 1943:

'All my recent landscapes are, as it were, recreations of one actual scene—the prospect as seen from the house I go to stay at on Boar's Hill where there is a wide window . . . looking across the garden to the Berkshire Downs on the horizon. Between the farthest woods and the downs rise up the twin hills of the Wittenham Clumps. . . .

Actually they are a long way from Boar's Hill and I have to look at them through my field glasses to get an adequate view of them. . . .

'The other considerable feature is the little avenue of cypress which runs off to the left in a slight curve: I generally exaggerate the proportions of this for my own ends. Then there are two or three more salient features—the three different levels in the foreground, the curving path down into the woods and the two flame-shaped bushes, yews I think. On the other side of the garden you get the wide stretch of grass, once lawn, between two long lines of rose bushes. Away behind this you have the view of the Clumps. Further to the right, outside the garden, there is a glimpse of wooded hills over the top of the beech hedge. But I don't bother what grows where very much. I find most things grow where I paint them.'

The Wittenham Clumps now finally assert themselves as the most powerful of his personal symbols on the earth; and in this Boar's Hill series they are frequently brought into conjunction with the most powerful of all his symbols, the inhabitants of the sky. Oddly enough, the drawing specifically called *Landscape with Inhabited Sky* (1946) has neither sun nor moon nor aerial flowers; the Clumps suffice, hanging cloud-like in the far distance. I shall not discuss those pictures where only the Place is rendered, not because they are inferior but because they do not directly carry forward the last stages of his symbolism, which I now consider my only remaining business.

'I suppose you might call these landscapes transcendental', Nash wrote of the Boar's Hill Series in *Picture History*. 'The same method applies to all. The same processes I have instinctively followed for a long time now I have enlarged perhaps over the series.'

But the series may be divided into two groups. The first involves the fungus, the second the sun and moon; but they so often overlap that I should not have made this division had not Nash written to Dudley Tooth about May 1943:

'I have something of a system in regard to these recent pictures. To a certain extent they are the result of a preoccupation mainly concerned with one landscape variously related to flowers and fungi [to] which it yields or to moods of weather or the seasons affecting it. Presently the whole scene will change but while it lasts it is as well to gently hammer away on the same note. Apart from this it is as well to keep all fungi together whatever their backgrounds.'

The fungus group related to Boar's Hill contains three outstanding works, beginning with *November Moon* (1942) (Frontispiece), an oil in which the foreground is inhabited by two giant fungi. The edge of the first terrace draws a sharp line beyond them, dividing their area from that inhabited by the other features of the garden, but most conspicuously by the cypress avenue, which is the way out. This picture also, of course, belongs to the second group by virtue of its ascendant moon. The second is *Landscape of the Brown Fungus* [1943], of which there are oil and water-colour versions. It is similarly divided, but the fungi are smaller and there are neither sun nor moon. Their place is taken by Wittenham Clumps which appear against the sky. In the third, on the other hand, the drawing called *Landscape of the Red Fungus* [1943], although it is again similarly divided, the fungi have become monstrous and the garden is belittled. Even the cypress avenue is suppressed, and indeed the garden is almost featureless and merges into the distance. The domed summit of a fungus alone penetrates the sky, and serves for Sinodun Hill or the upper half of a rising or setting sun or moon.

Landscape of the Puff Ball [1943] is a fine example of a fungus picture not in the Boar's Hill Series. The huge puff ball lies in the foreground among its satellites and the background is the Malvern distance. Sir Allen Lane chose this from among several drawings at Tooths', and Nash wrote to him on the occasion:

'It happens to be one of my favourite drawings and while I have wondered why someone didn't perceive its quality that set it just ahead of quite a few others, I was amused to realise that there must be something—what, subversive? perhaps *unwholesome* about the subject. One may paint mushrooms, and I have succeeded in selling the most suspicious people pictures of palpably poisonous fungi, but puff balls, no. They seemed to be taboo. It is a great relief to me to know the spell is now broken' (4 March 1944).

The symbolism of the poisonous fungi for Nash is self-evident. They have vegetable life, like flowers; but they contain death. Flowers are also symbols of death, but in them the skeleton is clothed in beauty: the fungus is naked. Some of the old herbalists derived the word 'fungus' from *funus* and *ago*. Many fungi are popularly called toadstools and we know the fearful reputation of the toad: many of their popular names are indicative—destroying angel (*amanita virosus*), death cap (*amanita phalloides*), and so on. The puff ball is not poisonous, but the *Lycoperdon Giganteum* which Nash painted, seems to have a bad name: the French peasant calls it *Tête de Mort*. In the poisonous plant, which we shall find again shortly, Nash combined the flower and the fungus symbols. Through both he planted death in his garden.

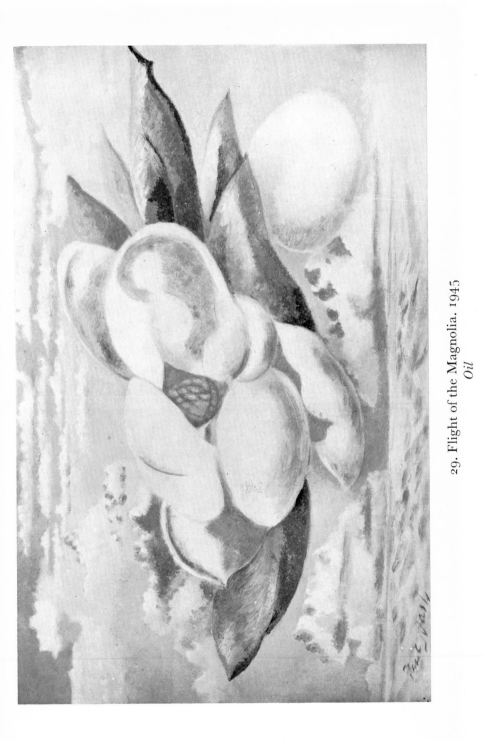

29. Flight of the Magnolia. 1945
Oil

30. Farewell. 1944

The group in the Boar's Hill series dominated by the sun and moon is always in relation to the garden and Wittenham Clumps. We have seen that some pictures, such as *November Moon* (Frontispiece), fall into both groups; but this picture is also part of a subordinate and also overlapping series concerned exclusively with the moon: *Landscapes of the Crescent Moon, of the Moon's First Quarter, of the Moon's Last Phase* and so on.

I shall not try to discuss the symbolism of the sun and moon. Their superficial significance is too familiar and their full significance too complicated; and I can only indicate a few particularly pertinent and well-known aspects of a vast subject. One aspect which is particularly pertinent is that in the sun myth the sun is the hero who escapes from the womb of earth for his journey of trials and dragon-slaying; and at the end of the day returns to the womb, to his own parish. The sun, then, may symbolize the life of man; but most usually, of course, it was identified with the creator of that life. Then, with the rise to a more spiritual religion, it inevitably became the symbol for Him. Nash must have remembered that Sir Thomas Browne had said in *Urne Buriall* that 'the sunne it self is but the dark *simulachrum*, and light but the shadow of God'. And yet, since we can see God only *sub cuiusdem caligine imaginationis*,[1] he could do no better than accept the oldest and most powerful image. It was no failure of imagination. Dante himself, the supreme imaginative artist, proclaimed the sun as the fittest image of God, since it illumines itself and then all else.[2]

The moon, which first receives this light, naturally became the symbol of the female principle, or the egg. At night, the sun is only manifest in its reflection, and that reflection, therefore, *at that time*, precedes the birth of the sun itself.

> *But the bright Sun was not as yet; he, filling all the expanse,*
> *Slept as a bird in the blue shell that soon shall burst away.*[3]

There are other relations of sun and moon which bear on Nash's use. For example, it was the *magnum opus* of the alchemists to produce the intersection of two principles, for which they took sun and moon, red and white, sulphur and mercury, soul and body, subject and object, male and female and other like pairs, as symbols. The final union was itself the symbol of man's mystical union with God.

[1] St. Gregory, *G. Mor.*, V, 53.
[2] *Convivio*, III, 12. For a full discussion of Dante's use of the sun symbol, in all its complexity, see *Symbolism of the Divine Comedy* by Jefferson B. Fletcher, Columbia University Press, 1921, Ch. I.
[3] Blake, *Vala*, Night the First.

However, the symbolism of sun and moon is not quite so simple and rational as that. There are variations of this neat pattern. In Egypt, for example, the moon was masculine and identified with Thoth, the pathfinder. The power of the moon was not completely passive in Diana, as goddess of fertility, whose light was not *all* borrowed; for she was creative as the body to the soul of the sun. And in other myths the borrowed light of the moon was considered as the soul of man, the spark from the divine light of the sun.

Nash was fascinated by these complexities. He constantly applied to his friends during his last years for information and advice on reading. The myths and rituals of Midsummer fires, Walpurgis night, St. John's Eve and all the rest of it, were filling his mind with images. He was not studying the subject scientifically, of course, but pursuing with delighted and awed excitement the record of how man, in all times and places, had celebrated the magic power of these symbols which he had discovered for himself by poetic intuition.

Writing in *Picture History* of the whole Boar's Hill series, Nash said that to describe one picture would explain all except *Sunflower and Sun*. He then went on to speak of *Landscape of the Summer Solstice* (1943):

'Actually there is nothing to it—the method is . . . taking visual facts in nature for visual use in a picture regardless of natural logic. Objects to me are all the same in the end, i.e. part of a picture, but primarily a pictorial part not merely symbolical. I may hunt out symbolical flowers to make a picture about the Summer Solstice but they must be useful pictorially, namely in colour and form. Thus the presence of the Orpine, a sedum, suggests the introduction of a stone. The queer pink of the flowers and the cold sea-green leaves are just what I want to build up my ochres and deep blues and give me the opportunity of tinting up my foreground of rough grass with a pink glow. Similarly the flowers of the mouse-eared hawksweed, very much exaggerated, are of great importance to echo the form of the sun and to repeat his image. The tall straight stem of St. John's wort, with its branching fronds and jets of bright yellow petals, makes a significant division where it is absolutely needed. And yet, for all this utility procedure, I am convinced the presence of these magic flowers somehow influences the atmosphere of the picture. That is a mystery, but I believe in it without question and without being able to explain.'

The inconsistency of this passage is flagrant. Nash begins by saying there is 'nothing in it', and ends with a mystery. And it is the mystery that mattered. He was making a verbal concession to a discarded aesthetic heresy; and trying to pass off a work of art as no more than an artifact. The mystery is in the colours and forms which *are* the symbols and in the symbols which *are* the colours and forms; for 'art is a true *aesthetic synthesis a priori* of feeling and image in the intuition, as to which it may be repeated that feeling without image is blind, and image without feeling is void'.[1] We may justly distinguish between what is expressed and the means of expression; but this is not a question of content and form. Means of expression are not form: they are means to express the form of the content without which the content does not exist.

Consider the picture in question. The stone and the magic flowers stand in a formal row across the foreground. Beyond them Wittenham Clumps rise in the centre. Above them the sun blazes. All that I have said about Nash goes for nothing, if it is not unmistakably clear that this is not a mere rendering into pleasant pattern of the seen, but a symbol of the unseen. And Nash knew it perfectly well. His position in English art is with Blake—I do not say on the same level but in the same household—and it is regrettable to find him, at this late stage, writing as if he were no more than a man of taste, matching his colours like an interior decorator.

On the back of a photograph of this picture, Nash wrote: 'The picture is meant to give a sense of heat palpitating throughout. The sun's zenith, the time of the year when the sun stands in the sky before he begins to descend in power.' And in a letter to Dudley Tooth he wrote: 'This is Midsummer Eve or nearly It is the peak of the suns climb, from now he begins to descend' [September 1943]. These notes, taken together, reveal the personal symbolism which is another 'layer' in the picture's significance. He was at the height of his artistic powers, and from them there was to be no decline but sudden extinction.

A second picture in the series of which Nash gave an account in *Picture History* is *Landscape of the Vernal Equinox* (Plate 26). There are three versions in oil, of which the first was certainly painted before August 1943.[2] It is perhaps Nash's most celebrated work. Unusual circumstances have contributed to this: it was bought by Queen Elizabeth the Queen Mother, which gave it great publicity; a lithograph was made of it by C.E.M.A. for distribution to the services; and it hung in the Lion and Unicorn Pavilion at the South

[1] Croce, *The Essence of Aesthetic*, p. 39.
[2] Nash also made a water-colour version, but spoilt and finally destroyed it. For the other versions, see Index of Pictures.

Bank Exhibition of the Festival of Britain in 1951 as one of four works representing British painting, of which the others were by Hogarth, Gainsborough and Constable. These honours may have given it undue prominence in Nash's work; but even so, it must certainly rank with his finest pictures. This is his account of it:

'Call it, if you like, a transcendental conception; a landscape of the imagination which has evolved in two ways: on the one hand through a personal interpretation of the phenomenon of the equinox, on the other through the inspiration derived from an actual place. In each case so-called truths of knowledge and appearance have been disregarded where it seemed necessary. Just as probably, it would not be possible to find a period (of day or night) when the sun and moon are in the relationship shown here, so it would be difficult to recognize features of the landscape in the natural scene. . . .

'The only forms and facts that interest the painter are those which can be used pictorially; these imagination seizes upon and uses in a quite arbitrary way.

'The phenomenon of the Spring Equinox, for example, presents the *fact* of equal day and night; which contains the idea of simultaneous sun and moon—a red disc and a white.[1] Again, the thought of division into light and darkness in equal parts suggests a divided space wherein a landscape, on one side, is lit by the setting sun, while the other lies under the influence of a rising moon. This, in turn, determines certain dominant colours. Red and deep yellows, with a range of fading and dying rose and pink, and blue from its palest cold tints, deepening to the tones of night.

'It is early spring. The woods are diffused with the glow of buds about to break. There is a beech hedge still in its winter leaf, pure "rouge Anglais". The line of rose bushes and the rough grass of the neglected garden are full of ghostly tints, from the mingling beams of sun and moon, where the rival illuminations merge in the sky; and over the distant view, the intermediate pale greens and green greys and subtelties of brown and blue come into play to complete the full harmony.'

Nash then described Wittenham Clumps and what they had meant to him since childhood, which I need not repeat, and he concluded: 'So the picture comes about. Of course it didn't get painted in the way the piece of writing may seem to suggest. It was painted suddenly and very quickly.'

But his description is not complete. There are unaccountable

---

[1] Red and white, we have seen, were among the alchemic terms for the two principles also represented by sun and moon.

omissions of the greatest significance. For example, on the foreground platform previously inhabited by the fungi and the magic flowers are two important objects. On the right is a structure of bare posts, once the supports of netting round a tennis court, which I see as the earlier skeleton forms and the mansions of the dead; on the left is a snake. One of the Clumps, rising in massive majesty against the sky, is lit by the moon, the other by the sun. This tends to identify the Clumps with the heavenly bodies, to get them finally into the sky. The moon is high on the left: the sun is low on the right.

Nash could have meant many things by calling this picture a 'personal' interpretation, and no doubt he did: it is a symbol, not an allegory. But among these meanings, surely one was a dichotomy: this is the propitious and germinating season *in the year*, which is the life of his creative genius; but it is also the evening *of the day*, which is the life of his body. Nash knew that. The sun here is not God, but the artist, the secondary light; but the artist is also the image of God because he is the maker of images, the creator analogically.

In October 1943, after completing the third version of the *Vernal Equinox*, Nash wrote to Dudley Tooth:

'I have certain paintings thought out which will bring this series to a close with the end of the year. All will be based upon the same place and I am spending the last week of this month up there. One will be a moonlit landscape—*Landscape of the Moon's Last Quarter*, another *Landscape of the Wittenham Clumps* with some odd ones with objects such as fungi, leaves and what not. . . .[1] After that a new business begins—all very aeriel and fiery—linking up with my new Bomber drawings which are due for the M of I. Chief pictures revolving in my head are *Walpurgis Night* and *Hallows'een* both very chaotic and alarming. Also a new lot of ghost drawings mostly aerial too.'

Clearly the ideas for the last uncompleted series of oils were already actively at work during this Boar's Hill period. We know that he had been reading Frazer during that summer because he had written to Clare Neilson in July: 'A great picture, the death of Balder is growing in my mind in terms of mistletoe and oak rather than odd gods I think.' In the February of 1944, just before his last visit to Madams, he wrote: 'We must get down seriously to this business of Balder when I am with you—also Druids—for God's sake call up all Druids on the book network . . . strange and awful fellows Druids with strange and awful practices.'

The form which these imaginings first took, in the spring of 1944,

[1] No omission.

was the new phase of Aerial Flowers. Nash was searching without rest. Ill and often depressed though he was, he remained courageously optimistic, 'I haven't done yet I hope,' he wrote to Bottomley in June, 'and I may yet have time to do better.'

The new adventure was announced to Clare Neilson in a letter which shows how he connected the Aerial Flowers with the Golden Bough:

'I am doing some strange new pictures. Giant flowers blooming among the clouds or sailing down the night skies like falling stars. . . . I was on the point of writing to you about a week back when—did you realize? our soldiers reached the lake of Nemi and must have been shooting their way through the Sacred Grove. Did they meet the King of the Wood I wonder—did anyone catch sight I wonder of a pale light burning in the depth of the wood where hung the Golden Bough. . . .[1] What a strange business. . . . Well, the Bough is about my next subject. The mistletoe-lightening bunch flashing in the storm sky' (8 June 1944).

The Rose of Death, which preluded the war years, was now developing to announce Nash's last flight. The study of flowers on earth, in the years of discipline, had prepared for their final identification with the inhabitants of the sky, the sunflower with the sun. But long before, it may be remembered, in 1913, he had seen a cloud as the Rose in the sky, the 'far off, most secret and inviolate Rose'. I hesitate to dwell on a symbol which has become so familiar in Christian usage that the Blessed Virgin is addressed as *rosa mystica*. In the *Roman de la Rose* all the Western world had learnt to see the rose as the symbol of earthly love and then Dante raised it to its higher significance.

> *Quivi è la rosa in che il verbo divino*
> *carne si fece . . .'*[2]

But with the fading of clarity and faith, the Rose became less specific in its symbolism. In Rilke, whose affinity to Nash I have indicated more than once, this growth to complexity is clearly stated:

> *Rose, du thronende, denen im Altertume*
> *Warst du ein Kelch mit einfachem Rand.*
> *Uns aber bist du die volle zahlose Blume,*
> *Der unerschöpfliche Gegenstand.*[3]

And of course that mystery is again and again expressed in Yeats, who had so early influenced Nash:

[1] No omission.
[2] *Paradiso*, XXIII, 73.
[3] *Die Sonette an Orpheus*, II, vi.

> *I can see nothing plain; all's mystery.*
> *Yet sometimes there's a torch inside my head*
> *That makes all clear, but when the light is gone*
> *I have but images, analogies,*
> *The mystic bread, the sacramental wine,*
> *The red rose where the two shafts of the cross,*
> *Body and soul, waking and sleeping, death, life,*
> *Whatever meaning ancient allegorists*
> *Have settled on, are mixed into one joy.*
> *For what's the rose but that? miraculous cries,*
> *Old stories about mystic marriages,*
> *Impossible truths? But when the torch is lit*
> *All that is impossible is certain,*
> *I plunge in the abyss.*[1]

In all the complexities, it is most relevant to point out that the Rose is also the Moon,

> *The moon like a flower*
> *In heaven's high bower*[2]

and the sun and the bombers. And in the end we are left with the old question: 'Who is she that looketh forth as the morning, fair as the moon, clear as the sun, and terrible as an army with banners?'

But for the male the transformation into the flower is the symbol of death as the way to life. Perhaps Nash knew that; certainly he felt it by intuition. The essay *Aerial Flowers*,[3] perhaps his finest piece of writing, ends with this passage:

'The great thing is to exercise constantly in the imagining of aerial images, probing tentatively always, not unlike those incredibly brave engineers who go ahead of the infantry in search of mines—feeling for death every foot. But it is death I have been writing about all this time, and I make no apology for mentioning it only at the end because anything written here is only the preliminary of my theme. . . .[4] Death, about which we are all thinking, death, I believe, is the only solution to this problem of how to be able to fly. Personally, I feel that if death can give us that, death will be good.'

It may be remembered that in his early story *The Dream Room* the girl who drew the hero up the stairs to face the sky and death had the

---

[1] W. B. Yeats, *The Shadowy Waters* (Acting version, 1911).
[2] Blake, *Songs of Innocence. Night.*
[3] Counterpoint Publications, 1947.
[4] No omission.

name of a flower not unlike the sunflower. The last flight of the soul, then, in the form of a flower, now clearly emerged as Nash's symbol for the mystery of life and death. He had passed through the forest and encountered the monster and now was on the final stretch of the way back to his own parish, to the sky where he first saw the face of a woman. We remember that when he described that face he spoke of it as 'like an immature flower, about to unfold . . . lit only by some other radiance which poured out of the eyes'. If we judge those early visions to have been no more than the projection into the sky of a particular girl's face with which his imagination was occupied, we must judge the Aerial Flowers as symbols of that other radiance, of some transcendental experience, which, again in our limited sense, we must call 'mystical'.

The appearance of the flowers in the sky had been prepared for unconsciously in all Nash's work. In 1944 several pictures announce them more immediately. The first is *Cumulus Head*, of which there are oil and water-colour versions, where the face in the sky reappears as a cloud, the Sibylline face of life and death, which has now taken the form of the thick coiled hair which had always fascinated him in his wife, who has the name of a flower like the sunflower. In *Battle of Germany*, which was finished in October, the smoke of destruction takes the form of towering cumuli. Nash described this work in *Picture History*:

'The moment of the picture is when the city lying under the uncertain light of the moon awaits the blow at her heart. In the background a gigantic column of smoke rises. . . . These two objects, pillar and moon, seem to threaten the spirit city no less than the army of bombers which are about to strike out of the red sky. The moon's illumination not only reveals the form of the city but, with the pillar's increasing width and height, throws its largening shadow nearer and nearer. In contrast to the waiting city and the quiet though baleful moon, the other half of the picture shows the opening of the attack. The entire area of sky and background and part of the middle distance are violently animated. Here forms are used arbitrarily and colour with a kind of chromatic percussion to suggest explosion and detonation. In the central foreground the group of descending discs may be a flight of paratroops or the crews of aircraft forced to bale out.'

Nash wrote in *Aerial Flowers* how once when he was breaking off the dead flowers from a poisonous plant in his garden, a distinct 'communiqué' came into his head: *Last night heavy and medium helle-*

bores bombed the mountains of the Moon. If, then, the bombing series can
be related to the Aerial Flowers; so, more obviously, can his long
fidelity to birds. It is the cumulus clouds again that form the water-
colour called *Cloud Cuckoo's Nest* as they had formed his first rose.

And so we arrive at the Aerial Flowers proper. In *Dawn Flowers*
(Plate 28.b) the roses are as thick in the sky as a battalion of para-
troops and stretch far into the distance over the flat land. In *Nocturnal
Flower*, one flower flies in the dark riven sky above the full moon. In
Sunset Flower, the red sun hangs small and low above the green water,
and the flower soars up triumphantly past the yellow, green and *lilac*
to the blue of the empyrean. It is a vision startingly like Emily
Dickinson's,

> *The lilac is an ancient shrub,*
> *But ancienter than that*
> *The firmamental lilac*
> *Upon the hill tonight.*
>
> *The sun subsiding on his course*
> *Bequeathes this final plant*
> *To contemplation—not to touch*
> *The flower of occident.*[1]

Though Nash had been introduced to her work by Conrad Aiken
he could not have read that poem, because it had not been published
at the time: but he could have read Wordsworth's two lines in *Ruth*:

> *He told of the magnolia, spread*
> *High as a cloud, high over head!*

and conceived his *Flight of the Magnolia* (Plate 29) from it;
although it is likelier that this is an instance of the same imagery
occurring to two artists. Wordsworth, of course, was only comparing
the magnolia to a cloud in metaphor: Nash compared the cloud to
the magnolia by turning it into one and so making a classic example
of a true symbol.

There are three versions of *Flight of the Magnolia*, the original
water-colour of 1944, a tracing of it and an oil painted in 1945. The
differences are slight. The huge flower, formed like a cumulus cloud
or the wings of a swan gently interfolded, stretching from side to side
of the picture, and bearing the quincunx of its seed pods at its centre,
flies softly and silently over the water. The pale colour, the quiet sky

[1] *Bolts of Melody*, No. 30, Cape, 1945.

barred with comfortable clouds, the whole tender and easy rhythm seem to convey that Nash had reached a centre of assuranced tranquillity. He might indeed have used of this picture his phrase: This rather gives me my Wings.

The Aerial Flower was to take its last and greatest form in the Sun and Sunflower sequence which his death interrupted. He had prepared himself for it in the drawings he had made at Cleeve Hill over Christmas 1944. In connexion with the exhibition in the following spring, he had written to Dudley Tooth:

'All these are called Studies. They are studies in the sense that an "étude" by Chopin is a study—at least they aspire to be—pieces complete in themselves *not* preliminary sketches. . . .

'Most collections of water colours after a country visit do not need much fuss but this last lot I think you will agree is different . . . they represent a new phase' [1945. Received 26 March].

The Studies are in two groups, *Sunset Eye* and *Sun Descending* (Plate 31), and are only distinguished by their group name and a number. The symbolism of the Eye as an image of God does not need elucidation at this stage, nor does the reference implicit in the sun descending.

These studies are amazing in their beauty and completeness, but they cannot be described in words: they are so fragile and so dependent on colour and on the precise touches of the brush, which note all that need be said and leave empty spaces full of the invisible. The Chinese drawings had shown him a way, and their problems were leading him to Turner. He was to write to Hartley Ramsden shortly before his death: 'In Turner's late work lies a great secret I believe. I feel it is for me to look for it. Presumption only may be but I shall persist nevertheless but how to come at it?' (25–28 April 1946).

We now approach Nash's last and unfinished enterprise—the sequence of four paintings planned under the title of *Sunflower and Sun*. It was a title which he had already used for three pictures. Two of them, an oil and a water-colour, were substantially the same in design and both were produced in 1942.[1] Nash described the oil in *Picture History* in a way which is applicable to both:

'This is the second of a series of paintings of the same conception. The idea behind the design is the mystical association of two objects which inhabit different elements and have no apparent relation in life. In the first picture called *Pillar and Moon*, the pale stone sphere

---

[1] The date 1943 given to the oil in *Nash: Penguin* is certainly wrong. It was delivered to Tooths' in December 1942.

on top of a ruined pillar faces its counterpart the moon, cold and pale and solid as stone. No legend or history attaches to such a picture; its drama is inherent in the scene. Its appeal is purely evocatory. That is to say, its power, if power it has, is to call up memories and stir emotions in the spectator, rather than to impose a particular idea upon him. Even so the animation of such a picture lies in its ruling design. Not only does this dictate the nature of the drama, it also expresses by its forms and colours the nature of its mystery.'

The picture Nash refers to is the Tate Gallery oil. It was begun in 1932, but I do not know to what state it was brought at that time. That was the year of the *Urne Buriall* designs when Nash, as we have seen, began to turn back to his 'mystical' interests. It was completed in 1942. But apart from the formal relationship between the stone sphere and the moon, the picture was, as Nash indicated, almost free from transcendental overtones. *Sunflower and Sun* was certainly not. He went on to describe it:

'Thus in the second picture, *Sunflower and Sun*, over a scene of wooded landscape dominated by twin hills, crowned with clumps of dense trees, a shaft of sunlight breaking through the cloud falls across the form of a giant sunflower bowed by the wind. I cannot explain this picture. It means only what it says. Its design was evolved from the actual landscape under much the same atmospheric conditions. There was such a sunflower and some such effect of sunlight. All the elements of this picture were present in more or less degree. But the drama of the event, which implies the mystical association of the sun and the sunflower, is heightened by the two opposing ellipses and by the other echoing forms of the sky which retaliate with the same apparent movement of outspread wings made by the leaves of the flower'

Although it is perfectly true that the body of the design was evolved from an actual landscape, which is, of course, the view from the Boar's Hill garden towards Wittenham Clumps, its *forma* is directly evolved from the landscape of his imagination. The symbolism was familiar to him, as it is to everyone, in Blake's poem *Ah! Sunflower*. As he had been previously fascinated by the convolvulus, now he encountered the sunflower, and the significance of them both is that they are what Sir Thomas Browne called 'solisequious and Sun-following plants'. In this picture, the hidden sun lances down its insistent invitation through the elliptic opening in the clouds and the sunflower turns towards it, opens its wings and prepares to fly.

Nash was also invited to the sun:

'En suivant la ligne même de son art, il tend sans le savoir à passer au delà de son art; comme une plante ignorante dirige sa tige vers le soleil, il est orienté, si bas qu'il habite, dans la direction de la Beauté subsistante dont les saints goûtent la douceur dans une lumière inaccessible à l'art et à la raison.'[1]

But he was not ready yet to follow his sunflower to the sun. The third picture called *Sunflower and Sun* is a completely different design. It is an upright water-colour almost filled with two giant sunflowers. They grow out of a rectangular bed which suggests the garden at Banbury Road, but instead of being imprisoned by its brick walls, they are surrounded by open country which stretches to far hills, *not* Wittenham Clumps. The diminutive sun, tucked away in a corner, is, like the hills, quite subordinated to the two assertive earth-bound plants. This drawing has been reproduced and exhibited since Nash's death as of 1943. If that is correct it was very early in the year because it was sold by Tooths' in February. But the important point is that it does seem to have succeeded the others with the same title, and to be an assertion of the body of the sunflower, repelling the sun and refusing to fly.

Sir Maurice Bowra has interpreted Blake's sunflower, which follows the sun with its head but remains rooted in earth, as a symbol of men whose lives are dominated and spoiled by a longing which they can never satisfy because they are earth-bound.[2] In this drawing Nash has made his sunflowers turn even their heads away from the sun.

These three pictures were followed by the Aerial Flowers, which were not sunflowers. *They* could take to the air for they were not identified with the sun: they retained their independence. It was not until 1945, with death very close, that Nash had the courage and assurance to tackle the identification—to cast off the sunflower to hawk at the sun. In March he wrote to Dudley Tooth that soon after his return from Cleeve Hill 'a new sequence had crystallized' in his mind and that the first two pictures were already designed and their canvases squared up. But there were long delays. In August no progress had been made; but by the beginning of November the two pictures were delivered. A long letter to Tooth announcing his retirement to a nursing home was accompanied by a note on the sequence:

'Four pictures in which the image of the Sunflower is exalted to take the part of the Sun. In three of the pictures the flower stands in the sky in place of the Sun. But in the *Solstice* the spent sun shines from its zenith encouraging the sunflower in the dual character of

[1] Jacques Maritain, *Art et Scolastique*, ed. 1935, p. 141.
[2] *The Romantic Imagination*, 1950, p. 45.

Sun and firewheel to perform its mythological purpose. The Sun appears to be whipping the sunflower like a top. The sunflower wheel tears over the hill cutting a path through the standing corn and bounding into the air as it gathers momentum. This is the blessing of the Midsummer Fire.

'The *Eclipse* explains itself. The withered flower head is a ghost of the flower in eclipse or just another sunflower time has destroyed and the tempest has torn up and scattered over the water.

'The other pictures are *The Sunflower Rises* and *The Sunflower Sets*.'[1]

Nash's imagination, long venturing alone in the creation of his own myth, has at last arrived, with what he found in *The Golden Bough*, at a most ancient and common myth which can serve him. It is outside my scope to speculate why he should have been content with a natural myth, centred in the mystery of terrestrial life, and have turned away from the supernatural, centred in the mystery of eternal life;[2] but so it was. The symbol of the Sunwheel was known to palaeolithic man, whose footprints he had so carefully traced. I can add little, at this stage, to what I have already written. It is too late now to rectify it, if I have failed to show that these pictures were the natural culmination of his whole pursuit. Of the *Eclipse of the Sunflower*, I am content to give the comment of a poem by James Kirkup with that title 'after the painting by Paul Nash':

> *Two suns there are, and each*
> *adoringly obscures the other.*
> *Both flowers live and die*
> *in mutual fascination.*
> *One, upon the rootless stalk*
> *of space; the other,*
> *bearing the blackened seeds*
> *of life's death-giving dream,*
> *burns out upon a stem*
> *too weak to bear its heavy ghost;*
> *that gropes already with a root*
> *spread like a human hand*
> *wearing the earth's great glove*
> *of clay, among the darkened*
> *heavens of another, longer day.*[3]

[1] They were never painted, but Mrs. Nash has a study for *The Sunflower Rises*.
[2] See Christopher Dawson, *Religion and the Rise of Western Culture*, Sheed & Ward, 1950, p. 41.
[3] *The Submerged Village and Other Poems*, Oxford University Press, 1951.

If Nash's body was soon to be, until the Resurrection, 'just another sunflower time has destroyed', his vital imagination is still embodied in the astounding power and abundance of the *Solstice of the Sunflower* (Plate 32). The sun, enthroned in concentric circles of light like the last vision of Dante, sent out the great sunwheel which is the Sunflower. It touched the earth on the top of a domed hill, one of a pair that are the hills at Wittenham, but without the dark and terrible Clumps. Now the tops are open to the intense blue of the sky and the splendour of the sun. The whole earth is covered with the golden corn and, at the moment it is caught in the picture, the sunflower has cut its path from the distant top to the foreground. It is very near us, on our right, bounding into the air with the exuberance of its fecundity.

Those who had complained that Nash's colour was too pale and tender, that his fancies were at times too fragile; who had found him hesitant, restless, experimental, probing here and there like the engineers in the mine-fields, had their answer in the fiery power of this last explosion.

Nash had no strength left except for a handful of water-colours. *The Sunflower Sets* was not painted but acted.

iv. Chronicle completed

The last few months of Nash's life can be almost entirely recorded in a sequence of extracts from letters. The first is to Conrad Aiken and his wife, and is written in pencil. It is dated from Oxford, 13 March 1945, which is, of course, an error for 1946.

'I have wanted to write to you for so long. I realise with a shock I have been ill eight weeks and many of those were strangely spent It appears I have had 3 quite important diseases Pneumonia and finally and most alarmingly what Margaret calls Endymion[1] . . . for me it was no less than incipient Elephantiasis and simply frightened the life out of me I still have a funny foot but it becomes less and less of a joke in appearance and otherwise I am almost normal—The medico is staggered by my progress and we all now have high hopes. Yesterday I began to draw again as I cut the pencil the smell of the cedar was the sweetest thing I could imagine! When I see you I will try to describe a few of the impressions that remain of a place I visited just the other side of this life but not at all like the usual conception— more like Thurber than most things—

[1] It was oedema, of which Nash gives further variants later.

'I cant write much (your and Ed's are my first letters) I get absurdly fagged but to feel like doing *anything* is heaven.'

Conrad Aiken might have answered from his *Preludes to Memnon*:

> *—You went to the verge, you say, and came back safely?*
> *Some have not been so fortunate—some have fallen.*

and the poem also gives Nash's answer with startling appropriateness:

> *Wreckage I saw, but also I saw flowers.*

The letter to Edward Burra was also in pencil. Its envelope is postmarked 15 March 1946.

'Yours is about the first letter I remember the other side of whatever has been happening these last months. It appears I have been wandering along the shores of "That Bourne from which . . ." in an inconsequent way and thrice turned my face to the other side and taken a step out and down and thrice changed my purpose and more or less firmly returned. I can remember quite a bit about it and shall try to record the experience which was very strange dearie.

'. . . Just beginning to try painting which in future I must always do sitting like a hen or, I suppose, suspended like a crocodile from the ceiling.'

About the same time—there is no close indication of date—Nash wrote to Bottomley:

'It is slightly unreal sometimes to be alive I was, apparently by all accounts so near being dead. . . . You and I between us have enough of illness to preclude exchange of confidences. . . . It was Margaret who insisted I couldnt die when the specialist said I must. You dont know him says she hes a creative artist and he still has some work to do—just like that! And the doctor seemed impressed. But, think of it, they all went home that night and left me quite alone to face the crisis. I was lightheaded and spent the hours in and out of some other world. Margaret was marvellously calm and by our side the old yeoman stock fought for us. . . .

'All this about myself, but how are you mon vieux? what have you been up to. . . . I often think about you.'

Nash also wrote to John Piper and his wife about the same date, sending them, he said, 'a small souvenir to celebrate my return from the shades. . . . The Other World of which I had a distinct glimpse is a rather baffling place'. There followed this letter to Richard Smart, dated 4 April 1946:

'My paste-pot and scissors have been taken away, my paints and my brush, now I have only my pen and (for writing only) my pencil.

'Well I shall try to make the best of it, and I will begin here.

'I must apologise for my somewhat incoherent "cri de cœur" over the telephone. I had come near the end of my tether: the full tyranny of the "book" had become unbearable. I felt I must stop this business or it will certainly stop me or so encompass my mind that I can think of nothing else. Also I was slipping back a bit. . . .[1] I was promptly taken in hand with the result you know. From now on—for a time at least—Margaret must take over. So I am writing this letter to start her off. These are my views . . .'

He then gave his proposals for unloading his part in the preparation of the Counterpoint book. From about the fourteenth to the twenty-ninth of April, the Nashes went to stay in rooms at 15 Parks Road to be free from domestic troubles; and from there he wrote to Mrs. Percy Withers on the twenty-seventh to thank her for a book on Russian ikons which she had given him in memory of her husband.

'You have struck a happy note for me as I particularly love the early Russian art. . . .

'Since you came to see us I have had a very serious illness and am only just recovering. Its a bore to talk about these things but it is enough to say I have been mercifully pulled through pneumonia, followed by two deadly complications. Now I am trying to rest intelligently enough to be able to start work again after months of idleness—I haven't painted since October. Forgive me if I don't write more. I have to do everything in small doses.

'My love to Audrey when you next see her. Again my thanks for a momento of Percy, so very satisfying to my memory of him.'

He also wrote from there a long letter in faint pencil to Hartley Ramsden dated from the twenty-fifth to the twenty-eighth. I give a long extract to display his persistent gaiety even at this oppressive moment:

'I am very much ashamed to have kept you so long for a letter in reply to so many of yours. I still am rather the prey to irrational phobias as to writing letters. I dont know why I worry myself about *not* writing when so easily I might be *writing*. If you only knew what a dent youve made sitting on my chest as it were. you see I always suffer most on account of those I most care about not getting letters because those are the long letters—ideally, and so they endlessly get postponed. [*Note in margin:* this is horribly involved] However, not another hour shall pass before I will start a letter to you at least.

[1] No omission.

31. Sun Descending. Study 7. 1945
Water-colour

'It is never easy to write letters if youre married to Margaret because she practically never writes letters. . . . So she is very liable to talk or perhaps read aloud out of the Paper or Ouida or Mrs Eddy or Trilby (this odd "masterpiece" we found in the room here) But this morning I am alone. . . . All is quiet and gloaming even the green parrot has ceased to call for help in his meaningless way—but hark I hear the taxi so for the moment must pause and postpone . . . perhaps 24 hours later—another try. Margaret has gone for a tatta with Richard Seddon and I am alone again waiting for the alarm to go off 12 midday which reminds me I must take my digitalin pill. We have been talking art and philosophy since mid-breakfast and I have done my bread and butter watercolour for the day (minuscle works based on odd notes and sketches) and now I must shave and dress so only these few words more to carry on the letter. hell, there goes the alarm. See you later.

'Well, this is day and half later because Richard Seddon came for a night and half the next day and I had a long tiring talk with my young musician-publisher (who is doing my book)[1] and by the evening I was rather whacked. But here goes once more. . . . We get back to the flat tomorrow where terriffic upsidedowness is quickly giving place to a new and beautiful order. . . . I am all tensed and crouched for a spring into my new studio—at the same [time] having to remember *not* to crouch and *not* to do in [?any] springing. Fancy the studio without that bloody great bed—oh boy (as someone once said)[2]. . . . Did I tell you how much I liked the honour you did *Winter Sea*—most interesting.[3] You know I am very anxious to study Turner somehow. . . .

[*Rings round coffee stain*] 'I beg your pardon I upset my coffee.

'I must fold up now and steal away silently. . . .'

The next letter is to Clare Neilson and is only dated 1946. Mrs. Neilson believes it to have been written about May.

'How awful not to have sent this[4] to its very inspiration sooner than now. Wasnt it our Charles who discovered Monster Field? he ought to have a special mention in the brochure but it might start all the other Ironmasters looking for monsters among the mines and pits and brew up a new labour trouble. Better keep Charles out of it, the

---

[1] Conrad Senat of *Counterpoint Publications*.

[2] The Nashes were going to sleep in the upper flat to give him more space in the garden studio.

[3] This must refer to a pre-view of the article by E. H. Ramsden in which Nash's *Winter Sea* is compared with Turner's *Storm off a Rocky Coast*. It did not appear until after his death. *World Review*, September 1946.

[4] The brochure, *Monster Field*.

Inspirator—the deus *ex* machina. . . . I mend slowly, am still very inclined to get exhausted and the asthma has been worse. Still I improve underneath I can feel I am getting stronger But life is unspeakably difficult we are both so tired and our precious money must be restored—about £300 that damned affair cost.'

A typed letter to Richard Smart, dated 25 June 1946, gives news of his movements and work:

'On the first of July Margaret and I retire to the shores of Boscombe seeking recuperation and maybe new inspiration for water colour paintings. Maybe a few small oils. Who knows? Anyhow it is a thrilling adventure for me because I shall see the sea again and I have not seen the sea for I can't remember how many years. Boscombe is next to Bournemouth, Bournemouth is next to Poole and Poole is next to Swanage. And there I am in my kingdom. . . .

'As to work—beginning work again after my illness has not been easy as I am sure you understand. So far I have not re-embarked upon oil painting, nor have I made any headway with the large water-colours. I was obliged to tear up the Bouncing Sunflower. It wasn't good enough. The only complete one is the Eclipsed Sunflower, as good as any one of the series so far.'

This is followed by a letter to Lance Sieveking, written in pencil on the inside of a foolscape envelope cut open. It is headed Florida Hotel, Boscombe Spa Road, but was sent in an envelope postmarked Oxford 30 June 1946.

'Well, as a matter of fact yes—I would prefer an easier introductory adjective to your Public old boy than say couth.[1] Because I cant help feeling that by the time they see the fun of one being called couth—not to say very couth (which will start a jingle in their heads very cooth in very sooth, very sooth in very couth—by then not only will they dislike me but will suspect your book, and I think rightly so. Again or as they will say—and *another* thing are you aware I have only just returned from the shores of Styx—do you know you unnatural helicoptural camel that your old friend is only just making an *unheard of* recovery from pneumonia Loss of speech Endema [oedema] or near elephantiasis dry pleurisy and 151 M & B tablets *Do* I feel nicely balanced and polished; and bane perhaps but scarcely *ur*bane. 11 weeks we wrestled but we have not come through quite immune—in fact I am a good deal mune still. And now God help us

<hr>

[1] The reference is to a draft dedication of Sieveking's *North American Binocular* (Sylvan Press, N.D.). The final dedication was as follows: I dedicate this book to one of my oldest and best loved friends PAUL NASH who suggested my writing a book about North America after having seen my photographs and having been very much taken with some of them particularly The Forest of Ventilators. I am sorry he did not live to see the book.

we go to Boscombe next Monday for 3 weeks. . . . I still only do things by halves or even quarters. . . . Figure to yourself I aint allowed to *stand*—Never must stand to paint again everything from the arse upward from now on feet up! Keep the feet up! knees up Mother Brown, feet up Mr Nash. . . .[1]

Yours mune and bane

Nash's last ten days were happy and busy. He drove about the country visiting Christchurch Priory where his great-uncle Zachary had been rector, Corfe and Swanage and Worth Matravers near Kimmeridge Bay. He began a fresh interest on finding himself in an hotel built on land that had once been Shelley property. He worked on the balcony which overlooked the Channel and the Isle of Wight and there made his last water-colour, of which he spoke in a letter to Viola Garvin, which is the last I have seen. It is only dated July 1946. He did not finish it, but his wife posted it after his death:

'Yes you told me about old Lady Shelley and the Urne with the heart. It is what Blake would call a Memorable image. I have often recalled it and now I think of it more often. I want you to be kind enough to tell me some more about all that. I don't know about Shelley but curiously, lately, I have come to be interested in him—apart from his poetry I mean. Did he live down here at any time, did he stay here, did he wander about the Park, stand on these cliffs, gaze out to sea? There is a derelict ancient pier opposite my window—a surprising affair! When you open the window the whole of the left hand view of houses and cliffs is reflected onto the image of the pier—you'll see it presently in some pictures. This window'

And with these two significant words the letter stops. The Nashes had arranged to visit Archibald Russell at Swanage on the eleventh of July. On the night of the tenth Nash drew from the balcony, wrote a letter to his brother and went early to bed, looking forward to revisiting an old friend and a familiar Place. He soon fell asleep. His wife did not and at about half-past one she heard him speak to her, and answered. Then she did sleep and when she woke at about eight o'clock, she found him dead. I have said very little directly of her long devotion to her husband, but I hope that it has always been implicit in their constant companionship. In the last years of his terrible illness, she had completely fulfilled her duty, giving her whole life to the care of him. Now she accompanied him to the churchyard at Langley Marish where he was buried at the foot of his father's grave among many Nashes; and since then her only care has been for his memory and his fame.

[1] No omission.

Bibliography

i. Writings and Illustrations by Paul Nash

A. Books by Paul Nash

1. PLACES / SEVEN PRINTS / REPRODUCED / FROM / WOODBLOCKS / DE-
   SIGNED AND ENGRAVED / BY / PAUL NASH / WITH ILLUSTRATIONS
   / 'IN PROSE'
   William Heinemann 1922. 8·8 × 11·2 in. 28 pp. Ed. 210 of which 1
   to 200 for sale. Dedication: 'To Margaret 1922.'

2. ROOM AND BOOK / BY / PAUL NASH
   Soncino Press 1932. 5·5 × 8·7 in. xix + 102 pp. 'Dedicated / to / Conrad Aiken / Poet and Mentor.' Six essays some of which had appeared
   previously. Nineteen plates of which two are of P.N.'s designs.

3. DORSET / SHELL GUIDE / COMPILED / AND WRITTEN BY PAUL NASH
   Architectural Press n.d. (Preface dated Dec. 1935.) 7 × 9 in. 46 pp.
   'Dedication / to / the landowners of Dorset / the council for the preservation / of rural England / the society for the protection / of ancient
   buildings / and / all those courageous enemies of "development" / to
   whom we owe what / is left of / England.' General ed. of series: John
   Betjeman. Articles on sport by Brig.-Gen. Patch and on flora and
   fauna by Archibald G. B. Russell. Thirty-two illustrations of which
   12 are from photographs and 4 from water-colours by P.N.

4. MONSTER FIELD / A DISCOVERY RECORDED BY PAUL NASH
   Counterpoint Publications, Oxford 1946. 8·7 × 11 in. 8 pp. Ed.
   1000. One colour plate on cover and 2 half-tone from water-colours
   by P.N. Three half-tone from photographs by P.N. Text in facsimile
   reproduction of P.N.'s manuscript.

5. AERIAL FLOWERS / BY / PAUL NASH
   Counterpoint Publications, Oxford 1947. 8·9 × 11·2 in. 8 pp. Ed.
   1000. 'This brochure was designed by Paul / Nash shortly before he
   died on / July 11th, 1946, and is now published by / his friends, one
   year later, as a / small tribute to his memory.' Photograph of P.N. on
   cover. One colour plate and 5 half-tone after water-colours by P.N.

6. OUTLINE / AN / AUTOBIOGRAPHY / AND OTHER WRITINGS / BY /
   PAUL NASH / WITH A PREFACE BY / HERBERT READ
   Faber and Faber 1949. 6 × 9·5 in. 272 pp. Dedication: 'To Mar-

garet 1914–1946.' Two colour plates after pictures by P.N. and 51 half-tone of which 34 are after pictures by P.N. Material selected by Margaret Nash includes extracts from P.N.'s war letters to her, P.N.'s notes for continuation of book and seven essays, all reprints except *Bombers' Lair*.

7. POET AND PAINTER. BEING THE CORRESPONDENCE OF GORDON BOTTOMLEY AND PAUL NASH EDITED BY C. COLLEER ABBOTT AND ANTHONY BERTRAM

O.U.P. 1955. Introduction by the eds. Texts of 270 letters with notes. Sixteen plates in half tone of which 11 are from drawings by P.N. and 2 facsimiles of letters.

B. Books Illustrated by Paul Nash

8. LOYALTIES / A BOOK OF POEMS BY / JOHN DRINKWATER

Beaumont Press 1918. 5·2 × 7·8 in. 44 pp. Ed: 30 on Japanese vellum signed by author and artist (1 to 30) 50 on cartridge paper (31 to 80) 120 on hand-made paper (81 to 200). Cover in black and yellow on blue paper and 10 decorations in black and white by P.N. P.N.'s own copy is inscribed: 'The plates in this book were coloured by Mr Beaumont without my assistance or instigation.' It is not known how many copies were coloured in this way.

9. IMAGES OF WAR / A BOOK OF POEMS BY / RICHARD ALDINGTON

Beaumont Press 1919. 5·2 × 7·8 in. 48 pp. Ed: as for *Loyalties*. Cover in black on red paper and 11 decorations in black and white by P.N.

10. COTSWOLD / CHARACTERS / BY / JOHN DRINKWATER / WITH FIVE ENGRAVINGS ON WOOD BY PAUL NASH

Yale U.P. London, Humphrey Milford, O.U.P. 1921. 5·2 × 7·6 in. 56 pp.

11. MISTER BOSPHORUS / AND THE MUSES / OR A SHORT HISTORY OF / POETRY IN BRITAIN / VARIETY ENTERTAINMENT / IN FOUR ACTS / WORDS BY / FORD MADOX FORD / MUSIC BY / SEVERAL POPULAR COMPOSERS / WITH HARLEQUINADE, TRANSFORMATION / SCENE, CINEMATOGRAPHIC EFFECTS, AND / MANY OTHER NOVELTIES, AS WELL AS / OLD AND TRIED FAVOURITES / DECORATED WITH DE-SIGNS / ENGRAVED ON WOOD BY / PAUL NASH

Duckworth 1923. 7·6 × 10 in. 128 pp. There are 12 engravings.

12. GENESIS TWELVE WOODCUTS BY PAUL / NASH WITH THE FIRST CHAPTER / OF GENESIS IN THE AUTHORISED / VERSION * THE NONE-SUCH PRESS / SOHO MCMXXIV

7·7 × 10·8 in. 28 printed pp. Ed: 375.

13. SHAKESPEARE'S / A MIDSOMMER / NIGHTS DREAME / NEWLY PRINTED FROM THE / FIRST FOLIO OF 1623 / LONDON 1924

Ernest Benn. 9·8 × 13 in. liii + 72 pp. excluding plates. This was a volume in the Player's Shakespeare. Art ed: Albert Rutherston. Introductions by Harley Granville-Barker. Ed: 100 signed copies for sale and 6 not for sale (1 to 100 and I to VI) on Batchelor's hand-made paper, hand-bound in vellum or oasis morocco. And 450 for sale and 50 not for sale (101 to 550 and VII to LVI). This constituted two editions. Five colour-plates in facsimile collotype and 9 line drawings.

14. WAGNER'S MUSIC DRAMA / OF THE RING / BY L. ARCHIER LEROY / WITH WOOD ENGRAVINGS / BY PAUL NASH
Noel Douglas n.d. (Preface dated 1925). 6 × 9 in. xxiv + 196 pp. Four engravings. Bound in pattern paper by P.N.

15. WELCHMAN'S HOSE / BY / ROBERT GRAVES / WOOD ENGRAVINGS BY PAUL NASH
Fleuron 1925. 6·2 × 8·2 in. x + 62 pp. Ed: 525 of which 500 for sale. Five engravings of which 2 printed twice.

16. SEVEN PILLARS OF WISDOM BY T. E. LAWRENCE Pte. publication 1926.

17. SAINT HERCULES / AND OTHER STORIES / BY MARTIN ARMSTRONG / WITH DRAWINGS BY PAUL NASH
Fleuron n.d. [1927]. 8 × 11·8 in. 70 pp. Ed: 310. Two full-page and 3 smaller drawings in pen and wash reproduced in colour.

18. SHAKESPEARE'S / THE TRADGEDIE / OF KING LEAR / NEWLY PRINTED FROM / THE FIRST FOLIO OF 1623 / LONDON 1927
All particulars as for *Midsommer Nights Dreame* except c × 110 pp.

19. NATIVITY / BY / SIEGFRIED / SASSOON / DESIGNS BY PAUL NASH
Faber and Gwyer n.d. [1927]. 4·7 × 7·3. 4 pp. Paper bound. No. 7 in The Ariel Poems. Cover in black on mauve and colour plate by P.N.

20. ABD-ER-RHAMAN / IN PARADISE / BY JULES TELLIER / TRANSLATED BY BRIAN RHYS / WITH WOOD-ENGRAVINGS / BY PAUL NASH
Golden Cockerel 1928. 6 × 9 in. 40 pp. Ed: 400 of which 200 issued by Random House, N.Y. Three full-page engravings and title-page decoration.

21. A SONG ABOUT / TSAR IVAN VASILYEVITCH / HIS YOUNG BODY-GUARD AND THE / VALIANT MERCHANT KALASHNIKOV / BY / MIKHAIL YURIEVITCH / LERMONTOV / TRANSLATED BY / JOHN COURNOS / WITH DECORATIONS BY / PAUL NASH
Aquila Press 1929. 7 × 10·8 in. 26 + viii pp. Four decorations in red and black by P.N. who also designed the binding and format. Ed: 750.

22. DARK WEEPING / 'AE' / DESIGNS BY PAUL NASH
Particulars as for *Nativity* except that cover black on grey and this is No. 19 of Ariel Poems.

23. URNE / BURIALL / AND / THE GARDEN / OF CYRUS / BY SIR THOMAS BROWNE / WITH THIRTY DRAWINGS BY / PAUL NASH
Cassell 1932. 9 × 12·2 in. xx + 146 numbered pp. Ed: 215. Illustrations in collotype coloured from stencils.

C. Contributions by Paul Nash to Periodicals and Books

This list does not include items where *only* illustrations from Nash's visual works appear. It is of his writings.

BIBLIOGRAPHY

The following abbreviations are used:

WER   = *Week-end Review*
LIS   = *The Listener*
ARCH. REV = *The Architectural Review*

1911

24. Under a Picture. A poem. *U.C.L. Magazine.* (The students' magazine of University College, London.)   March

1919

25. Dressing Gowns and Glue by Captain L. de G. Sieveking, D.S.C., with illustrations by John Nash. Introductions by P.N., G. K. Chesterton, Max Beerbohm and Cecil Palmer. Ed. by P.N., Cecil Palmer, n.d.

The following 15 items all appeared in the *New Witness*. They were signed Robert Derriman or R.D. except in the items indicated by (P.N.).

26. The Artist and the Public I. Harold Gilman and Groups.   25 April

27. The Artist and the Public II. What the Public Wants.   9 May

28. Art Notices and Reviews (Drawings and caricatures by Edmond X. Kapp. Cartoons by Raemaekers)   16 May

29. The Artist and the Public III. The Arts League of Service.   23 May

30. Art Notices and Reviews (Exns. by International Society of Sculptors, Painters and Gravers, C. J. Holmes and Pamela Bianco)   6 June

31. The Artist and the Public. A Plea for Picture Books   20 June

32. Art Notices and Reviews (Exns. by Walter Bayes and Sylvia Gosse)   4 July

33. An English Ballet (P.N.)   11 July

34. An English Painter in Spain (Exn. by Wyndham Tryon)   1 August

35. Letter answering objection by Leonard Baker in same issue   8 August

36. The French Exhibition at the Mansard Gallery (P.N.).   22 August

37. Letter answering objection by V. C. Lefanu in issue of 8 August.   5 September

38. Art. Books Popular and Precious I. Popular.   19 September

39. Art. Books Popular and Precious II. Precious.   17 October

40. 'A Loss to English Art' (Harold Gilman) (P.N.).   14 November

41. Introduction to 'Supplement of Drawings'. Signed Paul Nash. Notes on the Artists. Signed R.D. *Illustration*, House Organ of Sun Engraving Co.   Autumn

42. The Sun Calendar 1920. Arranged by P.N. with illustrations by Paul and John Nash and Rupert Lee. Sun Engraving Co. P.N. chose a poem and pen drawing for each month. 6 drawings and cover decorations are by him.   Autumn

1920

43. Letter of apology in reference to exposure by Frank Rutter of 'Derriman' incident in *Arts Gazette*, 27 Dec. 1919. *Arts Gazette.*   17 January

44. Dramatic Symbolism. A Note on Ibsen's 'Lady from the Sea'. P.N.'s design for Act III and his note on it. *Theatre-Craft.*   Spring

1922

45. Bad Plays, Bad Art. *Evening Standard.*   21 June
46. The Artist Outside the Theatre. *English Review. Theatre-Craft Supplement.*   August
47. A Note on the Cover Design. (Design for a stage by P.N.) *Drama* (organ of British Drama League).   December

1927

48. Woodcut Patterns. *The Woodcut: an Annual. No. 1.* Ed. by Herbert Furst. Fleuron Press. Bound in pattern paper designed by P.N.

1928

49. Introduction to *A Specimen Book of Pattern Papers Designed for and in use at the Curwen Press.* Fleuron Press. Reprinted in *Room and Book.*

1930

50. Contemporary English Drawing. *WER.*   6 December
51. I Look at the Theatre. *Theatre Arts Monthly* (U.S.A.).   December

1931

52. Back to the Sources. *WER.*   7 February
53. The Artist as Sportsman. *WER.*   18 April
54. Mr. Nash and his Critics. A letter answering Epstein's objections to the preceding article. *WER.*   25 April
55. Giorgio di Chirico. *LIS.*   29 April
56. The Artist as Sportsman. A letter continuing the controversy with Epstein. *WER.*   9 May
57. André Bauchant. *LIS.*   3 June
58. Savage Messiah. *WER.*   20 June
59. Picasso and Painting. *WER.*   27 June
60. English Humorous Draughtsmen. *WER.*   18 July
61. American Humorous Draughtsmen. *WER.*   8 August
62. Contemporary American Painting. *LIS.*   4 November
63. Peter Arno. *WER.*   14 November
64. Art and Photography. *LIS.*   18 November
65. Nature, Life and Art. *WER.*   5 December
66. The Painter and the Stage. *LIS.*   23 December
67. The Stencil. *The Curwen Press Miscellany.* Ed. by Oliver Simon. Curwen Press. Reprinted in *Room and Book.*
68. Introduction to catalogue of exn. called 'Page and Scene Designs' by P.N. Batsford Gallery. Reprinted *Nash: Eates,* p. 50.

BIBLIOGRAPHY

1932

69. The French Exhibition. *WER.*   9 January
70. The Artist and the Community. *LIS.*   20 January
71. The Pictorial Subject. *LIS.*   17 February
72. Review of Octavius Hill by Heinrich Schwartz. *LIS.*   24 February
73. 'Going Modern' and 'Being British'. *WER.*   12 March
74. The Artist in the House. *LIS.*   16 March
75. The Man with the Golden Voice. *WER.*   9 April
76. Modern English Textiles I. *LIS.*   27 April
77. Kit Wood: 1901–1930. *WER.*   30 April
78. The New Movement in the Theatre. *LIS.*   18 May
79. Advertising and Contemporary Art. *WER.*   11 June
80. Modern English Textiles II. *LIS.*   15 June
81. Nina Hamnett. *WER.*   18 June
82. The Meaning of 'Modern'. *WER.*   16 July
83. Photography and Modern Art. *LIS.*   27 July
84. Abstract Art. *LIS.*   17 August
85. The Building Centre. *LIS.*   21 September
86. The Artist and Industry. *WER.*   24 September
87. A Painter and a Sculptor. (Ben Nicholson and Barbara Hepworth.) *WER.*   19 November
88. Caricature. *WER.*   24 December

1933

89. Instruction in Art. *WER.*   28 January
90. Finding a Living in Art Today. *Journal of Careers.*   May
90A. Nature and Art. Letter to *The Times.*   19 May
91. Unit One. A New Group of Artists. Letter to *The Times.*   12 June
92. Art and the English Press. *WER.*   17 June
93. Unit One. *LIS.*   5 July

1934

94. Unit One. Letter to *The Observer.*   22 April
95. Unit One. Letter to *The Observer.*   29 April
96. The Laocoon of El Greco. *LIS.*   3 October
97. Contribution to *Sermons by Artists.* Golden Cockerel Press.
98. Contribution to *Unit One.* Edited by Herbert Read. Cassell.

1935

99. For, but not with. *Axis,* No. 1.   January
100. Review of *Art in America in Modern Times* edited by Holger Cahill and A. J. Barr, Jnr. *LIS.*   8 May

BIBLIOGRAPHY

101. Ben Nicholson's Carved Reliefs. *ARCH.REV.*   October
102. New Draughtsmen. *Signature*, No. 1.   November

1936
103. Swanage or Seaside Surrealism. *ARCH.REV.*   April
104. Experiments in Wood Murals. *Wood.*   April
105. Surrealism in Interior Decoration. *Decoration.*   June
106. Signs. *LIS.*   11 November

1937
107. Personal View. *Manchester Evening News.*   12 February
108. Surrealism and the Illustrated Book. *Signature*, No. 5   March
109. The Life of the Inanimate Object. *Country Life.*   1 May
110. A New Poetry. *News Chronicle.*   7 June
111. Introduction to exn. of P.N.'s works in various mediums, Redfern Gallery. Reprinted *Nash: Eates*, p. 53.
112. Swanage, or Seaside Realism (adapted from article published in 1936 in *ARCH.REV*) and The Nest of the Wild Stones. Contributions to *The Painter's Object*, edited by Myfanwy Evans. Gerald Howe.

1938
113. Unseen Landscapes. *Country Life.*   21 May
114. Openings. (Extracts from *Outline.*) *Signature*, No. 9.   July

1939
115. Landscape of the Megaliths. *Art and Education.*   March
116. The Giant's Stride. *ARCH.REV.*   September
117. Letter from Oxford. P.N. describes the Arts Bureau at Oxford. *LIS.*
                                                           30 November

1942
118. The Personality of Planes. *Vogue.*   March
119. Introduction to exn. of work by Eileen Agar, Redfern Gallery.

1943
120. Art and War. *World Review.*   May
121. Introduction to C.E.M.A. circulating exn. of applied design by P.N. Reprinted *Nash: Eates*, p. 57.

1944
122. An Artist's Revolution: The First Wave. *The Central Institute of Art and Design Bulletin.*   July

1945
123. Notes on the Picture Called 'Farewell'. *Transformation No. 3* edited by Stefan Schmanski and Henry Treece. Lindsay Drummond.   n.d.
124. Introduction to exn. of P.N.'s works in various mediums at Cheltenham Art Gallery. Reprinted in *Nash: Eates*, p. 59.

ii. Writings on Paul Nash

A. Monographs

The abbreviation given in brackets before each item is that which, preceded by the word 'Nash', is used in references throughout the text.

125. (B.A.F.) Paul Nash
No. III in *British Artists at the Front*, Country Life 1918. 9·6 × 12·3 in. Text 9 pp. + comment facing each plate. Introductions by John Salis (Jan Gordon) and C. E. Montague. Fifteen colour plates. 1 monochrome. Pencil portrait of P.N. by William Rothenstein. Paperbound with further colour plate on cover.

126 (A.B.) Paul Nash
In series *Contemporary British Artists* ed. by Albert Rutherston, Ernest Benn 1923. 7·5 × 10·1 in. 32 pp. excluding plates. Introduction by Anthony Bertram (signed A.B.). Thirty-four plates in monochrome. Frontispiece after wood-engraved self-portrait.

127 (Bertram) Paul Nash
No. V in *British Artists of Today*, Fleuron 1927. 4·8 × 6·3 in. 6 pp. excluding plates. Introduction by Anthony Bertram. Seventeen plates in monochrome.

128. (Read) Paul Nash
No. 1 in *Contemporary British Painters* ed. by D. A. Ross and A. C. Hannay. Soho Gallery 1937. 11·8 × 15 in. 14 pp. excluding plates. Biography by D.A.R. (D. A. Ross) and Introduction by Sir Herbert Read. Bibliography. Nine colour plates. 2 monochrome. Frontispiece photograph of P.N. Bound in stiff paper with further colour plate on cover.

129. (Penguin) Paul Nash
In series *The Penguin Modern Painters* ed. by Sir Kenneth Clark. Penguin Books 1944. 8·8 × 7 in. 16 pp. excluding plates. Introduction by Sir Herbert Read. Sixteen colour plates. 16 in monochrome.

130. (Eates) Paul Nash/Paintings Drawings and Illustrations
Edited by Margot Eates. Lund Humphries 1948. 9·3 × 11·8 in. xii + 80 pp. excluding plates. Essays by Sir Herbert Read, Sir John Rothenstein, E. H. Ramsden, Philip James and Richard Seddon. Chronology of life. Catalogues of P.N.'s exhibitions, etc. List of works in public collections. Select bibliography. Catalogue of plates. Twenty colour plates. 112 in monochrome.

131. Fertile Image
Edited by Margaret Nash. Faber and Faber 1951. 7·6 × 10·2 in. 32 pp. excluding plates. Introduction by James Laver. Notes on the plates. Sixty-four monochrome plates after photographs by P.N. Frontispiece photograph of P.N.

B. Selected Critical Essays on Paul Nash

This section is arranged alphabetically under the names of the critics.

BIBLIOGRAPHY

Except in very few cases press notices of current exhibitions, introductions to their catalogues which, except in one case included below, are reprinted in *Nash: Eates*, and reviews of books by or illustrated by P.N. are omitted.

132. ARMSTRONG, JOHN. The Present Tendency of P.N. *Apollo*, November 1932.

133. AYRTON, MICHAEL. P.N. A Memorial Exhibition at the Tate Gallery. *Spectator*, 16 March 1948.

134. BERTRAM, ANTHONY. P.N. *Architectural Review*, October 1932.

135. BERTRAM, ANTHONY. The Art of P.N. *Listener*, 9 November 1932. See also items 126 and 127.

136. BOTTOMLEY, GORDON. The Theatre Work of P.N. *Theatre Arts Monthly* (U.S.A.), January 1924.

137. BOTTOMLEY, GORDON. Many references in *A Stage for Poetry: My Purposes with my Plays*. Privately printed for the author by Titus Wilson, Kendal. Includes six colour plates and 7 half-tone after P.N. See also item 7.

138. BRADDELL, DARCY. The Textile Designs of P.N. *Architectural Review*, Craftsmanship Supplement, October 1928.

139. COURNOS, JOHN. The Ypres Salient. An Appreciation. *Land and Water*, 28 June 1917. An anonymous article quoting J.C. at length.

140. DIGBY, GEORGE WINGFIELD. Meaning and Symbol in three modern artists, Faber 1955.

141. EARP, T. W. The Work of P.N. *Apollo*, November 1928.

142. EVANS, MYFANWY. P.N., 1937. *Axis*, Early winter, 1937.

143. EVANS, MYFANWY. The Significance of P.N. *Architectural Review*, September 1947.

144. FLETCHER, JOHN GOULD. The Wood Engravings of P.N. *Print Collector's Quarterly*, July 1928. Contains complete catalogue to date.

145. FLETCHER, JOHN GOULD. P.N. *The Arts* (U.S.A), October 1928.

146. GAUNT, WILLIAM. P.N. *Drawing and Design*, October 1926.

147. GAUNT, WILLIAM. New Paintings by P.N. *Studio*, November 1928. (Signed Philip Spence.)

148. GAUNT, WILLIAM. P.N. The Man and his Work. *Studio*, December 1932.

149. GIBSON, WILLIAM. The P.N. Memorial Exhibition. *Burlington Magazine*, April 1948.

150. GORDON, JAN. Landscapes of Hell by Lieut. P.N. *Country Life*, 19 January 1918. (Signed John Salis.) See also item 125.

151. GRIGSON, GEOFFREY. A Metaphysical Artist. *Listener*, 1 April 1948.

152. GRIGSON, GEOFFREY. P.N. *Vogue*, April 1948.

153. HENDY, SIR PHILIP. P.N. *Horizon*, June 1943.

154. HENDY, SIR PHILIP. Introduction to P.N.'s exhibition, Temple Newsam, Leeds, 1943.

BIBLIOGRAPHY

155. HENDY, SIR PHILIP. P.N. The Memorial Exhibition. *Britain Today*, May 1948.

156. HOPKINS, GERARD. Two English Painters of Today. *The Landmark*, March 1933. (P.N. and Edward Wadsworth.)

157. LAVER, JAMES. P.N. in *Portraits in Oil and Vinegar*, John Castle, 1925.

158. LAVER, JAMES. Two Drawings. *Signature*, No. 2, March 1936.
    See also item 131.

159. MARRIOTT, CHARLES. The Indispensable Artist. *Land and Water*, 30 May 1918.

160. MORTIMER, RAYMOND. Nature Imitates Art. *Architectural Review*, January 1935.

161. NEWTON, ERIC. P.N. in *The 1943 Saturday Book*, ed. by Leonard Russell, Hutchinson, 1943.

162. NEWTON, ERIC. P.N. 1889–1946. *Listener*, 25 July 1946.

163. PIPER, JOHN. Recent Water-colours of P.N. *Town Flats and Country Cottages (Design for Living)*, May 1937.

164. PIPER, JOHN. New War Pictures. *Spectator*, 6 September 1940.

165. POPE-HENNESSY, JOHN. P.N. *Listener*, 12 May 1937.

166. RAMSDEN, E. HARTLEY. P.N: Surrealism in Landscape. *Country Life*, 2 January 1942.

167. RAMSDEN, E. HARTLEY. In Memoriam: P.N., July 11, 1946, in series Contrasts and Comparisons between Old and New Masters. *World Review*, September 1946. (P.N.'s *Winter Sea* compared with Turner's *Storm off a Rocky Coast*.)
    See also item 130.

168. READ, SIR HERBERT. Introduction to cat. of P.N.'s exn., Leicester Galleries, 1938. Reprinted *Nash: Eates*, p. 54.

169. READ, SIR HERBERT. P.N.: A Modern Romantic. *Picture Post*, 10 April 1948.

170. READ, SIR HERBERT. P.N. in *The Philosophy of Modern Art*, Faber and Faber, 1952. Composed from essays in *Nash: Penguin, Nash:Eates* and *Outline*.
    See also items 128 and 129.

171. RUSSELL, JOHN. The Vision of P.N. *Listener*, 18 November 1948.
    SALIS, JOHN. See under GORDON, JAN.

172. SEDDON, RICHARD. P.N. *The Artist*, August 1942.

173. SEDDON, RICHARD. P.N. 1889–1946. *Studio*, March 1948.

174. SHAND, P. MORTON. Object and Landscape. *Country Life*, 3 June 1939.

175. SITWELL, OSBERT. Three Drawings by Lt. P. N. *Colour*, March 1918. (Signed O.S.)

176. WILENSKI, R. H. Carpaccio and P.N. *Studio*, December 1930.

317

Index of Pictures

———❦———

This index includes all the pictures mentioned in the text, but it does not include book illustrations except where issued as separate prints or where the reference is to an original drawing or independent variant; nor does it include theatrical, commercial or industrial designs. These will be found in the General Index under *Nash, Paul: Designs by*.

I regret that I have not been able to give the complete particulars of all pictures. The exact dating of Nash's works is exceedingly difficult. He was not accurate himself and subsequent dating has been even more unreliable. The same picture will sometimes be found with two or three different dates in *Nash: Eates*, and *Outline* will often give a further variant. Therefore, where I have no incontrovertible evidence, I have given the date which I consider most probable in square brackets. In very few cases have I made my own measurements. Here also several variants are sometimes given in different sources, or even in different references in the same source. Owners are continually changing at present and, apart from public galleries, I am uncertain where some of the pictures now are. I give the latest owner of whom I have evidence. The chief use, therefore, of much of this information will be to offer starting points for the very extensive research which any compiler of a catalogue raisonnée would have to undertake. My general experience has been that none of the hitherto published sources can be wholly relied on.

Abbreviations

Bib: This indicates that the picture is reproduced in the item of the Bibliography of which the number is given. Where a picture is not reproduced in any item, the reference to a publication where it can be found is given in brackets.

D: Dated in Nash's hand.   *S:* Signed in full.

Mon: Signed with monogramme.   *W-C:* Water-colour.

Above the Clouds. See *Follow the Führer*.

Aerial Composition. Alternative title for *Mansions of the Dead*. Oil.

After the Battle. *SD*. 1918–19. *W-C*. $18 \times 23\frac{1}{4}$. Imperial War Museum. 103.

Air Fight at Wyschaete. 1918. *W-C*. and chalk. 10×14. G. H. Nevill, Esq. (*Bib*. 125). 102.

Alice. See Daglish.

Andante. *Mon. c* 1935. *W-C*. $11\frac{1}{2} \times 15\frac{1}{4}$. Sir M. Culme-Seymour, R.N. 244.

Angel and Devil or The Combat. 1910. Pen and chalk. $13\frac{5}{8} \times 9\frac{3}{4}$. Mrs. P. Nash. 61, 62, 280.

Archer, The. See *Night Landscape*.

Archer, The. *S*. 1930–42. Oil. $28\frac{1}{4} \times 36$. Edward le Bas, Esq., A.R.A. (*Bib*. 129). 168.

Archer Overthrown. *S*. [1937]. Oil. 20×36. Private Collection. (*Bib*. 169). 168, 169.

Arches. 1926. Wood-engraving. (*Bib*. 144). 152.

Arrival of the Stirlings. 1943. *W-C*. 15×22. Air Ministry. 277.

At Littlington. *SD*. 1924. *W-C*. $22\frac{1}{2} \times 15\frac{1}{2}$. A. Knyvett Lee, Esq. 134.

Atlantic. *SD*. 1932. *W-C*. 22×15. Miss Macaw. (*Bib*. 129). 214.

Autumn Crocus. *Mon*. [1928]. Oil. Royan Middleton, Esq. (*Bib*. 130). 158.

Backwater. [1919]. *W-C*. $10\frac{7}{8} \times 15$. Manchester City Art Gallery, Rutherston Loan Collection. 134.

Badbury Rings. 1935. *W-C*. $11\frac{1}{4} \times 15\frac{1}{4}$. Mrs. Booker. (*Bib*. 3). 222, 238.

Balcony, Cros de Cagnes. *Mon*. [1927]. Oil. 29×19. Miss Winifred Felce. (*Bib*. 130). 134.

INDEX OF PICTURES

Hill, Plain and Clouds. *Mon.* 1945. *W-C.* 11¼ × 15½. Sir John Parkinson. 284.

Hill 60. *S.* 1918. *W-C.* 15¼ × 19½. Imperial War Museum. (*British Artists and the War* by Sir J. Rothenstein, 1931). 102.

Hill 60 from the Cutting. 1918. *W-C.* (*Bib.* 125). 102.

Hills, The. *SD.* 1921. Pen and *W-C.* Joseph Holbrooke, Esq. (*Bib.* 126). 136.

Hudson. *S.* [1931]. *W-C.* 215.

In the Tunnels. 1918. *W-C.* Late John Drinkwater. (*Bib.* 175). 101.

Incident at Madams. [1944]. *W-C.* 15½ × 22½. Mrs. Charles Neilson. 282, Plate 27.

Inhabited Landscape. [1937]. *W-C.* 5 × 9. Mrs. Vyrnwy Biscoe. 246.

Interior. *Mon.* [1925]. Oil. 20 × 24. Madame Marguerite Prassinos, Paris. (*Bib.* 127). 156.

Iron Sea. First title for *Totes Meer.*

Kensington Gardens. *S.* [1943]. *W-C.* 7½ × 10¾. Duncan Norman, Esq. 282.

Kimmeridgian Ghost. *S.* [1942]. *W-C.* 15 × 22. Mrs. Harvey Phillips. (*Bib.* 130). 286.

Kinetic Feature. *SD.* 1931. Oil. 26 × 20. Mrs. P. Nash. (*Bib.* 130). 214.

Lake, The, Black Park. *SD.* 1928. Pencil. Mrs. P. Nash. 155.

Lake, The. First title for *Chestnut Waters.*

Lake in a Wood. *S.* [1916]. *W-C.* 9¾ × 13¼. Mrs. Kathleen Dodd. (*Bib.* 126). 83, 154.

Landscape. *S.* 1929 or 1930. Oil. 20 × 30. Mayor Gallery. (*Bib.* 173). 163.

Landscape. *Mon.* [1929]. Oil. 20 × 27. Miss Macaw. 163, Plate 10.

Landscape after Frost, The. 1945. *W-C.* 15½ × 22½. Rt. Hon. Vincent Massey, Esq., Canada. 284.

Landscape at Fulmer. *SD.* 1919. *W-C.* 11 × 15. Miss Ruth Clark. (*Bib.* 130). 136.

Landscape at Iden. *S.* 1928. Oil. 27½ × 36. Tate Gallery. (*Bib.* 130). 163.

Landscape at Pen Pits. *S.* [1934]. *W-C.* 15⅝ × 23. Victoria and Albert Museum. 238, Plate 16.

Landscape at Wood Lane. *S.* 1913. *W-C.* and chalk. 22 × 14½. Manchester City Art Gallery. (*Bib.* 130). 82.

Landscape Emerging. 1945. *W-C.* 11¼ × 15½. R. C. Pritchard, Esq. 284.

Landscape from a Dream. *Mon.* 1937. *W-C.* Private Collection. (*Architects Journal*, 13 May, 1937). 247n.

Landscape from a Dream. *S.* [1938]. Oil. 26½ × 40. Tate Gallery. (*Bib.* 130). 247.

Landscape of Bleached Objects. *S.* [1933]. Oil. 15 × 20. Lost in France in 1940. (*Bib.* 130). 244.

Landscape of the Brown Fungus. [1943]. Oil. 20 × 30. H. J. Tapperson, Esq. 288.

Landscape of the Brown Fungus. *S.* [1943]. *W-C.* 15½ × 22½. A. Zwemmer, Esq. (*Bib.* 130). 288.

Landscape of the Crescent Moon. *S.* 1944. Oil. 20 × 30. Toronto Art Gallery, Canada. (*Bib.* 173). 289.

Landscape of the Death Watch. *S.* [1938]. *W-C.* 11 × 15½. J. G. Barrow, Esq. (*Bib.* 130). 245.

Landscape of the Megaliths. *S.* [1934]. Oil. 19¾ × 28½. British Council. (*Bib.* 129 and 130). 240.

Landscape of the Megaliths. *S.* [1937]. *W-C.* 19¾ × 29¾. Ardler Gallery, Buffalo, U.S.A. (*Bib.* 130). 240.

Landscape of the Megaliths. [1937]. Lithograph. 195, 240, Plate 18.

Landscape of the Moon's First Quarter. *S.* 1943. Oil. 25 × 30. Birmingham City Art Gallery. 289.

Landscape of the Moon's Last Phase. *S.* 1944. Oil. 25 × 30. Walker Art Gallery. Liverpool. (*Studio*, February 1949). 289.

Landscape of the Moon's Last Quarter. First title of *Landscape of the Moon's Last Phase.* 293.

Landscape of the Puff Ball. *S.* [1943]. *W-C.* 15 × 22. Sir Allen and Lady Lane. (*Bib.* 130). 288.

Landscape of the Red Fungus. *S.* [1943]. *W-C.* 15½ × 22½. Lionel Massey, Esq., Canada. (*Bib.* 130). 288.

Landscape of the Summer Solstice. 1943. Oil. 28 × 36. R. Cameron, Esq. (*Bib.* 130). 290.

Landscape of the Vale: Dawn. *S.* [1943]. *W-C.* 15½ × 22½. Birmingham City Art Gallery. 283.

Landscape of the Vernal Equinox. *S.* 1943–4. Oil. 28 × 36. H.M. Queen Elizabeth the Queen Mother. 262n, 291, Plate 26.

Landscape of the Vernal Equinox. 1943–4. Oil. 25 × 30. Mrs. P. Nash. 291.

Landscape of the Vernal Equinox. *S.* 1943–4. Oil and *W-C.* 21¼ × 29. Sir Allen and Lady Lane. 291, 293.

Landscape of the Wittenham Clumps. *S.* 1946. *W-C.* 7 × 10. Richard Seddon, Esq. 293.

Landscape under Mist and Frost. 1945. *W-C.* 15½ × 22½. National Gallery of Victoria, Australia. 284.

Landscape: West Dorset. 1935. *W-C.* (*Bib.* 3). 238.

Landscape with Inhabited Sky. 1946. *W-C.* 8 × 11¼. Mrs. P. Nash. 287.

Landscape: Year of Our Lord 1917. 1918. *W-C* and chalk. 10 × 14. National Gallery, Ottawa, Canada. (*Bib.* 130). 102.

Lares. *Mon.* [1929]. Oil. 24½ × 15½. Mrs. W. N. Sherratt. (*Bib.* 176). 163.

Lavengro Teaching Isopel Armenian in the Dingle. *S.* 1912. *W-C.* and chalk. 17½ × 14. Sir Gerald Kelly, P.R.A. (*Bib.* 6). 65.

General Index

INDEX

Blake, William, 60, 78, 116, 133, 183, 246, 282n., 300, 307
   Compared with PN, 15, 55, 56, 121, 130, 132, 204, 208, 291
   Influence on PN, 14, 62, 80, 117, 118, 165, 212
   of his Pictures, 51, 57, 63, 67
   of his Poetry, 50, 58, 67, 231, 273, 299
   PN's Illustrations to, 128
   Quotations from, 59, 129, 162, 289, 295
Blunden, Edmund, 100
Boar's Hill, 211, 259, 286–90 passim, 293, 299
Boccaccio, 54
Bolt Court, 36, 51, 73
Bonaventura, Saint, 211n.
Bone, Sir Muirhead, 39
Borrow, George, 43, 50, 65, 113
Boscombe, 306, 307
Boswell, James, 26n.
Botticelli, 55, 56, 114, 121, 165
Bottomley, Emily, 86, 87
Bottomley, Gordon, 33, 38, 67, 70, 78n., 86, 87, 111, 124, 240, 262, 263
   Influence and help, 37, 39, 123, 124, 316
   Letters from, 32, 34, 57, 69, 73, 125, 230, 254
   Letters to, from PN, 41, 44, 75, 94, 107, 142, 145, 162, 170n., 254, 263, 303
   on: French Art, 135; G. B.'s Influence, 93, 136; Landscape and figures, 78, 80, 81, 128n., 131; Mysticism, 206; Pre-Raphaelites, 55, 255; Shows, 72, 133; Teaching, 109, 115; Theatre, 123–7 passim; Training, 40, 63; War (1914), 85, 89, 96; Work before 1914, 54, 62, 64, 65, 68, 82, 84, 103; Work after 1914, 104, 112, 120, 128n., 139, 294
   PN's description of, 73, 77
   Portraits of, 73, 78n.
Bournemouth, 306
Bowra, Sir Maurice, 203n., 300
Bradell, Darcy, 192n., 316
Bradhurst, Christine, 54
Brancusi, Constantin, 242
Braque, Georges, 133
Breton, André, 167
Bridges, Robert, 212
Bristol, 227, 233
Britain Today, 317
Brittany, 39
Brooke, Rupert, 77, 86
Brooks, Ivan Wilkinson, 40
Brown, Yeats, 170
Browne, Sir Thomas, 142, 194–201 passim, 289, 299, 310
Browning, Elizabeth B., 59
Browning, Robert, 50
Bruni, Leonardo, 56
Buchan, John (Lord Tweedsmuir), 94, 98
Buchanan, Bertram, 109, 113, 134, 141, 186n.
Buchholz Gallery, N.Y., 267
Bullet, Gerald, 175
'Bunty', see Nash, Margaret

Burchfield, Charles, 172
Burke, Edmond, 163
Burlington Magazine, The, 316
Burne-Jones, Sir Edward, 41, 54
Burra, Edward, 33, 146, 147, 148, 170, 177, 183, 219, 221, 224, 259, 303
Butler, Abbot, 205
Byron, Robert, 180
Bystander, 223

Cabinet Maker and Complete House Furnisher, 192n.
Caen, 167n.
Calico Printers Association, 192
Calvert, Edward, 255
Camberley, 89
Camden Town Group, 76
Canada, 103, 104, 108
Cannan, Gilbert, 88
Cardiff, Maurice, 249
Carfax Gallery, 51, 70, 72
Cahill, Holger, 313
Carline, Sydney, 109
Carlyle, Thomas, 50
Carnegie Institute of Pittsburgh, 171, 174
Carnegie International Exhibition, 146
Carrington, Noel, 192n.
Carroll, Lewis, 22, 270
Castlemaine, Lord, 40n.
Cattley, Caroline, 19
Cecil, Lord David, 249
C.E.M.A., 54n., 132n., 188n., 260, 291, 314
Central Institute of Art and Design Bulletin, 314
Ceuta, 220
Cézanne, Paul, 135, 154
Chalfont St. Peter, 96
Chance Brothers, 192
Chapman, Mrs. George (Susan Mary Nash, Aunt Molly), 25
Chelsea Polytechnic, 35, 38
Cheltenham, 266
Cheltenham Art Gallery, 267, 268, 314
Cheltenham Ladies' College, 74
Chesterton, G. K., 80, 311
Chicago, Exhibition at, 267
Chiltern Hills, 107, 133, 283
Chinese Art, 114, 283, 284, 298
Chirico, Giorgio de, 234, 312
Christchurch, Hants, 18, 307
Christ Church, Oxford, 264
Clark, Sir Kenneth, 212n., 249, 250, 256, 263, 273, 278, 315
Clark, Ruth, 87, 143, 145, 146n., 147, 148, 153, 175, 176, 216
   Letters to, 217–20 passim, 223, 228, 252, 254, 263, 265, 267, 274
Cleeve Hill, 266, 267, 298, 300
Clifton, 227
Clutton Brock, A., 94
Coates, Wells, 176, 177
Colchester Pageant, 54
Coleridge, S. T., 50, 131, 203
Colet Court, 29, 30
Coliseum, 126
Collignon, Raymonde, 108, 142

INDEX

INDEX

INDEX

INDEX

INDEX